A

Philip E. Lilienthal

BOOK

The Philip E. Lilienthal imprint
honors special books
in commemoration of a man whose work
at University of California Press from 1954 to 1979
was marked by dedication to young authors
and to high standards in the field of Asian Studies.
Friends, family, authors, and foundations have together
endowed the Lilienthal Fund, which enables UC Press
to publish under this imprint selected books
in a way that reflects the taste and judgment
of a great and beloved editor.

The publisher and the University of California Press Foundation gratefully acknowledge the generous support of the Philip E. Lilienthal Imprint in Asian Studies, established by a major gift from Sally Lilienthal.

AMERICAN EXODUS

AMERICAN EXODUS

SECOND-GENERATION CHINESE AMERICANS IN CHINA, 1901–1949

Charlotte Brooks

UNIVERSITY OF CALIFORNIA PRESS

University of California Press
Oakland, California

Library of Congress Cataloging-in-Publication Data

Names: Brooks, Charlotte, 1971- author.
Title: American exodus : second-generation Chinese Americans in China 1901-1949 / Charlotte Brooks.
Description: Oakland, California : University of California Press, [2019] | Includes bibliographical references and index. | "In the early twentieth century, between one-third and one-half of all native-born Chinese American citizens left the United States for China under the assumption that they would never permanently return to the land of their birth. American Exodus explores this little-known aspect of modern Chinese and American history through the lives of the thousands of Chinese Americans who settled in Shanghai, Guangzhou, Hong Kong, and the Pearl River Delta"—Provided by publisher.
Identifiers: LCCN 2019002611 (print) | LCCN 2019001395 (ebook) | ISBN 9780520302679 (cloth : alk. paper) | ISBN 9780520302686 (pbk. : alk. paper) | ISBN 9780520972551 (Epub)
Subjects: LCSH: Chinese Americans—China—20th century. | Chinese Americans—Ethnic identity.
Classification: LCC E184.C5 B735 2019 (ebook) | LCC E184.C5 (print) | DDC 305.895/1073—dc23
LC record available at https://lccn.loc.gov/2019002611

Manufactured in the United States of America

28 27 26 25 24 23 22 21 20 19
10 9 8 7 6 5 4 3 2 1

For Pam

And with tremendous gratitude to the millions of immigrants, past and present, who have helped make a better America

CONTENTS

Illustrations ix
Acknowledgments xi
Note on Sources, Names, Data, and Translations xv

Introduction 1
1. New Lives in the South: Chinese American Merchant and Student Immigrants 13
2. The Modernizers: US-Educated Chinese Americans in China 41
3. The Golden Age Ends: Chinese Americans and the Rise of Anti-imperialist Nationalism 75
4. The Nanjing Decade: Chinese American Immigrants and the Nationalist Regime 115
5. Agonizing Choices: The War against Japan, 1937–1945 152
Conclusion 190

Epilogue 194
Notes Abbreviations 205
Notes 207
Bibliography 273
Index 297

ILLUSTRATIONS

1. US citizen immigrants Ng Ah Tye and Ng Lee Ting Tye with their sons, Herbert Spencer Tye and Leland Stanford Tye, and their daughter, Van Gesner Tye / *14*
2. California native Louey Shuck while a comprador in Hong Kong / *20*
3. Students of Canton Christian College's Wa Kiu (Overseas Chinese) School during the 1923–1924 school year / *33*
4. The Hawaiian-born Jun-ke Choy in the late 1910s, after his graduation from Columbia University / *49*
5. The aviator Tom Gunn the year before his departure for China / *50*
6. Pilot Arthur F. Lym while a student at the Curtiss School of Aviation in San Diego / *51*
7. New York architect Poy Gum Lee in front of the Sun Yat-sen Mausoleum in Nanjing / *65*
8. New Yorker Chu Shea Wai's Form 430 application / *90*
9. San Francisco native and Nationalist Chinese diplomat Samuel S. Young in the late 1930s / *107*
10. and 11. Well-known Shanghai American lawyer and athlete Wai Yuen "Nick" Char / *110*
12. Lynne Lee Shew, founder of the Heungshan Benevolent Hospital / *125*
13. The 1932 Yenching University women's baseball team, including several players from Honolulu / *131*

14. Pilots Virginia Wong and Hazel Ying Lee shortly before their departure for China / *137*

15. The 1935 Ilimokilani Club of St. John's University, Shanghai / *140*

16. The June 1941 marriage of ophthalmologists James Yee and Marian Li / *146*

17. Honolulu native and St. John's University graduate William Yukon Chang in front of Jimmy's Kitchen, Shanghai / *167*

18. Boston-born lawyer Russell Bates Shue Chen as a member of the collaborationist Reformed Government of the Republic of China's Legislative Yuan / *170*

19. Ruth K. Moy in the late 1930s / *182*

20. Dr. James Yee with his sons, Robert and James, right after World War II / *197*

ACKNOWLEDGMENTS

In 1936 the Ging Hawk Club of New York City sponsored an essay contest about a question of great importance to thousands of second-generation Chinese American high school and college students: "Does My Future Lie in China or America?" Almost eighty years later, I assigned the winning essays to my Asian American History class, and while our resulting discussion involved thorny issues of transnationalism and second-generation identity, at the end of the day one of my students had a far simpler query: "What happened to these people? Did they go to China or did they stay in America?" That student's question inadvertently launched one of the most engrossing projects of my career. I am thankful to her for asking it and to the many other people and institutions whose support and assistance helped me to answer it.

I could not have completed this book without generous support from numerous sources. In addition to a sabbatical from Baruch College, I was fortunate enough to receive a Scholar Incentive Award and a Weissman School of Arts and Sciences Dean's Office Travel Grant. A PSC-CUNY grant helped fund most of my research in China, while a Harvard-Yenching Travel Grant enabled me to luxuriate in the tremendous resources of that wonderful library. I spent a very rewarding semester as a CUNY fellow at the CUNY Graduate Center's Advanced Research Collaborative (ARC). Finally, a National Endowment for the Humanities Fellowship for University Teachers allowed me to complete the book manuscript. Any views, findings, conclusions, or recommendations expressed in this book do not necessarily reflect those of the National Endowment for the Humanities.

Research for *American Exodus* took me to institutions around the United States and across the Pacific Ocean. I wish to thank the archivists and librarians who assisted me at the Stanford University Library Special Collections; the Hoover Institution; the C. V. Starr East Asian Library and the Asian American Studies Library at the University of California, Berkeley; the C. V. Starr East Asian Library at Columbia University; the New York Public Library; the Museum of Chinese in America; the Yale Divinity School Library; the Shanghai Municipal Archives; the Harvard-Yenching Library; the University Library Special Collections at the Chinese University of Hong Kong; the Hong Kong Collection at the University of Hong Kong Main Library; the Hong Kong Public Records Office; the National Taiwan University Library; the Academia Historica; and the National Archives and Records Administration (NARA) facility at College Park, Maryland. I am particularly grateful to Kelly McAnnaney at the New York NARA facility, Charliann Cross at the Seattle NARA facility, and Bill Greene at the San Bruno NARA facility for pulling scores of Form 430 application files for me, and to Deborah Rudolph at Berkeley's C. V. Starr East Asian Library for her assistance with Jiang Kang-hu's autobiography.

I am thankful as well to the many people who shared their family papers and their memories with me, including Richard Chan Bing, William Yukon Chang, Wayne Hu, Curtis Joe, Jane Leung Larson, Kim Liao, Vincent Ma Padua, Weyman Wong, and Robert D. Yee. I am particularly grateful to Dallas Chang for inviting me to help organize her father William Yukon Chang's papers for donation and for sharing with me so many of his photos and documents.

The support of friends and colleagues around the country has been crucial to making this book a reality. Shana Bernstein, Melissa Borja, Kristin Cellelo, Richard S. Kim, Erika Lee, Cindy Loebel, Vanessa May, Jonathan Soffer, Lara Vapnek, Scott Wong, and Ellen Wu read sections of the chapters and conference papers that became part of the final manuscript. Patti Gully generously supplied a copy of her biography of Art Lym. Kerri Culhane, Stella Dong, Becky Nicolaides, Scott Seligman, and Helen Zia offered encouragement and research assistance. Tansen Sen, Jianming Ye, and Psyche Zeng Yuanyuan helped me gain access to archives in the People's Republic of China. Carol Berkin, John Cox, Bert Hansen, and Madeline Hsu gave me valuable suggestions for improving my book proposal, and Shana Bernstein, Nancy MacLean, Scott Wong, and Ellen Wu offered moral support and much-needed perspective at key moments.

At the University of California Press, Reed Malcolm shepherded this book through the publication process, while editorial assistant Archna Patel patiently answered my never-ending questions about photos. I also wish to express my gratitude to Dr. Parks Coble and the anonymous reader at the press for their suggestions and comments on the manuscript.

In addition, I am deeply appreciative of the support and help I received from my colleagues in the CUNY system. At the CUNY Graduate Center, Don Robotham made ARC an incredibly supportive intellectual community, while Kay Powell ensured its smooth functioning. The work of spring 2016 fellows Cristian R. Aquino-Sterling, Timothy Amrhein, Marcella Bencivenni, Verónica Benet-Martínez, Medhi Bozorgmehr, Claudia Diehl, Mary Gibson, Christine Hélot, Juliet Hooker, Janet Elise Johnson, Leslie McCall, Kim Potowski, Patrick Simon, and Christina Tortora gave me new perspectives on my own. Ava Chin, Eva Shan Chou, and Ying Zhu offered useful advice and assistance; C.J. Suzuki and Ky Woltering helped with Japanese and German-language translation questions; and Seiji Shirane provided valuable materials about Chinese collaborators. Baruch College interlibrary loan librarian Emma Raub managed to fulfill the vast majority of my requests for research material, no matter how unusual or rare. This book would also not have been possible without the help and support of my history department colleagues. I am particularly indebted to Carol Berkin, Ana Calero, T.J. Desch-Obi, Vince DiGirolamo, Bert Hansen, Elizabeth Heath, Thomas Heinrich, Brian Murphy, Martina Nguyen, Kathy Pence, Mark Rice, and Clarence Taylor.

Finally, I am tremendously thankful for the love and support of my family, including Marlene and Jim Bentzien; Joy Brooks; Jill Brooks-Garnett and Paul Garnett; Glenn, Jennifer, and James Tucker; Nancy Bowman; Michelle Purrington; Lisa Brooks; Shannon Brooks Mann; Dara Griffith; and Teresa Golden. Even in the worst of times, Lou Griffith-Brooks's wagging tail always made me smile. Most of all, I am grateful for the love and encouragement of my wife, Pam Griffith, a tireless advocate for immigrants and a fierce warrior for social justice.

NOTE ON SOURCES, NAMES, DATA, AND TRANSLATIONS

SOURCES

The primary source material in this book reflects the often uncomfortable and marginalized position of Chinese Americans in prewar Chinese and American society. US immigration laws stigmatized Chinese Americans but also allowed them to create paper trails in order to facilitate their reentry to the United States. The disorder of the Pearl River Delta in the warlord years and the existence of extraterritoriality also encouraged them to assert their citizenship while in south China. As a result, US consular and State Department records, together with Form 430 applications and the appended preinvestigation interrogations, form one of the main source bases for the book. Because of the centrality of Hong Kong to what I call the "overseas Chinese world," this study also incorporates British Foreign Office records and Hong Kong government reports, which offer numerous insights into the lives of the Chinese American citizens who immigrated to south China in the prewar years.

The Chinese-language sources for this book further reflect the importance of Hong Kong and Shanghai to Chinese American immigrant life, but they also demonstrate the difficulties of doing research in China. While the book contains some material from mainland Chinese archives, including the Shanghai Municipal Archives, it is limited because foreign scholars' access to such archives is quite restricted. In addition, the Second Historical Archives of China, which holds so many republican-era documents, was still closed for digitization when I conducted my archival research in the People's Republic of China. Fortunately, several Chinese archives have published substantial compilations of the documents in their collections, and I use these throughout the book. In addition, republican-era governments at all levels circulated numerous journals dealing with overseas Chinese affairs and education; I have included many of these as well. Taiwan restricts foreign scholars' access to republican-era archival material much less than the PRC does, so this book makes considerable use of Taiwan's archival holdings, particularly the papers of the Ministry of Foreign Affairs in the Academia Historica.

Perhaps fittingly, though, material about Chinese American citizens is far scarcer in Chinese government archives on either side of the Taiwan Strait than it is in the Chinese- and English-language journals, newspapers, directories, school records, and commemorative volumes produced in China's colonial and semicolonial spaces, including Shanghai and Hong Kong, before World War II. This material, which I accessed largely at the Chinese University of Hong Kong, Hong Kong University, the Yale Divinity School Library, and the Harvard-Yenching Library, is crucial to this book and to any understanding of the prewar overseas Chinese world.

TERMINOLOGY

Throughout this book, I use the term *overseas Chinese*, despite the fact that it is an occasionally controversial term with a somewhat fraught history. A translation of the term *huaqiao*, *overseas Chinese* came into use at the turn of the twentieth century, and at its broadest, it simply means anyone of Chinese ancestry living outside of China. However, historians such as Wang Gungwu and Huang Jianli have astutely noted the potential dangers of the term for ethnic Chinese citizens in other countries, since it has at times implied loyalty to China (such as during the Cold War). At the same time, they and others have struggled to come up with more satisfactory terminology.

The Chinese Americans I discuss in this book routinely used the term *overseas Chinese* in the broadest sense, applying it to themselves and to all of their ethnic Chinese friends born outside of China (in Australia or Canada, for example). As this book demonstrates, those who employed the term often resisted various governments' attempts to enforce a particular definition of loyalty or "Chineseness." For this reason, I also use the phrase *overseas Chinese* without making any arguments about loyalty to China, because no term captures better the way Chinese Americans understood their own identities and their relationships to other ethnic Chinese.

DATA

US Census Bureau and US Immigration Bureau statistics suggest that between one third and one half of all native-born Chinese American citizens emigrated from the United States to China between 1901 and 1941. However, both sets of data are admittedly flawed. Under US law, "legally domiciled" China-born merchants had the right to bring family members to America to reside with them, while the China-born children of US citizens were themselves citizens because they derived their citizenship from their fathers. In the early twentieth century, China-born merchants and Chinese American citizens (or those purporting to be members of these groups) often claimed to have fathered sons during their visits to their wives in China, creating a "slot" they could later sell to someone who wanted to enter the United States. Thousands of these "paper sons" (and a few paper daughters) immigrated to the United States during the early twentieth century.

This book focuses only on native-born citizens and not derivative citizens, many of whom were paper sons born and largely raised in China. Unlike the native-born Chinese American citizens I discuss, derivative citizens—especially paper sons—generally wished to emigrate to the United States, not leave it for greater opportunities elsewhere.

The US census could not and did not distinguish paper sons and daughters from actual native-born people. The yearly compendium of immigration statistics did not consistently separate derivative from native-born citizens, and the US Census Bureau generally classed all of them as native-born. In order to address these statistical problems, I extrapolate when necessary the actual percentage of native-born Chinese Americans by using the reported numbers of "natives" and then correcting that total by relying on other census and immigration data points (such as education, years spent in the United States, etc.).

Finally, a very small number of the men and women I call "native-born people" may in fact have been China-born people who very effectively misrepresented their status. If this is the case, it is mainly true of the very earliest generation of Chinese Americans who traveled to China. They came of age in an America in which women often gave birth at home, birth certificates were far from universal, customs collectors at the ports largely ran the immigration system, and Chinese Americans returning to the United States frequently underwent habeas corpus proceedings to establish their right to land in

America. By the 1910s and 1920s, the Chinese Americans at the center of this book usually possessed solid documentation of their US birth (especially birth certificates), which they established in the preinvestigation hearings that were also an early-twentieth-century innovation.

TRANSLATIONS AND NAMES

The vast majority of Chinese immigrants to the United States, as well as many of their descendants, spoke one of the dialects of Chinese belonging to the Yue dialect family and used in the Pearl River Delta of Guangdong Province and in Hong Kong. However, there was no standard way of romanizing Yue dialects in the first half of the twentieth century. To further confuse matters, scholars generally transliterate written Chinese using the *Pinyin* system developed in the PRC. *Pinyin* is a romanization system for "standard Chinese," or *putonghua*, a dialect spoken around Beijing that is today the language of education and government in mainland China.

In this book, I use *Pinyin* to transliterate most place names in mainland China but give both the *Pinyin* and Yue dialect names for Pearl River Delta villages. For personal names, I use *Pinyin* only when no record exists of the way the name was commonly transliterated at the time (a transliteration that would almost certainly have reflected a Yue dialect pronunciation rather than a northern Chinese pronunciation). When a person used different names in English and Chinese, I have referred to that person by the name that he or she used in English. Finally, I use the old postal and Wade-Giles systems (widely employed before 1979) in cases where older versions of particular names are widely recognized in the United States (Chiang Kai-shek instead of Jiang Jieshi, for example).

In Chinese, full names always begin with the surname, but some Chinese Americans used their given names first, while others used their surnames first. Rather than standardize names, I have written them the way each individual seems to have done at the time (the index lists all by surname, of course). Scholars of Chinese American history often mistakenly assert that the given name of many women was "Shee," a Cantonese transliteration of the character *zhi* (氏), which essentially means "surnamed" (so "Fong Shee" means "surnamed Fong"). When possible, I have attempted to find and use women's full birth names and have only employed the word "Shee" when no record of any other name exists.

Unless otherwise noted, all translations in this book are mine.

Introduction

Louey Shuck was an American immigrant, but he did not immigrate to America. The son of merchant parents from south China, Louey was born in 1872 in the tiny gold mining town of Weaverville, California. His birth on American soil made him a US citizen, but his ancestry left him extremely vulnerable in his native land. During his youth, Congress barred Chinese aliens from naturalizing, while anti-Chinese violence surged across the western states. By the 1890s, Louey had joined the Chinese merchant elite of San Francisco, where he lived with his Chinese American wife and children. Though they were citizens, their legal status did not protect them from the egregious racial discrimination that limited the residential, social, educational, and economic choices of all ethnic Chinese in the United States. Having previously traveled to Asia, Louey Shuck knew that it offered opportunities unavailable to his family in America, so in 1907 the Loueys left the United States and settled in south China to build lives and careers far from the land of their birth.[1] The collapse of the Qing dynasty and the establishment of a new republic in 1912 quickly complicated their plans, choices, and identities, however. By the early 1910s, Louey Shuck had gained prestige and prominence in Hong Kong and Guangzhou as a comprador (*maiban*), a foreign firm's senior Chinese employee and its go-between with Chinese officials, individuals, and businesses. After 1919, though, many Chinese patriots criticized compradors as disloyal tools of foreign imperialism, casting a shadow over Louey and others like him.[2] Soon after, the Chinese Nationalist Party (Guomindang/GMD) targeted the Loueys as part of the newly suspect overseas Chinese merchant class, despite the fact that Louey Shuck had supported the GMD after the 1911 revolution. While the Nationalists denigrated their patriotism to China, Louey Shuck and his family simultaneously fought to make US officials acknowledge their American citizenship and right to protection. Still, by the 1930s, most of the Loueys had retreated to Hong Kong or to the foreign-controlled areas of Shanghai; weary of Chinese politics and American racism, they sought homes in the few places that offered any space for their complex identities and affinities.

This is a book about the thousands of Chinese American citizens who, like the Loueys, moved to Asia in the early twentieth century for better lives and choices than they could expect in the United States. This exodus was largely a response to America's anti-Chinese movement, its white supremacist politics, and its Chinese exclusion laws. Pushed by powerful forces in the western states, the Chinese Exclusion Act of 1882 barred the immigration of laborers from China for ten years and prohibited the naturalization of all Chinese aliens.[3] Congress extended the Act in 1892 and made it permanent in 1904, but the Supreme Court confirmed in its 1898 *United States v. Wong Kim Ark* decision that Chinese born on US soil were American citizens.[4] Chinese merchants could still legally enter the United States after 1882, meaning that the small Chinese American citizen population consisted mainly of merchants' offspring. Despite belonging to a comparatively privileged class of Chinese Americans, these citizens and their parents faced antagonistic immigration agents, racist legislators, and hostile police and neighbors. White Americans generally refused to hire people of Chinese ancestry, regardless of citizenship or education, for any work that was not menial labor.[5] In the early twentieth century, thousands of second-generation Chinese American citizens responded by emigrating to China and seeking a future in which race did not so completely limit their lives.

Federal attempts to quantify the effectiveness of Chinese exclusion inadvertently captured the size of Chinese American citizen emigration too. In 1880, when the ethnic Chinese population of the United States numbered around 104,500, only about 1,100 (or around 1 percent) of those people were American born. In 1900, almost two decades after the Exclusion Act's passage, the ethnic Chinese population of the American mainland dipped to 90,000 (an additional 30,000 Chinese lived in the new American territory of Hawaii), but the American-born part of that population grew to 9,000, or 10 percent of the whole (with an additional 4,000 in Hawaii). By 1910, when the ethnic

Chinese population of the mainland and Hawaii fell to around 94,000, the native-born population numbered 22,100, or about 23 percent of the whole.[6] Between 1900 and 1916, around 1,300 of these native-born Chinese Americans departed the United States each year, while only about 1,000 returned annually.[7] In other words, by 1916 close to 5,000 Chinese American citizens had moved to Asia—about one-quarter of the entire citizen population at that time. After a pause during World War I, the exodus resumed at an even faster clip. Census and immigration statistics for this period suggest that up to half of all native-born Chinese American citizens may have relocated to China between 1901 and World War II.

The racism that these Chinese Americans encountered almost everywhere in the United States deeply shaped their ideas about the China to which they emigrated and Chinese identity in general. White supremacist politicians routinely used racial arguments to justify the Chinese Exclusion Act of 1882 and its subsequent renewals. US officials, journalists, and academics drew a stark line between the nation and the state and denied that people of Chinese ancestry could be real Americans, whatever their formal citizenship status. On the West Coast especially, critics took pains to portray all Chinese in the United States as uniquely undesirable, inassimilable, and odious.[8] San Francisco mayor James Phelan, who later served in the US Senate, scoffed that "of such stuff citizens fit for a republic cannot be made."[9] Sociologist Sarah E. Simons called the Chinese a "servile class" and one of the "elements whose racial point of view is so utterly different from ours that our civilization has no effect on them."[10] Such commentators treated the citizenship of American-born Chinese as a legal misfortune at odds with common sense. The racism and racialization with which Chinese Americans grappled in the United States thus encouraged them to view their Chineseness in primordial, biological ways, even as they rejected overt white supremacy. Meanwhile, China-born parents countered the prevailing racism by encouraging their American offspring to take pride in their Chinese ancestry and to identify with China. Exiled Chinese reformers and revolutionaries who raised money abroad in the late nineteenth and early twentieth centuries also praised the "overseas Chinese" and described them as part of a future Chinese nation.[11] In these ways, parents, Chinese political activists, and white supremacists alike convinced Chinese Americans that they were part of the Chinese nation, even as they claimed citizenship in the American state.

Chinese Americans' complex feelings about belonging and citizenship put them at odds with the governments of both the United States and China, where officials during this era worked to define citizenship in exclusive ways and their populations in strict racial and ethnic terms. The trend was most pronounced in the United States. Between 1906 and 1924, the American government barred all Asian immigrants from citizenship and, eventually, from entering the United States. Legislators also slapped harsh quotas on Southern and Eastern European immigrants, deeming them undesirable though not as racially distasteful as Asians or other people of color. Numerous eugenics activists supported the use of sterilization to "improve" the US population and succeeded in convincing scores of state legislators of this view. Others favored brutalizing southern blacks through Jim Crow laws and disfranchisement, applying literacy tests to voters in states across the country, and denying Asian immigrants the right to own land. The Naturalization Act of 1906 and the Expatriation Act of 1907 reaffirmed the racial basis of American citizenship and stripped a woman's citizenship away if she married an alien.

China's approach was less punitive but also rooted in ideas about race and blood as central to citizenship and belonging.[12] Despite prohibitions on leaving the empire, Chinese subjects had traveled to Southeast Asia for hundreds of years and to the Americas, Africa, and South and Northeast Asia since the nineteenth century. But the context of such population flows was changing, and not just because the Qing dynasty finally allowed emigration in 1868.[13] By the early twentieth century, the Qing sought to transform China into a modern nation as part of its attempt to maintain its sovereignty in the face of Western and Japanese imperialism. This effort required imperial jurists to define citizenship; in 1909 the Qing government issued its first nationality law, which declared all children of Chinese fathers to be Chinese subjects, wherever they were born.[14] The early republican governments and eventually the Nationalist regime continued to adhere to and build upon this idea.[15] The many Chinese Americans who felt tied to both the Chinese and American nations thus received little encouragement for their hybrid identities from either side.

Chinese Americans' formal citizenship was divorced from membership in a racialized American nation to which they could never belong, but those who actually traveled to China often came to question just how Chinese they really were. The first generation of Western-educated Chinese American immigrants certainly appreciated the tremendous opportunities they received in China, even as they struggled to overcome cultural and linguistic barriers there. Still, by the 1920s Chinese Americans came to realize that numerous

Chinese politicians and leaders viewed the overseas Chinese with suspicion and disdain, seeing their habits, complicated identities, and experiences abroad as evidence of insufficient Chineseness and even of disloyalty. As scholar Soon Keong Ong asserts, overseas Chinese "were defined as Chinese while abroad and thus permanently tied to China, and yet deemed not Chinese enough to be allowed to fully reintegrate into Chinese society when they returned to China."[16] Such treatment worsened over time and especially under the GMD.

Although fully welcome in neither China nor America, Chinese American citizen immigrants still helped shape Sino-American relations, the development of key economic sectors in China, the character of social life in its coastal cities, debates about the meaning of culture and "modernity" there, and the US government's approach to citizenship and expatriation. Chinese Americans' experiences with racism, imperialism, and conflicting Chinese regimes also pushed many second-generation people to reject the monogamous, exclusive view of citizenship popular with their China-born and white American contemporaries. Instead, they learned to question and at times avoid or resist the various Chinese regimes that claimed them, and they also demanded representation from a US government intent on abandoning them. In the process, many Chinese Americans came to understand that their economic and social opportunities and futures existed in between, rather than inside, these competing nations.

This realization helps explain the disappearance of Chinese American citizen immigrants from the histories of both China and the United States. Narratives of the US past are particularly silent about these people, whose decision to emigrate calls into question the popular mythology about immigration to America during this era.[17] Thousands of Chinese American citizens moved to Asia in the very same years in which millions of Europeans poured into US ports. Both groups shared the same goals—better economic opportunities and, often, happier and freer lives in a new country—but racial discrimination meant that only the Europeans could realistically achieve these aspirations in the United States. Of these two parallel movements, then, the massive European influx alone made an impact on the national consciousness, feeding a self-congratulatory and still potent narrative of America as a magnetic land of unequalled opportunity.[18] Common terminology has inadvertently shored up that narrative. Historians know that around one-third of the Europeans who arrived in America between the 1890s and 1924 eventually returned to their homelands or traveled back and forth across the Atlantic multiple times, yet scholars routinely label both those who stayed and those who left "immigrants"—a term that implies the intent to reside permanently and assumes America's status as the preferred final destination.[19] Chinese American citizens who intended to reside permanently in China, even though their plans sometimes changed, were certainly immigrants as well. But their immigration stories undermine rather than reaffirm American mythology.

The realities of Chinese American citizen emigration also challenge scholars' assumptions about the link between immigration and socioeconomic mobility in the twentieth-century United States. Historians typically assert that immigrants who chose to stay in America were almost uniformly able to give their children better lives and opportunities there than in the "old country."[20] The underlying message is that immigrants' sacrifices were worthwhile, at least for their offspring, who had every incentive to stay in the United States and did so. This powerful and appealing narrative of opportunity and a rooted and rising second generation has also inadvertently obscured the Chinese American exodus. In the United States, our national self-esteem seems to demand recognition of an American exceptionalism that includes limitless upward mobility, unending political progress, and rewards for immigrant effort. Yet the backgrounds of many Chinese Americans who emigrated during these years contradict such ideas.

The citizen emigrants were frequently the offspring of economically successful China-born people who could not imagine a similarly bright future for their children in the United States. Grinding discrimination and the continual extension of Chinese exclusion instead convinced many parents, like the China-born entrepreneur Wong Fee Lee, that their children would struggle to achieve wealth or status in America. Wong arrived in Deadwood, South Dakota, during the 1870s Black Hills gold rush, worked in mining, opened a dry goods store in the town, and eventually prospered as a businessman and property owner. But in 1902, after Congress voted to extend Chinese exclusion for another ten years, all eight of his children applied for documents to travel to China.[21] Other parents desired to give their children the kinds of educational opportunities denied them in America. In San Francisco, home to the largest Chinese American population in the United States, Chinese parents for many years had little choice but to send their children to the segregated Oriental Public School; it offered no organized classes for students above grade 5, and its teachers often refused to issue certificates of promotion to Chinese Americans who wished to proceed to high school.[22] Disgusted, in 1912 the San Francisco-born merchant Lee Yuk Sue took his five American citizen children to China, where they studied in academies in Hong Kong and Guangdong.[23] Many China-born people believed that if their American children emigrated to China, they would enjoy the kind of social mobility their parents never achieved in America.[24] When the successful China-born ticket merchant Hong Sling retired, he took his Chicago-born children Willie, Harry, and Jenny to Hong Kong, where they attended exclusive schools and became part of the colony's business and social elite.[25] For Chinese American citizens, especially merchants' children, remaining in the United States meant experiencing almost certain downward social and economic mobility in the land of their birth. Strivers like Hong Sling, Lee Yuk Sue, and Wong Fee Lee refused to accept such a future for their offspring.

While the Chinese American citizen exodus upends both scholarly and popular myths about the universality of social mobility and opportunities for immigrants and their children in the United States, it simultaneously challenges China's own nationalist narratives. Political leaders and scholars in both the People's Republic of China (PRC) and the Republic of China on Taiwan (ROC) have frequently celebrated the overseas Chinese who "returned to the nation" in the early twentieth century, and they have strongly criticized the racial discrimination and exclusion that Chinese migrants faced overseas.[26] But like their American counterparts, Chinese scholars and officials largely ignore the sizable Chinese American citizen immigration of the prewar era. They do so because few Chinese Americans who left the United States for Asia chose to remain there after 1949, at least in the ROC or the PRC. Even before World War II, most found opportunities and a sense of legitimacy in Chinese contexts but outside of the Chinese nation-state itself, whether in foreign-controlled concession areas in China, European colonies such as Hong Kong and Macao, or warlord-run provinces in the south. Furthermore, Chinese American immigrants often expressed hostility to the Chinese Communist Party while also depending on family- and place-based networks that operated largely outside the Chinese Nationalist state, and sometimes in opposition to it. These networks spanned the globe, linking the Pearl River Delta of Guangdong to Shanghai, New York, Honolulu, Saigon, Singapore, Lima, Sydney, Cape Town, Malacca, and numerous points in between.[27] However, the central node in such networks was not China itself but the British colony of Hong Kong.[28]

In other words, Chinese American citizen immigrants have largely disappeared from both Chinese and American history because their choices and identities defied government objectives in the prewar and wartime years and subverted nationalist narratives in the postwar era. The existence in republican China of a group of people with dual citizenship, complicated affinities, and relative mobility frustrated two generations of American consuls and Chinese authorities. After 1945 and especially 1949, the history of Chinese American citizen immigration called into question the nationalist narratives of the PRC, the ROC, and the United States, whose Cold War strategies involved proclaiming the superiority of their governmental systems and ways of life.[29] The United States government in particular promoted in its Cold War propaganda the idea of America as a nation where freedom, opportunity, and a democratic, capitalist system attracted people from every nation and allowed them to prosper. The country's actual history of both emigration and racist immigration laws contradicted this comforting narrative, which officials and many community leaders hoped would help thwart communist propaganda about the existence of racial, ethnic, and religious discrimination in America.[30]

While Chinese American citizen emigration is a forgotten chapter in US history, it is one with significant parallels in other American communities. Most famously, the small but persistent Back to Africa movement reflected black frustration with the brutality of the post-Reconstruction South and the racism of the early-twentieth-century North.[31] Less obviously, the Immigration Act of 1917 confirmed a larger, ongoing exodus of Americans when it mandated that the government collect statistics about native-born and naturalized citizens permanently departing the country.[32] The intent of the clause in the act is unclear, and to make matters even more confusing, the data collected often mixed different types of people together: citizens starting new lives abroad, missionaries, American-born children accompanying foreign-born parents home, and businesspeople and their families moving abroad for work, just to name a few. Still, the resulting numbers are eye opening. In 1921, when around 800,000 people immigrated to the United States, more than 64,000 native-born American citizens reported that they were permanently departing.[33] After temporary and then permanent immigration restrictions went into effect between 1921 and 1924, the number of native-born Americans permanently departing varied annually between 10 and 25 percent of the number of immigrants arriving in the United States. Americans of all ages and professions reported plans to move to every part of the world, from Austria to Australia to Canada, India, and the West Indies. Some were the young children of immigrants returning to Europe, but even more were adults when they chose to depart.[34] The peak years of the Chinese American exodus also paralleled those of the Great Migration of African Americans from the Jim Crow South to the urban North, which blacks often called "the promised land" and which seemed almost like another country to many of them. Both groups left their native homes for the same reasons: to escape racism, gain access to educational opportunities, and enjoy better job opportunities. About fifteen percent of the entire black population of the South migrated to the North between 1915 and 1930 alone.[35] An even larger percentage of Chinese American citizens emigrated to China in the same years.

American Exodus examines the transnational lives that these Chinese American citizens led in China, which they believed would be their own promised land. It also explores the complex sense of identity and nationalism they developed in response to the nation-building goals of the two countries they claimed. The book discusses Chinese American citizens across China but looks mainly at the two areas that attracted more of these immigrants than anywhere else: the city of Shanghai and the relatively compact triangle of the Pearl River Delta bounded roughly by Guangzhou to the north, Hong Kong to the southeast, and Toisan (Taishan) to the southwest.

The book also focuses on two distinct groups of Chinese American immigrants. The first consisted of US-born children and adults who sought educational and business opportunities mainly in Hong Kong and Guangdong Province, moving there through the same Cantonese migrant networks that brought their parents to America. The second, whom I call the "modernizers," were Chinese American graduates of US colleges and technical schools who imagined themselves transforming their parents' homeland with their skills and training while gaining acceptance there as "real" Chinese. As the book explains, these categories broke down somewhat by the 1920s and 1930s but never fully lost their meaning. In structure, this study moves forward in a roughly chronological fashion as it discusses how changes in the Chinese American population, China's own government, and American government and business practices propelled and shaped the Chinese American Great Migration.

Chapter 1 introduces the entrepreneurs and students who, beginning in the 1890s, moved to China and Hong Kong for business or to seek a "Chinese education." Compared to the modernizers, these students and merchants seemed the far more "traditional" group as they traveled back through the well-worn Cantonese migration circuit and adapted to Asia as it was, rather than trying to change it. But China was changing, and the rapidly shifting political situation, particularly in Guangdong, influenced and often transformed these immigrants' original plans. Chapter 2 examines the golden era of the modernizers as well as their limited vision of what "modernizing" China involved. Encouraged by the Qing dynasty's "New Policies," hundreds of college-educated Chinese Americans began to emigrate to China after 1901, and they continued to move there in the early republican years. Their bilingual skills and Western educations enabled them to enjoy meteoric careers, but they struggled to understand the massive cultural and political upheavals that the New Culture and May Fourth Movements set in motion.

Chapter 3 focuses on the years between 1923 and 1928, when Chinese Americans grappled with the fallout from anti-imperialist nationalism and the relative success of the Guomindang's attempts to unite the country. American-born merchants and students in the south became increasingly alienated from Sun Yat-sen's Guomindang regime once it allied with the Soviet Union; many left Guangdong for Hong Kong or Shanghai as the political climate worsened and the Guomindang began to criticize overseas Chinese as agents of imperialism. And as the GMD moved north from its base in Guangdong to unify much of China and establish Nanjing as the new national capital, the party began a lengthy wrangle with the United States and other Western countries over the citizenship status of ethnic Chinese. This led to the formalization of the US government's policy of refusing to protect Chinese American citizens in China.

Chapter 4 explores the "Nanjing Decade" and the souring relationship between Chinese American citizen immigrants and the new Nationalist state. Because of racial discrimination and the Great Depression, Chinese American job seekers continued to arrive in China as late as 1940, while many cash-strapped Chinese parents in the United States sent their children to Guangdong for school. Chinese American émigrés often felt the presence of the GMD regime in repressive ways that reinforced their sense of themselves as outsiders, treaty port Chinese, overseas Chinese, or "returned students"—anything but ordinary Chinese citizens. Chapter 5 examines the dilemmas that such people faced during the Japanese invasion and occupation of China. Most initially identified as loyal Chinese who supported the Nationalist regime, but as the conflict dragged on, they faced difficult choices, especially once American officials essentially ordered US citizens to leave China. Many stayed on, unwilling to desert China-born spouses whom American immigration laws barred, or to abandon careers they could never have built in the United States. After Pearl Harbor, they found themselves cut off from any American protection and under pressure to collaborate with Japanese occupation forces. The book's conclusion and epilogue examine the aftermath of the war, when hundreds of Chinese American youths poured out of the Pearl River Delta and mid-career adults returned to an America that often had no place for them or their skills.

At the heart of this book is a specific contradiction: the coexistence in the United States of a powerful, institutionalized racial nationalism and a legal system that grudgingly recognized the formal citizenship status of ethnic Chinese born on American soil.[36] Beginning in the 1920s, US officials, especially in the State Department, attempted to eliminate this contradiction by acknowledging and protecting only membership in the imagined racial nation rather than in the formal American state. They never fully succeeded, but neither did the lawmakers whose far more salutary repeal of Chinese exclusion in 1943 and national origins quotas in 1965 changed the racial basis of US immigration policy.

Instead, the contradiction between formal state and imagined racial nation continues to shape the politics of immigration and citizenship in the United States today, as the recent and alarming resurgence of open white nationalism in American civic life demonstrates. In the first half of the twentieth century, thousands of Chinese American citizens traveled to China for work because their race and ancestry supposedly made them "inassimilable" and undesirable in America. Such people usually spoke, read, and wrote English better than they did Chinese. Most were far more familiar with American cultural and social norms than with Chinese ones. A significant number were Christians, and scores possessed degrees from the finest universities in the United States. Most ached to belong somewhere, whether to China or the United States. While they were often more comfortable in the latter, they knew they could never truly "assimilate" in America. The San Francisco journalist Gilbert Woo once explained why this was, when he argued that in the minds of many white Americans, the only satisfactory method for a Chinese American to achieve assimilation would be "to go to a plastic surgeon and get a face lift and a nose job and have one's eyes turned blue."[37] In other words, when white Americans complained about another group's culture—or legal status, language, or religion—what they really complained about was racial difference, and what they really meant was that only white people could ever be "real" Americans. A century later, this cancerous fiction remains politically potent.

CHAPTER I

New Lives in the South

Chinese American Merchant and Student Immigrants

Ng Ah Tye was born in Portland, Oregon, in 1871, just as the anti-Chinese movement began to catch fire across the Pacific Coast. Entrepreneurial from a young age, he opened the "Japanese Bazaar" in central Oregon's Prineville when he was only eighteen. Although the store dealt mostly in dishes and trinkets from China, Ng likely chose its name both because of a contemporary vogue for Japanese product stores and because of the anti-Chinese fervor still powerful in the West. The business proved successful enough to enable Ng to marry San Francisco native Lee Ting in 1895, but six years and three children later, a rising anti-Japanese movement with roots in the old anti-Chinese campaigns threatened the family's prosperity. In 1901 the "Tyes," as they called themselves, boarded a ship for Hong Kong, where "N. A. Tye" built a successful confectionary importing business using his American knowledge and his Chinese connections. Except for a few visits, he and his family never returned to the United States.[1]

This chapter explores the lives and choices of the thousands of Chinese American citizen merchants and students who, like the Tyes, relocated to China in the first two decades of the twentieth century. Rather than remaking China as the "modernizers" hoped to do, these immigrants relied on and planned for futures within the well-established professional, family, and native-place networks that bound south China to Chinese migrant communities around the world. Like Ng Ah Tye, many were entrepreneurs and merchants who sought greater economic opportunities and social mobility; others, such as the Tyes' children, hoped to study the Chinese language, gain cultural

FIGURE I. A 1906 passport photo of Chinese American citizens Ng Ah Tye and Ng Lee Ting Tye with their sons, Herbert Spencer Tye and Leland Stanford Tye, and their daughter, Van Gesner Tye. After moving to Hong Kong in 1901, the Tyes never permanently returned to America. Records of the Immigration and Naturalization Service, National Archives and Records Administration, Washington, DC, File Unit 14603/22.

competency, and forge relationships with the children of other merchants, including the offspring of other Chinese living abroad.[2] As this chapter demonstrates, their relationships with the political groups attempting to transform China into a nation-state eventually affected their business and educational plans and their evolving identities as Chinese and Americans.

While the merchants and students imagined that developing lives and successful careers would be far easier outside of the United States than within it, few ever fully rejected the land of their birth, despite the fact that US officials often cast them as members of a devious race loyal only to China.[3] American authorities translated such attitudes into discriminatory policies: in the late nineteenth and early twentieth centuries, Chinese American citizen travelers had to seek a writ of habeas corpus to reenter the United States; after 1908 they needed to complete an "Application of Alleged American-born Chinese for Preinvestigation of Status," commonly known as a Form 430, before leaving the country for China and submit to interrogation upon their return.[4] Ethnic Chinese were the only group of US citizens forced to undergo such an ordeal, but their willingness to do so reflected not just their recognition of the benefits of US citizenship but also their attachment to the land of their birth, despite the discrimination they faced there.[5]

However, nationalists and governments on both sides of the Pacific increasingly rejected this kind of transnationalism, especially by the 1910s. The citizen students' and merchants' sense of identity lacked the exclusivity that white, native-born, Protestant Americans demanded of immigrants and their children during this period.[6] Similarly, the citizen merchants and students often felt little of the exclusive Chinese nationalism that their Western-educated "modernizer" peers commonly expressed and that political activists and officials in China eventually demanded. Instead, they frequently identified as culturally Chinese, were often just as culturally American, usually felt a deep sentimental attachment to the United States, and saw no contradiction in their overlapping affinities. Unlike the modernizers, most of the students and merchants were not committed statists or even conventional nationalists before they left for China. Except for a few fleeting moments, such as in 1919, their experiences in the south encouraged such ambivalence about central authority and monogamous identity. However they saw themselves, most also remained acutely aware of the importance of their US citizenship to their mobility and opportunity; their relationships with Chinese migrants from other parts of the world had taught them that citizenship status could mean protection, access to economic opportunity, or particular vulnerability.[7] But preserving the value of their citizenship became ever more difficult over time, as Chinese authorities attempted to exert authority over them, often with the help of a US government eager to ignore their rights as Americans.

HONG KONG, CAPITAL OF THE OVERSEAS CHINESE WORLD

The Chinese American citizen merchants' and students' initial and sometimes ultimate destination was Hong Kong, which China ceded to Britain in 1842 after losing the First Opium War. Hong Kong began to prosper in the second half of the nineteenth century, as hundreds of thousands of Chinese immigrants left Guangdong Province and Fujian to labor in countries and colonies around the world. The vast majority departed from Hong Kong, which became the central hub that connected them to their ancestral villages in south China. Emigrants, foodstuffs, opium, print media, and other goods flowed through the British colony to Chinese communities in the Americas, Australia, Africa, and East and Southeast Asia, while Hong Kong's firms also received and processed remittances and letters from Chinese abroad. As Hong Kong prospered, its population grew quickly, while Britain's conflicts with China increased the colony's territory: between 1860 and 1899, Britain obtained Kowloon by cession and the New Territories by lease, more than quintupling the colony's size. Urban Victoria on Hong Kong Island remained the colony's business and residential center, with colonnaded trading houses and shops lining its waterfront and the streets behind it; large, airy homes clustering in the Midlevels; and mansions dotting the exclusive, whites-only Peak.[8]

The colony emerged as the capital of the far-flung overseas Chinese world in these years not just because it connected global trading and migrant networks but also because it offered unique social and economic opportunities for "returned merchants." Beginning in the 1880s, as Australia, South Africa, Canada, and the United States limited Chinese immigration, Hong Kong attracted Chinese returning from such places with capital to invest.[9] Many settled permanently in the colony rather than in their old villages because of Hong Kong's greater stability, higher standard of living, and financial opportunities. Even better, as historian Elizabeth Sinn notes, "in the absence of the literati-gentry class that for centuries had dominated Chinese society, Chinese merchants in Hong Kong were able to play top dog in the local community and among Chinese abroad."[10] According to historian John M. Carroll, by the turn of the century "the Hong Kong Chinese business elite had become a full-fledged bourgeoisie," even in the face of colonial racism.[11]

Hong Kong's private schools enhanced the colony's attractiveness for successful Chinese merchants living not just in the colony itself but in other English-speaking countries and territories. Most wanted their sons, and, increasingly, their daughters, to receive both a Chinese- and an English-language education that included exposure to westernized subjects such as science and math. This kind of mixed education would enable their offspring to deal not just with other ethnic Chinese but with the South Asian merchants, Western traders, and colonial officials who also moved in Asian business circles. Mainland China's schools largely proved unequal to the task, since elite Chinese there continued to educate their sons (but not their daughters) to take the traditional civil service exams until the Qing court abolished the system in 1905. Until then, studying the Confucian classics for regurgitation on the exams remained a major route to wealth and power in Chinese society and the focus of most family academies, schools, and tutors.[12] Missionary schools operated in many parts of Guangdong before the 1911 revolution, but they tended to focus on proselytizing as much if not more than on Western subjects. They also drew most of their students from poorer and more marginalized groups in Chinese society.[13] Many prosperous overseas merchants thus preferred to place their offspring in Hong Kong's Western-style academies. Most of these schools, although church affiliated, had a very different social meaning than their mainland counterparts: they catered to the children of the colony's elite, and they not only trained students for a future in the overseas Chinese world but also reinforced their parents' social status.[14]

Mainland China's instability added to Hong Kong's allure for Chinese merchants returning from abroad in the late nineteenth and early twentieth centuries. By then, the Qing dynasty was tottering as it struggled to deal with the Western and Japanese imperialism that compounded China's internal problems, from increasingly disobedient provincial officials, to famines, droughts, and floods, to multiple and often catastrophic peasant uprisings. In 1898 conservatives at the Qing court crushed attempts by Kang Youwei and Liang Qichao, Guangdong-born advisors to the Emperor Guangxu, to promote reform; two years later, the powerful Empress Dowager Cixi threw her support to the "Boxers," an anti-foreign sect that murdered hundreds of missionaries and Chinese Christians before laying siege to the foreign legation quarter in Beijing. After a combined Western and Japanese military force ended the siege and sacked the city, the Qing court negotiated a peace treaty, and Cixi finally launched economic, educational, and political reforms.

As part of this process, the cash-strapped imperial court sought to attract investment from Chinese abroad and improve the business climate for it, yet such attempts inadvertently demonstrated the hold of the hidebound bureaucracy and the growing anti-Qing sentiment in the south. Despite orders to embrace reform, imperial bureaucrats after 1901 made investment difficult at best with their red tape and corruption.[15] Furthermore, overseas Chinese were becoming some of the most fervent opponents of Qing rule, and of Cixi in particular. By 1905 Liang Qichao and Kang Youwei, and their archrival, the revolutionary Sun Yat-sen, had each traveled across the world raising hundreds of thousands of dollars for their causes from the Chinese abroad.[16]

THE LURE OF HONG KONG

Like many returned merchants from Australia, South Africa, Southeast Asia, and Latin America, second-generation Chinese American merchants who emigrated to Asia before 1911 flocked to Hong Kong rather than the Chinese mainland. They appreciated the colony's flexibility and its social and economic opportunities, for they possessed few if any of the educational credentials that meant status in late Qing China.[17] Instead, many had some money as well as existing connections to Chinese businesspeople in the colony through professional, family, and ancestral village networks.[18] When Louey Shuck arrived in Hong Kong, he relied on the Chui Cheong Loong company, a *jinshanzhuang* (literally, Gold Mountain firm) that exported Chinese goods to the United States and arranged remittances from overseas Chinese to the Pearl River Delta.[19] Much of Chui Cheong Loong's Hong Kong staff consisted of Louey's relatives, while Louey Shuck himself had once been the San Francisco branch's bookkeeper. The firm was one of dozens of Hong Kong companies that served overseas Chinese in San Francisco, Honolulu, Sydney, and Melbourne and whose staff usually consisted of family members or men from the same village or district. Hundreds of similar companies in Hong Kong specialized in trade and remittances for overseas Chinese from other parts of the world, including Havana, Calcutta, Lima, Penang, Singapore, and South Africa.[20]

The Chinese American population of Hong Kong grew quickly after the turn of the century, as scores of citizen merchants and students left the United States for greater opportunities in Asia. In 1901 the Hong Kong government's census counted only two Chinese Americans in the colony, but by mid-1911, that number had increased to 202.[21] Relatively few of these Chinese American citizens bothered to register with the US consulate, but if the data it collected about those who did applied to their unregistered peers, as many as sixty or seventy of those listed in the Hong Kong government census were students, and perhaps ninety or more were merchants or entrepreneurs. Members of the latter group almost invariably possessed at least some money or a trade, although few were truly rich. Usually the children of merchants, they sought continued upward mobility by moving to Hong Kong; ordinary laborers earned far less in the colony than in the United States, so Chinese American citizen adults without money or skills generally stayed in America.[22]

In Hong Kong, Chinese Americans with some education or capital could work in a wide variety of professions, unlike in the United States. A few rose to the lucrative position of comprador, including Louey Shuck, who represented a number of San Francisco firms in Hong Kong and became the comprador for the US shipping company Struthers and Dixon (later Struthers and Barry).[23] Most Chinese Americans never became compradors, but the colony's importance as a port still pushed them into trade-related fields, where their language skills and cultural knowledge gave them a distinct advantage. Well-heeled brothers Dong Wing and Dong Toy represented San Francisco's Quong Lun Company in the colony, while a number of more middling Chinese American citizen immigrants clerked for the smaller trading houses that lined Queens, Des Voeux, and Connaught Roads in the Central District.[24] Not all Chinese American citizens worked directly in trade. Though N.A. Tye founded an import-export business, he also opened a retail confectionary store that sold American soft drinks, gum, and candy on busy Pottinger Street. One San Francisco-born herbalist even set up a Chinese medicine shop among a number of similar practitioners on Wing Lock Street.[25]

While seeking to tap into existing overseas networks, a number of Chinese American merchants and entrepreneurs also brought US business practices to Hong Kong and South China. They became particularly prominent in banking in the region, where before the 1911 revolution "native banks" with their own set of practices served Chinese customers, and foreign banks catered to white-run firms. In early 1912, brothers Look Tin Eli and Look Poong Shan, two American citizens prominent in San Francisco business circles, founded the first bank in Hong Kong underwritten solely with (overseas) Chinese capital but relying on what its chief accountant termed "strictly Western methods" for its "customs and usages." Leading Hong Kong businesspeople and the governor of Guangdong alike expressed their hopes that this new Bank of Canton would spread such practices throughout China and make overseas investment there easier.[26] Highlighting the institution's strong overseas Chinese connections, Look brought in another American—Louey

FIGURE 2. Louey Shuck (also known as Louey Po Sang), a native of tiny Weaverville, California, emigrated to China with his family in 1907. Louey not only became a comprador in Hong Kong but also gained entry to the colony's elite Chinese social circles. National Archives and Records Administration, San Bruno regional facility.

Shuck—to serve as the bank's auditor.[27] Not to be outdone, in 1917 the Hawaiian-born Jun-ke Choy and several of his friends helped raise capital for yet another institution, the Industrial and Commercial Bank, Ltd.; the institution sought investors among overseas Chinese, especially in the US-controlled Philippines, and worked to encourage Chinese in Hong Kong to put their money in savings accounts.[28] The next year, brothers and Quong Lun Company representatives Dong Toy and Dong Wing founded the Chinese Merchants Bank to take advantage of the growing market for

Western-style banks.[29] The three institutions channeled overseas Chinese investment into the colony and south China until the mid-1920s.

As they moved in the Chinese business networks that converged in Hong Kong, many Chinese American merchants also placed their children in the colony's schools, just as so many overseas Chinese did in these years. One of the first young Chinese Americans to attend a Hong Kong academy was the son of Liao Zhubao, the San Francisco agent for the Hong Kong and Shanghai Bank. In 1894 Liao sent his American-born son Liao Zhongkai, later a leader of the Guomindang, back to the colony to enroll in Queen's College, the oldest public school in Hong Kong.[30] Just a few years later, longtime US resident Hong Sling arrived in Hong Kong and placed his Chicago-born sons Willie and Harry Hong Sling at Queen's College, where they became standout athletes, playing an Anglo-American blend of sports that included cricket, lawn bowling, and baseball.[31] Avoiding the colony's girls public school, which served a significant population of poor children, Hong Sling instead enrolled his daughter Jennie in the prestigious St. Stephen's Girls School, where she hobnobbed with young women from Hong Kong's most powerful Chinese families.[32] Many returning merchants preferred this kind of church-sponsored education for their American-born children, who soon flocked to elite private academies such as the Diocesan Boys School, the Diocesan Girls School, and the Italian Convent School.[33] After all, the right school conferred prestige on children and parents alike, and many of them craved that kind of recognition, so often denied them in America.

EDUCATING CHINESE AMERICAN CHILDREN ON THE CHINESE MAINLAND

Unlike returned merchants in Hong Kong, China-born parents who stayed in America while sending their offspring to China for an education almost always preferred schools on the mainland. In the 1900s and 1910s, hundreds of US-based Chinese fathers and mothers dispatched their American children to China for an education in their ancestral villages. A cigar manufacturer and a local restaurateur who lived just a few feet apart in New York's Chinatown enrolled their sons in schools in their native places, seventy miles away from each other.[34] Wong Fee Lee, the Deadwood landowner, sent seven of his offspring to attend school in his native village, as did scores of other China-born parents from cities and towns across America.[35] All of them rested easier knowing that their children were living under the supervision of their relatives and attending classes with their cousins.

Many of these parents framed their educational decisions in purely cultural terms, but their definition of culture was an expansive one. Some wanted their children to grow up as they themselves had, in homes where extended families lived under a single roof. Language immersion would also benefit young men who seemed destined to work among other Chinese, whether in Asia or the United States, and to marry in China because of the gender imbalances in US Chinese communities. But the Seattle merchant Albert King hinted at some of the less obvious reasons for dispatching children to China when he explained, "I will send my children back to China first to get that education, the Chinese customs and the Chinese ideals."[36] Most large Chinese American communities had long since organized their own culture and language schools, but such institutions were not particularly effective at instilling certain "customs" and "ideals."[37] In particular, parents often saw village schools as an antidote to the contaminating influence of urban American culture, with its sexual overtones and lack of esteem for elders.[38] "The children here have no respect for the old people," claimed one Los Angeles merchant in a typical lament. "It is not so in China[;] there they respect the old people. But here, if you are old, they think you ought to die."[39]

Many parents especially hoped that a "Chinese education," which included not just coursework at a local school but immersion in village life far from the United States, would make their daughters more manageable and perhaps more marriageable.[40] In US cities especially, Chinese parents frequently clashed with daughters who wanted to behave like other urban American girls. "My parents seem to think that I should not go out, at least in the evenings," one such Chinese American woman explained. "Chinese parents tend to restrict their daughters."[41] Whatever their own desires, young women also felt considerable pressure from parents who "believe . . . in that old Chinese idea that all girls must eventually be launched into matrimony," as another noted.[42] Compounding this burden, China-born men in the United States often complained about second-generation women, dismissing them as profligate and uninterested in raising large families. "This country you know, girl too independent. Go out in the evening, dance, spend money, don't like stay home much," alleged a longtime Chinese resident of Seattle. "Girls [in] this country don't make so good wives as girls in China."[43] At least some parents saw a Chinese education as the solution to this "problem" and assumed that life in China would discipline their daughters out of their American ideas.

These Chinese American children, dispatched to the mainland for school in the twilight of the Qing dynasty, entered an educational environment undergoing rapid transformation. Donations from Chinese abroad enabled many villages in the Pearl River Delta to open primary schools by the early twentieth century.[44] The quality of these institutions varied, however, and reflected the spotty nature of recent Qing educational reforms. Chinese social activists had since the turn of the century pushed for universal education, including education for females, and the introduction of Western subjects such as math, science, and geography. Educators also debated replacing classical Chinese with vernacular Chinese, as well as the degree to which new subjects should supplant older curricular staples. The results were hardly coherent: in Guangdong, officials actually forced the closure of some newly established women's schools after 1904, and they also sought to push imperial degree holders and other traditional literati into new teachers' colleges, with mixed results.[45]

Institutional turmoil aside, Chinese American students often struggled in the local primary schools, where instruction was completely in Chinese. Wong Fee Lee's children, who attended an ordinary village school, "started . . . late and had a difficult time catching up," according to Wong's grandson Edward Wong.[46] Eloise Fong remembered that after some time in Guangzhou, her grandfather eventually "figured out we were not learning much" and sent her and her cousins to a special overseas Chinese school.[47] After the 1911 revolution, when Chinese American students began to attend missionary schools in larger numbers, teachers there noticed the problems that Chinese American and other ethnic Chinese children from abroad seemed inevitably to encounter. The Canton Christian College argued that its "usual [feeder] schools could not receive these irregular students" because of their low Chinese language level.[48] Provincial and national education officials also struggled for years to deal with the problems overseas Chinese students encountered in village schools. During the early 1920s, the National Education Federation passed resolutions asking the various provinces to create "special type" schools specifically for overseas Chinese students.[49] A decade later, the Nationalist regime, which sought to register and regiment the school system, still grappled with the issue, eventually arguing that "the children of overseas Chinese . . . shouldn't be recruited if their levels are too low" and recommending special cram schools and exams for other youths from abroad.[50]

For some Chinese American students, the solution was to seek education in China but at least partly if not wholly in the English language. In the years before 1911, a handful of Hawaiian Chinese Christian parents sent their children to Shanghai to study at St. John's College (later St. John's University), at that time something of a preparatory academy where the medium of instruction was English.[51] As a religious institution, St. John's recruited Hawaiian youths through the islands' Anglican networks, particularly Rev. Kong Tet-En's St. Peter's Church and Anglican schools like the Iolani School.[52] In 1895 a handful of Chinese Americans from Honolulu led by Philip Tyau Ahung (an Iolani graduate) became the first group of Hawaiians to enroll in St. John's, and a trickle of other Hawaiian Chinese boys, including Paul Ball Young, Andrew Fong Zane, and T. M. Li, followed in the next decade.[53] After 1905 and especially 1911, the fact that St. John's used English for instruction increasingly attracted the children of Shanghai's business classes. The school's resulting links to the region's bourgeoisie also broadened its appeal to less religious Chinese American students, especially those from Hawaii who sought entry into Shanghai business and society.[54]

THE COLLAPSE OF THE QING DYNASTY

The brief "Xinhai Revolution," which began in 1911, led to the end of China's last imperial dynasty in 1912.[55] When news of the revolution reached him in the United States, Sun Yat-sen, the Cantonese revolutionary whose Tongmenghui (Revolutionary Alliance) counted members around the world, rushed back to China to participate. A group of provincial delegates named Sun the provisional president of the new Republic of China, but he soon bowed to the inevitable and stepped aside for strongman Yuan Shikai. Unlike Sun, Yuan wielded real military power as the former commander of the "new style" Beiyang Army that Qing reformers had created in the late nineteenth century.[56] Quickly, the new president worked to suppress the Guomindang, the political party that Sun created out of the old Tongmenghui after the revolution and that dominated the new parliament. The eventual Guomindang-Yuan clash pushed Sun and other leaders into exile, and in 1915 Yuan Shikai even attempted to declare himself emperor.[57]

Against the backdrop of this political upheaval, Chinese American citizen merchants and students continued to pour into the south. The fall of the Qing dynasty prompted little concern among the Chinese parents who had sent their American-born children to study on the mainland, since Guangdong seemed far safer than other parts of China in 1911 and 1912. In central China, fighting between Qing and revolutionary troops erupted and led to the slaughter of Manchus in several cities.[58] At Shanghai, a number of St. John's students joined the revolution, while others disrupted campus life to such a degree that administrators suspended them en masse.[59] Because of the chaos, some of the early Hawaiian students left St. John's for good, either finishing school in Hong Kong or returning to Hawaii.[60] In contrast, the Pearl River Delta remained calm, with the revolution initially making almost no impact on Chinese American children in the village schools there. Early optimism about the republic and its economic potential also prompted a number of Chinese American citizen merchants to move from the United States or Hong Kong to Guangdong in 1912 and 1913. One of the new enthusiasts, Louey Shuck, even briefly joined the Guomindang after his arrival in Guangzhou.[61]

Despite this early excitement about the revolution, the new regime quickly alienated many Cantonese, including Chinese American citizen merchants. Once the last Qing governor fled the province in late 1911, Guangdong sputtered along under a hastily composed group of Sun Yat-sen's followers, led by Hu Hanmin. The insolvency of the new government, which zealously borrowed money from Guangzhou businesspeople, soon made it unpopular in the region. Many Chinese in the south thus approved when President Yuan Shikai crushed Sun Yat-sen's Guomindang during the Second Revolution of 1913 and stationed General Long Jiguang and his troops in the province. Their relief proved short-lived: through his financial extractions, Long made himself more loathed than the rulers he replaced. He eventually lost his grip on power when Yuan died, China spiraled into warlordism, and a group of Guangxi militarists, including Lu Rongting, ejected Long from Guangdong. They proved just as adept at gouging local people for money to pay for their own armies but equally uninterested in actually providing security for the region.[62] Chinese American citizens were hardly immune from the problems that resulted.

By 1917 China was falling apart, with local warlords ignoring the internationally recognized but weak government in Beijing (itself warlord controlled) and fighting against each other for control of the country's different regions. Determined to rule China, Sun Yat-sen in these chaotic years lent his name and prestige to a string of willing strongmen in the south. In 1917, with the support of Lu Rongting, Sun gathered in Guangzhou with remnants of the old parliament, which elected him generalissimo of a new military government. When Lu withdrew his backing the next year, Sun had to flee to Shanghai. In 1920 he returned to Guangzhou with the support of warlord Chen

Jiongming, but the two men fell out over Chen's support for federalism, prompting Sun to flee the province again. In 1923 Sun was back, supported by warlord troops from Guangxi and Yunnan provinces. In between Sun's short-lived regimes, southern warlords extracted money from and sparked terror in Guangdong's long-suffering residents.[63]

As public order disintegrated in the south, Chinese American citizens there found that bandits, warlord troops, and corrupt authorities alike often targeted them and their families for their perceived wealth. One American complained that people in his parents' village were attempting to extort money from him. The next year, burglars broke into the village home of another Chinese American, stealing not only his possessions but also taking his nephew and demanding HK$1,000 in ransom for the boy's return. At the insistence of the American consul, local magistrates ordered troops to assist the man, but a few months later, the same soldiers shot and killed a Chinese Hawaiian while he was strolling along a local road.[64] As the incidents demonstrated, sometimes the line between lawbreakers and law enforcement officials disappeared entirely. Police in one Pearl River Delta village kidnapped Chinese American citizens, demanding hefty ransoms for their release, while in another district, authorities openly arrested a number of immigrants and confiscated their belongings.[65]

News about brigands and officials who levied arbitrary "fines" and "taxes" now reached Chinese American communities in the United States with alarming frequency, temporarily dampening enthusiasm for emigration. Beginning in 1916, the number of Chinese American citizens with Forms 430 returning to the United States exceeded those leaving the United States for the first time since immigration officials began to collect such statistics. By 1918 the number of preinvestigated Chinese American citizens leaving the United States dipped to a mere thirty-five.[66] In part this was the result of World War I and new wartime passport restrictions, but it also reflected the disorder into which South China had plunged since the revolution.[67]

DEFINING CITIZENSHIP

During the same period, the south's political turmoil also transformed the relationship between Chinese American citizen students and merchants and the governments in both China and the United States. Since corruption had permeated Chinese officialdom in the twilight of the Qing dynasty, southerners hoped for a cleaner or at least a more efficient government after the revolution.

Instead, the opportunism of Sun Yat-sen and the behavior of his followers in these years alienated much of Guangdong's business class, which by the 1910s included a growing number of Chinese American citizens. A hotel owner from San Francisco described how during one of Sun's periods of authority in the province, Guangzhou's "police department . . . demanded the usual squeeze."[68] American banker Jun-ke Choy similarly explained that "some of the public land of the city had been stolen and sold by influential members of the Kuomintang."[69] By 1921 the Hawaiian-born journalist Hin Wong lamented that "not a few Cantonese merchants and citizens . . . are still in Hongkong and Macao so as to avoid possible persecution in Canton upon their return."[70] The other regimes that alternated with Sun's attempts to regain power simply heightened Chinese American disillusionment with all the south's authorities. "The soldiers [here] have mixed themselves with bands of robbers and are raiding the districts," complained Boston native Kwok Min in a typical lament.[71]

As corruption mounted and public order collapsed, Chinese Americans who found themselves in trouble began to demand help from the US consulate in Guangzhou. Initially, consular authorities complied, writing letters appealing for assistance or justice to local magistrates, district commanders, *dujun* (military governors), and whatever officials were running the government in Guangdong at that moment. Among other arguments, consular staff asserted that as American citizens, Chinese Americans enjoyed protection from fines and taxes because of extraterritoriality (often shortened to "extrality").[72] A system that the foreign powers had imposed on China in the mid-nineteenth century, extrality meant that if a foreigner was accused of committing a crime in China, Chinese officials had to hand him or her over to representatives of his or her nation for trial (and, if convicted, imprisonment) under that nation's laws.[73] Increasingly, though, consular staff discovered that Chinese magistrates, police, and other authorities pushed back against such claims, asserting that Chinese Americans had no rights as American citizens.[74] Beginning in 1909, China used a jus sanguinis system that based citizenship on ancestry and considered all children with Chinese fathers to be Chinese citizens, whether they were born in China or not. In contrast, the United States, Britain, and a handful of other nations used variations of the jus soli system, in which birth within the borders of the nation conferred citizenship, regardless of ethnicity.[75] This meant that Chinese American citizens were dual citizens, and under international law, when dual citizens were within the boundaries of one of their two nations, that country exercised jurisdiction over them unless a treaty between it and the other nation stipulated differently.[76] No such treaty existed between the United States and China. This did not prevent some consular officials from pressing for the release of arrested Chinese Americans or the seizure of their kidnappers, but even sympathetic Chinese authorities often had little real power to help. Far more had no desire to do so.

In Guangzhou, a growing number of US officials showed similar tendencies, moving to exclude Chinese Americans from the full benefits of citizenship in a manner reflective of initiatives underway in the United States. In reality, consular staff might have rejected local authorities' attempts to claim jurisdiction over Chinese Americans, based on the simple fact that the US government recognized the Beijing-based "Beiyang" regime as the official government of China; a succession of southern governments that tried in vain to gain international recognition thus had less potential ability to assert power over Chinese American citizens. But like many white Americans, numerous Guangzhou US consular officials had little incentive to look for loopholes for Chinese Americans. Instead, they dismissed such people's citizenship claims on racial and ethnic grounds. Consul Albert W. Pontius fumed that Chinese American citizens "come and go as Chinese purely and have little regard for American ideals or institutions."[77] Consul F. D. Cheshire complained to colleagues that "these American Chinese are Chinese when it suits their purposes to be Chinese, and when they get into trouble they defy the Chinese authorities and claim American protection. . . . If a half dozen of them were shot it would probably have a very good effect."[78]

Most consular officials did not similarly endorse the murder of Chinese Americans, but they still found ways to show contempt for such people's citizenship claims. As Guangdong descended into chaos, consular staff created a variety of excuses to reject Chinese Americans' pleas for almost any kind of assistance and recognition. Some staff members turned away Chinese American citizens who wished to register their businesses with the US consulate because the firms "[had] the aspects of a Chinese rather than an American enterprise." Other US officials demanded that Chinese Americans communicate with their consulates only in English.[79]

In reality, during the last years of the Qing dynasty and throughout the republican period, many Chinese American citizens did use their dual status as Chinese citizens to their advantage. Dual citizenship provided potential protection and a competitive edge as China descended into revolution and political chaos. Some Chinese government agencies barred foreigners from certain jobs, yet Chinese Americans occasionally sought and received these positions.[80] China's treaties forbade non-Chinese citizens (except foreign missionaries) from living or owning property outside of the treaty port areas, but Chinese Americans often inherited or purchased property in their ancestral villages and lived there.[81] Chinese Americans also participated in Chinese political parties, served in the Chinese military, and worked for a variety of Chinese regimes, all while maintaining their US citizenship and occasionally seeking refuge in it.[82] Some could not speak, read, or write in English, especially those who had come to China as children or had grown up without access to US public schools. The phenomenon of passing as a purely Chinese citizen was not limited to Americans but was common practice among many different overseas Chinese, especially those born in Southeast Asia's European colonies. In fact, even ethnic Chinese leaders in Hong Kong complained about the behavior of British subjects from the colony and the Straits Settlements: "While in China they exercise all the rights and privileges of Chinese citizens without any regard to their duties as British subjects; but when they come into conflict with the constituted Chinese authorities, they immediately seek the privileges of British citizenship, and claim British protection."[83]

Still, at a time when social and political order were crumbling in China, Chinese Americans who "passed" acted no better or worse than those among whom they lived in the Pearl River Delta. Like other people in China, they sought whatever security advantages they could gain in the chaos of the late Qing and early republican years. They were also following the lead of white Americans who while in China skirted meddlesome laws and regulations and relied on their citizenship status to shield them.[84] Unsurprisingly, US consular officials did not write off the entire "white race" for exploiting extrality, but American authorities routinely dismissed Chinese Americans for similar behavior and excoriated them for lacking loyalty to a nation, the United States, that had shown them almost none in return.

Worst of all, consuls and the State Department essentially revoked the citizenship of some Chinese Americans by refusing to issue passports to a number wishing to escape the turmoil of the south and return to the United States. Such cases involved Chinese American citizens who had lived in China for many years; the consuls who examined them did not contest their birth on US soil but simply argued that these people had expatriated themselves through long residence abroad.[85] In fact, US law stipulated that the only way lengthy residence abroad could result in expatriation was if the person in question was a *naturalized* citizen. The law, which was silent about dual citizenship, specified that native-born people could only expatriate if they served in a foreign military or government, naturalized in a foreign state, or, if female, married a man who was not a US citizen.[86] Regardless, consuls appear to have seen extended Chinese American residence abroad as equivalent to "naturalization" in China, stripping from people of Chinese ancestry their citizenship rights without the slightest intervention of a court.[87]

THE CHANGING MEANING OF A "CHINESE EDUCATION"

The disintegration of order in the Pearl River Delta not only changed the relationship between Chinese Americans and the governments of both the United States and China, but it also transformed the meaning of a "Chinese education" for at least some youths. As political and social instability increased in mid-1910s south China, Chinese and Chinese American parents who wished to educate their US-born children on the mainland faced a real dilemma. Village schools frequently offered an essentially classical Chinese education with just a smattering of newer subjects and pedagogies.[88] Worse yet, villages and the schools that served them now appeared frighteningly insecure in an era of widespread banditry, kidnapping, and official abuses.

Most Chinese American parents who educated their children in China continued to send them to village schools in order to ensure the proper supervision of their sons and daughters, but fewer dispatched them alone. Sometimes, both parents accompanied their young children to China, retiring to their home villages or Guangzhou and seeking to acclimate their offspring to life there.[89] More often, mothers brought Chinese American children home to raise and educate in the village while Chinese merchant fathers stayed in the United States.[90] But even parents who could not accompany their children to China continued to send them to vulnerable villages to live with grandparents or cousins. Despite the rise of banditry and kidnapping in the Pearl River Delta, these parents often believed that obtaining a "Chinese education" for their children was worth the risk involved, especially if such schooling helped counteract some of the behaviors their offspring had learned in Jazz Age America. As a Seattle merchant argued, "if they don't have this old country education, they [are] no good."[91] Chinese merchant parents in America kept sending their children to south China's village schools as late as 1940, two years after the Japanese occupation of Guangdong began.[92]

But as the social and political fabric frayed in the province, a growing number of US-based Chinese parents turned from village schools to the Western institutions in and around Guangzhou that were beginning to groom a new generation of Guangdong elites. Founded by missionary organizations, these Western academies and Christian colleges had grown increasingly popular with local merchants after the end of the exam system. They usually enjoyed some US government protection, offered curricula distinct from traditional village schools, and included excellent English instruction. By the late 1910s, many US-based Chinese parents recognized both the social and physical advantages of such schools. Some transferred their children from village schools, while others withdrew offspring from Hong Kong academies to enroll them in the increasingly prestigious Guangzhou institutions.[93] Louey Shuck shifted his sons Louie Jung Yan and Louie Hong How from Hong Kong institutions to the middle school affiliated with Canton Christian College (CCC) in the mid-1910s to prepare them for university in America.[94] During the same period, many other Chinese American youths, along with scores of overseas Chinese children from other parts of the world, sought admission directly to Guangzhou's Western-style academies, bypassing village schools altogether.

The timing of this surge demonstrates just how much the lack of security in south China enhanced the popularity of special overseas schools across the country. The Qing-founded Jinan Academy, a school for overseas Chinese that closed after the revolution, reopened in 1917 to meet the new demand.[95] In Beijing, Tsing Hua College, created with US Boxer Indemnity money and initially intended to groom Chinese students for American universities, began admitting the sons (but not, apparently, the daughters) of overseas Chinese after 1917.[96] The Chinese government promised to administer exams to them in their native countries and, when possible, offer them scholarships.[97] But Guangzhou-area Western schools remained the most popular with overseas parents. In 1918 CCC created a middle school especially for overseas Chinese; within five years, the number of students enrolled in its classes quadrupled, eclipsing the growth in almost every other department of CCC.[98] During the same period, True Light Middle School's new facility in Pak Hok Tung, Guangdong, became known for the large numbers of overseas Chinese female students it attracted.[99] By the early 1920s, a Chinese organization in Guangdong had even formed to help lobby for the creation of special overseas Chinese schools there.[100]

The influx of Chinese American and other overseas Chinese children and teens into westernized Chinese schools changed the entire meaning of going to China to receive a "Chinese education." A series of Chinese governments after 1900 had pushed for the establishment of special Chinese schools in places outside of China but with large ethnic Chinese populations, especially Southeast Asia; the purpose of these institutions was to counter European officials' attempts to encourage overseas Chinese to attend Western schools and identify with colonial rulers.[101] Now, however, many overseas Chinese students who came to China enrolled in institutions at which instruction took place at least partly in English, attendance at prayer services and chapel on Sunday was a requirement, and the westernized curricula bore little resemblance to what most ordinary village schools offered.[102] For instance, Tsing Hua strove to prepare young Chinese to study in the United States and reflected what scholar John Israel calls a "whole-hearted commitment to the American model" of education.[103] Christian schools in Shanghai and Guangzhou strained the idea of a "Chinese education" even more. Certainly, they sought to improve the Chinese fluency of overseas students, whose grasp of academic Chinese fell far short of their peers', but the experience was hardly akin to immersion. Although Chinese Christians worked at almost all of the missionary schools, many of the teachers whom Chinese Americans encountered at St. John's, Pui Ying, Pui Ching, Pooi To, True Light, and other Christian schools were themselves fairly recent arrivals from the United States—often enthusiastic young, white, American Protestant participants in the Student Volunteer Movement, steeped in the Social Gospel crusade that inspired so many of their peers in this era to enter foreign mission work.[104]

Parents who enrolled their American-born children in schools such as CCC and its feeders likely saw these institutions as educationally beneficial in a changing economy and nation, but they understood even more clearly the social advantages their offspring could gain. The Western-style, partly English-language education so many of these schools offered attracted wealthy members of coastal China's merchant class. In 1915 the American-educated Chinese Christian Fong F. Sec commented proudly on "the prestige, which St. John's University, Peking University, the University of Nanking, Soochow University, the Canton Christian College and institutions of similar grade at present enjoy," explicitly comparing these missionary-run, westernized colleges to far less popular government schools.[105] "Eighty-five percent of [our] . . . students are from non-Christian homes," noted Herbert E. House of CCC.

OVERSEAS SCHOOL 1923-24 "WAKIU" School. Students in this school are born outside of China and sent back for their education. C. K. Tse, one time Commandant of the School reports that he sometimes had to have his orders translated into six languages to accomodate these boys. They are the sons of wealthy parents in most cases

FIGURE 3. By the late 1910s, Cantonese from around the world were sending their children to Canton Christian College (later Lingnan University) and its associated schools, including the "Wa Kiu" (Overseas Chinese) School. This photo of Wa Kiu students was taken during the 1923–1924 school year, right before the exodus of American students from Guangzhou. The caption notes that the former head of the school "sometimes had to have his orders translated into six languages to accommodate these boys," who were "the sons of wealthy parents in most cases." Reprinted with permission of the Lingnan Foundation (archived at Special Collections, Yale Divinity School Library).

"Most of these are of the leading people."[106] CCC's administration admitted, "Our relatively high tuition fees have not caused a diminution of enrollment in our own Middle School," which attracted scores of students whose parents could easily afford to pay the costs involved.[107]

Canton Christian College gained a simultaneously cosmopolitan and extremely regional feel as it mixed local elites with overseas merchants' children. By the early 1920s, preparatory and college students at CCC came from Malacca, Borneo, Tasmania, Bangkok, New York, Penang, Denver, Yokohama, Honolulu, and Java, but also from Hong Kong, Macao, Guangzhou, and many of the smaller towns of the Pearl River Delta. Students' parents included ministers and missionaries, to be sure, but also bankers, traditional scholars, a former Nationalist assemblyman, a one-time governor of Guangdong, and a large number of wealthy merchants and entrepreneurs, including the overseas Chinese Christian families behind the Sincere and Wing On department stores of Hong Kong and Shanghai.[108]

Despite CCC's ostensibly global profile, what bound its student cohort together was a shared regional ancestry. All but a handful of the students traced their roots to the Pearl River Delta, and Cantonese fluency was a social necessity on campus.[109] Reinforcing a regional-overseas identity, the college offered what was probably the world's first course on the history of "Chinese immigration into foreign countries," or in the words of the Chinese bulletin title, "Overseas Chinese history."[110] By 1919 the college was also busy erecting a dormitory especially for overseas Chinese students, and donations from overseas merchants were crucial to the success of the institution as a whole.[111] The schools that fed CCC, including Pui Ying, Union Middle School, Pui Ching, Pooi To, and True Light, reflected the same demographics and attracted many Chinese American students by the early 1920s, from Tak Shin Hung and Tak Sang Hung of Kohala, Hawaii; to Edward Fook Leung of Atlantic City, New Jersey; to Foot Jung Lew of San Francisco.[112]

THE OVERSEAS CHINESE WORLD OF THE SOUTH

Despite the political chaos of this era, Chinese American citizen merchants and students in the early 1920s played an increasingly visible role in Guangdong's education system, social circles, and economy. Scores invested in the city of Guangzhou, which managed to thrive in the midst of chaos. In the first years of the 1920s, groups of overseas Chinese that included Americans bankrolled a cotton spinning works, a cement factory, a drug company, and a new branch of the Sincere Department Store.[113] Sid Bock Yin, Gee Chuck, and other Chinese Americans even created their own *jinshanzhuang*, the China Agency and Trading Company, to take advantage of the growing US immigrant presence in Guangzhou.[114] Chinese American citizen entrepreneurs also scrambled to meet an increasing demand for Western-style products driven by returned overseas workers with a taste for foreign goods and services.[115] The American immigrants opened Western-style pharmacies, a hotel, a hospital, and a school for chauffeurs, and they produced local versions of popular Western products at new factories.[116] Bilingual and bicultural

Chinese Americans also served as direct agents for foreign products, working for a variety of American and European companies such as Asiatic Petroleum, Anderson Meyer, Purnell and Pagett, British American Tobacco, and Standard Oil. People of Chinese ancestry at this time could never imagine landing such jobs in the United States, but in China they were valuable employees.

Savvy educational decisions, together with financial security and merchant connections, also enabled many Chinese American citizen merchants and students in this era to enter a particular kind of Chinese high society—one anchored in cosmopolitan port cities, enmeshed in networks linked to European colonies, heavily Cantonese, and deeply dismaying to ardent nationalists. Scholar Soon Keong Ong argues that "in the eyes of Chinese politicians and Chinese intellectuals, [overseas Chinese] could never be the equivalent of those Chinese who never left China," especially in terms of their cultural and social level.[117] But even if northern intellectuals and politicians looked down on the overseas Chinese, the commercial classes of the central and southern coastal cities embraced those with enough money and polish.

Louey Shuck, a native of a tiny California town, was a prime example. In 1921 his daughter Frances Yuk Yung Lui (whose siblings spelled their surname Louie—none used Louey) wed David W.K. Au, the son of Andrew Au Ben, a wealthy emigrant from the Pearl River Delta to Australia and a founder of the Sincere Company department stores of Hong Kong and Shanghai.[118] Just three years later, Louey's son Jung Yan Louie married Theodora Yen, the niece of a Chinese railroad executive and of Shanghai publisher and diplomat W. W. Yen.[119] During the same years, Louey sat on the board of Hong Kong's Tung Wah Hospital, which in the colony signified the pinnacle of social success, and joined the YMCA, another way for Chinese in Hong Kong to establish their status.[120] Louey may have been born in Weaverville, but his decision to relocate to Asia allowed his family to avoid the social and economic limitations that Chinese faced both in Gold Rush country and in San Francisco.

For Chinese American women, the fluidity and mores of the China coast world were often even more liberating. Growing up in the United States, most envisioned a future centered on marriage and children, but few desired the limited freedoms and large families their own mothers endured. "Because of my American training I feel the restraints imposed by the Chinese traditions," confessed a Chinese American woman from Los Angeles. "I feel the restrictions imposed upon the girls; we are not permitted to go out to socials or to have good times as the American girls have."[121] Some young women who wished to attend high school and college also clashed with parents who saw little value in educating female children, while men in their communities often derided them as too modern and Americanized.[122] Arriving in Guangzhou in the late 1910s and early 1920s, these merchants' daughters found friends and allies in their quest to live differently than their mothers had.

Indeed, they discovered that younger Cantonese and overseas Chinese from other parts of the world often saw their "American" traits in a positive light. Lynne Lee Shew, a Chinese American from the Bay Area who moved to China to found a hospital, enthused over the "freedom of choice, equal opportunity of education, and . . . fair chance for doing her parts in society" that she saw for women in Guangzhou and the other urban coastal areas she visited.[123] Many students on the campuses of the China coast schools and colleges supported these "new women," reflecting the influence of the New Culture Movement of the 1910s and the May Fourth Movement on young, educated Chinese. Participants in both movements envisioned women's emancipation as integral to China's modernization, and the new literary and political journals they published supported individualism and romantic love while opposing the repressive aspects of the traditional family.[124]

For the more privileged Chinese American citizen women, then, Guangzhou offered the kinds of educational and social opportunities and validation they could only dream of back in the United States, or in their ancestral villages in more remote areas of the Pearl River Delta. In Guangzhou, they could attend modern schools, read the new women's magazines, and participate in women's clubs. They could also mix with Chinese men of similar backgrounds, whether on the campus of Canton Christian College, at the Guangzhou YMCA, or in the Sincere Department Store. In fact, a good number who attended CCC met their future husbands there—fellow students who were often the sons of well-heeled Guangzhou import-export traders or of wealthy merchants from Australia, South Africa, or Canada.[125]

THE PERILS OF POLITICS

Although they relished the economic and social opportunities of the treaty port world, these Chinese American citizen immigrants, especially the students among them, entered Chinese schools and coastal society at a fraught moment in the country's history. Patriotic Chinese had hoped that China's participation on the victorious Allied forces' side in World War I would convince the major Western powers to return the German-held concession at Jiaozhou in Shandong Province to China. Japan, another member of the Allies, occupied the concession beginning in 1914 and wanted to retain the territory for itself. A web of secret agreements involving the major powers, Japan, and the Beiyang regime resulted in that outcome, much to the dismay of many Chinese. On May 4, 1919, as the terms of the Treaty of Versailles became public, students from several Beijing-area colleges took to the streets in protest. Despite the northern regime's attempts to suppress them, the student protesters in Beijing sparked a major political, literary, and social movement that became known as the May Fourth Movement and in many ways marked the birth of the modern Chinese nation. Simultaneously, Chinese across the country and the world flooded the northern government with angry letters and telegrams protesting the treaty.[126] Youths living in Guangdong similarly excoriated the northern regime and enthusiastically supported the May Fourth activists, even receiving some support from southern officials.[127]

At first, Chinese American and other overseas students joined their local classmates in expressing hatred for Japan and patriotism for China. For these Americans, a group whose attachment to China had previously been fairly apolitical, the new movement signaled a potential turning point. Guangdong's Student Union organized enthusiastic branches at heavily overseas campus such as Canton Christian College, Pui Ying, Pui Ching, and True Light.[128] Students at CCC, like those across the city, created a speakers' bureau in their quest to "save the nation," and they urged fellow citizens to participate in a national boycott of Japanese goods.[129] Students from the missionary schools also played key roles in organizing boycott parades, while a youth from CCC chaired a Student Union committee seeking to raise money to build a factory for the manufacture of local goods to undercut Japan.[130] The boycott activities eventually spread to more remote parts of the Pearl River Delta, including heavily overseas Chinese areas such as Toisan, where students at village schools organized townspeople to boycott Japanese products.[131]

However, as the boycott continued and the protests in Guangzhou intensified, fissures developed in the movement, exposing the uneasy position both of the students at the Western missionary schools and of the overseas Chinese merchants in south China. In early June 1919, during a massive march connected to the boycott, students entered the three largest department stores in Guangzhou—two of them (Sincere and the Sun) owned by overseas Chinese—and ordered them to stop dealing in Japanese products. At Sincere, managers agreed to student demands, but demonstrators still caused problems outside the store; at the Sun, a guard shot a blank round into the air to frighten off the crowd, which responded by breaking the shop's windows and causing several thousand dollars in damage.[132] Both stores soon became targets of new boycott pressures, causing considerable dismay among CCC students. Some happily participated in the anti-Sincere activities; others explicitly avoided these affairs because their families owned shares in the stores, and because Ma Ying Piu, who controlled the company, was a prominent overseas Chinese Christian, CCC trustee, and college donor.[133] More radical members of the Student Union increasingly excluded from their activities all CCC students and many youths from other Christian colleges, including the American citizens among them, because such people refused to attack Sincere during rallies.[134]

The Sun and Sincere incidents, which hinted at the future anti-imperialist trajectory of Chinese nationalism, marked the beginning of the end of widespread Chinese American student activism in the south. When protesting Japan, overseas Chinese students easily found common ground with local youths from schools and colleges that lacked any Western affiliation. But once the protests targeted not just actual Japanese but those Chinese who did business with them, and then imperialism in general, the most ardent local participants began to cast overseas Chinese merchants and networks as unpatriotic. Similarly, by helping revive the languishing campaign to use and buy "national products," the movement called into question the activities of ethnic Chinese who traded in foreign goods, represented foreign companies, or possessed foreign citizenship.[135] As May Fourth activism grew increasingly anti-imperialist, Chinese American students in and around Guangzhou retreated into the overseas Chinese circles in which their own complex affinities and affiliations remained not just acceptable but the norm.

IDENTITY CRISIS

Despite the political unrest and social disorder in south China, Chinese American emigration to Guangdong increased during the early 1920s as US politics became ever more xenophobic and anti-immigrant. According to the US census, the Chinese American citizen population of the United States rose from 18,500 in 1920 to 31,000 in 1930. However, many of these people were unlawful entrants claiming derivative citizenship through citizen fathers who were not their actual parents. During the same decade, almost 9,000 nonderivative native-born Chinese Americans declared to immigration officials that they were "permanently departing" from the United States and moving to China or Hong Kong.[136] In other words, about half of all truly native-born Chinese Americans may have left for China during this decade—a remarkably high percentage.

These Chinese American immigrants developed a sense of "Chineseness" that reflected regional and class identities as much as a national consciousness. By the 1910s, significant numbers of Chinese American citizens were arriving in China to attend Western-style schools, where they often studied in English and sometimes struggled with their "native" tongue. Furthermore, as Canton Christian College's experience showed, these new schools also became magnets for the children of local compradors, wealthy merchants, and other members of the south China coastal elite, undeterred by the presence of so many overseas Chinese students. The merchants of Guangdong proved far less likely than northern elites to express concern over such a mix of students, given their frequent involvement in the import-export trade and their family and professional ties to overseas Chinese. Instead, shared schools, friends, and social activities helped Chinese Americans in south China forge close ties to these other mercantile families, both overseas Chinese and local, enhancing their social status in the region and their identification with its merchants.

At the same time, though, the American-born students and merchants participated in social circles, made educational choices, and picked careers that placed them on a collision course with some of China's most fervent nationalists. When they protested the Treaty of Versailles and Japanese goods, Chinese American students began to confront head-on the involvement of overseas Chinese merchants in activities that other Chinese increasingly considered unpatriotic. The Chinese American citizen adults who relocated to south China in these years frequently developed similarly conflicted identities, working in the import-export business, in *jinshanzhuang*, as dealers of foreign goods, and, sometimes, as agents of foreign companies. By the mid-1920s, their choices became ever more problematic as anti-imperialist politics convulsed the region and, eventually, the country as a whole.

Chinese American citizen immigrants' involvement, both individually and in groups, in Guangdong's and Hong Kong's economic life bound their identities closely to the south's merchants. While they saw themselves as Chinese and supported patriotic national movements, their closest relationships in

China were often with other ethnic Chinese from abroad, or with local Chinese whose major business ties were overseas. Intermarriage, shared schools, and similar economic interests thus cemented a sense not just of being Chinese but of being a particular kind of Chinese—an overseas Chinese, a China coast dweller, a treaty port Chinese, or a Cantonese—as did a lack of connection to the distant, Mandarin-speaking intellectuals and officials of the North. The political disruption and fragmentation of the warlord era simply enhanced such feelings and provided a kind of protection for those who shared them. But by the mid-1920s, the reinvigorated Nationalist movement began to consider such sentiments to be threats to China's sovereignty and integrity.

CHAPTER 2

The Modernizers

US-Educated Chinese Americans in China

Renowned aviator and San Francisco native Tom Gunn was halfway across the Pacific when he heard the news. In the summer of 1913, troops loyal to Sun Yat-sen and the Guomindang (GMD) rebelled again Yuan Shikai, the increasingly dictatorial president of the new Republic of China. This "Second Revolution" ended when Yuan's forces crushed the GMD and its allies. Sun, who had invited Tom to China to help develop aviation there, now fled to Japan.[1] Rather than continuing on to Shanghai as planned, Tom traveled instead to Hawaii and the Philippines, where he held a series of flying exhibitions. As Chinese politics shifted quickly over the next few years, Tom secretly joined the Guomindang during a visit to Tokyo, established an aviation corps in warlord-controlled Guangzhou, staged airplane demonstrations for charity in Macao and Hong Kong, offered testimonials for a Chinese oil company, imported cars from America to sell in China, tried to breed horses and police dogs there, and helped the warlords of Guangxi develop their own air force.[2] Although Tom's colorful and varied exploits won him an unusual degree of fame, he was just one of the hundreds of skilled and educated Chinese American adults who traveled to China in the first two decades of the twentieth century to develop their careers and serve their parents' homeland.

This chapter follows these American-educated Chinese American adults who moved to China and explores the ways that their skills and credentials, ideas about the meaning of modernity, and views of citizenship shaped their lives and opportunities there. Unlike the thousands of Chinese American citizen merchants and students who left the United States to work or study in Hong Kong or south China, Tom Gunn and his Western-trained US citizen counterparts, whom I call the "modernizers," planned to use their education and skills to transform their new home into a "modern" nation. Beginning in 1901, the weak and floundering Qing dynasty finally launched a series of far-reaching reforms, but it lacked a critical mass of scientists, technicians, and other experts to build infrastructure, exploit natural resources, guide economic development, shape public health efforts, and overhaul hidebound institutions.[3] This situation offered Western-educated Chinese American citizens the chance not only to work in their fields but often to rise quickly, even meteorically, to positions of leadership and influence.[4] The 1911 revolution and the political fragmentation of the later 1910s also meant that opportunities proliferated for Chinese Americans as various regimes competed to woo talent and develop modern armies and infrastructure.

Still, these immigrants from America tended to take a fairly limited, even conservative, view of the modernizing project in early-twentieth-century China. During the 1910s and 1920s, many Chinese intellectuals came to believe that in order to modernize, China needed not just to embrace Western technology and science but, more significantly, to reject the Confucian past and create a completely new culture.[5] The revered writer Lu Xun caustically commented that "the instincts of those who have not read the works of the sages still sprout from time to time under the axe of Confucian morality; and this is why the Chinese, although going downhill, have not perished."[6] US-educated Chinese Americans, on the other hand, often dreamed that immersion in "Chinese culture"—which they envisioned as a static, hoary entity imbued with the wisdom of Confucius and the sages—would enable them to be authentically Chinese and thus to belong somewhere at last. In contrast, most China-born modernizers in the early republican years took a far more radical view of what modernization entailed.

Differing concepts of citizenship and its development also divided Chinese Americans from Chinese modernizers. The latter group generally believed that modernizing China involved transforming subjects into citizens, making China a modern nation-state in part by teaching the Chinese to prioritize their membership in the nation above other ties, whether religious, familial, regional, or professional. This, they believed, would change China from what Sun Yat-sen called a "sheet of loose sand" into "hard concrete," enabling the nation to participate on equal terms in the international arena.[7] Many Chinese Americans viewed the building of a strong, modern China more literally: as a process of introducing new technology and weapons, and perhaps new legal and financial systems. A large number also saw Western-style education, Christianity, and monogamous, companionate marriage as reforms that China required in order to be "modern." Certainly, they agreed with Chinese intellectuals that China needed to become a unified nation with an engaged citizenry, but their position as skilled outsiders meant they often focused disproportionately on the role of technology in changing China. Their resistance to exclusive definitions of citizenship further cemented their status as a group apart, even as it enabled them to exploit the political fragmentation of China in the 1910s and 1920s to build careers while retaining the prerogatives that came with an American passport.

For the Chinese American second generation, then, the late Qing and early republican era was a golden age of opportunity that greater unification, the anti-imperialist movement, and political consolidation ultimately destroyed. By the early 1920s, the end of their golden age was already in sight. Unrest in the inland areas and the south prompted many to relocate for safety to Shanghai, a place that represented the height of Chinese modernity, from its glittering stores to its cultural and literary scene to its turbulent industrial sector. Seeking homes and work in Shanghai and similarly developed cities changed these Chinese Americans from modernizers into people seeking recognition as modern professionals—a recognition denied them in the United States.

A BLEAK OUTLOOK IN AMERICA

Most of the modernizers belonged to the educational elite of a generation that the Chinese Exclusion Act of 1882 had deeply shaped. Like the Chinese American citizen merchants and students, the modernizers' fathers were usually merchants, one of the only categories of Chinese men still allowed to enter the United States after 1882. However, while the merchant and student immigrants hailed from towns, cities, and villages across America, modernizers almost always grew up in large urban centers, where they attended school at a rate not only higher than that of foreign-born white Americans but often comparable to that of native-born white Americans, the best-educated group in the US population.[8] Few "merchants" in these communities were truly wealthy, so they often sent their children to the public universities of the West Coast, but others could and did pay to educate their children at exclusive private colleges, including Harvard, Yale, Columbia, and Stanford.[9]

After earning their degrees, however, Chinese American citizens faced downward mobility in the United States. In 1910, around 1,200 Chinese American citizens were attending high school or college in the US mainland and Hawaii, but the professions and occupations open to them remained depressingly limited: official statistics that lumped all native and foreign-born Chinese and Japanese in the country together showed that in the mainland United States, only fourteen were engineers; four were college professors; eighteen were lawyers; two hundred or so were physicians of all kinds (including herbalists); a few score were teachers, usually in community language schools; and five were architects. The numbers for women were even worse, as were the figures for Hawaii, despite its large Asian American population. To Chinese American citizens in US high schools and colleges, the future in the land of their birth looked bleak indeed, and their opportunities over the next decade actually shrank. By the 1920s, there were more Chinese American citizen lawyers, engineers, and doctors in the city of Shanghai than in Hawaii, California, Oregon, and Washington combined.[10]

The experiences of Anthony Leefong Ahlo, Frank William Lee Chinglun, and Samuel Sung Young, all early modernizers who served in the Republic of China's diplomatic corps, vividly illustrate the way even the most well-educated Chinese American citizens struggled in the land of their birth. The men were born and grew up within just a few years of each other in Honolulu, New York, and San Francisco, respectively—the three largest centers of late-nineteenth-century Chinese American life. All sons of people who arrived from China before exclusion became law, they were slightly older than most members of the first sizable Chinese American citizen generation. Still, their experiences mirrored those of younger counterparts who grew up in a society with few prospects and much disdain for them.

Anthony Leefong Ahlo, the oldest of the three, had the most privileged upbringing of all. Born in 1876 in the Kingdom of Hawaii, which attracted considerable Chinese trade and immigration beginning in the mid-nineteenth century, he was the son of a Hawaiian woman, Lahela Kehuokalani, and a poor Cantonese laborer, Lee Ahlo, who eventually became a leading merchant in the islands.[11] Despite Anthony Ahlo's mixed ancestry and lack of Chinese fluency, he identified closely with his father's homeland; at his graduation from Oahu College (now Punahou School) in 1897, the young man "spoke with intense earnestness of a great future for China."[12] That year, Ahlo left for England, eventually receiving his bachelor of arts degree from Cambridge, marrying the granddaughter of an English peer, and becoming an enthusiastic supporter of exiled Chinese reformers Kang Youwei and Liang Qichao.[13] While crossing the United States to return to Hawaii in 1901, he promoted Chinese reform in San Francisco and accused agents of the Qing government, which opposed his cause, of searching his luggage and harassing him.[14]

The son of a very wealthy man, Anthony Ahlo lived a privileged life, yet he and his family's inability to escape either casual or institutionalized racism seems to have pushed him to embrace reformist activism and his Chinese identity with particular zeal.[15] In the mid-1890s, he watched key members of Hawaii's white planter elite depose the islands' queen (a family friend) and deny suffrage to all Asian immigrants.[16] The 1898 US annexation of Hawaii brought American immigration law as well, particularly the Chinese Exclusion Act of 1882. Now, Ahlo had to obtain special paperwork to prove his birth in the islands and his right to travel freely in the United States. While he was at Cambridge, officials in Honolulu blamed a bubonic plague outbreak on the Chinese population and cordoned off Chinatown, where his parents lived. Board of Health authorities then attempted to burn down the dwelling of an infected Chinese resident and ended up destroying the entire Chinese district, including the Ahlo family home.[17] In 1901 Ahlo returned to Hawaii, where he tried practicing law, but despite his wealth, polish, and education, he could not woo clients from the island elite or join its ranks; that was possible only for white Anglo-Saxon Protestants.[18]

Frank William Lee Chinglun felt the sting of social opprobrium in a different way. Because of strict immigration laws, Chinese men in Manhattan tended to seek marriage partners locally, so Lee, like Ahlo, was of mixed ancestry.[19] Born in 1884 on Mott Street, the heart of New York's emerging Chinatown, he was the second son of notorious tong leader Tom Lee and his German-American wife, Minnie.[20] Tom Lee led the On Leong Tong in Manhattan during a period when it fought violently with other tongs to control gambling establishments, brothels, and the opium trade in the city. The elder Lee routinely bribed policemen and city officials to ignore his organization's activities, while in return the corrupt sachems of Tammany Hall, Manhattan's Democratic Party machine, appointed Lee a deputy sheriff of New York County.[21] The honor delighted Tom Lee, but it did not make him the least bit "respectable" in the eyes of Manhattan's more genteel residents. Nor did his race or his mixed marriage. Frank Lee's conversion to Christianity against his father's wishes, and his almost rigidly upright life, may have been subconscious attempts to live down Tom Lee's criminal reputation.[22]

Although the child of two Chinese parents, Samuel Sung Young, also born in 1884, was far less typical of his generation than Lee or Ahlo. His parents were Woo Ah Tin and Walter Ching Young, immigrants and devout Christians from south China. Walter Young, who received a Christian education in Guangdong and some seminary training in the American Midwest, established an Episcopal mission in San Francisco's Chinatown in 1879. At a time when Chinese Christians routinely faced scorn and hostility both in China and in Chinese American communities, Rev. Young "never seemed to gain much influence or standing with the members of his race, and accomplished little" in San Francisco, at least in the opinion of diocesan officials.[23] He and his wife likely struggled to defend their foreign religion to other Chinese at a time of immense violence toward such people in California. Still, Rev. Young's position enabled him to place Samuel in the church's Trinity School, ensuring that the boy received a racially integrated and comprehensive education during a period in which the only school open to most other San Francisco Chinese Americans was the very limited Oriental Public School. This superior education later helped Samuel S. Young to thrive at the University of California, Berkeley, but it did very little for him in America after his graduation.[24]

IN THE WAKE OF THE BOXERS

Developments in China unexpectedly opened new possibilities to Ahlo, Lee, Young, and hundreds of their peers. In 1900 the Empress Dowager Cixi threw the struggling Qing dynasty's support to the "Boxers," an anti-foreign sect that emerged from drought-ravaged Shandong Province in the late 1890s to rip up railroad tracks, tear down telegraph wires, vandalize Christian cemeteries, and murder hundreds of native Christians and foreign missionaries. When the Boxers laid siege to the foreign legation quarter of Beijing, an international expeditionary force of British, Japanese, Italian, German, Russian, Austro-Hungarian, French, and American troops moved in to relieve the legations and pillage the capital. The Qing court fled to the northwest city of Xi'an, where Cixi remained until her representatives signed the humiliating Boxer Protocol.[25] Upon her return to Beijing, Cixi surprised many foreigners by embracing a series of reforms far more extensive than those her nephew, the Emperor Guangxu, had attempted in 1898 before she placed him under house arrest. The resulting New Policies (*xinzheng*, also known as the "New Government" Movement) sought to transform China through centralization, the recovery of economic rights previously ceded or sold to foreigners, the encouragement of chambers of commerce, and the development of a constitution.[26]

The New Policies quickly impressed many Chinese American citizens and influenced their plans for the future. Some reformers, including Anthony Leefong Ahlo, became reconciled to Cixi's regime because of the new initiatives.[27] The creation of chambers of commerce and the rise of economic nationalism also converged in the 1905 merchant-led boycott of American products—a movement that Chinese Americans in the United States supported and that made a deep impression on second-generation people.[28] But the Qing government's 1905 elimination of the civil service examination, the thousand year-old route to social status, influence, and power in Chinese society, played a far more important role in the lives of many Chinese American citizen youths. The dynasty sorely lacked the Western-educated Chinese it needed to put the New Policies into action. The Qing government scrambled to remedy this by establishing new schools and sending Chinese to study overseas, but imperial officials also sought to recruit Chinese born and educated abroad.[29]

Such rapid developments transformed the prospects and plans of hundreds of Chinese American teens and young adults, both university graduates and those who had never seriously considered college before. Generally bilingual in spoken Cantonese and English, large numbers of these young men and women had also learned to read and write Chinese at night or weekend academies.[30] Many with university diplomas already in hand—degrees that had attracted little interest in the American job market—now prepared to leave for China, while perceptive high school students set to work studying the subjects they saw as crucial to building careers while building China, such as engineering, medicine, education, aviation, and military science.[31] The number of people of Chinese ancestry entering college thus quadrupled between 1900 and 1910.[32] During the same years, the Chinese Students' Alliance, which formed on the West Coast in 1901, discovered that the desire to modernize China shaped the educational choices of both China-born and Chinese American citizen students: between 1905 and 1909, the only liberal arts majors among these people were those studying political science or economics. Engineering proved far more attractive, while finance, medicine, law, agriculture, and education were other top choices.[33] Given the extreme racial discrimination in the US job market, such statistics suggest that most if not all of the Chinese American citizen college students from this group were planning to use their degrees in China, not the United States.

The narrow range of majors that Chinese American citizens chose during the New Policies years reveals how they defined "modernization" and believed they could contribute to it, a vision that scarcely changed in the two decades after the fall of the Qing dynasty. Hawaiian Jun-ke Choy, who attended Columbia University on a Guangdong provincial government scholarship with many Chinese students in the mid-1910s, complained that "materialism and the almighty dollar were what attracted these students," and that "many of my engineering friends ridiculed the studies I was taking [in government and law]."[34] The popularity of mining and railroad engineering reflected the impact of the rights recovery campaign then ongoing in China; it also suggested the influence of Yung Wing, the first Chinese graduate of Yale (class of 1854) and a voice favoring the reform of China's educational system. Chinese and Chinese American students almost certainly snapped up copies of Yung's autobiography when it first appeared in 1909, and they could not avoid his argument that Chinese students needed to study the "physical, mechanical, and military sciences" in order to build a better China.[35] One of Yung's American citizen sons, Bartlett Golden Yung, worked as the China representative for Colt Firearms; the other, Morrison Brown Yung, became a mining engineer.[36] So did a host of Chinese American citizens who came of age at this time, including Chee S. Lowe, Young Chan Chun, William A. Wong, Pond Shuck Wu, Coon Ai Yee, and In Young.[37] The inaugural publication of the Chinese Students' Alliance of Hawaii even featured a lengthy article about the field and prospects for Chinese Americans who hoped to use their metallurgy training in China.[38] To these young Americans, modernity and technology were inextricable.

Chinese American Christians' vision of a modern China often included not just technological advancements but also missions and churches spread across the land. As anti-Christian sentiment in China began to abate to some degree during the post-Boxer years, a number of Western-educated Chinese Americans decided to focus on evangelizing the country. Some, including Frank Lee, sought formal seminary training as they prepared to Christianize China, while a handful chose missionary careers after their arrival in Asia.[39] Chinese American women had little access to seminary training, yet Samuel Young's sister, Grace Young, and a number of her peers determinedly set out for China in order to establish Christian institutions.[40] Other Chinese American Christians accepted "practical" jobs in China while finding ways to express their religious faith in their free time. Mining engineer Chee S. Lowe and his wife, Bessie Ahtye Lowe, were avid volunteers for the Guangzhou

FIGURE 4. The Hawaiian-born Jun-ke Choy traveled to China for the first time in 1912, served briefly in the Guangdong assembly, and then received a scholarship to study at Columbia University. Upon his return to China in 1916, he spent the next two and a half decades as a banker, financier, and government official with various regimes. National Archives and Records Administration, San Bruno regional facility.

YWCA and YMCA, while ophthalmologist T. M. Li, who graduated from the University of Pennsylvania's medical school in 1909, became a medical missionary at nearby Canton Christian College's University Medical Center.[41]

Chinese American modernizers who worked in cultural fields unrelated to the Christian church often did so by chance, however. Henry Loo Kong took a job teaching English at a Chinese school in Guangzhou when he was unable to find another position.[42] Ernest Kee Moy purchased chiropractic degrees from two correspondence schools but struggled to launch a successful medical career, so he eventually headed to Shanghai and became a journalist.[43] A handful of other Chinese Americans with journalism experience, such as the Chicago-born political activist Moy Quong-poy, also moved to China to run newspapers that advocated their vision for a new China.[44] Among the modernizers, though, such

FIGURE 5. Tom Gunn at a 1912 aviation exhibition in San Diego, about a year before he left for China. Demonstrating his loyalties, Tom is holding both the American flag and the blue sky/white sun flag that the Guomindang favored (as opposed to the five-barred flag that the Republic of China had adopted a few months earlier). Smithsonian Museum, National Air and Space Museum Archives.

people were in the minority, since few young Chinese Americans saw such occupations as important to the modernization of China.

In contrast, nothing seemed as modern in the 1900s and 1910s as airplanes, and a steady stream of newly minted Chinese American pilots moved to Asia to build China through aviation. San Francisco natives Tom Gunn and Art Lym were the two most famous. After high school, Lym helped edit the reformist *Chinese World* newspaper, which his brother-in-law owned, but he enjoyed mechanical tinkering far more than journalism. Both Tom and Lym came of age just as the Wright brothers successfully tested their first plane, and aviation quickly captured their imaginations. After meeting in the small world of Bay Area flying enthusiasts, they became close friends, despite their political and temperamental differences: Lym was cautious, while Tom was daring to an almost reckless degree and eventually joined the Tongmenghui, the rival to Lym's reformist group. In the early 1910s, both young men graduated from the new Curtiss School of Aviation and gained renown in flying exhibitions around California. Sun Yat-sen was particularly taken with Tom Gunn, inviting him to come to China after the revolution, and Lym eventually followed.[45]

FIGURE 6. Arthur F. Lym in 1913, while a student at the Curtiss School of Aviation in San Diego, California. Like his friend and fellow Curtiss graduate Tom Gunn, Lym left for China within a year of graduation. Smithsonian Museum, National Air and Space Museum Archives.

SERVING THE QING DYNASTY

Although Western-educated Chinese Americans saw themselves as Chinese patriots, self-interest shaped their view of politics, service, and modernization. Unlike the Chinese American citizen students and merchants, the US-educated modernizers largely avoided settling in Hong Kong, even before the 1911 revolution. The colony's stability and business climate attracted numerous overseas Chinese wary of the Qing bureaucracy or hostile to the regime itself. In contrast, Western-educated Chinese Americans expressed far more interest in helping to build a new, modern China than in standard entrepreneurial success, particularly in a British colony. The allure of China was not just its position as the "motherland," however. Because Qing authorities controlled and financed the development of China's infrastructure and natural resources, Chinese Americans who hoped to find work in these fields necessarily accepted the unpopular dynasty and made it the focus of their loyalty.

The revolutionary activism bubbling in Chinese communities across the globe complicated such claims. In the last years of the Qing dynasty, Chinese across the United States and many other parts of the world divided between reformers who continued to support a constitutional monarchy for China and revolutionaries who favored the complete overthrow of the Qing and the establishment of a republic.[46] Although more and more ordinary Chinese Americans leaned toward the revolutionaries and their leader Sun Yat-sen, Chinese American students continued to favor the Qing regime.[47] Lacking territory and money, the revolutionaries could not offer jobs to the growing ranks of engineers, teachers, and other young Chinese American professionals, which helped such people focus their patriotism on the one entity that could: the Qing state.

Still, the modernizers described their motivations for serving the Qing government in strictly patriotic terms. In 1911, Honolulu native Charles Wong Ahfook, the first president of the Chinese Students' Alliance of Hawaii, described his China-born and Chinese American peers this way: "At heart, we are patriotic citizens of China, and we need . . . to exert ourselves to work for the glory of our common country."[48] Organizations such as the Chinese Students' Alliance reaffirmed such ideas. According to historian Weili Ye, students from China founded the group in order "to instill patriotism in local, American-born Chinese youth, whose loyalty to China the students from the home country had found wanting."[49]

As a result, the two groups of Chinese American citizen immigrants—the students and merchants, and the modernizers—moved in separate economies and often in different social and political circles before the 1911 revolution. Young Chinese American citizens who left for Asia to study there were less culturally Americanized than college-educated men and women who spent far more of their lives in the United States before departing for China. The citizen merchant immigrants also tended to work outside the Chinese state, relying on webs of relationships that might involve some state actors but generally centered on family, place, and professional ties in both south China and Hong Kong and spanning Southeast Asia. Students traveling to China to obtain a Chinese education sought it in village schoolhouses often underwritten with overseas Chinese money, or in Christian academies that foreigners had founded; the end of the old exam system further distanced them from the imperial government. In contrast, the attempts of the Qing government during the New Policies years to centralize power and to direct and bankroll economic development put access to skilled positions in mining, on railroads, and in new colleges into the hands of government officials. So did the record of failure that private companies compiled in these fields.[50] Western-educated Chinese Americans who wanted to build a modern China—or simply find a prestigious position—through the development of natural resources, new universities, or railroads could only realistically do so if they worked for Qing government bureaus. A few, such as Samuel Young and Anthony Leefong Ahlo, even sought traditional social legitimacy by taking the new national examinations that aimed to award the old degree of *jinshi* to people with Western training.[51]

Further tying these Chinese American modernizers to the Qing regime, many arrived in China to discover that their American educations entitled them to jobs unimaginable even for white Americans of comparable age and experience in the United States. The tottering Manchu regime aggressively recruited ethnic Chinese with Western educations to staff fledgling ministries, bureaus, and government ventures, giving Chinese Americans hired in the last years of the dynasty considerable influence over various New Policies initiatives.[52] Samuel S. Young graduated from UC Berkeley in 1905, joined both the Ministry of Education and the Ministry of Communications in 1908, and by 1910 was president of the Tangshan Engineering and Mining College.[53] In 1904 Anthony Ahlo planned to participate in the Qing dynasty's new reform program by developing mining concessions. After arriving in Shanghai, he practiced law instead, took one of the early exams that the Qing court administered to Western degree holders, and was named a justice of the country's supreme court in Beijing soon after.[54] Yue Ching, a Hawaiian with a PhD from the University of Chicago, became treasurer of Guangzhou's Department of Public Works as well as a professor at a teacher's college within a year of his arrival in China.[55] Dr. S. Pond M. Jee, one of Chee and Bessie Lowe and Samuel Young's Berkeley classmates, was appointed chief medical officer of a hospital in Manchuria less than two years after graduating from medical school; his brother, the Harvard-trained economist Shien-Yien Luther M. Jee, became a professor at the Imperial College of Finance and a member of the Ministry of Finance when he arrived in China in 1910.[56] Little wonder that these rising stars avoided any taint of revolutionary political involvement.

REVOLUTION

The 1911 revolution, and the rise to power of Yuan Shikai in 1912, created new opportunities for many of these technocrats. Although numerous modernizers lost their high positions in Qing bureaus and ministries after 1911, many easily made the transition to jobs with the Yuan regime or other levels of government. Samuel S. Young moved swiftly from his position as a college president into a new post at the National Oil Administration, while Luther Jee left the Qing Ministry of Finance to work for the republican Ministry of Finance.[57] Dr. Pond Jee moved from the government-run Mancouli Hospital in Manchuria to more comfortable Tianjin, where he became an eye surgeon for one of the railway lines.[58] The revolution did not end Chee S. Lowe's teaching duties at the Liangguang Coal Mining College; in fact, he found additional work at the Guangdong Cement Company, a new state-owned firm.[59]

The financial woes of Yuan Shikai's regime paradoxically strengthened the position and influence of many of these Chinese Americans. In order to pay his government's ballooning expenses, Yuan initially depended on foreign loans—their political unpopularity helped spark the Guomindang's 1913 revolt—and, after the outbreak of World War I, domestic and Japanese loans. As security for this debt, Yuan's government used the proceeds from the Beijing-Zhangjiakou railway, the Hanyang iron foundries, Hubei's coal mines, the salt tax, and similar sources of revenue.[60] Chinese American citizen employees of agencies such as the Salt Gabelle and the Hanyang Iron Works consequently enjoyed unusual job security despite the financial problems of the Yuan regime.[61]

In contrast, the handful of Chinese American citizen immigrants active in the Guomindang faced repression and, generally, exile. The 1911 revolution launched the political career of Frank Lee, the New York-born minister who came to China in 1908 to teach at Guangzhou's Chinese-run Baptist Academy.[62] While still in the United States, Lee secretly joined Sun Yat-sen's Tongmenghui and after the revolution became the Guangdong provincial government's minister of foreign affairs.[63] In 1913 he also renounced his US citizenship, a vote of confidence both in the new regime and in the Nationalists' view of citizenship as exclusive. Despite Lee's public plea to other Chinese American citizens, however, none appear to have followed his lead.[64] In any case, the abrupt and disorganized Second Revolution of 1913, which Yuan Shikai's forces quickly crushed, sent Lee fleeing back to the United States. Unable to return to China until 1917, he spent four years in Chicago working as a pastor for a small Chinese congregation there.[65] In 1913 the Chicago-born newspaper editor Moy Quong-poy, another close comrade of Sun Yat-sen, escaped to Hong Kong, only returning to the mainland after 1916. Although Moy found refuge in Hong Kong, the colony's authorities rejected the more well-known Liao Zhongkai, another American-born Guomindang leader and Sun confidante. Liao and his family eventually followed Sun to Japan.[66]

Not all American-born Guomindang sympathizers suffered in the republic's first years, especially if they showed some political flexibility. Despite the initial setback of the Second Revolution, Tom Gunn finally arrived in Hong Kong in 1915, flew a series of exhibitions in the colony, and accepted an invitation from Long Jiguang, the governor-general of Guangdong and a Yuan Shikai supporter, to set up an aviation school in Guangzhou.[67] Tom, who had secretly joined the GMD a year earlier and originally came to China at Sun Yat-sen's request, now publicly disavowed politics and expressed his desire simply to train pilots to serve China.[68] Regardless of Long's initial enthusiasm for aviation, the project sputtered and died for lack of funding, made worse by the fact that Yuan Shikai distrusted the involvement in aviation of overseas Chinese, among whom anti-Yuan political parties remained a vibrant force.[69]

Frustrated with Guangdong's fickle rulers, the entrepreneurial Tom sought other backers and developed private ventures at the same time, building his career on the disintegration of China into feuding fiefdoms. After the ouster of Long Jiguang, Tom and his Chinese American citizen wife, Lily Tom Gunn, paid a social call on the new military governor, Lu Rongting. With Lu's support, Tom applied to the southern government for financing for his long-deferred aviation school and then traveled to the wartime United States to purchase airplanes for it. Agents of the northern regime attempted to frame Tom as a German sympathizer, prompting British officials in Hong Kong to detain him. American authorities eventually arrested Tom as well for attempting to export forbidden military technology to China in 1918. However, they eventually dropped the charges, and Tom returned to Guangdong in time to help his friend Art Lym use their airplanes to bomb the forces of Tom's old boss, Long Jiguang. Late in 1919, Tom accepted the invitation of General Ma Chi, the adopted son of Lu Rongting, to build an air corps in Guangxi. Meanwhile, Tom and a group of other Americans created the South China Development Company, supposedly to develop mining but also, apparently, to traffic in the kinds of munitions that by international agreement China could not legally import. At the same time, Tom sought Guomindang funds for a shipping company, imported cars into south China, and used his now famous name to endorse products. The Guangdong-Guangxi War, which broke out in 1920, sorely tested Tom's many and varied loyalties and business interests—particularly because the Guomindang was now fighting against the Guangxi group. Eventually, Tom refused to fight in the Guangxi forces against the military of his ancestral province, though after the war's end, Guangxi leaders invited him back to open an aviation school anyway. By 1923 Tom was serving a new commander, Zhao Hongdi, who just three years later fought against the Guomindang.[70] When Tom died mysteriously in 1924, many mourned, but few were surprised.

GOING INLAND

Tom Gunn's exploits highlight not just his own hunger for adventure and money but also the fragmentation of China in the years he lived there. By the late 1910s, as China plunged into warlordism, local strongmen ignored the central government and exerted authority across the different regions of the country. Some formed alliances with other warlords or groups of warlords, seeking military advantage and new sources of revenue. A few paid lip service to the need for national unification but showed little interest in forfeiting their own power. Sometimes they attempted to seize Beijing, capital of the internationally recognized government known as the Beiyang regime, or the "northern government." In the 1910s and early 1920s, control of the Beiyang regime shifted among a number of rival warlord factions, including the Anhui, Zhili, and Fengtian groups.[71]

The disintegration of the country revealed the nature of the modernizers' patriotism, which focused on the people and land of China rather than any one government but which also included self-interest and personal ambition. Chinese American engineers in particular traveled wherever they found work, including into warlord-held territory. In 1913 San Francisco native In Young started his China career in Nanning, Guangxi, as a mining engineer; became an engineer on a railway in Yichang, Hubei, a year later; and by 1917 was engineer-in-chief of the Daye iron mine downriver near Wuhan. By then, Hubei had passed into the hands a military governor who paid lip service to the Beiyang regime but acted independently of it.[72] When Pond Shuck Wu, a civil engineer, registered with the US consulates closest to his many jobsites, he listed his employer as "the Chinese government," yet he worked under at least three and probably more different warlord regimes, moving from Hankou to Changsha to Beijing and Tianjin within just a few short years.[73] In the process, he encountered a number of Chinese Americans whose affiliations with foreign-backed institutions offered them protection from warlord abuses in China's inland. These included three Chinese Hawaiian doctors, including Dr. T. M. Li, who before decamping to Beijing practiced at the Yale hospital in Changsha and treated the many victims of the northern regime's brutal attempts to exert control over Hunan.[74]

As these modernizers accepted work across China, they came to wield considerable influence over numerous aspects of the fragmented republic's development, politics, and "modernization." A Hawaiian aviator who studied flying under Glenn Curtiss organized the Guomindang's first air corps in 1917.[75] In Fujian, his fellow Curtiss graduates Art Lym and Tom Gunn pioneered the use of aerial bombing while serving under Chen Jiongming and the "Constitutional Protection Movement."[76] In the north, Beiyang official Samuel S. Young coordinated with American engineers to conduct the first detailed, scientific surveys of the Yellow River and surrounding areas.[77] Nearby, Peking Union Medical College's Dr. T. M. Li not only introduced scores of Chinese medical students to the field of ophthalmology but also helped fit the former Qing boy emperor Puyi with his first set of eyeglasses.[78] Hin Wong edited the southern government's *Canton Times*, directed that regime's intelligence bureau, served as president of Guangdong College, and helped found the Boy Scouts in Guangdong.[79] In Young's work as chief engineer of the Daye iron mines placed him at the head of the largest producer of iron ore in China.[80] Dr. Andrew Wu Gayson helped found the Western-style Wai Wah Hospital and Medical College in Guangzhou, as well as the Southern Hospital, where treatments included Chinese medicine and which retains a significant role in that field even today.[81] Wu's experience was unusual, however, for most Western-educated Chinese Americans saw little value in China's ancient technology. To them, modernization meant the American science and technology they were introducing to China.

RETURNED STUDENTS

Mingling with a small but growing number of Western-trained experts born in China, Chinese American modernizers came to share the former group's identity as "returned students" whose training in European and American universities set them apart, even from those who had attended school in Japan. The returned students were a self-consciously elite group who viewed the modernization of China as their special burden and task. One of them noted in 1915, "We are told, and truly told . . . that we are to play the leading role in regenerating our country and that China's destiny is in our hands."[82] A few years later, the Chinese diplomat Alfred Sao-ke Sze, a graduate of Cornell, captured the returned students' sense of their importance to the future of China when he proclaimed that "the Chinese students who have been educated abroad have exerted on their return home an inestimable influence on the various branches of the government, on the social conditions of China, on education and on the habits and mode of thinking and living."[83] But the westernized habits and expectations of the returned students often created a painful cultural and social gulf between them and their fellow Chinese. They coped by banding together both formally and informally. "Through their common memories of both carefree and troublesome times, they established lasting bonds that kept them from feeling rootless in a bicultural world," argues historian Stacey Bieler.[84]

Chinese American citizen modernizers had an even greater interest in establishing such bonds because they were more bicultural, rootless, and alienated from other Chinese than were their China-born returned student peers. In the United States, China-born students who worried about the patriotism of Chinese American citizens had formed branches of the Chinese Students' Alliance; once in China, Chinese American citizens proved equally intent on preserving the special status of the "returned students" and emphasizing their mission to modernize the nation. To do so, Chinese American citizens in the years following the revolution helped organize "returned student" clubs in a number of China's major cities. In 1912 a group of Chinese Americans and China-born returned students in Guangzhou formed the Euro-American Returned Students' Association, followed by the Western Returned Students Association in 1913, also in Guangzhou; the American Returned Students' Association of East China in Shanghai in 1915; the Association for the European and American Returned Students in Beijing the same year; the Chinese Western Returned Students Club of Hankou in 1918; and the Returned Chinese Women's Club in Shanghai in 1921.[85] Members and leaders of returned student groups from across northern China flocked to Beijing in 1918 to attend a regional returned student conference there, with a larger national conference attracting even more such people to Shanghai the next year.[86] Chinese Americans continued to shape these groups, particularly in the south. Most of the Guangzhou Euro-American group's officers in the late 1910s were US-born people, including Art Lym, Hin Wong, and Chee S. Lowe.[87]

Although these modernizers developed a far different sense of the country and their place in it than the Chinese American citizen students and merchants who settled mainly in Guangdong and Hong Kong, they often nurtured similar social aspirations. By shaping the culture and contours of returned student culture and society, Chinese American modernizers guaranteed themselves a place in an emerging, Western-educated coastal elite, just as the émigré students and merchants had done in the south. In addition to the special returned student organizations, they helped found many of the US college alumni clubs that popped up across China in these years. In the north, they played a major role in creating the American College Club and the University of California Alumni Club, and they also helped form Columbia, NYU, and University of California groups and the larger American University Men's Club in Shanghai (a China branch of the American Association of University Women followed a few years later).[88] Such associations included some white Americans, but they drew their memberships largely from Chinese returnees and Chinese Americans. Chinese American citizens also joined and led branches of numerous organizations that other Chinese associated with westernization and returned students, such as Christian churches and the YMCA and YWCA.[89] They founded and led new Chinese sports leagues, particularly those focused on American favorites like football, baseball, and tennis.[90] By the late 1910s, Chinese American citizens even helped create new provincial and national professional organizations that sought to promote emerging professions such as law, Western medicine, and architecture.[91]

The residential choices of Western-educated Chinese American citizens reflected not only the ways they identified with the China-born returned students but the literal place both groups sought in Chinese society. In Guangzhou, Chinese American citizens and returned students clustered together in what they often called the "Tungshan Colony." Tungshan (Dongshan) was a popular residential area for foreigners who disliked the stuffy Shameen (Shamian) concession area, where several foreign legations stood.[92] It was also home to the Pui Ching and Pooi To academies, favorite choices of overseas Chinese parents. In Shanghai, returned students and Chinese American citizens frequently lived in the French Concession (or, less often, in the more commercial International Settlement), an area that was relatively safe from the meddling of the Chinese government and that offered a higher standard of living and more Western amenities than other parts of the city.[93]

Although Chinese American modernizers focused overwhelmingly on technical rather than cultural fields, the social and cultural flux of China during these years enabled them to enter coastal urban China's elite circles in ways that would have been far more difficult at another time. During the first decades of the twentieth century, Chinese leaders and intellectuals argued ferociously over Chinese identity. Some educators suggested romanizing China's writing system, while others pushed for the use of vernacular Chinese in schools instead of the traditional classical Chinese.[94] During the New Culture Movement, which began in 1915, and the May Fourth Movement, which erupted in 1919, young writers jettisoned older forms of literature, debated the virtues of different political systems, and challenged traditional family norms in their lives and work.[95] Sun Yat-sen and his adherents rejected many of the ideals of such people as corrosively individualistic and potentially threatening to national unity.[96] Other politicians and scholars continued to defend Confucian values or embraced anarchism, socialism, pragmatism, and other "isms".[97] The shifting, contested, and unfixed nature of Chineseness in these years not only helped Chinese Americans stake their own claim to a place in Chinese society but also allowed them to influence the cultural and social organizations and norms of other Western-educated people.

SHANGHAI

In Shanghai, Chinese American modernizers came into contact with the epitome of Chinese modernity. Literary scholar Leo Ou-fan Lee describes Shanghai in these years as "a world of splendid modernity set apart from the still tradition-bound countryside that was China."[98] During World War I, China's economy grew substantially, especially when imported goods became scarce and local industry stepped in to fill the void.[99] In Shanghai, the country's industrial center, output also surged in the early 1920s, and a new commercial culture coalesced around Nanjing Road, the city's major shopping street then and now. New department stores, often built with overseas Chinese capital, brought a vast array of foreign luxury goods to Chinese consumers with the money to purchase them.[100] In his novel *Midnight*, the May Fourth Movement author Mao Dun described the resulting cityscape as "a shock of wonder on the roof of a building a gigantic NEON sign in flaming red and phosphorescent green: LIGHT HEAT POWER."[101]

But Shanghai also symbolized imperialism and humiliation to many patriotic Chinese. Beginning in the mid-nineteenth century, the Western powers provoked and won a series of wars that forced China's ruling Qing dynasty to sign numerous unequal treaties compromising the empire's sovereignty. As part of that process, Western nations and eventually Japan seized pieces of

China's territory and carved out large chunks of Shanghai and other Chinese cities, including Guangzhou, Tianjin, Xiamen, and Hankou, as foreign "concession areas." Shanghai's French Concession was largely residential, while the International Settlement was home to the Asian headquarters of hundreds of foreign-owned businesses.[102] Tens of thousands of Chinese citizens resided in the foreign concessions, which boasted high living standards, but the Chinese government exercised almost no power there: in the Shanghai International Settlement, for example, an elected council of foreign residents known as the Shanghai Municipal Council governed, while foreign police patrolled and kept the peace.[103] The British had traditionally dominated foreign Shanghai, but by the late 1910s, more and more Americans streamed into the thriving city, setting up their own businesses and institutions and creating a distinctive social life there.[104]

Chinese nationalism also surged, and it shook the city during the early 1920s. The political ferment of the May Fourth Movement produced a steady flow of new publications, manifestos, and political organizations. In 1921 the Chinese Communist Party secretly held its founding national congress in a house in the French Concession, and Sun Yat-sen met in Shanghai with Adolph Joffe less than two years later to discuss possible Soviet support for the Guomindang. Communist-backed strikes at foreign-owned companies also roiled the city, and the growing nationalism of many different groups of Chinese resulted in (somewhat self-serving) merchant calls for the use of "national goods."[105]

In the late 1910s and early 1920s, this booming, shiny, tumultuous city began to attract an increasing number of Chinese American immigrants, many of them professionals seeking outlets for their training. Growing US business interests drew many young Chinese American lawyers, including Nicholas Char and Russell Chen, who arrived within a few months of each other in 1922.[106] Numerous well-educated Chinese American men and women, from bankers to engineers, brokers, architects, and clerks, also relocated to Shanghai in the early and mid-1920s.[107] A local newspaper noted that in early 1921 alone, "more than 1000 San Francisco Chinese have departed for the Orient" because of "poor business and their inability to find work" in California.[108] While the postwar US recession hardly helped Chinese Americans' employment prospects, their larger inability to obtain suitable positions in the land of their birth was the result of deeply ingrained racial discrimination there. Although the American economy boomed by the mid-1920s, well-educated Chinese Americans continued to flow into China and eventually gravitate to Shanghai.

FEMALE IMMIGRATION

Chinese American women made up only a small number of these professionals in the 1920s and found their opportunities limited to a handful of fields, such as teaching. Chinese American girls often faced parental opposition to their educational aspirations to begin with; those who made it to college found that universities also discouraged and sometimes outright barred women from studying the subjects so many Chinese Americans saw as vital to China's modernization, such as law, engineering, and medicine. Like many other female college students, Chinese American women thus frequently chose majors that allowed them to enter teaching, nursing, or social work.[109] Chinese American women's concentration in such fields also reflected the fact that Chinese Christians often proved more willing than other Chinese to educate American-born daughters and allow them to travel alone to China for work—at least if such positions were church or mission related and thus involved some degree of protection and supervision.[110]

In the 1920s, then, the most visible cohort of US-educated Chinese American citizen women in Shanghai and other treaty ports worked for Christian institutions, such as hospitals, schools, and branches of the YMCA and YWCA. These women tended to be single and to secure their positions before leaving the United States. Caroline Huie and Alice Huie, both daughters of New York clergyman Huie Kin and Louise Van Arnam Huie, received their parents' complete support to study education at Columbia and work for the Chinese YMCA in Shanghai.[111] Marguerite Chiu James, the daughter of two Christian parents, took a position at the YMCA in New York City before the "Foreign Work" department of the organization sent her to Shanghai.[112] Ethel Lee Toma, a devout Christian and the daughter of a Honolulu cigar merchant, taught school in Hawaii before attending college in the Midwest, after which she sailed for China to teach in a mission school.[113]

The handful of Chinese American women who worked outside of Christian institutions in 1920s Shanghai had far fewer job options than their male peers, and the work they found tended to be of the "pink collar" variety. Dora Kam Tom of Hawaii served as a clerk at the US immigration station in Honolulu before sailing for Shanghai. Ambitious and savvy, she billed herself as a businesswoman and a "buying and selling commission agent" who planned to import Hawaiian products to China. The *North China Herald* hailed her as an example of the "further emancipation of Chinese women" and quoted a "friend" of hers (possibly Tom herself) as saying that "the Chinese girls in Shanghai ought to be proud to learn that among them there are quite a few bright intellectual ones . . . [who are of] true value and thus give their best to the world."[114] In reality, Tom supported herself by working behind the counter of Shanghai's Delmonico Sweet Shop, and she returned to Hawaii after the store's owner ran into legal trouble.[115] Gertrude Chew Wu, who left her China-born returned student husband when she discovered that he already had a wife in his village, struggled to make ends meet in Guangzhou and moved to Shanghai, but life did not get easier there. "It was hard to get a decent job in Shanghai without thoroughly knowing Chinese," she admitted, and she only just managed to support herself and her son by finding occasional work with the city's English-language press.[116] Olive Young, the Missouri-born daughter of an American-trained Chinese doctor, avoided tedious clerical work and fulfilled her dreams of acting by starring in films that the Chinese studios in Shanghai produced. This success came at a high social cost, however: she scandalized many Chinese who believed that "good" women did not work as actors, and like Dora Tom, she eventually returned to the United States.[117]

If a Chinese American woman married, she almost always left her job, publicly demonstrating her husband's ability to support her on his income alone and helping firm up his social position through her participation in Shanghai's active social scene. Chinese American women married to professional men frequently volunteered with Chinese women's organizations, planned dances and parties for American university alumni organizations, and helped raise money for the flood and famine relief campaigns that became a regular feature of urban Chinese life in the 1920s.[118] Such activities brought these women together with China-born women, many of them American-educated, whose husbands were also westernized professionals. Some of these Chinese and Chinese American women had been friends since college in the United States, but more often they met as part of the new, Western-educated Shanghai elite that coalesced after World War I.

BRIDGE BUILDERS

In the process, these women created a rare bridge between foreign and Chinese social circles at a time of growing anti-foreign sentiment in China. Historian Jeffrey Wasserstrom has contended that scholarly understanding of Shanghai "will remain incomplete . . . until we know a good deal more about how border-crossers and Sino-Foreign associations—and the transnational networks they were part of and helped to extend—influenced the transformation of the treaty port's most economically significant and robustly cosmopolitan sectors."[119] In interwar Shanghai, Western-educated Chinese American citizens were the ultimate border crossers, participating in Chinese organizations as well as in groups composed largely of white Americans. H. C. Mei, a San Francisco-born lawyer and devout Christian, helped lead the Chinese YMCA in the city, contributed articles to Western missionary magazines and Chinese legal journals, and served with a host of Chinese and foreigners on the board of the Shanghai Civic League.[120] The Chinese Hawaiian accountant Yue Ching not only taught for the YMCA but also helped found the Society for the Promotion of National Products, while Honolulu native Johnny Zane drew cartoons for the English-language *China Press* while exhibiting more serious work with a patriotic art organization in Shanghai.[121] Poy Gum Lee, a New York–born former YMCA architect, worked as the finishing architect on the Sun Yat-sen Mausoleum in Nanjing, founded his own firm to serve both Chinese and foreign clients, and eventually led the new Chinese Architects' Association.[122] His sister Ida Lee served as vice president of the large, multinational Shanghai Business and Professional Women's Association, which drew together Western and Chinese women.[123] While practicing at St. Luke's missionary hospital, Dr. Edward En-Young Kau played on the baseball team that represented China in the Far Eastern Olympics and refereed for the new Chinese sporting federation.[124] Kau and numerous other Chinese American citizen physicians practiced at Western missionary hospitals while participating in the new, exclusively Chinese national medical association.[125] Of course, Chinese Americans also founded and flocked to college alumni associations in the city, mixing with both Chinese and foreign graduates.

The large number of educated Chinese Americans in the city's professional circles, and their frequent "border crossing," demonstrated how Shanghai's development in these years created unusual social and cultural opportunities for Americans of Chinese ancestry. Historian Bryna Goodman has described the resilience and adaptability of traditional networks in Shanghai, and certainly some Chinese American citizens moved in these networks: both Jun-ke Choy and Dr. Andrew Wu Gayson joined and eventually served as officers in Shanghai's powerful Cantonese Residents' Association, and Russell Chen did legal work for the group.[126] In fact, much of the entrepreneurial and

FIGURE 7. New York architect Poy Gum Lee (left) with an unknown man in front of the Sun Yat-sen Mausoleum in Nanjing. Lee served as the finishing architect for the mausoleum after its original architect, Li Yanzhi, died during construction. The commission helped make him one of the most sought-after architects in the country. Courtesy of the Lee Family, Museum of Chinese in America (MOCA) Collection.

comprador class of Shanghai hailed from Guangdong, the province to which almost every Chinese American could trace his or her own ancestors.[127] However, as historian Wen-hsin Yeh notes, "in the 1920s a new elite emerged in Shanghai. . . . [that] cut across conventional lines of social divisions, built a dense network of relationships, and interacted with each other in multiple capacities."[128] The emergence of this new network, much of it rooted in westernized organizations such as the YMCA, offered a significant point of entry and influence for Chinese Americans in Shanghai.

So did the importance of returned students in the new elite. Indeed, the prestige of being a "returned student" encouraged at least some Chinese Americans to pretend they possessed better credentials than they really had. Ernest K. Moy, the failed chiropractor turned journalist, claimed at various times to have graduated from the University of Chicago and to have received a doctorate from NYU, though neither school has any record of him.[129] His brother Herbert, a high school dropout who came to China in 1932, carried on the family tradition, boasting of his Columbia degree or, if he was in a different mood, his years at Harvard.[130] By attempting to claim "returned student" status, the Moys tried to signal that they were not simply ordinary overseas Chinese but men entitled to move in Shanghai's elite Chinese social circles.

MARRIAGE AND THE PROBLEM OF CITIZENSHIP

Chinese American modernizers married into the treaty port elite with considerable frequency in the 1920s and early 1930s, but these unions had different meanings and implications for men than they did for women. In the 1920s, the China-born wives of American citizen men could visit the United States temporarily but not immigrate there permanently, while Chinese American citizen women lost their US citizenship irreversibly if they married foreign nationals. After 1931 Chinese American citizen women retained their US citizenship upon marriage to a China-born man and could even petition to regain lost citizenship. Still, they could not bring China-born spouses into the United States permanently, unlike male peers who married China-born women before 1924 and benefitted from a 1930 revision of the immigration law. Either way, the decision to wed a China-born man or woman generally signified a Chinese American modernizer's commitment to a future in China.

Male modernizers' marriages to China-born women reflected the considerable fluidity of treaty port society in this era. Being a "returned student" enhanced the marriage prospects of Chinese American men even from quite modest backgrounds. Philip Lin Ho, the son of an Oahu shopkeeper, and Jun-ke Choy, whose laborer father barely made enough to feed his large family, both wed the daughters of successful Shanghai businessmen, and they were hardly alone in their ability to climb the city's social ladder.[131] Chinese American citizens from families considered successful in America could also improve their social standing through marriage into China's treaty port elite. Attorney Russell Bates Shue Chen was the son of well-off Boston merchant

Charles K. Shue, whose friendship with Massachusetts governor John Bates not only inspired him to name his son after the politician but to run for Congress himself.[132] Still, Boston's Chinese community was tiny, and the younger Chen's star rose far higher after he arrived in Shanghai and met Julia Sih Tong, the daughter of a wealthy, politically connected sharebroker whose prominent friends crowded into the couple's wedding ceremony and reception.[133]

Many Western-educated Chinese American women who married China-born men did so with the expectation that such unions would offer an unusual degree of personal fulfillment and companionship. People in their birth communities constantly claimed that second-generation females were too extravagant, too independent, and too modern. Such women often had to fight for the right to attend college, and those who envisioned careers faced particular hostility.[134] Chinese American men, even those who attended college, frequently said they preferred "old-fashioned" women, but numerous male students from China disagreed, to the delight of Chinese American women collegians.[135] Flora Belle Jan, a Chinese American "flapper" from Fresno, chafed at the reactionary attitudes she encountered from older Chinese Americans both in her hometown and in the Bay Area, where she attended college. After she transferred from the University of California, Berkeley, to the University of Chicago, though, she "met a whole handful of Chinese Northerners; they are all enthusiastic about adding a new girl to their roll." Within a year, she married a psychology graduate student from Henan, and the couple moved to China in 1932.[136] Jan married late enough to retain her citizenship, but Lily Soo-hoo did not. The San Francisco native left the Bay Area for college in the East, studied at Oberlin, participated in Chinese student activities there, and developed great esteem for the students from China. They were "of high scholarship, of high resolve, of ambition,—loyal, earnest—in other words, men and women of high hopes and aspirations," she explained. She felt a particular fondness for a St. John's graduate named William Zu-liang Sung, whom she married and followed to Shanghai in 1924. Like scores of other Chinese American women, she forfeited her citizenship in the process, a sacrifice that seemed worthwhile for a kind of happiness and acceptance so difficult to achieve in America.[137]

CHINESE MODERNS

The post–World War I growth of Chinese nationalism began to create some tension between these Chinese Americans' desire for acceptance as real

Chinese and their Western educations, American citizenship, and self-identification as "returned students." To a certain degree, this reflected a wider questioning of the usefulness of Western education during the later warlord period; even Y. S. Tsao, the Western-educated president of Tsing Hua College, argued in frustration that "THIS IS WHAT THE CHINESE STUDENT TRAINED ABROAD HAS ACCOMPLISHED[:] DESTRUCTION, NOT CONSTRUCTION. CHAOS, INSTEAD OF ORDER. SUFFERING, NOT HAPPINESS. POVERTY, NOT PROSPERITY."[138] But these tensions also flared around questions of patriotism and loyalty, particularly for the many Chinese Americans and China-born people who chose westernized lifestyles. Acceptable Chineseness, although still in flux, was beginning to harden into something that excluded foreign elements, at least in the minds of many ardent nationalists. Shanghai's *Shih Shih Hsin Pao* newspaper complained of the returned students that "in their outlook on life there is no trace of Chinese ideals. . . . What China is absorbing to-day is not a superior civilization but merely its vulgar excrescences."[139] Even H. C. Mei, the American-born Shanghai lawyer, lambasted "all this slavish following of things foreign, with the almost complete ignoring of native talent and material," and wondered, "Can we rightfully say that China is truly making progress, or do we observe in it a perniciously degrading tendency that is retarding the growth of a real national consciousness and national patriotism?"[140]

Such condemnation stung, particularly since most modernizers did not end up serving China in quite the heroic ways they had imagined before their arrival there. In the United States, the Chinese Students' Alliance regularly exhorted its members about their patriotic duties to China and the crucial roles they would play in its future. The winner of two of the alliance's annual oratorical contests urged his fellow students to remember that China "looks upon you to be the torchbearers of truth and the apostles of progress, to exemplify and spread . . . patriotism."[141] An editorial in the alliance's monthly journal similarly urged members to "return to our country with our eyes open only to the ideal of service and blind to every consideration of material interest and pleasure, forgetting ourselves in our efforts to help our fellow men and be of service to our country."[142] Despite sharing such feelings, Chinese American citizens arriving in China *needed* to consider their material interests in order to survive. Young, inexperienced, and lacking investment capital, Chinese American citizens who could not set up their own professional practices in medicine, architecture, or law in Shanghai had little choice but to work for others, including foreign employers in need of bilingual and bicultural staff. And this kind of work rarely offered them the chance to act as "torch-bearers" or "apostles." In addition, despite imagining themselves as modernizers, Western-educated Chinese Americans who were not engineers discovered that outlets for their training existed largely in China's already "modernizing" places, especially Shanghai but also Guangzhou, Tianjin, Hankou, and Hong Kong.

These same Chinese American citizens had absorbed the widespread American view of an ancient, hoary, unchanging Chinese essence, developing in the process a conception of China's culture as static and distinct from its politics, educational system, economy, and major cities. Newly arrived in China, Dorothy Gee enthused to a friend that the country "is beautiful, glorious in her great ancientness of everything," before admitting that "of course, as you know . . . China is practically a stranger to me."[143] Another recent Chinese American arrival noted, "I am beginning to see the superiority of some Chinese customs and habits to some American customs and habits . . . [and] I look forward with great joy and fascination to living in China."[144] In conceiving of China's culture as both superior and changeless, such people could peel it away from the other areas of Chinese life they believed were in need of reform. In other words, they could square their role as modernizers with their desire to become more Chinese through immersion in China's real—and ancient—culture.

This compartmentalized conception of China's problems contrasted markedly with the beliefs of most New Culture and May Fourth Movement activists, who generally saw traditional Chinese culture as a negative, pernicious influence, not as a venerable object.[145] "Our country's culture is today on the brink of bankruptcy," declared Hu Xiansu in the moderate journal *The Critical Review*.[146] The far more radical Chen Duxiu, who cofounded the Chinese Communist Party in 1921, proclaimed the year before that "the New Culture Movement, which believes the old culture is deficient, is a movement to greatly improve science, religion, ethics, literature, art, and music" as well as to influence military affairs, politics, and production.[147] As historian Lung-kee See notes, the "May Fourth generation" saw itself "confronted . . . with the task of demolishing the moribund Chinese culture, while burdened with the mission of national salvation."[148] Chinese Americans rarely shared this sense that national salvation required demolishing Chinese culture; if anything, they saw that "moribund" culture as part of their own salvation.

This view for years shaped and limited the way Western-educated Chinese Americans understood China's modernization project. While China-born artists, writers, and activists across the country demanded deep cultural changes, Chinese Americans focused on using their technical and professional expertise to reform their new home. Few could do otherwise: born and raised in the United States, they had little exposure to the cultural debates raging in China's academic circles, especially among intellectuals who hailed largely from northern and central China. New Culture Movement writers helped widen the gap: those who took refuge in Shanghai's foreign concessions often criticized such places and their Chinese residents for their decadence and worship of all things Western.[149] Chinese Americans' social, residential, and marital choices obviously aligned them with the targets of these artists because their closest Chinese friends were usually returned students educated in America. Such people had grown more conservative and apolitical than the China-born youths who studied in American schools right after the 1911 revolution and far more than the May Fourth activists inside China itself.[150]

By the 1920s, then, the Chinese American modernizers who moved to China in search of purpose, opportunity, and a sense of belonging had unwittingly become "treaty port Chinese" and increasingly the targets of nationalist scorn and disdain.[151] Leftists and rightists alike criticized them as "somehow less patriotic, less worthy representatives of their country than the more parochial people of interior China," according to scholar Lucien Pye.[152] Their training and biculturality meant that a growing number depended for their livelihood on the companies, institutions, and statutes that underpinned foreign power on the China coast. Even many Chinese American professionals inadvertently supported the foreign presence: large numbers of Chinese American doctors worked in Shanghai's missionary hospitals and taught in its Western universities, while most of the American-born lawyers practiced in the US Court for China, which existed because of extraterritoriality. Chinese Americans also worked for a host of foreign companies, from Standard Oil to Asiatic Petroleum to British-American Tobacco, which Chinese businesspeople saw as threats to indigenous firms and national independence.[153] Chinese American women frequently found jobs in the kinds of institutions, including the YMCA and Christian schools and colleges, that segments of the re-emergent Guomindang viewed as unwelcome purveyors of a foreign faith.[154] Even many Chinese American citizens who secured positions with Chinese-owned companies could not escape the taint of foreign influence and decadence: some worked at the new Western-style department stores like Sincere and Wing On; others distributed and acted in films that shocked conservative Chinese; one or two ran gambling houses that cemented Shanghai's decadent image; and several managed the new financial institutions intent on undermining the old native banks.[155]

By the late 1920s, Western-educated Chinese American citizens also found themselves in an uncomfortable spot not simply because they were part of the "modern" China so often associated with Shanghai but because they were also overseas Chinese linked to Western imperialism. In other words, they faced a dilemma similar to the Chinese American citizen merchants and students in the south. Scholar Marie-Claire Bergère notes that "the development of the treaty ports was not only a triumph for the West," but also empowered "a cosmopolitan and entrepreneurial China" that had long been a "marginal and minority section of Chinese society."[156] Other Chinese, including nationalists, expressed deeply mixed feelings about the emergence of this segment of society. Furthermore, according to historian Hanchao Lu, "ambivalence towards the city in general and Shanghai in particular reflected earthbound China's contradictory feelings towards things new, unorthodox, and foreign."[157] Educated Chinese American citizens saw themselves as Chinese, but their value as employees was largely due to their understanding of the "new, unorthodox, and foreign"; indeed, many other Chinese viewed them as unorthodox, foreign, and tied to Western and Japanese colonialism. Successive regimes helped fuel suspicions of overseas Chinese by simultaneously seeking donations and loyalty from them while acting as if they were inferior to "real" Chinese born on the mainland.[158] In Shanghai and other cities on the coast, Chinese American citizens could largely escape such attitudes, but only because they found a home in a social class similarly implicated in its ties to Western companies, colonies, schools, lifestyles, and trade.

CONVERGENCE, DIVERGENCE

By the late 1920s, the elite of the Chinese American modernizers and the citizen students and merchants had begun to converge to a certain degree as a result of China's internal disintegration and its uneven economic development. Some Chinese parents still sent their American-born children to the Pearl River Delta to study at village schools before they ever had a chance to attend school in the United States. However, after the inauguration of the

New Policies, and particularly with the increasingly visible flow of China-born students into the United States after 1905, more and more US-based Chinese parents sensed the value of providing their children with both a Western and a Chinese education. The deteriorating security of overseas Chinese areas of Guangdong in the late 1910s also encouraged Chinese parents in America to choose protected Western schools in Guangzhou or Shanghai (or even Beijing) for their offspring. A growing number kept their children in US schools until late in high school, then sent them to China to enroll in one of the westernized universities such as Canton Christian College, St. John's, or Yenching, where English was a major medium of instruction. After college, these youths often returned to the United States for graduate school before moving once again to China, the only place where they could realistically hope to build careers.

By the 1920s, then, Chinese American citizens immigrating to Shanghai moved in social and economic circles that mixed China-born returned students, Chinese American citizens, the children of earlier citizen immigrants, local graduates of westernized universities like St. John's, and well-to-do overseas Chinese from Southeast Asia, Canada, and Australia. The children of Louey Shuck and Hong Sling exemplified this overlap. After attending school in south China, at least two of Louey's sons and one of his daughters traveled to the United States for college, but all returned to China, where the men entered business.[159] Another of Louey's daughters married the Australian-born overseas Chinese David Au of the Sincere Department Store family, and after a stint in New York, where Au studied at Columbia, she eventually settled with him in Shanghai.[160] The Hong Slings followed a similar trajectory. After completing Queens College, Harry Hong Sling attended Yale and Bill Hong Sling chose the new University of Hong Kong, but both became well-known businessmen in Hong Kong. Louey Shuck's son Edward Louie eventually worked for Harry Hong Sling at a company the latter created in the colony.[161]

Despite such convergence at the top, economic interests and political differences continued to divide most of the modernizers from the less elite Chinese American citizen students and merchants of the 1920s. The latter group, still concentrated in the south, often developed a very different relationship with and view of the state than their Western-educated counterparts. The modernizers had absorbed the language and ideas of strong sovereignty and nationalism while studying in American universities, where what the historian Prasenjit Duara calls an "extraordinary preoccupation with the omnipotence of the state" dominated fields such as law, history, and political science in the late nineteenth and early twentieth centuries.[162] Such ideas resonated with Chinese Americans concerned about China's weakness during the last Qing years and its disintegration in the 1910s and early 1920s. Guomindang members also embraced these ideas, with Sun Yat-sen arguing that nationalism would be "the salvation of the country," and that "after China has established a powerful government, we must not be afraid, as Western people are, that the government will become too strong and that we will be unable to control it."[163] Whether they supported the GMD, the northern government, or another option for the country, Western-educated Chinese Americans tended to agree that China needed a powerful central authority to combat the devolution of their era.[164] Their professional ambitions bolstered this view, since many worked in fields that benefitted from state investment and oversight, such as engineering, education, and infrastructure.

In contrast, the experiences of ordinary Chinese American citizen merchants and students, especially in Guangdong, left them far less enamored of the strong state concept and statist ideas in general. While Western-educated modernizers sought positions in Qing and republican government bureaus, Chinese American citizen students and merchants moved in family, professional, and native place circles largely outside of the state. Few opposed a unified China, and some even supported Sun Yat-sen for a handful of years after the 1911 revolution. Still, by the early 1920s, they had suffered through a series of southern regimes whose major focus seemed to be shaking down the Cantonese, especially overseas Chinese, for their wealth. In addition, the economic fortunes and social lives of overseas Chinese merchants and students in China were bound far less to the country's rural interior than to diaspora networks that spanned the Pacific and were anchored in colonial Southeast Asia and Hong Kong. Those in this group who were American citizens, British subjects or Protected Persons, or in possession of some other kind of foreign citizenship found that this status offered them more protection than whoever controlled the south after 1911. Unsurprisingly, then, their loyalties to whatever regime claimed to govern China, or Guangdong, were sometimes tenuous, and their view of centralism rather dim. The Guomindang's activities in the south thus alienated Chinese American merchants even as Western-educated Chinese American citizens continued to support the party, or at least the strong state idea.

Over the course of the 1920s, the resurgence, transformation, and, ultimately, the political success of the Guomindang sorely tested both the modernizers and the citizen merchants and students, who represented two different but equally problematic visions of Chineseness to the Nationalists. The merchants' and students' mobility, connections to colonialism, dual citizenship, and alienation from the party rendered them suspicious at best. The modernizers' social, cultural, and residential choices and attachment to their US citizenship made them prime targets for Nationalist critics of Western "degeneracy." For both groups, the golden era was beginning to come to an end. What did not stop, however, was the exodus of Chinese Americans to China.

CHAPTER 3

The Golden Age Ends

Chinese Americans and the Rise of Anti-imperialist Nationalism

In August 1925, assassins in Guangzhou shot and killed Liao Zhongkai, the San Francisco-born Guomindang leftist.[1] Sun Yat-sen had died from cancer just a few months earlier, and the murder of Liao, Sun's close friend and comrade, worsened Guangdong's already tumultuous political climate. In 1923 Sun had announced that he would accept aid and advisors from the Soviet Union and allow Chinese Communist Party members into the Guomindang.[2] The next year, he had also dismissed the doubts many overseas Chinese expressed about this alliance and suggested that the naysayers lacked both sophistication and loyalty. "These overseas Chinese live in places under the jurisdiction of imperialist governments," he argued, "and they are greatly influenced by the imperialist nations' poisonous propaganda denigrating the Russian Revolution."[3] Sun's words and actions worried not only Guangdong's China-born merchants, especially those with ties to overseas networks, but also many of the Chinese American citizens who made their homes in the south.[4] Between 1923 and 1925, scores of these people fled Guangdong, and after Liao's death, their migration seemed particularly wise: following the assassination, leftist military cadets swept into Guangzhou and arrested a large group of suspects, including Americans Moy Quong-poy and Chu Shea Wai.[5] The men's arrests and trials showed how a dismissive State Department, together with a Guomindang that viewed all ethnic Chinese possessively, threatened Chinese Americans' US citizenship rights and their future prospects in China.

This chapter examines the way that anti-imperialism became central to Chinese nationalism in the 1920s, creating a crisis for Chinese American citizens whose claims for protection were increasingly rejected by the US government.[6] Many of the Chinese Americans who sought to preserve their US citizenship rights also worked for Western companies and had friends and colleagues who were "returned students," other overseas Chinese, or members of the westernized business classes of the treaty ports. A series of events that convulsed the country in the mid-1920s exposed the shaky, uncertain status of all such people. The May Thirtieth Incident of 1925, in which members of the foreign-controlled Shanghai Municipal Police fired on Chinese demonstrators, sparked a massive anti-imperialist movement across the nation; it also led to the 1925–1926 Hong Kong-Guangzhou boycott and strike, which forced Chinese merchants and laborers in the British colony to choose between Britain and an increasingly leftist Guomindang. Soon after, the GMD's Northern Expedition to reunify China directly threatened the treaty ports and foreign-controlled concessions and institutions in which growing numbers of Chinese Americans were finding economic, social, and educational opportunities.

Pressed by the Nationalists to renegotiate unequal treaties and extraterritoriality, US officials now found that ignoring Chinese American rights enabled them to preserve the illusion of an equal Sino-American relationship while actually safeguarding the privileged status of white Americans in China. In the late 1890s, Secretary of State John Hay drafted the "Open Door" notes in an attempt to preserve American access to China's markets; in the years afterward, however, the US government and much of the public came to view this basically self-serving policy as a shining example of American fairness to and friendship with China.[7] The rise of anti-imperialist Chinese nationalism thus threatened not just Chinese American citizens and US institutions in China but also a political fiction beloved in America. To help protect that fiction, as well as American business and philanthropic interests in China, the State Department increasingly abandoned Chinese Americans citizens there, withholding protection from them in almost every case. This new policy also reflected the racial nationalism of American officials in both Washington and China. Between 1921 and 1924, nativists in the US Congress successfully pushed through legislation that ended all Asian immigration and slapped harsh quotas on Southern and Eastern European immigrants. The legislation was overtly discriminatory, as its supporters readily admitted.[8] In the mid-1920s, key foreign service personnel used their authority to enforce such ideas in China by working to undermine the US citizenship status of Chinese Americans there.

The exclusive nationalism of the resurgent GMD also created new problems for Chinese American citizens, whose understandings of Chineseness, patriotism, and nationalism were far more complex and less monogamous than the party's. Although deeply frustrated by the discrimination they faced in the land of their birth, Chinese Americans often felt tremendous affection for the United States. Most were generally resigned to the divergence between their simultaneous citizenship in the American state and their exclusion from the imagined racial nation, but like their predecessors in the 1900s and 1910s, they valued their citizenship status and their roots in the United States. The modernizers in particular embodied this duality: crusaders for American science, technology, and democracy, they saw themselves both as Chinese and as representatives of the American spirit. But the new GMD government expressed little enthusiasm for such hybrid identities. Bent on claiming authority over Chinese Americans based on their Chinese "blood," the GMD simultaneously treated such people as inherently untrustworthy and even dangerously unorthodox. By 1928, as the Nationalists consolidated their power, Chinese Americans discovered that their golden era in China had come to an end.

"RED" GUANGDONG

In 1922, Chen Jiongming, the warlord who controlled most of Guangdong, staged a coup against Sun Yat-sen, the man he had allowed to return to the south in 1920 to help govern and to restore the old national parliament. Despite their onetime alliance, Chen and Sun had always seen China's future in very different ways, with the former an advocate of federalism as the basis for a reunited China and the latter a proponent of stronger central authority. During Chen's coup, Sun fled Guangzhou with the help of rising military commander Chiang Kai-shek. George Y. S. Bow, a Chinese American soldier and engineer from tiny Grass Valley, California, helped Sun's wife, Song Qingling, escape separately.[9] Sun then combined the forces loyal to him with warlord soldiers from Yunnan and Guangxi, and by early 1923 he had successfully expelled Chen Jiongming from Guangzhou. Having failed to convince any other foreign power to support him, Sun in 1922 also began negotiations with Soviet representative Adolph Joffe, who promised military and financial support to the Guomindang in its quest to unify China. As part of the 1923 agreement the two men signed, the Guomindang incorporated Chinese Communist Party members into its ranks.[10]

The Guomindang's alliance with the Soviets unnerved many overseas Chinese merchants in Guangzhou, as did the party's newly adopted stance that imperialism was one of the major threats to China. Large numbers of overseas Chinese lived throughout Southeast Asia, working in European colonies as traders, planters, and laborers. As historian John Fitzgerald notes, "overseas party members . . . were sensitive to the implications of [the anti-imperialist] policy for their position in the colonies and metropolitan centers targeted by the anti-imperialist movement, rightly fearing that they might become targets of imperialist reaction." The Guangdong party organization, many of whose members had close ties to overseas Chinese, protested the anti-imperialist language now part of the party program, citing specifically the impact it would have on overseas Chinese. Sun dismissed such pleas.[11]

Chinese American citizens were particularly alarmed at the newly sharp rhetoric, which promised to intensify Guomindang initiatives that challenged the Americans' legal status. Such people held tightly to their US citizenship for sentimental and practical reasons while usually regarding themselves as Chinese at the same time. However, during the GMD collaboration with Chen Jiongming, civil and military authorities had begun dismissing Chinese American citizenship claims. Frank Lee, the New York–born commissioner of foreign affairs, showed almost no tolerance for dual citizenship; having renounced his own American citizenship in 1913, he seemed determined to make other Chinese Americans do so as well.[12] By late 1921, Lee was refusing to affix visas to the US passports of Chinese American citizens seeking to travel outside the treaty ports, even as the United States consulate in Guangzhou urged all citizens to obtain such visas if they wished to proceed inland.[13] Arguing that Chinese American citizens were Chinese under China's own laws, local officials also continued their former habit of ignoring such people's extraterritoriality claims. In the early 1920s, authorities arrested numerous Chinese American citizens on charges ranging from illicit earthmoving to opium smoking. Local governments held them in prisons for lengthy periods and often confiscated their property or demanded the payment of "fines" for their release.[14] Although not complicit in these demands for bribes, Frank Lee appears to have encouraged what was once an unorganized and occasional practice of rejecting Chinese American citizenship. He likely saw this as a declaration of China's sovereignty and a way to strike at extraterritoriality (extrality), however weakly.[15]

When Sun returned to power in Guangdong in late 1922, casual demands for bribes and fees became systematized tax levies as he scrambled to satisfy his newest warlord backers and to fund an army to reunify China. Chen Jiongming had barred the sale of opium, but Sun's government overturned that law and created an opium monopoly farmed out to the highest bidder. Officials continued to collect the substantial "flower tax" on prostitution, sold off public lands, collected many taxes years in advance, and confiscated the landholdings of charitable institutions. In addition to negotiating a loan from Chinese in Hong Kong, Sun strongly "encouraged" the Guangzhou Chamber of Commerce and local guilds to contribute hundreds of thousands of dollars to his regime. His government also "encouraged" landlords to hand over a month's rent and laborers to pitch in part of their wages.[16] Municipal officials pressured the director of the Chinese American citizen-backed Sunning Railroad for a "loan" to Sun even though the line was deeply in debt. The Chinese Hawaiian journalist Hin Wong publicly criticized such practices, focusing in particular on the regime's use of extraprovincial armies, the arbitrary taxes it levied, and the overall cost of the Nationalist establishment in the south. His articles prompted the Yunnanese and Guangxi forces supporting Sun to arrest Wong, releasing him only after a number of American citizens and officials pressed them to do so.[17]

The new taxes, fees, and property seizures deeply affected the Chinese merchant class with which many Chinese American citizens in Guangdong were aligned, heightening the tension that had been building for a number of years between Guangzhou elites and Sun Yat-sen. After a decade of shifting regimes and the disintegration of order in the south, Guangzhou's merchants had grown tired of Sun's costly ambitions and constant demands for new funds. In addition, many merchants rejected the party's new rhetoric about imperialism, and almost all of them deplored the continued abuses of the Guangxi and Yunnanese troops.[18] A member of the banned opposition Chinese Constitutionalist Party, which drew adherents almost exclusively from local and overseas merchants, complained after a visit to Guangdong that "Sun would rob hell if he could. . . . I am disgusted with the mess his government has made."[19]

Local merchants and overseas Chinese in Guangdong grew increasingly alarmed in late 1923, when Sun unsuccessfully demanded that his government receive part of the revenue from the foreign-run Chinese Maritime Customs Service. At the time, all of this money went to support the internationally recognized, Beijing-based Beiyang regime. The Maritime Customs Service dated to the mid-nineteenth century, when the Qing government was unable to collect customs revenues due to the catastrophic Taiping Rebellion. Organized by foreigners and still largely run by them, the Customs Service provided substantial revenue in the 1920s to the northern warlords bent on crushing Sun's government in Guangzhou.[20] Few merchants viewed Sun's demand for part of the surplus as irrational. "The more-enlightened Cantonese . . . support . . . Dr. Sun Yat-sen in the reasonableness of the claim that no more Cantonese money shall be used by Peking to further disturb the peace of Canton," noted Hin Wong, who considered merchants the "enlightened" class. But such people balked when Sun threatened to use force to seize the Guangzhou customs money, and the foreign powers dispatched gunboats to the city's harbor to make him back down.[21] Warlord conflicts were bad enough for Guangzhou; foreign intervention would be catastrophic.

The merchants also distanced themselves from the groups of students and laborers who responded to the foreign show of force by parading through the city and calling for a boycott of British and American goods. Hin Wong dismissed such actions and contended that "thinking Cantonese" did not hate foreigners at all, especially since their institutions were more trustworthy than those of war-torn China:

> The biggest retail stores in Canton, the Sun, the Sincere, and the Chen Kwong are companies registered at Hongkong and with British consular protection. . . . There are more Chinese funds in one foreign bank in Shameen than in all the three large modern Chinese banks along the Bund in Canton. Canton parents prefer missionary to government schools for their children. Foreign insurance companies and agencies underwrite more policies in Canton than native concerns. . . . The anti-foreign agitation in Canton does not truly represent Cantonese sentiment.[22]

Given Guangzhou's long history as a center of foreign trade, its people may have been less xenophobic than Chinese elsewhere. But Hin Wong was also describing the kind of networks and ties that Sun Yat-sen was beginning to paint as threats to national integrity and sovereignty.[23] And in listing the ways certain Cantonese relied on foreign institutions, Hin Wong inadvertently revealed that he spoke for a privileged class with investment capital, the means to educate children, a surplus to put in the bank, and property to insure. Indeed, as the son of a successful overseas Chinese merchant, he was speaking for his own people, and he became such a thorn in the regime's side that in mid-1924, Sun ordered Wong's arrest and banishment from Guangdong for ten years.[24] The move indicated that Sun had no intention of toning down his criticism of the merchant classes or their overseas Chinese members.

THE MERCHANT CORPS INCIDENT

By mid-1924, Guangzhou merchants' disillusionment with Sun had crested, as the Soviet advisors in the new government became more visible and the Guomindang's First National Party Conference sanctioned the need to "overthrow imperialism."[25] Local merchant elites pushed back forcefully when they moved to consolidate their old volunteer corps. Initially organized for self-protection after the 1911 revolution, the Guangzhou Merchant Volunteer Corps now became a more centralized group linked to similar forces across the province. Corps leaders also purchased a new batch of arms from abroad.[26]

The arrival of the weapons in August 1924 provoked a showdown that demonstrated the tenuous place of overseas Chinese and their merchant allies in the new Nationalist order. Sun Yat-sen instructed his soldiers to confiscate the shipment and then demanded a fee for each gun, prompting the merchants to threaten a commercial strike. In October, when negotiations between the merchants and the government broke down, Sun sent three thousand troops to attack and subdue the Merchant Corps-controlled Xiguan district of Guangzhou.[27] A distraught Hin Wong, who witnessed the ensuing violence, accused the Guomindang's Soviet advisors of encouraging the spilling of "the blood of aged and young who were too weak to endure the rage of a Red Sun which pierced through them in the form of daggers and bayonets and kerosene oil, the power of which has left a monument of hundreds of blackened walls standing over the debris." He also accused another Chinese American, Liao Zhongkai, of having directed "squads . . . of unemployed coolies" to burn the district down.[28] In the end, the government's shelling of and attack on Xiguan destroyed about a third of the area and led to the deaths of hundreds, and possibly more than one thousand, residents.[29]

Chinese Americans in the United States responded to the Merchant Corps Incident and Guomindang attempts to place blame for it on overseas Chinese by withdrawing almost all of their support from the party. As historian Michael Tsin notes, after the Merchant Corps Incident, the Guomindang leadership accused the merchant elite of the city of acting "as mere accessories . . . of the imperialists and their allies, the warlords."[30] In a rambling speech about a month later, Sun essentially blamed merchant traitors for China's internal chaos, claiming that British commercial agents had manipulated the leader of the Merchant Corps in order to help keep China semi-colonized.[31] The earlier flap over anti-imperialism in the Guomindang program had already driven many overseas Chinese out of the party; now, membership declined further, and contributions from Chinese in the United States dropped from hundreds of thousands of dollars in 1922 to just a few hundred dollars in 1924 and 1925.[32]

The Merchant Corps Incident angered numerous Chinese in the United States, but it terrified Chinese Americans in and around Guangzhou. Under Chen Jiongming, many of them had prospered, founding new businesses or using their skills and education in government agencies and bureaus. At least some of them sensed the dangers inherent in Frank Lee's US citizenship policy, but most still viewed banditry in the villages and piracy on the Pearl River as their most pressing concerns. Sun's new regime, with its high and sometimes arbitrary taxes and turbulence, frustrated many Chinese Americans, especially when the government's new property confiscation policies threatened to wreck the city's economy.[33] But the violence in Xiguan was far worse than anything they had previously experienced. Fearing for their lives and property, a large number during and after the initial attack appealed to the US consul general for protection.[34] A Chinese American businessman admitted he was "afraid the soldiers might loot his house," while the wife of another US citizen pleaded for help after he was "arrested, while walking in one of the streets in Sai Kwan, by Yunnanese soldiers . . . [and] suspected of being a member of the Merchant Volunteers."[35] Even non-US citizens began to approach the US consulate to ask if they could pay to fly the American flag for protection.[36]

The aftermath of the Merchant Corps Incident further stunned and disillusioned Chinese Americans, who could hardly avoid noticing that overseas Chinese received much of the blame for the debacle. The attack had rendered concrete the anti-imperialist fulminations of Guomindang leaders who had been hinting at overseas Chinese disloyalty since the February 1924 party conference. Sun Yat-sen justified the attack on Xiguan in part because of murky rumors that the hated British imperialists were backing the Merchant Corps. Mainly, though, he blamed the incident on the city's "compradors and the grande bourgeoisie." For further clarification, he singled out two of Guangzhou's most prominent overseas Chinese merchants as the major villains: Chen Lianbo, a Hong Kong–educated silk merchant, and Jian Jinglun, a member of the overseas Chinese family that owned the Nanyang Brothers Tobacco Company.[37]

RETREAT FROM THE SOUTH

The Guomindang embrace of anti-imperialism, together with the Merchant Corps Incident, prompted a stream of Chinese Americans to flee Guangdong for the assumed safety of Shanghai and Hong Kong. Western-educated Chinese American professionals still supported the idea of a strong central government in the abstract, but fewer seemed to have the stomach for the Guomindang after its radicalization. Jun-ke Choy was one of the first to leave, relocating with his family to Shanghai after his work for Guangzhou's city government resulted in threats on his life. By the mid-1920s, a stream of modernizers followed Choy, moving to Shanghai as politics in the south grew more radical. Pushed out of the government, Frank Lee left the south to take a position at Shanghai College. The Soviet advisors' growing influence in the provincial military also convinced the pilot Art Lym and his fiancée, the San Francisco-born Sarah Chuck, to relocate to Shanghai, where Lym quit flying to manage a popular wallpaper store on Nanjing Road.[38] Chinese American citizen merchants and students left the south as well. George Kin Leung, who was studying literature and theater privately in Guangzhou, boarded a boat to Shanghai, where he translated Lu Xun's *The True Story of Ah Q* into English and became a highly regarded drama critic. His brother dropped out of the Pui Ching Academy and went north too, along with a number of other Chinese American citizen youths abandoning their studies for safety. This migration was part of a larger shift of the Chinese American population from less secure areas of the inland and the south to Shanghai, which offered both jobs and greater physical safety. Engineers In Young and Mon Yin Chung, businessman Luther Jee, and physicians Henshaw Jee and Edward Kau were just a few of the Chinese Americans who left more remote provinces like Hunan and Guangxi for Shanghai during the 1920s.[39]

The continued deterioration of public order and the Guomindang's radicalism also made parents in the United States reconsider sending their children to the area. In addition to a dozen or more kidnappings of Chinese American adults in 1924 and 1925, bold groups of criminals seized young students at the Canton Christian College (CCC) and the Union Middle School and demanded hefty ransoms for them. In the late 1910s and early 1920s, both institutions had seemed like safe havens for overseas Chinese children studying in China.[40] Now, however, nowhere was really safe.

Unlike Western-educated professionals, most Guangzhou-based citizen merchants did not enjoy a particularly high degree of geographical mobility.

Their networks and family ties were in the south, and despite their unease about Sun's regime, many of them had far too much of their capital invested in businesses and property in Guangzhou and the Pearl River Delta to move out of the region completely. Although many citizen merchants and students stayed in the south, for the first time since the 1911 revolution the Chinese American population of Hong Kong began to rise, doubling between 1921 and 1931.[41] Unable or unwilling to leave south China completely, many Chinese American merchants appear to have at least moved their families to the safety of the British colony, despite its higher cost of living.

By 1925 hundreds of potential Chinese American emigrants also began to delay plans to leave the United States for China. In 1922 more than 150 Chinese American citizens declared to US officials that they were merchants permanently departing the country for China, and almost all settled in south China, where they had strong family, business, and native-place networks. Just two years later, that number dropped by more than two-thirds. An unusually large number of short-term visitors and longtime residents also left China in the mid-1920s: in 1923, about 1,600 Chinese Americans returned to the United States from China, but in 1925 that figure almost doubled, while the number of citizens declaring their plans to leave permanently for China dropped by half.[42] Explaining the changed plans of Chinese Americans in his own community, Los Angeles restaurateur George Lem noted, "There is nothing for them to do because [south China] is so unsettled now that not much work of any kind can be done."[43]

THE STRIKE: HONG KONG

Chinese Americans who sought safety in Shanghai or Hong Kong could not escape the convulsions of Chinese politics, which increasingly meant anti-imperialist and anti-Western politics. In March 1925, Sun Yat-sen died of cancer, setting off a power scramble within the Guomindang and a new debate about the party's political course. Sun's three closest allies—Liao Zhongkai, Wang Jingwei, and Hu Hanmin—differed greatly in their views of the Soviet alliance's desirability.[44] Meanwhile, labor unrest surged in Shanghai, especially at foreign-owned factories.[45] In May 1925, Chinese workers broke into a Japanese plant in the city to demand jobs and to destroy machinery. The mill's Japanese guards opened fire, killing a communist labor activist and sparking a wave of demonstrations against foreign imperialism during which police in the International Settlement arrested several students. On May 30, more students from area colleges rallied inside the settlement and demanded the release of their comrades; instead, a British police inspector ordered his men to open fire, killing several Chinese and badly wounding many others. The May Thirtieth Incident, as it became known, touched off a national wave of protests, anti-foreign riots, and anti-imperialist anger.[46]

In the process, the incident helped reinvigorate the GMD government in Guangdong, especially after machine gun fire from the foreign concession on Guangzhou's Shameen Island killed Chinese demonstrators. The GMD government quickly called for a boycott of British Hong Kong and for Chinese there to leave. After the party leadership promised to support those who came to Guangzhou, between 100,000 and 250,000 abandoned the colony, essentially crippling Hong Kong's economy. As these workers flooded into Guangzhou, Guomindang officials recruited hundreds and eventually thousands to be "pickets." Their job was now to enforce the boycott by examining incoming and outgoing merchandise in Guangzhou.[47]

Chinese who stayed in Hong Kong during the strike thus signaled their loyalty to Britain, or at least their acquiescence to its colonial rule. This was especially the case for Hong Kong's Chinese elite. Historian John Carroll notes, "Fighting the strike enabled the leaders of the Chinese bourgeoisie to present themselves as allies, to show their loyalty to the colonial government, and to prove themselves as Hong Kong Chinese." Doing this also put them in direct conflict with the anti-imperialist GMD. Party activists in Guangzhou castigated the British loyalist Chinese in Hong Kong, calling into question their very Chineseness as the Nationalists defined it. Nevertheless, much of the Chinese merchant elite of the colony rejected this criticism, stayed put, and pressed for an end to the strike.[48]

Chinese American citizens who stayed on in Hong Kong during the strike also aligned themselves with the hated British imperialists, whether willingly or unwittingly. Some appear to have had little interest in politics or making a statement: one recently arrived Chinese Hawaiian, who had just left a job in north China to avoid strikes and warlord troops there, proved unwilling to move yet again.[49] Other Chinese Americans more purposely aligned themselves with the Hong Kong Chinese merchant elite and refused to participate in the strike.[50] While some of his old Queens College friends voted to support the strike, Bill Hong Sling joined a University of Hong Kong student group aligned with anti-strike Chinese leaders.[51] Some Chinese Americans in Hong

Kong made their opposition even clearer. San Franciscan Tsai Yan Lum, sub-manager of the overseas Chinese–owned Sincere Department Store in Hong Kong, publicly denied rumors that the firm had asked employees to contribute to the strike fund for Guangzhou.[52] This statement of neutrality was hardly neutral.

Whatever their view of the strike, Chinese American citizens in Hong Kong often felt its harsh economic impact, and some of their firms either collapsed totally or sustained losses from which they never fully recovered.[53] Likely prompted by leftists in Guangzhou, a popular newspaper there printed rumors during the strike that Look Poong Shan's Bank of Canton was about to fail, prompting a run on the institution.[54] Shops in the Central District, including Ng Ah Tye's confectionary on Pottinger Street and the Chinese American–owned Blue Bird candy store on Pedder Street, lost customers and thousands of dollars as food costs climbed and Chinese workers left the colony.[55] Chinese American citizen employees of British, American, and Chinese companies all sat idle with no idea when or if the strike and boycott would end.[56]

THE STRIKE: GUANGZHOU

In Guangzhou, the strike frightened both foreigners and, increasingly, the Chinese business community, which became a target of the pickets and of new forces that GMD activists helped mobilize in the province. Guomindang leftists and especially communists organized thousands of Guangdong peasants and laborers into unions whose leaders were avowedly anti-imperialist and outspoken in their opposition to local elites.[57] In Guangzhou itself, the government essentially lost control over the pickets, who wielded their power with near impunity. Some took bribes or helped themselves to the contents of local stores and banks, much to the consternation of Chinese merchants. Still, few in the business class spoke out about this. As a Chinese Australian visitor noted, "persons found dealing with the 'imperialists,' acting as the 'running dogs' of the foreigner, or offending the extreme labour unions in any way are rounded up, chained together and marched through the streets a couple of times a day as a warning to others."[58] Strikers also targeted foreigners, sometimes seized their food and other goods, and fired at foreign-flagged ships. Several months of such incidents prompted US Consul General Douglas Jenkins to complain of "the indignities to which American citizens are now being subjected at the hands of the strikers."[59]

As the strike divided Guangzhou's contending social and political classes, the pickets treated Chinese Americans as just another group of Chinese merchants conspiring with the hated imperialists. The relative of a Chinese American citizen reported that the man "was taken prisoner by the strikers, when on a visit to Chinsan. . . . and the amount of $5000.00 was asked for ransom."[60] Another woman described how "a couple of workmen striker pickets rush in. . . . saying that my [Chinese American husband] is smuggling Chinese to Hong Kong . . . [and] my husband was then sent to Tungyun and detained with chain and cuffs, as a criminal."[61] The strikers also targeted Louey Shuck, a wealthy man who embodied the comprador image: "a very prosperous looking merchant . . . fur-lined silk coats, etc.," according to one acquaintance. To thwart the pickets, Louey hoisted an American flag and a placard affirming his US citizenship outside his property, but this probably just encouraged the strikers to target him. Indeed, the pickets appear to have focused on these Chinese Americans because they seemed such apt representatives of the semi-Westernized overseas merchant class whom Guomindang leaders viewed with suspicion. Little wonder that Louey Shuck cursed his old party and its pickets as "Bolsheviks."[62]

The Guomindang also encouraged local activists to target US-backed missionary institutions, making the many Chinese American citizens affiliated with such establishments increasingly vulnerable and uneasy as the strike and boycott dragged on. Between 1925 and 1927, numerous foreign-backed institutions in the south became the targets of activists bent on ridding Guangdong of Western imperialism. By early 1926, large crowds of Chinese had already entered and looted missionary property on Hainan Island and in Wuzhou, Guangdong, often as government soldiers watched but refused to intervene.[63] Later that spring, strikers also surrounded the American-financed and -staffed Canton Hospital, urged the Chinese employees to leave, and refused to allow in food and other supplies.[64] Almost simultaneously, a small group of leftist students tried to convince the student body of CCC to stage a walkout.[65] The move affected not just China-born people but also the thirty-one Chinese Americans and 187 other overseas Chinese students enrolled in CCC and its lower schools that year. Indeed, anti-imperialist agitation threatened to affect the overseas Chinese studying or teaching at numerous other area schools, including the Noyes Memorial Academy, Pui Ching, Pui Ying, True Light Middle School, and Pooi To.[66]

In other words, Guomindang policies now directly exposed and questioned Chinese Americans' ties to those whom the party labeled its enemies, both foreign and domestic. CCC's overseas students could not escape the school's association with Western military power after the Shameen crisis, because a US Navy gunboat began to escort the college launch up and down the river to ensure its safety. The college's refusal to bow to government pressure and to readmit the students it suspended for trying to organize a campus strike cast anyone who sided with the administration as an enemy of the party. But foreign institutions with considerable merchant support, like CCC, were also irresistible targets for party leaders simply because they enabled the GMD to accuse the local merchant elite of enabling imperialism.[67] Overseas Chinese considering such institutions for their children increasingly balked at such attacks. The number of ethnic Chinese from abroad studying at Canton Christian College had fallen from 277 to 218 between 1923 and 1925.[68] The exodus continued in 1926, when many of the remaining Chinese American youths at Guangzhou's missionary colleges withdrew from school and returned to the United States.[69] By 1927 not a single Chinese American student was registered at the regular Canton Christian College schools, although a few likely remained in the overseas school. Far more now chose the much safer Hong Kong branch, which not coincidentally announced its expansion in 1925.[70]

The vast majority of Chinese American students who fled Guangzhou in these years acted not out of disgust at Western imperialism but because they supported the missionary institutions and feared for their own safety as a result. Strikers and their backers in the regime shut down CCC briefly in 1927, but they received almost no student support for their actions; instead, most youths and their parents stoutly defended CCC against what they considered creeping Bolshevism.[71] "For many years our university has been criticized as a sort of non-patriotic, if not imperialistic educational institution," wrote college administrator Chan K. Wong after the school finally reopened. "Especially since the recent national movements [we] have suffered severe antagonism from outside students for being a foreignized group not desiring to meet the national aspirations."[72] In these two sentences, Wong neatly summed up a problem that not only CCC students but the overseas-linked China coastal merchant classes and Chinese Americans had all faced since the anti-Sincere demonstrations of 1919: the perception, now part of the GMD platform, that the local and "returned" merchants who moved in the networks of the overseas Chinese world were both unpatriotic and pro-imperialist.

By making the struggle against foreign imperialism central to the nationalist movement, the Guomindang after 1923 attempted to enforce a narrow and exclusive definition of patriotic citizenship at odds with the often hybrid identities of the southern coastal merchant class, including its Chinese American members. Like Chan K. Wong, much of this group embraced an expansive, transnational idea of Chineseness that deeply troubled Guomindang activists. The overseas-linked merchants' sense of Chinese cultural identity was obviously strong, and they supported the creation of a modern China from the ashes of the decrepit Qing empire. But they had also learned to thrive in a world of colonies, blurred boundaries, and competing citizenships. A decade of warlordism had further weakened their political attachment to centralizing authorities, even those who claimed the republican mantle; in the 1910s and 1920s, Guangdong experienced not only endemic banditry and piracy but also the depredations of the different armies that fought for control of the south. Although every group of Cantonese suffered under these conditions, merchants, because of their perceived wealth, often became the particular targets of soldiers, rapacious officials, and bandits.[73] Now, the Nationalists had labeled many of these same merchants imperialism's servants, casting their links to Asian colonies, their citizenship status, and their cultural practices as un-Chinese.

ABANDONMENT

US officials tacitly endorsed the Guomindang's exclusive view of citizenship in the aftermath of Liao Zhongkai's assassination. On August 25, 1925, New York native Jo Nom Wing appeared at the US Consulate in Guangzhou to ask for help. Soldiers had broken into his mother's home looking for Jo's half brother, Chu Su Gunn, a Chinese citizen and the editor of the *Guomin Xinwen* newspaper. Failing to find Chu Su Gunn, the soldiers instead seized Jo's brother Chu Shea Wai and alleged that he had some connection to the assassination of Liao Zhongkai. A frightened Jo requested that the consulate intervene with the Chinese authorities, and he continued to repeat this plea for months afterward. "My brother's case is nothing but framed up, as I understand the Canton Government has no real evidence and witnesses," Jo contended. But more importantly, he noted, Chu Shea Wai's arrest "is obviously contrary to the treaty between the United States and China," because extraterritoriality protected US citizen Chu from arrest and imprisonment by Chinese officials.[74]

The Chu family was well known both in Guangzhou and in overseas Chinese circles. Chu Shea Wai's father had been a merchant in New York for

Form 430 APPLICATION OF ALLEGED AMERICAN-BORN CHINESE FOR PREINVESTIGATION OF STATUS TRIPLICATE

U. S. DEPARTMENT OF LABOR
IMMIGRATION SERVICE

N. Y. No. 32~~[illegible]~~/480

Office of Chinese Inspector in Charge,
Port of New York, N. Y.
June 3, 1916.

To H. R. Sisson,
Chinese and Immigrant Inspector,
New York, N. Y.

SIR: It being my intention to leave the United States on a temporary visit abroad, departing and returning through the Chinese port of entry of San Francisco, California I hereby apply, under the provisions of Rule 16 of the Chinese Regulations, for preinvestigation of my claimed status as an American citizen by birth, submitting herewith such documentary proofs (if any) as I possess, and agreeing to appear at such time and place as you may designate, and to produce then and there witnesses, for oral examination regarding the claim made by me.

This application is submitted in triplicate with my photograph attached to each copy, as required by said rule.

Respectfully,

Signature in Chinese 簽唐字名 趙士偉
Signature in English 簽番字名 Chu Shea Wai
Address 具禀人之住址 33 Mott St., New York, N.Y.

管理外人入口委員知之我現欲暫離美國出遊外邦今由華人出入之港埠而去將來亦即由該埠而回玆依三十九欵之例在美國出世所有之憑據呈上查驗亦親與證人到委員之公辦房詢問口供照例簽名稟上並附相三幅

NO. 32 / 4330

U. S. Immigrant Inspector.

Bureau of Immigration,
Washington, D. C.
JUN 18 1916, 19

Respectfully returned to
H. R. Sisson,
Chinese and Immigrant Inspector,
New York N.Y.

With the information that I am prepared, on the basis of the evidence submitted with the original of this application, to approve said application.

A. Caminetti
Commissioner-General.

14-73

FIGURE 8. Chu Shea Wai's Form 430 application. In 1925 leftist Guomindang cadets arrested the New York–born Chu for his alleged involvement in the assassination of party leader Liao Zhongkai. The US State Department used Chu's case as a precedent for refusing to invoke extraterritoriality in cases that involved Chinese American citizens in China. National Archives and Records Administration, New York regional facility.

several decades before retiring to China around 1918.[75] Several of his American-born children followed, including Henry Joe Young, Chu Shea Wai, Laurand Chu, Ow Wing Chu, and Jo Nom Wing, who was probably most well known in Manhattan for having run away with the Ringling Brothers circus as a teenager.[76] Chu Shea Wai's China-born half-brother Chu Su Gunn was a far more serious youth; he joined the Tongmenghui (the forerunner to the Guomindang) in New York, edited party papers in San Francisco and Manhattan, and published a historical novel about the Tongmenghui that received praise from Sun Yat-sen himself.[77]

In 1925 Chu Shea Wai's only crime was his relationship to the controversial Chu Su Gunn, one of several overseas Chinese conservatives in the party's leadership ranks. In the early 1920s, Chu Su Gunn headed the Liangguang Salt Commission and drew criticism for his management of the agency, but he became particularly notorious for running a newspaper that opposed the influence of Soviet advisors and Chinese communists in the Guomindang.[78] His allies included Hu Hanmin, the most conservative of Sun Yat-sen's three leading political heirs.[79] From his Manhattan years, Chu Su Gunn also knew Frank Lee, the New York–born Guomindang diplomat who left Guangzhou for a position at Shanghai College in late 1922 because of the rise of leftists in the party.[80]

Despite his half-brother's ties to Chinese politics, Chu Shea Wai's own China, like that of so many Chinese American citizens in the south, was as much, if not more, a part of the overseas Chinese world stretching from Guangzhou to Hong Kong to Singapore, Honolulu, San Francisco, and New York, than it was of the Chinese nation with its capital in Beijing. In addition to being the son of a prosperous merchant, Chu had attended primary school and a year of high school in Manhattan. In 1921, at age 18, he traveled to China with his young sister Laurand to stay with their retired father and to prepare to enter a mainland university by studying Chinese in Guangzhou. At one point before his arrest, he even lived with his family on a lane known as "Overseas Merchant Street" in the Tungshan (Dongshan) area.[81]

In other words, Chu belonged to the overseas-connected class that the Guomindang now considered of dubious loyalty, and leftists in the party used the Liao murder to cast further doubt on such people specifically, as well as on party rightists in general. After a brief trial, a specially appointed judge condemned to death Liao's actual killer, a local man named Chan Shun, and gave one of his accomplices a death sentence as well.[82] But soldiers also placed rightist Hu Hanmin, whose brother had called for the "removal" of Liao just a few days before the assassination, under "protection," and Hu soon left the country.[83] Senior party leaders then arrested Chicagoan Moy Quong-poy and arranged for the military to court-martial him because he was one of the assassin's commanding officers.[84] Chu Su Gunn was another rightist with overseas connections, and the cadets who broke into his family's house apparently seized Chu Shea Wai in order to force his stepbrother to surrender; when this failed, they instead charged Chu Shea Wai with swindling, based on Chu Su Gunn's alleged misuse of state funds.[85] They also occupied the Chu home to put further pressure on the family. As Chu Shea Wai's brother Henry Joe Young complained, "there are soldiers living in my mother's house and I still have a little sister there . . . I am sure my mother and sister is scare to dead [*sic*]."[86]

Unlike Moy Quong-poy, Chu Shea Wai immediately invoked his American citizenship after his arrest. Moy had relied on his American birth to shield himself in the past, most notably during his days as a journalist in 1910s Shanghai.[87] But now, the circumstances surrounding his detention undercut any claim he had to citizenship under US law: by accepting a commission in the GMD government's military forces, he had expatriated himself as defined in the 1907 Expatriation Act and could no longer appeal to the American consulate. Chu Shea Wai, on the other hand, expected assistance as a student who had continually registered with the US consulate in Guangzhou in order to maintain his citizenship.[88] Even better, his closest siblings were also US citizens determined to get him the help he needed: his brother Henry Joe Young traveled to Hong Kong to plead with the consular officials there, while Jo Nom Wing sent a letter directly to the US minister in Beijing.[89] Indeed, after Jo explained Chu Shea Wai's plight to US officials, they did make token inquiries into the case and even decided that the accusations against Chu Shea Wai were almost certainly baseless.[90]

RACIAL NATIONALISM AND CHU SHEA WAI

Unfortunately for Chu Shea Wai, the racial nationalism now ascendant in American politics and immigration law deeply influenced the consular staff with whom his brothers dealt. The previous year, Congress had passed the explicitly racial Immigration Act of 1924, which President Calvin Coolidge endorsed in part because he believed that "Nordics deteriorate when mixed with other races."[91] But as historian Mae Ngai points out, by allowing in small numbers of Southern and Eastern Europeans but no Asians at all, the 1924 act actually "constructed a white American race, in which persons of European descent shared a common whiteness that made them distinct from those deemed to be not white." In contrast, the law affirmed the belief that Chinese and other non-Europeans were "unalterably foreign and unassimilable to the nation."[92] This brand of racial nationalism deeply influenced the approach of the two American officials—Guangzhou consul-general Douglas Jenkins and Beijing minister John V. MacMurray—who worked directly on Chu's case. The men shared a racial and cultural disdain for the rights of Chinese American citizens, whose legitimacy they increasingly felt emboldened to deny.

MacMurray, a 1925 Coolidge appointee, set the tone for staff in China as the senior US diplomat there. A former assistant secretary of state, MacMurray impressed his new British colleagues with what they considered his lack of traditional American sentimentality about China, and especially the Guomindang. He also supported immigration restrictions that favored "Nordics" and viewed rising Chinese nationalism as the result of an "inferiority complex which under the stress of an almost nation-wide excitement prompts [the Chinese] to a hysterical self-assertion."[93] His ideas about Chinese Americans were even less charitable.

MacMurray, with Jenkins's assistance, set out to use Chu's case as a precedent for excluding all Chinese Americans in China from US protection. The State Department had long argued that "it is a generally recognized rule . . . of international law, that when a person who was born with dual nationality is residing in either of the countries of which he is a national, that country has the right to assert its claim to him without any interference by the other."[94] Before 1925 some consular officials cited this principle in order to completely ignore Chinese American citizen pleas, but most staffers generally decided whether to intervene on a case-by-case basis. US authorities' conduct over time suggests that at least some felt a sense of obligation to respond to every citizen's request, while others acted because of pressure from the (usually white) friends of well-connected Chinese Americans. The unsettled situation in much of China also gave them some room for discretion: the United States until 1928 recognized the Beiyang regime as the government of China, but most Chinese Americans made requests for assistance after interacting with one of the southern regimes. Now, however, Jenkins and MacMurray tacitly ended the old flexibility and enforced a definition of protectable citizenship that excluded Chinese Americans.

Jenkins and MacMurray believed that while ethnic Chinese claimed privileges based on their formal membership in the American state, only members of the racial and cultural *nation* really deserved US protection. For this reason, the men grounded their opposition to helping Chu and other Chinese Americans not in the State Department's policy on dual citizenship but in the explicitly cultural and racial ideas of the era. For his part, MacMurray saw a deep gulf between the civilizations of "east and west," and to him, Chu and other Chinese American citizens stood firmly on the eastern side of that divide.[95] Jenkins not only shared such ideas but drew an even clearer line between legal status and actual belonging. "While Chu is undoubtedly an American citizen and possesses a valid passport," Jenkins argued, "he has many Chinese relatives and was living as a Chinese, and may possibly have had some connection with politics, although there appears to be no proof of this."[96] A month later, Jenkins made the case even more emphatically: "Chu is a Chinese and it is quite possible that he was implicated in Liao Chung-k'ai's [Liao Zhongkai's] assassination." In fact, no new evidence linking Chu Shea Wai to the murder had come to light since Jenkins's earlier statement, but the consul apparently felt the need to justify his unsubstantiated complaint that "it seems extremely unfortunate that we should be bound under our law to attempt to protect these people who come back to China and not only live as Chinese, but become involved in Chinese politics."[97]

The State Department fully backed Jenkins's cultural and racial criteria for protection, because officials in Washington had helped lay the groundwork for them in the wake of the racially motivated immigration laws of 1917 and 1921. Beginning in 1922, the department listed several factors for determining whether Chinese American citizens had in particular "abandoned [their] ties with the United States."[98] Actually, the 1907 Expatriation Act explicitly described the only ways a native-born citizen could expatriate, so the State Department's criteria had no basis in law; it simply reflected officials' bias against a particular group.[99] Nevertheless, the department saw symptoms of abandonment in "marriage to a Chinese women," although under US immigration law China-born women could not enter the United States or naturalize, and interracial marriage was illegal in most states; "establishment of business [in China]," although the department encouraged white Americans to establish businesses in China (and Chinese Americans faced egregious job discrimination in the United States); and "raising a family who from their manner of dress apparently follow Chinese customs," a vague and subjective standard at best.[100]

MacMurray even resurrected outdated policies to justify his racial and cultural disdain for Chu and other Chinese American citizens. According to MacMurray, the State Department claimed that it "of course is unable to grant passports to Chinese persons born in the United States proper or in its insular possessions without regard to the length and permanence of their residence in China, as it is a well established principle that the right to protection is reciprocal with the performance of the duties of citizenship."[101] In citing this "well established principle," MacMurray was actually relying on a defunct late-nineteenth-century State Department practice to deny passports to native-born or naturalized citizens who seemed to be residing abroad permanently. In defending this practice, Theodore Roosevelt's secretary of state, John Hay, had used former Secretary of State Hamilton Fish's 1870s definition of expatriation. Fish had based this partly on residence, "there being no legislative definition of what constitutes expatriation."[102] But the Expatriation Act of 1907 cleared up this problem, and in 1910 the acting secretary of state, Huntington Wilson, changed the department's overall position on the matter:

> The department has come to the conclusion that. . . . a [native-born] American citizen may now have a permanent foreign residence and yet contribute, indirectly if not directly, to the wealth and strength, the prestige and general welfare of his country, so that as long as he maintains a true allegiance to this Government and is ready, if need be, to come to its defense, he may be entitled to its protection.

In any case, Wilson maintained, before the State Department withdrew protection from an American, he or she should have the chance to "show that he is still a true citizen of the United States."[103] Jenkins and MacMurray never gave Chu Shea Wai this opportunity.

Instead, Jenkins, MacMurray, and the State Department not only relied on racial and cultural norms to justify withdrawing from Chu Shea Wai's case but also formalized the decision into a concrete policy for the future. The secretary of state and his staff henceforth cited the case of Chu Shea Wai—a native of New York who possessed a valid American passport and had registered continuously in Guangzhou—as a precedent for not intervening in any other Chinese American cases.[104] In Shanghai, where the status of the International Settlement and the French Concession complicated issues of jurisdiction and what constituted "China," consuls continued to intervene in certain instances. But outside such areas, Chinese Americans were now on their own and at the mercy of the Chinese government, whether they recognized themselves as its citizens or not.

SACRIFICIAL LAMBS

The Chu decision not only reflected the way racial nationalism influenced State Department policymaking but also showed Jenkins's shrewdness in using a maligned and largely powerless group to help preserve the status of white Americans in China. While Jenkins and MacMurray both opposed the protection of Chinese American citizens in China, MacMurray's main motivation was his view that such people were not real Americans. Jenkins shared this belief, but unlike MacMurray, he also understood the growing power of the Guomindang and the appeal of its anti-imperialist rhetoric.[105] From the very beginning of the Guangzhou–Hong Kong strike, Jenkins argued that the issue prompting much of the anti-foreign agitation was extraterritoriality, a symbol of imperialism and national humiliation that the Guomindang wanted to abolish. Like MacMurray, Jenkins did not favor dismantling the system, but he argued that "there can be no real stability and friendliness in China's relations with foreigners until some plan is found and put into effect for the readjustment of China's status with the Powers."[106] The problem Jenkins contemplated was how to preserve as much of extraterritoriality as possible while finding some way to placate the Guomindang, especially if it managed to eventually establish a functioning national government. Chu Shea Wai was part of his attempt at "readjustment."

By openly abandoning Chu Shea Wai and other Chinese American citizens, Jenkins demonstrated to Guomindang officials his country's respect for China's citizenship laws and its willingness to compromise on some aspects of extrality, even as he resisted the southern government's demands in areas he considered far more important. The difference between his treatment of Chinese Americans and of US business interests in south China revealed his approach. When the Standard Oil Company complained that the Guangzhou regime was slapping a treaty-violating tax on the corporation, Jenkins promised to support the firm if managers imposed a sales embargo on Guangdong. At one point, he even asked the State Department for permission to request US naval protection for a company convoy heading upriver to Guangxi Province.[107] While Chu Shea Wai, abandoned by his country, sat in a jail cell at Whampoa, Jenkins energetically threw himself into defending the profits of one of the largest corporations in the world. Little wonder that Chu Shea Wai's mother finally fled to the safety of Hong Kong with her American-born daughters Laurand and Oi Wing Chu.[108]

Jenkins and MacMurray actually proved more willing to defend the rights of Chinese citizen representatives of American companies than actual Chinese American citizens. When local officials taxed Standard Oil's Chinese agents in Sichuan, MacMurray asked the State Department for the right to lodge a formal protest against the warlord there.[109] In contrast, Jenkins rejected Louey Shuck's pleas for help when Guomindang officials in Guangzhou arrested Louey's wife and son because of his refusal to pay special war taxes on his property. Louey must have been quite surprised at the State Department's change in attitude. He had asked the Guangzhou consulate for assistance with a similar issue in 1923, and at that time Vice Consul Howard Bucknell Jr. not only settled the matter but also advised Louey never to pay any war taxes in order to preserve his status as an American citizen. During the same period, Douglas Jenkins himself wrote to Louey to assure him that "your family will not be annoyed in the future."[110] By 1926, however, with the Guomindang threatening extrality and the Chu Shea Wai case as a precedent, Jenkins both refused to assist Louey and also criticized his failure to register his second marriage (his first wife had died a few years earlier) or the birth of his "alleged son" with American officials. Jenkins also found fault with Louey because he "continued to reside indefinitely in China," although Louey actually lived in Hong Kong, had registered his first wife's death and youngest son's birth, and represented the American shipping firm Struthers and Barry. Furthermore, Louey paid a substantial amount of annual US taxes, or what Hamilton Wilson once would have called a contribution "to the wealth and strength" of the United States.[111] Nevertheless, Louey had no choice but to settle with the Guomindang regime, especially when he realized that his own government had no intention of assisting him.[112]

DIFFERENT NATIONAL APPROACHES TO ETHNIC CHINESE CITIZENSHIP

Unlike the United States, Great Britain, whose Asian colonies contained millions of ethnic Chinese, sought for as long as possible to preserve the status of such people in China as British Protected Persons or British subjects. Officials in the British Foreign Office and the US State Department shared many of the same racial and racist attitudes.[113] Still, while the United States possessed an Asian colony (the Philippines), American identity and prestige were not bound up with a territorial empire the way Britain's were.[114] The United States certainly used law and policy to segregate and stigmatize segments of its own population on the basis of race and ancestry (among other categories), but it also steadfastly maintained the fiction of individual equality. Britain's empire rendered most nonwhite subjects as subordinate and inferior, yet its open hierarchy also forced the British government to act as protector when Chinese authorities arrested or mistreated Anglo-Chinese.[115] Not all British officials agreed with that policy, of course. "Defeats in these futile disputes tend to render ineffective our efforts to protect genuine British interests of far greater importance," complained a British consular officer. "If the Foreign Office alone had been concerned we should long ago have adopted the American attitude in this matter."[116] But the Foreign Office was not the only concerned party. The British Colonial Office and the governments of heavily Chinese Hong Kong and the Straits Settlements demanded the Foreign Office try to protect Anglo-Chinese in China. They believed that the prestige of these governments, of the empire, and of white British power in Asia all depended on Foreign Office intervention.[117] As a result, the Foreign Office negotiated for several years with the Beiyang regime to push it to recognize Anglo-Chinese as British subjects.[118]

As the northern government faded, the British took up the issue with representatives of the Guomindang government but discovered that it completely rejected any recognition of Anglo-Chinese subjects. Party leaders argued that ethnic Chinese who wished to claim foreign citizenship needed to comply with the Nationalists' legal code by applying for denaturalization from China. When Anglo-Chinese attempted to do so, however, the Nationalists proved unwilling in almost every case to allow them to renounce their Chinese citizenship.[119] In part for this reason, staff of the Foreign Office continued to monitor and attempt to protect Anglo-Chinese in China.

In stark contrast, the US State Department made the question of Chinese Americans' status in China part of its negotiations with the new Nationalist regime not to protect such American citizens but to formalize its abandonment of them. During a session in which the major foreign powers discussed with Nationalist diplomats the future of extrality, the American representative suggested that foreign governments withhold protection from their ethnic Chinese citizens if such people stayed in China for more than six months. Of course, the American delegate claimed, these ethnic Chinese citizens could avoid this fate if they simply obtained a "denationalization" certificate from the Chinese government.[120] But the US negotiator fully understood that this stipulation was meaningless: an American consular official had admitted to British colleagues that the GMD regime operating in the south simply would not issue such certificates. In reality, the official explained, "in order to terminate the long and exasperating correspondence which American consuls have had to conduct on this subject, the State Department has admitted the principle of dual nationality and has ceased to intervene on behalf of Chinese Americans in China."[121] Simply put, the department stopped recognizing Chinese American citizenship in China in order to avoid inconvenience and extra work. By 1927 the files of the Canton consulate, once stuffed with Chinese American protection cases, thinned as consular officials cited the Chu Shea Wai precedent to ignore all Chinese American citizen protection claims. Presumably, Guangzhou consular authorities enjoyed the additional leisure time they gained.

In addition to creating a depressing precedent for Chinese Americans, the trials of Chu Shea Wai and Moy Quong-poy exposed the factional undercurrents of the Guomindang government during the spring and summer of 1926. As communist and leftist activists continued to organize segments of the province's population, different party leaders struggled for supremacy and debated how to respond to new warlord rumblings from the north. Still, describing Guangzhou in early 1926, American journalist Hallett Abend remembered that, despite the city's physical ugliness, oppressive climate, and anti-foreign tone, it pulsed with a "stirring purpose." In March 1926, Chiang Kai-shek, the ambitious commander of the Soviet-subsidized Guomindang military academy at Whampoa Island, responded to what he claimed were threats on his life by putting a number of Russian advisors under house arrest, moving against some of the communists, and curbing the power of the strike pickets. Despite this early power grab, Chiang publicly professed support for the GMD-communist alliance and his Soviet advisors. With their blessing, he launched in mid-1926 the long-awaited "Northern Expedition" against the warlord armies of central and northern China. Bent on reunifying the country, Guomindang and allied soldiers now flowed out of Guangzhou, taking some of the pickets with them as porters. "Canton, by the end of June, was like a squeezed lemon," recalled Abend. "All the juice and flavor was gone." Soon afterward, the Hong Kong–Canton strike began to wind down while Abend himself left newly sleepy Guangzhou for lack of news to report.[122]

GATHERING STORM

On the surface, Shanghai's Chinese Americans in 1926 seemed detached from and largely unconcerned by Guangzhou's radicalism and the Northern Expedition, which moved swiftly toward the Yangzi River. On the French Concession's ballfields, attorney Nick Char played in local football and baseball leagues, often with his fellow Hawaiians. In the US Consular Court, George D. Wing stood trial for allowing opium smoking and gambling to take place in a hotel he ran. At the newly reopened Carlton Café on Ningpo Road, the "American-born Chinese Band" played jazz and Hawaiian music to swaying dancers each evening. The well-regarded architect Poy Gum Lee married Pansy Choye, the daughter of a Hong Kong comprador, at the old Cantonese Baptist Church (Lee accepted a commission to design the new one in 1930). The lawyer H. C. Mei carefully untangled the complex estate of another son of San Francisco, the late Tom Gunn. Elsie Lee of Portland, Oregon, found a leading role in *The Willow Patterned Plate,* a film underwritten by British American Tobacco, while Missouri native Olive Young starred in the new movie *Filial Piety.* And Kam Yee Moon and Nina Moon of Hawaii scandalized Chinese American Shanghai when their nasty divorce hit the newspapers.[123]

Still, since the May Thirtieth Incident, relations between Chinese and foreigners in Shanghai had been particularly strained, and many Chinese Americans struggled to balance their multiple, overlapping loyalties in this tense atmosphere.[124] Largely the children of merchants, few felt much sympathy for communism, whether for religious, economic, or political reasons. At the same time, many of them expressed an unmistakable, if conservative, Chinese nationalism. H. C. Mei embodied this view: he deplored Chinese who worshipped everything foreign and Western and classed the "Bolshevistic doctrines and communistic leanings throughout this country at the present time" as evidence for this negative tendency.[125] Frank Lee agreed, condemning communism but explaining its attraction as a "patriotic appeal [that is] extremely potent with all Chinese who feel China's humiliating position in the family of Nations."[126] Nor was this conservative Chinese nationalism the sole province of the Nationalist right; in 1926 Lillian Ying Loo Kiang, the American-born wife of socialist professor Jiang Kanghu, helped lead a ceremony in which attendees raised the old five barred republican flag and sang the "national" anthem of the Beiyang regime.[127]

These Chinese American citizens certainly understood the attraction and raw power of Chinese nationalism far more than the non-Chinese with whom they mixed in the clubs, stores, restaurants, and courtrooms of the treaty ports. Unlike most such people, Chinese American citizens, especially in Shanghai, crossed borders, socializing with China-born residents, participating in new and solely Chinese professional organizations, and often finding places in the new, westernized Chinese elite of the coastal cities.[128] Furthermore, Chinese Americans had grown up in a racially unequal and segregated society and, particularly in Shanghai, still encountered on occasion the same kinds of attitudes from white Americans and Europeans. More than other foreign citizens, Chinese Americans understood Chinese resentment over imperialist aggrandizement—the foreign-controlled and policed concessions, the parks that forbade local (but not overseas) Chinese entry, the clubs that barred non-Europeans, and the courts that existed because of extrality.[129]

The post-May Thirtieth struggles in Shanghai galvanized and sometimes radicalized many of these Chinese American citizens. In the wake of the shooting, one young Chinese American donated money to the resurgent and increasingly anti-imperialist Shanghai Student Union, while another plunged into leftist activism and eventually attracted unwanted attention from right-wing Guomindang members.[130] Even establishment figure Loy Chang, a Hawaiian-born Hong Kong banker, took a public stand. After leaving the colony during the 1925–1926 strike and boycott, he spoke out for tariff autonomy for China at a national bankers' meeting in Shanghai, helped draft a resolution calling it the only outcome that would "satisfy the national aspirations of the Chinese people," and essentially blamed the strike in the south on the British governor of Hong Kong.[131]

Russell Chen's transformation was the most dramatic and long lasting, even though it took place quietly and initially out of the sight of his white colleagues in the Chinese courts. A third-generation Chinese American and a native of Boston, he briefly served in the US Army during World War I before completing his education at Boston University, Columbia University, and New York University Law School.[132] Arriving in Shanghai in 1923, he practiced business law and became a fixture in the Mixed Court and the US Court for China, two institutions that owed their existence to the "unequal treaties" that nationalists loathed.[133] Chen also met Lawrence Klindt Kentwell, the Hong Kong–born son of an English father and a Chinese mother. An Oxford- and Columbia-educated attorney, Kentwell was a boyhood friend and onetime business partner of the Chinese American lawyer Anthony Leefong Ahlo, with whom he attended preparatory school in Hawaii.[134] Except for two years in the British armed forces during World War I, Kentwell had spent most of his adult life practicing law in Shanghai, where he encountered considerable discrimination because of his partial Chinese ancestry. As John B. Powell, the American publisher of the *China Weekly Review*, explained, Kentwell "has had a difficult time because of his mixed blood [and] probably has never seen the inside of any of the clubs maintained by foreigners on these shores . . . [or] the inside of many foreign homes, the reason for this being the damnable social standards prevailing in the treaty ports."[135]

Kentwell may not have been wholly responsible for Russell Chen's growing Chinese nationalism, but he played a major role in shaping and channeling it. With protests over the May Thirtieth incident ongoing, British residents of Shanghai began to suspect that Kentwell sympathized with the Nationalists despite his own British citizenship. Kentwell only stoked such suspicions by publicly criticizing British attitudes in China, calling a white lawyer a racist, and refusing to pay taxes on land he owned in the International Settlement until Chinese ratepayers received representation on the foreign-run Shanghai Municipal Council (SMC).[136] Acquaintances of Chen and Kentwell likely knew that they were friends, but the former surprised many of his colleagues when he appeared at Kentwell's side during the SMC's annual ratepayers' meeting in early 1926.[137] Although of Chinese ancestry, both men could vote in the meeting because they were foreign citizen ratepayers.[138] Chen stood to second and argue for Kentwell's motion for an amendment to an SMC resolution that, after years of stalling, granted local Chinese ratepayers three seats on the council. Kentwell and Chen's amendment demanded that Chinese representation reflect the actual numbers of Chinese in the Settlement—a change that would have resulted in Chinese control of the council.[139]

Unsurprisingly, the issues of race and anti-imperialism that motivated Kentwell and Chen failed to move their fellow ratepayers. At the SMC meeting, Chen argued that proportional representation, rather than the three seats the council was proposing, would "erase all signs of any racial difference or inequality which [Chinese residents have] claimed is prevalent in the method under which they are governed in this Settlement at present."[140] Kentwell had just finished making a similar argument, provoking what a reporter described as "outbursts of laughter in the gathering that at one time verged almost to jeers forecast[ing] the fate of the amendment."[141] Only four of the more than three hundred ratepayers in attendance supported Kentwell's amendment, delivering a stinging rebuke to the two men. Perhaps not coincidentally, Kentwell after the meeting became the target of a prolonged lawsuit over financial fraud and in 1927 lost his right to practice in front of the Mixed Court. In the process, he publicly renounced his British citizenship.[142]

Chen avoided the kind of career damage that Kentwell sustained after the SMC meeting, but his friend's experiences and the ratepayers' jeers deeply affected him. After spring 1926, Russell Chen never again appeared in either the Mixed Court or the US Court for China. Chen hardly rejected Shanghai's cosmopolitan society—he continued his social rounds in the YMCA, the American University Men's Club, and the NYU Club, and he was single-handedly responsible for introducing Moxie soda to China—but he now focused his law practice entirely on business questions. His 1927 marriage to the socially prominent Julia Sih Tong and his friendships with local elites such as T. W. Kwok of the Wing On department store family likely helped him find clients outside the foreign courts.[143] He also quietly continued his activism. In 1927 Kentwell and Chinese editor Francis Zia began publishing a new, pro-Nationalist, anti-British newspaper called the *China Courier*. Incensed by the anti-British tone of Kentwell and Zia's paper, British detectives from the Shanghai Municipal Police investigated the journal's personnel in an attempt to tie them to communist elements. In the process, they discovered that Russell Chen had registered the paper as a US company, helping shield it from Chinese officials and British pressure.[144] Chen continued to support Kentwell and his politics for the next fifteen years, even as Kentwell drifted into collaborationism during the Japanese occupation.

THE GUOMINDANG TRIUMPHANT

By early 1927, the Guomindang's National Revolutionary Army (NRA) was nearing Shanghai, much to the consternation of foreign officials and residents who closely watched the NRA's northward march and its impact on other foreign enclaves and interests in China. In Sichuan, Hunan, and Hubei, civilian supporters of the NRA seized foreign-run institutions and forced their staffs to flee. In response, British gunboats on the Yangzi fired indiscriminately into populated areas and killed hundreds of Chinese, after which Britain's rumored support for anti-GMD forces prompted a new round of attacks on foreign institutions. NRA troops then captured foreign concession areas in

Hankou and Jiujiang, while NRA sympathizers looted missionary properties in Fuzhou and drove foreigners out of Hangzhou. When the GMD's military stormed Nanjing, either NRA troops or men wearing their uniforms killed several foreigners and sent scores of others fleeing to foreign gunboats, which shelled both the attackers and heavily populated Chinese residential areas.[145] Wary of provoking foreign intervention in Shanghai, Guomindang leaders and NRA forces occupied Chinese-held areas of the city while specifically avoiding any engagement with the recently bulked up international military units in the concession areas.[146] Thousands of foreigners in the city breathed a sigh of relief; for now, their way of life continued.

The Guomindang's unity did not survive the Northern Expedition, for Chiang Kai-shek and his loyalists swiftly turned on their communist allies in a bloody purge. By mid-April 1927, Chiang's men had killed hundreds of communists, including many of the labor leaders whose organizing acumen enabled the NRA to capture Shanghai with relative ease. The purge divided the party: Guomindang leftists under Wang Jingwei declared themselves the legitimate government of China with Hankou as their capital, and Chiang established his new capital at Nanjing. Eventually, the left and right GMD factions papered over their rift once the former group purged communists from its ranks in the middle of 1927. Still, Wang and Chiang remained rivals for party and national leadership for the next decade.[147]

In addition to transforming China's politics, the Nationalists' unification of large areas of the country ended a relatively open and fluid era for Chinese American citizens there. Under Chiang Kai-shek, who led the nation during much of the "Nanjing Decade," the Guomindang largely shut Chinese Americans out of positions in the ministries so instrumental to developing the nation's infrastructure, education system, and natural resources. Chiang often gave preference to people from his native province, Zhejiang, or from his base of power in the Yangzi Delta.[148] Even T. V. Soong, a Cantonese and the party's most influential finance official, tended to favor the entrepreneurial elites of Zhejiang and Jiangsu as he sought support for his policies.[149] Jun-ke Choy recalled that "when the [Guomindang] took over the government this splendid system of good civil service [created under the Beiyang government] was abolished and the administration became a party affair."[150] To make matters worse, Chinese American citizens by the late 1920s were starting to compete for work with a growing number of Western-educated China-born people with far better political connections than the average overseas Chinese.

For Chinese American modernizers, these developments ended the golden era in which a series of governments had been willing to pay well for their rare talents and to place them at the head of prestigious colleges, powerful ministries, and important agencies.

Modernizers who had served the northern government were some of the first to get the cold shoulder. Among those who lost their jobs were Chinese American citizen translators who had faithfully served the Beiyang government for many years.[151] American-born engineers, the darlings of Qing, Beiyang, and warlord governments alike, now struggled as well. Young Chan Chun and Pond Shuck Wu, veterans of previous government agencies, found no takers in the Guomindang's new bureaus, nor did Warren Wong Achuck.[152] Even longtime GMD loyalist Ernest Moy, the head of the Kuo Min News Agency in New York, could not secure a job with the new regime when he arrived in China in 1930. "I am grateful to you for your expression of approval regarding my work," Moy told his friend Paul Linebarger at that time, but "it would go a long way to facilitate matters if you wrote to such men as Dr. C. T. Wang, and Dr. Sun Fo, and to Dr. H. H. Kung whose ministries are most concerned with foreign publicity."[153] Whether or not Linebarger complied, none of the ministries opted to hire Moy.

Those Chinese Americans who managed to get or keep government jobs in and after the late 1920s generally did so because they had forged close relationships with a powerful patron within the GMD, where different factions dominated particular agencies and ministries. Sun Yat-sen's son Sun Fo, who led the Guomindang's "Crown Prince" faction, appointed his old friend Jun-ke Choy to work for him in Hankou until the GMD split; after the restoration of party unity, Sun recruited Choy to serve in the Railroad Ministry, where the Hawaiian eventually suffered a nervous breakdown from overwork and the stress of juggling party factions.[154] Mon Yin Chung, a Hawaiian-born engineer trained at Columbia, was one of the lucky few Chinese American protégés of T. V. Soong, who in 1931 appointed Chung to help oversee the National Mint.[155] Soong also brought his friend and Harvard classmate Loy Chang into the Ministry of Finance, where Chang's easy rapport with H. H. Kung, Soong's brother-in-law and rival, helped the Hawaiian stay employed after Soong left.[156] Lau Waan-wai, a San Francisco–born professor, similarly owed his job managing key sections of central China's railway system not just to his skill but to a Cornell classmate who was the well-connected director of the Shanghai-Nanjing Railroad.[157]

The Guomindang leadership retained only a handful of experienced Chinese Americans in the new diplomatic corps, where the best and most prestigious positions went to China-born people with political connections. After Nationalist ally Yan Xishan captured Beijing in mid-1928, the GMD government began to win international recognition from the foreign powers. During the northern regime's long twilight, however, representatives of both the Beiyang and Guomindang governments together negotiated a new commercial treaty with the United States.[158] The GMD sent as its envoy Frank Lee, who left his position as vice president of Shanghai College to travel to the United States for the talks. In essence, the American-born Lee served as the GMD's first ambassador to the United States, though his title was "commissioner," and in 1929 the Guomindang regime replaced him with an actual ambassador, the much more influential and well-connected C. C. Wu. Lee's support for Chiang Kai-shek and his long tenure in the party preserved his diplomatic career; still, his lack of a powerful backer meant that after the establishment of the Nationalist state, he never rose beyond a series of lesser ambassadorships in Mexico, Poland, and Portugal, and second-tier and acting positions within the foreign ministry.[159] One of Frank Lee's new colleagues in the Nationalist diplomatic service was Samuel S. Young, who for most of the 1920s served the Beiyang government, including as its last consul general in New York in 1928. He appears to have survived as a GMD diplomat because the cash-strapped Guomindang regime had no representative in New York that year. But for Young, the cost of serving the new regime was high. During his long service to the Beiyang regime, he steadfastly held on to his American citizenship, but the Guomindang government apparently pressured him to give it up. Despite his sacrifice, the new regime kept him at arm's length through minor postings to Mexico and Brazil.[160] Anthony Leefong Ahlo, the former Qing supreme court justice who had once served the Beiyang government as its minister to Samoa and North Borneo, experienced a similarly limited career under the Nationalists. In 1928 he received a new posting to serve as commissioner of foreign affairs in Changsha, but like Young, he never rose much further. Eventually he quit to join the semi-independent Guangdong government of Chen Jitang.[161]

Like Ahlo, many of the modernizers who once had dreamed of transforming China into a strong, unified nation through government service discovered after 1928 that connections suddenly mattered far more than experience. Lacking patrons in the new leadership circles, they scrambled to find work

FIGURE 9. San Francisco native Samuel S. Young served as the northern government's last and the Nationalist regime's first consul in New York City. Young retained his US citizenship during his first two decades of service to various Chinese governments but had to give it up when he accepted a position in the Guomindang's diplomatic corps. National Archives and Records Administration, New York regional facility.

with the handful of foreign-dominated agencies still willing to hire them. A few took positions with the Salt Administration, which foreign advisors helped run until 1949.[162] Ernest Moy finally landed a deanship at the Customs College, also partly managed by foreigners.[163] Other Chinese American immigrants served warlords and local strongmen. GMD loyalists George Y. Bow and Moy Quong-poy (the latter rehabilitated after the rightist purge) lost their jobs when the GMD government moved to Nanjing, and they ended up working for Guangdong General Li Jishen until Chiang Kai-shek arrested the general.[164] Of course, private employment remained an option for these modernizers, but the government's attempts to dominate infrastructure and resource development narrowed their options.[165]

FUNDING THE NEW REGIME

Factionalism and power struggles not only shaped the Guomindang's hiring but also its approach to raising money, a perennial problem for the party. During the Northern Expedition, Chiang Kai-shek used Shanghai business-people's fear of labor unions and communists to push bankers in the city to loan him money.[166] Eventually, they began to resist his constant pleas for more funds, prompting him to use coercion instead. In this, Chiang enjoyed the backing of powerful allies in Shanghai's underworld, especially Du Yuesheng of the notorious Green Gang, the organization that helped Chiang purge the communists in April 1927.[167] Chiang now either openly or through his gangster associates forced leading businesspeople to make "contributions" and loans to him. On occasion, Chiang ordered his troops to arrest those who defied him and to accuse them of being communists until they bought their way out of these charges. In other instances, Chiang had the Green Gang kidnap holdouts and demand ransom from their families.[168]

The youngest victim of Chiang's ransom scheme was Lincoln Au, the three-year-old son of David W. K. Au and Francis Lui Au and the grandson of Louey Shuck. In the early summer of 1927, a soldier dressed in a northern military uniform accosted Frances Au in Shanghai's Zhabei district, pointed a pistol at her, and forced her to hand over her toddler. When David and Frances Au discovered why the kidnapping had occurred, they "donated" Y500,000 to the Guomindang for the return of the little boy.[169] As the wave of kidnappings continued, the *China Weekly Review*, usually sympathetic to Chinese nationalism and the Guomindang, commented tartly, "We are beginning to have increasing difficulty in believing that all those who profess allegiance to the [GMD's] 'principles' are really actuated by motives which the late Dr. Sun Yat-sen would recognize."[170] Louey Shuck might have disagreed. Just a year earlier, the southern "Bolsheviks" had arrested his own wife and son because of Louey's unwillingness to pay new taxes on his property in Guangzhou. The Guomindang's approach had not changed very much since the move north.

The party's kidnappings, factionalism, and favoritism signaled the increased marginalization of the "treaty port" Chinese, especially the overseas Chinese among them, under the new regime.[171] This marginalization was somewhat ironic, given the importance of overseas Chinese in pushing for modernization and reform in the late Qing dynasty, as well as their prominence as early backers of Sun Yat-sen. But such people had far weaker connections to the Yangzi Delta elite who increasingly controlled the nation's government than they did to the merchant networks of the south. Chinese Americans were a prime example of this. Historian Christian Henriot describes 1920s Shanghai as a place with "a composite bourgeoisie that had both a local and a national dimension."[172] The networks of this China-born bourgeoisie were both horizontal and vertical, encompassing their Shanghai lives but also linking them back to villages and up to the capital (although these ties weakened under the Nationalists). Chinese American professionals managed to join the new Shanghai elite in the 1920s through marriage and entry into the professions and local social organizations, but they counted few ties beyond the treaty ports. Instead, their connections were almost wholly horizontal.

As a result, Guomindang factionalism and favoritism pushed Chinese American modernizers ever deeper into the treaty port economy and the foreign-dominated organizations and agencies there. Chinese American professionals who immigrated to China in the late 1920s now entered business in the treaty ports, rarely finding the kinds of positions in academia, extractive industries, the judiciary, the diplomatic corps, or the other government-controlled sectors in which the first modernizers had enjoyed such a meteoric rise in the 1900s and 1910s. Writing in 1936, Robert Dunn, a Chinese American citizen who debated whether or not to move to China, noted that his Massachusetts Institute of Technology–trained brother had actually found work with the government in Nanjing, but only because "he was lucky to have a sister who is married to someone connected with the government [and thus was] given a 'pull' up the ladder, a necessary force which most overseas Chinese do not have."[173]

CHINESE AMERICANS AND EXTRATERRITORIALITY IN SHANGHAI

The Nick Char case signaled the end of the modernizers' golden age. In 1929 the Hawaiian-born attorney and several friends from his baseball team got into a fight with some Chinese football players on the French Concession's Pioneer Field. When one of the brawlers claimed that Char had badly injured him, the case ended up in the Provisional Court (formerly the Mixed Court), and the Chinese magistrate ordered Char to pay a Y300 fine. But the plaintiff was unsatisfied and appealed the case, after which the court sentenced Char to three months in prison. At this point, Char invoked his American citizenship, prompting Shanghai US consul Edwin Cunningham to intervene and declare that the Chinese government could not imprison Char.[174] The attorney initially remained safe from Chinese authorities because he stayed inside the foreign concession areas. But in July 1929, Char called up Xu Mo, the Nationalist commissioner of foreign affairs, to discuss the case of a Korean citizen who was Char's client. Xu invited Char, supposedly his friend, to meet at Xu's

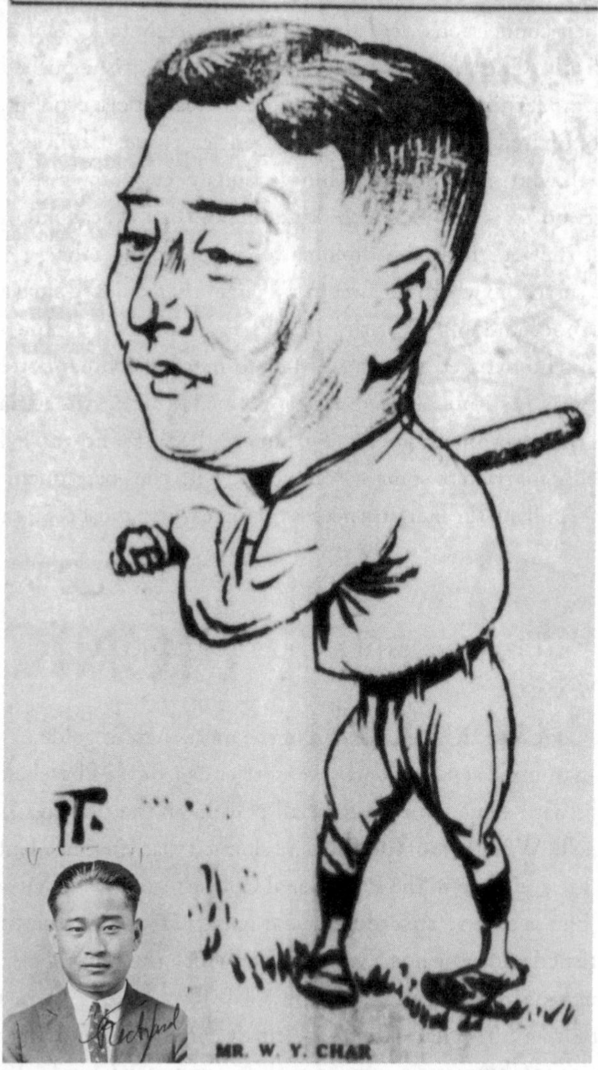

FIGURES 10 and 11. Before his July 1929 arrest, Chinese American attorney Wai Yuen "Nick" Char was a popular athlete in Shanghai, captaining the Chinese Baseball Team and organizing an American football squad as well. Cartoon reprinted from the *China Press*, June 24, 1928; photograph from the National Archives and Records Administration, San Bruno regional facility.

office to discuss the case; once Char arrived at the office in the Chinese sector of the city, Xu summoned Chinese police officers. They arrested Char and placed him in a Chinese jail, where he was "reported to have two notorious criminals and a horde of bed bugs for companions."[175]

As the Char case unfolded, it demonstrated once again how Chinese American citizens in late 1920s China were caught between a Chinese regime determined to use them to strike against extrality and an American government unwilling to defend their membership in the US nation. Privately, Cunningham expressed disgust at Char for "endeavoring to carry water on both shoulders"—claiming US citizenship but also serving as an advisor to the Ministry of Finance and representing Chinese clients in the Provisional Court, both privileges denied to foreigners. In his application for these positions, Char listed himself as a "native" of Zhongshan, Guangdong, his father's home county, using a Chinese term whose definition is vague about actual birth location. Still, Char was hardly "living as a Chinese," as Douglas Jenkins had argued in the Chu Shea Wai case. A graduate of an American university, Char, who did not speak Chinese, was a popular baseball and football player, a US Army veteran of World War I, and a member of the American Legion. His law partner, H. D. Rodger, was also an American citizen. Each of these factors pushed Cunningham to intervene. So did his alarm at the methods used to trick Char into leaving the concession area, as well as the fact that by placing Char in an ordinary jail, Chinese authorities had violated the Provisional Court rendition agreement, which specified imprisonment in the jail attached to that court. But Cunningham's biggest concern was that "it would [not] be unreasonable to presume that [the Char case] will be cited as a precedent affecting American citizens having no consanguineous relations with China."[176] In other words, the Nationalists could conceivably use the Char case to ignore extrality even for white Americans.

Cunningham's attitude echoed Jenkins's and MacMurray's mindset, but it also increasingly diverged from the goals of the State Department, which after 1928 sought to bolster and accommodate the Nationalists. In Guangzhou in 1925, Douglas Jenkins has abandoned Chu Shea Wai in order to conciliate Chinese officials without compromising extrality for white Americans. Now, Edwin Cunningham fought for Nick Char's release for the same reason: he wanted to avoid the creation of a precedent that would hurt white Americans. Cunningham, like Jenkins and MacMurray, shared the suspicion so many Americans in China had about the fairness of the legal system there during these years. However, the State Department in Washington, DC, had since the mid-1920s been rejecting American residents' demands for a robust and muscular defense of US treaty rights in China.[177] Secretary of State Henry Stimson thus wired Cunningham and instructed him to drop any defense of Char, although he did allow the consul to lodge a complaint about the violation of the Provisional Court agreement.[178]

For their part, Chinese officials used the Char case to publicly reiterate their authority over all ethnic Chinese, affirm the legitimacy of the Nationalist regime, and score points with local patriots who deplored extrality, treaty port Chinese, and foreign privilege. Char's case came at a perfect time for the Guomindang government, enabling it to show its patriotic credentials at no cost to its own security. "We cannot understand why [Char] should have conducted himself as a Chinese citizen under Chinese jurisdiction and then finding things not to his liking claimed his American citizenship," snapped the *China Critic*, which called the episode "one more reason why [extrality] should be abolished."[179] Nationalist officials agreed—they had been demanding the immediate end of extrality for years—but they lacked the military power and governmental stability to force the larger issue.[180] Still, they could and did use Char's arrest as a public demonstration of their commitment to upholding Chinese laws and sovereignty in the face of imperialist resistance. Simultaneously, GMD officials invoked the diplomatic principle that gave them jurisdiction over Char, a dual citizen, while he lived in China, thus showing that the Nationalist regime understood and abided by international law. The Char case even offered the GMD government yet another chance to cast aspersions on overseas Chinese loyalty. The incident was so symbolically useful that representatives of the regime exploited it as long as possible, quietly refusing to respond to Cunningham's queries and, often, to meet with him at all.[181]

In the end, Char's fate came down to his personal connections, yet another reminder of the way the new Nationalist regime functioned. Nick Char's father was a leader in the Hawaiian branch of the Guomindang's Overseas League, one of many such groups the party had established in foreign cities with large Chinese populations. Late in the summer of 1929, as his son sat in a Chinese jail, the elder Char arrived in Shanghai and then traveled upriver to Nanjing. There, he made a personal plea to Chiang Kai-shek to release Nick Char, whom Chinese authorities finally freed from prison after he had served two months of his three-month sentence.[182] In October 1929, Nick Char returned to Honolulu, leaving behind Shanghai and his thriving career and social life there. He never again set foot in China.[183]

END OF AN ERA

Beginning in the early 1920s, both the United States government and the Guomindang regime narrowed the requirements for membership in their respective nations in ways that forced Chinese American citizens to make difficult and even impossible choices about identity, security, and loyalty. Officials in both countries viewed Chinese Americans as lacking the traits necessary for full membership (as opposed to formal citizenship) in the American or Chinese nations. Ironically, US and Chinese authorities frequently deplored the same set of attributes: the "foreign" behaviors and tastes of Chinese American citizens, their relative mobility, their suspicious ties to a foreign country, their dual citizenship, and their use of a foreign language. The rising, often xenophobic nationalism in both countries left little room for such ambiguous cultural and national identities—the same identities that had originally created so many opportunities in China for Chinese American immigrants. Racism in the United States had pushed thousands of Chinese American citizens to improve their economic, social, and educational prospects by moving to China. Now, the emerging nation to which they had immigrated was hardening its boundaries as well.

This process differed from American racial exclusion in that the Nationalist government did not overtly reject Chinese Americans but instead encouraged suspicion about their loyalties, traits, and behavior. This soft attack reflected tensions between Guomindang reliance on overseas Chinese financial support and leaders' concerns that overseas Chinese were of dubious loyalty because of their involvement in transnational networks beyond the party's control.[184] Throughout the Nanjing Decade (1927–1937), GMD leaders and government officials seemed most comfortable with overseas Chinese who remained overseas, even as the party publicly called on such people to invest their capital in China.[185]

These contradictions deeply shaped the lives and experiences of the Chinese Americans who immigrated to China during the Nanjing Decade. Largely shut out of the public sector of the economy, Western-educated Chinese Americans increasingly sought work with Western firms in the treaty ports. While these professionals generally remained supportive of a unified China under the GMD, the party's treatment of them sometimes frayed their loyalty to the nation. Chinese American merchants and students in the south felt even greater ambivalence about the project of national unity, since so many had experienced both the strike of 1925–1926 and the even more radical Guangzhou commune of 1927. Yet both groups kept coming to China in the late 1920s and through the 1930s, driven by the Great Depression, an economic catastrophe that made a viable future in the United States hard to imagine.

CHAPTER 4

The Nanjing Decade

Chinese American Immigrants and the Nationalist Regime

In 1933 Jin Gun Oy and her husband, Yee Ting, shuttered their Akron, Ohio, hand laundry to escort their seven American-born children to Jin's home village in Guangdong. "Conditions have been very bad here and I want to go home to see our relatives and leave a few of the children there to get a little Chinese education," Jin explained.[1] The Great Depression prompted scores of Chinese parents to follow Jin's example, sending their children to China not just for educational purposes but because the cost of raising them there was so much lower than in America. This newest generation of students joined hundreds of other Chinese Americans who moved to China in the 1930s to avoid the worst ravages of the Depression in the United States.

This chapter examines these immigrants' lives, careers, and relationship with the GMD government during its ten years in Nanjing. During this so-called "Nanjing Decade," scores of teens from Hawaii and the mainland enrolled in St. John's University, Lingnan University (formerly Canton Christian College), Yenching University, and other westernized colleges and feeder schools popular with China's coastal business classes, whose ranks many hoped to join. Other new arrivals, from high school dropouts to graduates of American colleges, came to China looking for decent jobs, and although some still saw themselves as "modernizers," their ranks now included hairdressers, stock brokers, sales clerks, jazz singers, and other people whose primary goal was simply to find work. Driven both by economic necessity and their own widening ambitions, more Chinese American women than ever before also made the trip. Most of the immigrants did not bother seeking positions with the Nationalist regime, which courted overseas Chinese investment and donations but excluded from its growing workforce those without the right connections. Together with GMD cultural and social policies, this exclusion actually strengthened the new immigrants' identification with coastal merchants and returned students rather than the party and the larger nation it claimed to represent. In fact, the GMD government, which bragged about uniting the country after a decade of chaos, was less successful at binding Chinese Americans to it than the failed regimes it had replaced.

Since the turn of the century, racial discrimination in the job market had pushed adult Chinese American citizens to immigrate to China, and the Depression and demographic shifts in the United States simply worsened an already dispiriting situation. In a cruel twist, America's native-born Chinese population was growing faster than ever before, meaning that a large number of Chinese American citizens came of age and entered the workforce just as the US economy collapsed.[2] Of course, since the late nineteenth century, most Chinese in the United States had flocked to jobs that white American men avoided, working as domestics, operating hand laundries, running chop suey restaurants, importing goods from China, and selling souvenirs to tourists visiting Chinatowns. But the Depression affected even these sectors of the economy.[3] Hawaii offered no respite, either: despite facing less overt racism than on the mainland, Chinese Americans in the islands had limited access to the professions, regardless of their education. Many opened stores instead, but as the second generation grew, a glut of shops competed for Honolulu's scarce consumer dollars.[4]

Chinese Americans who despaired of finding work in the United States sought to take advantage of a Depression-linked boom in China. While the era's economic catastrophe eventually touched almost every area of the world, it began in the United States and Europe several years before it affected China. The West's crisis caused international silver prices to fall deeply in the late 1920s, a time when China, unlike most other countries, still clung to a silver monetary standard. The decline in silver prices essentially devalued China's currency, making its exports cheap and foreign imports into the country expensive and uncompetitive, all while loosening credit and encouraging foreign investment there. As a result, China avoided the Depression until 1931 and did not suffer a truly deep downturn until about 1934.[5] China's unusual boom drew a steady stream of Chinese American job seekers, who continued to come even after the Depression hit the country hard.[6]

Desperate for funding and legitimacy, the new GMD regime during these same years publicly promised to protect "overseas compatriots" but put far more effort into finding ways to economically exploit and politically influence such people. In meetings, committees, and official journals, the regime expressed leaders' desire to register all Chinese schools abroad, compile information about overseas newspapers, convince wealthy overseas Chinese to bankroll industries and infrastructure, set up an official Overseas Chinese League, and build a guesthouse for overseas delegations visiting Nanjing.[7] Although some of these plans focused on returnees from abroad, GMD leaders greatly preferred "overseas compatriots" who remained overseas to those who moved to China with their "foreign" habits, ideas, and identities. During the Nanjing Decade, Guomindang leaders mandated exclusive citizenship, outlawed other political parties, adopted aspects of fascism, and cast the GMD as the epitome of the nation. Chiang Kai-shek's New Life Movement also attacked Western cultural trappings as decadent, degenerate, and unpatriotic. Unsurprisingly, party leaders thus saw nothing of value in the era's influx of Chinese Americans—economically middling jobseekers from a Western nation with contested elections, a robust public school system, and a free press, none of which Nationalist China possessed.

For their part, Chinese American immigrants during this period professed their loyalty to China but resisted GMD cultural and political control and the regime's attempts to enforce a particular definition of Chineseness. When GMD cultural policy made Chinese Americans' social lives and practices problematic, most gravitated toward others who shared their same "foreign" tastes and language, usually ethnic Chinese born in the United States, Australia, or Canada. Even more than in the 1920s, Chinese Americans clustered in foreign concessions, warlord states, and Hong Kong, places that often represented to China-born people the regrettable persistence of Western imperialism. To a certain degree, economic need dictated such residential choices: most Chinese Americans lacked the necessary connections to land jobs with the GMD bureaus that increasingly controlled the fields in which they hoped to work. Often lacking Chinese fluency or local knowledge, large numbers thus settled instead in places like Shanghai, where they found positions in foreign companies or in firms that served expatriates, overseas Chinese, and returned students.

While earlier modernizers had felt some degree of alienation in China, their intangible compensation included widespread admiration for their skills and for American cultural forms and political systems in general. In the 1930s, however, this esteem was becoming increasingly rare, especially within the Guomindang. Its leaders often admired fascism and disdained Western liberalism and individualism. The GMD's seeming lack of interest in the skills, education, and ideas of the newest arrivals from America also contrasted jarringly with the attitude of previous Chinese governments. Chinese Americans' growing preference for lives in concessions and colonies sometimes reflected the disgust with which the newest arrivals responded to China's low living standards, their own defensiveness about their Chinese language ability, and, occasionally, their feeling of superiority to local people. But it also exposed their nagging sense that China's cultural, economic, and social development was moving away from what they represented and could offer.

THE NANJING DECADE: AN OVERVIEW

The Nanjing Decade, which began in 1927 and ended with the 1937 Japanese invasion of China, was the period during which the Guomindang ruled much of the central and eastern part of China from the new national capital at Nanjing. During these years, the party strove to build a strong nation-state through economic, political, and cultural policies designed to ensure one-party control, forge a modern Chinese identity, create a disciplined citizenry, and foster the development of industry and infrastructure. In reality, the party struggled to achieve most of its goals because of political infighting, corruption, and a lack of funds, among other problems. The national reunification process had actually created many of these issues. The GMD (particularly Chiang Kai-shek's faction) during the Northern Expedition cut deals with warlords in order to co-opt them and their armies. The administration that emerged in Nanjing thus mixed committed party members with opportunistic newcomers determined to enrich themselves and enhance their own power; the ensuing corruption, nepotism, and incompetence undermined the Guomindang's popularity. Meanwhile, GMD taxation policies transferred scarce resources from struggling rural areas to the country's cities and encouraged the further impoverishment of the peasantry. The rivalry among party leaders Chiang Kai-shek, Wang Jingwei, and Hu Hanmin also created ongoing tensions that destabilized the government at several key moments during the Nanjing Decade.[8]

To make matters worse, Japanese encroachment, a constant in these years, provoked passionate disagreements between Chinese leaders and ordinary citizens about how to thwart or at least slow it. In 1931 the Japanese created a pretext to invade and occupy Manchuria, transforming it into the puppet state of Manchukuo under the supposed rule of Puyi, the last Qing emperor. In 1932, after anti-Japanese incidents in Shanghai, Japanese aircraft bombed part of the city, provoking a bloody two-month war there. In the years that followed, Japan also used military pressure and manipulation to expand its hold on China's northeast and reduce Nationalist influence in that region. Despite criticism from many Chinese intellectuals, students, and left-leaning urbanites, Chiang Kai-shek—the most powerful of the rival Guomindang leaders and the head of the Nationalist military—preferred to negotiate with rather than confront the Japanese. Chiang believed that the Communist Party posed a greater threat to his regime and the nation than did Japan, and for much of the Nanjing Decade, he conducted and sought funds for "bandit extermination" campaigns to wipe out the communists once and for all. However, the Nanjing government's failure to stop Japanese aggression undermined the regime's legitimacy in the eyes of many Chinese.[9]

OVERSEAS CHINESE POLICY

The Guomindang regime attempted to shore up its legitimacy in part through its overseas Chinese educational, social, and cultural policies. These policies enabled the party both to claim that all ethnic Chinese—wherever they lived—were Chinese citizens and to assert that the GMD regime was the only legitimate focus of their patriotism. Beginning in 1928, delegations from ethnic Chinese communities across the world visited the new capital at Nanjing for official conferences and tours.[10] Party leaders encouraged wealthy overseas entrepreneurs to invest in factories and infrastructure and to donate generously to schools, hospitals, and similar institutions.[11] The regime loudly and publicly defended Chinese in Mexico, Thailand, the Dutch East Indies, and other places where local governments treated them with disrespect or harassed them.[12]

Guomindang outreach to overseas communities focused heavily on reinforcing the Chinese identity of children abroad through Chinese schools meant to counter the education such youths received in their local schools. Nationalist officials urged "overseas compatriots" to make "outstanding efforts to develop into a superior and strengthened race" through such Chinese schooling.[13] They pushed US-based Chinese parents in particular "to first enter children in overseas Chinese schools and only afterwards in Western schools" so that youths would not "find the principles of the Chinese language distasteful" and avoid studying them.[14] "We want to develop the spirit of the Chinese race, we can build our own skills, and we have our own willpower," a party activist exhorted overseas Chinese. "Receiving Chinese education with our sons and daughters will cultivate our race's patriotic thinking."[15]

Official enthusiasm about "racial spirit" and "completing the revolution" did not include exhortations to attend school in the "homeland." When education officials addressed overseas Chinese students, they focused largely on regulating the curricula and fees at the growing number of Chinese schools *outside* the nation's borders and using these institutions to spread party doctrine among the overseas population. GMD ministers demanded that Chinese schools abroad follow the domestic practice of honoring Sun Yat-sen's portrait and studying his Three People's Principles. While denying to European colonial governments in Southeast Asia that Sun's teachings were in any way political, party bureaucrats also emphasized the need to instill Nationalist ideology in teachers sent abroad to work in such institutions.[16] Although education officials drafted regulations to guide China's school officials in dealing with students from abroad, they did so largely to control and channel a surge of school-age children whose unemployed parents were returning from economically depressed areas, especially Southeast Asia.[17]

Youths from abroad might someday contribute to China's modernization, but the Nationalist regime seemed to view them as at best a drain on scarce resources and at worst a potentially disruptive presence for social and political reasons. In early 1928, the Nanjing regime issued its first overseas educational directives, which dissuaded rather than invited prospective students. Those interested in traveling to China to attend a government-controlled school now needed to obtain an introduction from relevant overseas Chinese educational authorities in their home countries and to undergo investigation. At government-controlled universities, students from abroad who cleared these hurdles then reported to ad hoc committees charged with supervising them. Three years after the initial regulations, education officials reissued and tightened the rules to discourage academically unqualified children and to add additional levels of investigation. The government also allowed only a tiny number of carefully selected overseas Chinese to attend special schools such as the Central Military Academy.[18] Officials' experiences with the students at Jinan University, an institution set up as the Jinan Academy during the late Qing dynasty to educate overseas Chinese youths, suggest some of the reasons for this caution. The Nationalist regime inherited the school, which by the late 1920s was a hotbed of political activism, from the Beiyang regime. When police arrested a Jinan professor in 1930 for allegedly receiving communist literature in the mail, most of the student body went on strike in protest. Jinan students also joined student protests in Shanghai and Nanjing, and a few years later they clashed violently with local townspeople.[19]

Regardless of such problems, the party could not resist using the desire of overseas Chinese to study in China to reaffirm the regime's legitimacy. Nanjing collected and trumpeted statistics on returnees, as in 1934, when the central government bragged about the large numbers of "overseas Chinese students who have enthusiastically returned to the nation to study just this year."[20] More subtly, officials debated that same year about whether to offer Fujian and Guangdong a subsidy to help pay the school fees of overseas Chinese students in the two provinces. At a time when both places operated independently of central control, the proposal enabled Nanjing to show overseas Chinese that it represented their interests better than local governments. Provincial leaders certainly realized as much and struck back by drawing up their own plans for building schools and reclaiming wasteland for returned overseas families.[21]

THE DEPRESSION EXODUS TO GUANGDONG

While these national and provincial authorities focused largely on returned overseas Chinese from Southeast Asia, the worldwide economic crisis prompted thousands of Chinese Americans to immigrate to south China in these years as well. The Yee family's experience was a typical one in which financial anxiety and physical stress eventually provoked the kind of Depression-era crisis that many non-Chinese Americans would easily have recognized. Herbert Yee, his wife, Fong Shee, and their six young children lived in Detroit, where they operated a hand laundry—a physically demanding business even at the best of times. As the Depression deepened, Fong Shee began to show signs of an illness that doctors diagnosed as heart disease. She kept working until mid-1935, when she collapsed and died while ironing clothes. Fong's illness and death depleted most of the family's savings, but Yee finally found and purchased a laundry that he could run by himself. Raising a family alone was another matter, however. "It costs me too much to take care of my children here and I [think] it best to take them home and let my mother take care of them," he explained, and in late 1935, he and his six children boarded a boat for Hong Kong, with Dai Din Pong village in Toisan their eventual destination.[22] During the Great Depression, poverty and hardship compelled hundreds of thousands of Americans to migrate to other parts of the country in the hopes of improving their situation.[23] The Yees and other Chinese American families were unusual only in that they sought economic relief outside the United States.

By the 1930s, two generations of US-based Chinese families had sent their children to China for education, but America's economic catastrophe, Nationalist rhetoric about patriotism and schooling, and the relatively settled and stable situation in Guangdong now combined to make the prospect especially attractive. During the 1910s and 1920s, banditry and piracy plagued many areas of the Pearl River Delta, while the Guomindang's leftist policies there alienated thousands of overseas Chinese. Ironically, the party lost direct control of Guangdong in the years after it launched the Northern Expedition from Guangzhou. Provincial governor and general Li Jishen wielded most of the power in Guangdong until removed by Chiang Kai-shek in 1929, but his ouster enabled Chen Jitang, another military commander and nominal Guomindang supporter, to eventually become the province's warlord. Known as the "King of the Southern Skies" or the "King of the South," Chen focused mainly on strengthening his military, but he also built thousands of miles of new roads, reduced banditry, and helped modernize the city of Guangzhou before he lost power in 1936.[24]

The relative stability of the south, combined with the worsening depression in the United States, made life in the Pearl River Delta more attractive to Chinese American immigrants than it had been since the end of World War I.[25] In 1930 the number of Chinese American citizens leaving the United States exceeded the number returning for the first time since 1924, the year Sun Yat-sen began to cast the overseas Chinese as imperialist dupes, and this growth continued over the next few years.[26] Hundreds and probably thousands of Chinese American citizens arrived in Guangdong during this period, most of them leaving from Vancouver, Seattle, or San Francisco, disembarking at Hong Kong, and taking a launch upriver to the Pearl River Delta counties. These American-born immigrants came from a range of communities, including cities such as New York, Philadelphia, and Portland, Oregon, and smaller towns like New Castle, Pennsylvania, and Minter City, Mississippi.[27] Village schools remained the choice of the majority, especially for large families grappling with the Depression, but pricier institutions like Pui Ching Academy and True Light Middle School continued to attract a handful of wealthier youths. Some even picked Hong Kong institutions such as St. Paul's Girls' School and the colony's Lingnan University branch school.[28]

Chinese Americans of all ages discovered that they could not always outrun their economic and personal woes by moving to China. In 1932 brothers Louis and William Wang of Brooklyn arrived in Guangzhou with a cousin of theirs to study Chinese. The cousin lost or spent all their money, leaving the two other boys stranded and unable to pay for school while their parents apparently lacked the funds to enable their return to the United States.[29] Yam Yau Sing studied at Pui Ching Academy until his father stopped sending money to support him, at which point his stepmother in Guangzhou threw him out; finding his way to Hong Kong, Yam initially survived as a manual laborer but then became a petty thief.[30] Economic desperation in the United States sometimes turned visitors into immigrants: one Chinese father sent his two American-born sons to China in 1932 for a short-term stay but then failed to provide any passage money for the boys' return. They were only able to go home in 1939.[31] Nor could many adults find the economic second chance they sought in south China. One unemployed Hawaiian who emigrated to Guangdong attempted to farm and raise birds there, while another sold cloth and tried to open a grocery store, but neither man's venture proved successful.[32]

Furthermore, despite Guangdong's relative security, the Depression made life there less financially comfortable for the newest generation of immigrants than it had been for their predecessors in the tumultuous 1910s and 1920s. Since the nineteenth century, residents of Toisan and several other Pearl River Delta counties had relied heavily on remittances from Chinese abroad. Their funds supported a relatively high standard of living, created a local market for Western products and styles, and endowed schools and other institutions.[33] But during the Depression, remittances slowed because hundreds of thousands of overseas Chinese simply could not afford to send funds to China anymore.[34] The most destitute returned home, sometimes driven not just by unemployment but by anti-Chinese campaigns in places such as Mexico.[35] By 1935 local sources in Guangdong reported that overseas Chinese were pouring into the province at a rate of about ten thousand per month.[36] Families that once depended on remittances from members working overseas now found themselves supporting returned relatives, like the Yee children of Detroit.[37]

Doing so became even more difficult after 1934, when south China began to experience the worst effects of the Depression, which cost hundreds of thousands of jobs in the province.[38]

Still, during much of the Nanjing Decade, Guangdong's political estrangement from the central government made it a magnet for Chinese American merchants and students who remained skeptical about the GMD. Such people bitterly recalled the way the GMD's anti-capitalist and anti-imperialist policies had targeted their families in the 1920s, and they often resented the party's unwillingness to acknowledge their foreign citizenship. Furthermore, the GMD not only left Guangdong saddled with debt from its 1920s Guangzhou government and Northern Expedition but also attempted during the Nanjing Decade to impose detrimental tax and industrial policies on the province.[39] Chinese American citizen immigrants with deep connections to local merchants and entrepreneurs not only understood the impact of the GMD's indifference and even hostility to provincial concerns but often felt similarly about the party.

AMERICAN-EDUCATED IMMIGRANTS IN GUANGZHOU

The GMD-controlled central government also managed to inadvertently encourage separatist feelings in the well-educated immigrants who came to Guangdong in the 1930s. Before the Nanjing Decade, few such people had shared the merchants' and students' sense of estrangement from the GMD state, but far more now came to experience it themselves. The party continued to show no interest in the Americans' educational credentials. In addition, warlords from Yan Xishan in Shaanxi to Li Zongren in Guangxi to Chen Jitang in Guangdong portrayed themselves as supportive both of national unity and of regionalism and provincial loyalties, which they cast as perfectly compatible.[40] Such rhetoric caught the ear of patriotic, well-educated Chinese Americans. Though most still believed that China needed a strong central government to stand up to external enemies, the GMD government continually accommodated Japanese expansion, while warlords like Chen were increasingly critical of Japan.

The substantial overseas Chinese institutional infrastructure that existed in Guangdong helped absorb considerable numbers of these Chinese American professionals. After the Northern Expedition ended, the south's westernized and missionary schools, hospitals, and similar establishments began to

FIGURE 12. University of California–educated Lynne Lee Shew spent more than a decade fundraising among ethnic Chinese in North America to build a hospital in Xiangshan, her ancestral district. She finally opened the Heungshan Benevolent Hospital in 1934, while Guangdong was still under the control of Chen Jitang. National Archives and Records Administration, New York regional facility.

reopen, and modernizers who moved to Guangdong in the years that followed often found work at such institutions. Rev. Stephen Gum Mark arrived in the province in the early 1930s to work at the True Light Middle School and to spread Christianity in Guangzhou. Sarah Elaine Lee, the daughter of an Oakland, California, Christian minister, traveled to Guangdong in 1933 and taught at the Pui Ching Academy until the Japanese arrived in the province in 1938. Richard Lam, a farming expert, came in 1934 to teach at Lingnan University, where donations from overseas Chinese funded a modern school of agriculture. And Lynne Lee Shew finally achieved a goal that had driven her since her brother, a medical student, died when both siblings were in college: founding a modern hospital in his memory in their ancestral district. Having spent a decade raising funds for the institution from overseas Chinese across the Americas, Shew opened the Heungshan Benevolent Hospital in 1934.[41] In establishing such an institution in breakaway Guangdong, the UC Berkeley–educated Shew showed that in the south, modernizers no longer rejected provincial loyalties as harmful to nationalism.

Since Chen Jitang's regime offered employment to very few Chinese American university graduates, those who did not find positions in overseas educational or medical institutions generally worked for foreign firms, overseas Chinese companies, or returned student enterprises. Joseph Yuk Woon Tseu, a former merchant, took a position as the business manager of the new

Canton Daily Sun, an English-language newspaper run largely by returned students.[42] After completing school in the south, Carolyn Chinn accepted a job with Carlowitz and Company, a German import firm that valued her bilingual skills, while Hawaiian-born chemist Edward Shim became a representative for a foreign fertilizer company.[43] Chinese American citizens expressed little resentment at this narrow field of opportunity, since few expected as much from the breakaway region as they did from the Nationalist regime. When the *Canton Daily Sun* griped about the plight of overseas Chinese jobseekers, it ignored Chen Jitang's government completely and contended instead that the corrupt GMD regime was wasting the talent of the returned foreign-born Chinese. "There are too much [*sic*] party politics and various cliques to overcome," the paper carped, and "when an official gets into power he will hire his relatives, schoolmates or personal friends no matter whether they are qualified or not."[44]

In keeping with his restricted agenda, Chen Jitang employed only the handful of Chinese Americans who could contribute directly to his political and military ambitions.[45] The experiences of his US citizen employees suggest how the GMD's rejection of Chinese American immigrants during the Nanjing Decade alienated them and pushed them toward separatist regimes. On the civilian side, the most prominent Chen employee was Anthony Leefong Ahlo, who now simply called himself "Lee Fong" (or Li Fang). A onetime Beiyang official, Ahlo quit the Nanjing government's diplomatic corps in 1931 after a short and fairly frustrating career with the regime. He found the Guangdong government far more appreciative of his talents: in 1932, he became the commissioner of foreign affairs for Guangdong, and by 1934 he was director of the provincial department of reconstruction, representing Chen Jitang in his negotiations with foreign banks in Hong Kong. Ahlo even created a new Bureau of Information for the province.[46]

On the military side, Chen Jitang's emphasis on aviation also made Guangdong the first choice of most Chinese American pilots, another group of modernizers who chose their ancestral province over the GMD's new nation.[47] The most famous of the Guangdong fliers was Art Lym, the San Franciscan who helped build the Shaoguan airfield in the province during the late 1910s. In 1929 he left his life as a wallpaper salesman in Shanghai to accept a position as commander of the Nanjing government's aircraft repair facility, but in 1931 he resigned and returned to the south to fly for Chen. Never tremendously ideological, Lym knew that Chen's air force was developing into the best in

China. Chen's investment in aviation, together with Lym's fame, soon attracted numerous other Chinese American citizen pilots who immigrated to China to fly for the provincial air force rather than for the central government.[48]

With the Japanese threat looming, most of the south's modernizers voiced their support for the GMD government after Chen fell from power in 1936, yet their tenuous attachment to the regime reflected a larger problem for the party. When the Japanese invaders arrived in Guangdong in 1938, most of the province's Chinese Americans chose not to follow the GMD government inland. Many stayed put, others fled to Hong Kong or the United States, and a small number collaborated with the enemy. In its decade in power, the GMD had not managed to convince such people that its government deserved their sacrifices or loyalty.[49]

HONG KONG RESURGENT

In another reflection of the modernists' changing patriotism, many well-educated American immigrants chose Hong Kong over the mainland in the 1930s. Simple issues of security helped motivate some of the Chinese Americans who picked the British colony: war between Chen Jitang and Chiang Kai-shek seemed likely, and few Chinese Americans had the stomach for such conflicts. Even Guangzhou booster Joseph Y. Tseu kept his family in Hong Kong.[50] Economic opportunities also attracted a growing number of Chinese American citizens because in the early 1930s, Hong Kong's economy remained relatively healthy.[51] Even when the colony's economy faltered, however, few Chinese Americans saw British imperialism as so odious that it prevented them from working in Hong Kong.

Of course, some of the American immigrants who moved to Hong Kong in these years had deep roots in the colony. Born in Oregon, Leland Stanford Tye grew up in Hong Kong, traveled to the United States as a young man, and finally returned to the colony to work as an assistant at N. A. Tye and Brothers, his father's import firm.[52] San Francisco–born banker Look Poong Shan's son Look King studied in America but eventually went back to Hong Kong to work at the Bank of Canton.[53] Edward H. T. Louie, one of Louey Shuck's sons, studied auto mechanics in America before returning to Hong Kong to work for Chicago native Bill Hong Sling's new South China Motor Car Co.; the men knew each other through their families' deep links to the colony's overseas Chinese networks.[54]

But the GMD's policies eroded the belief among other well-educated Chinese American professionals, most of whom had no roots in Hong Kong, that patriotic people should move to the mainland rather than the colony. During the twilight of the Qing and the early years of the republic, modernizers avoided working in Hong Kong, preferring instead to serve China, preferably through state positions. The last imperial and first republican governments had also recruited young, talented Chinese Americans who dreamed of making their fortunes while helping build a new China. In contrast, the Guomindang simply asked for donations from the older, established overseas Chinese who had built their wealth elsewhere.[55] Their patriotism largely thwarted, many Chinese American professionals, including a growing number of single and married women, simply went where they could find work most easily. Even engineers, who in previous decades were the most recruited group of modernizers to travel to the mainland, now helped build the Shing Mun Dam in the New Territories and expand the Hong Kong Shipyard instead.[56]

A large number of Hawaiians also moved to Hong Kong with the hope of finding jobs, since Chinese American professionals enjoyed so few decent prospects in the Depression-era islands.[57] The new arrivals entered a variety of sectors, including banking, civil engineering, retail sales, and trade.[58] A growing number were professional women who had found little or no opportunity to use their talents in Honolulu. Sau Ung Loo Chan, a graduate of Yale Law School, arrived in the colony in 1928 with her San Francisco–born husband, Hin Cheung Chan, and practiced law, one of the first women in Hong Kong to do so. Loo's sister, the Honolulu-born dental surgeon Nancy Ngan Sin Loo, came to the colony six years later to set up her own practice there; like Loo Chan, she was almost certainly one of the first women in this field in Hong Kong.[59] The Loo sisters managed to succeed in their professions even when the Depression finally hit Hong Kong, but not every Hawaiian was so fortunate. When his Union Petroleum Company closed, Samuel B. Luke ended up importing trinkets from mainland China to sell to tourists at the Star Ferry in Kowloon.[60] Luke was hardly the only immigrant to eventually struggle in Hong Kong as the economy worsened; advertisements from educated Chinese Americans seeking white collar work routinely appeared in colony newspapers' classified sections by the mid-1930s.[61]

While the streets of Hong Kong were hardly paved with gold, many Chinese Americans in the 1930s saw a job in the colony as a legitimate and respectable alternative to one on the Chinese mainland. A decided break with the past, this attitude also suggested that provincial loyalties and complicated identities now shaped the views not just of the US-educated immigrants to Guangdong but also of those who moved to Hong Kong. After all, patriotic China-born people, including many Guomindang leaders, expressed a particular hatred for Britain, which they blamed for reducing the country to semi-colonial status over the course of the nineteenth century.[62] People such as Nancy Loo certainly thought of themselves as Chinese patriots too—during World War II, Loo even lived briefly in the Nationalist capital at Chongqing—but their brand of patriotism suggested only a tenuous connection to the GMD.

THE SHANGHAI COMMUNITY

Chinese American citizens' sentiments about China and its government were also evolving in Shanghai, a major magnet for immigrants during the Nanjing Decade. During the Depression years, scores of Chinese American citizens moved to the city, then China's most important industrial, educational, and commercial center. In 1930 the records of the Shanghai US Consulate listed about 120 Chinese American household heads, some of whose children and spouses were also American citizens.[63] By January 1937, the Consulate estimated that more than three hundred Chinese Americans lived in the city, with an additional forty in the surrounding areas.[64] As in the past, many of the new arrivals were prospective students or college-educated men seeking better career opportunities than existed in the United States. Now, however, numerous university-trained women joined them, and so did less-educated people, especially job seekers from Hawaii. In the early 1930s, these immigrants took advantage of Shanghai's boom, which the silver-linked depreciation of Chinese currency helped create. Even after the Depression began to affect China, though, they kept coming, a reflection of just how few opportunities Chinese Americans could expect in the US job market of the 1930s.

In larger numbers than ever before, Chinese American immigrants from the US mainland streamed into the universities of Shanghai and other parts of central and northern China, seeking language skills and social relationships that would smooth their entry into regional and national business circles. Most of the new students came from Hawaii, even though attending one of China's missionary colleges cost far more than the highly affordable University of Hawaii.[65] In the 1930s, more than forty Chinese Hawaiians attended pricey

St. John's University or its middle school in Shanghai, joining other Chinese Americans from states like Washington and California, which also ran excellent and cheap public universities. A dozen hopeful Hawaiians enrolled in St. John's University Medical School, including Flora Seu Tai Liu, the first American woman to study there.[66] By 1934 about twenty Chinese American citizens were attending Beijing's Yenching University, the premier missionary college of north China and, like St. John's, a congenial place for people more comfortable using English than Chinese.[67] A handful of Hawaiians and US mainlanders enrolled in other Western-backed Chinese universities, including the University of Shanghai, the University of Nanjing, and Ginling College, while Chu Shea Wai, released from prison after the rightist shift in Guangzhou, moved to Shanghai to attend the Chinese-founded Daxia University.[68] Most of these Chinese American students hoped to both earn a degree and develop the kinds of relationships and connections necessary for securing decent work in China after graduation.[69] Even the best public universities in the United States could not offer such intangible benefits. The students' focus on forging connections and joining the commercial classes, particularly of Shanghai, reflected their acceptance of the fact that under the Nationalists, American modernizers no longer enjoyed the same opportunities for positions in government as they had during the late Qing and early republican years.

The immigrants whose services GMD agencies and leaders still sought were those who had built distinguished reputations and careers in previous decades. Loy Chang, the Harvard-educated Hawaiian protégé of T. V. Soong and, eventually, H. H. Kung, continued to rise in the Nationalists' Ministry of Finance, becoming head of the national bond lottery and chief of customs between 1933 and 1935. Hin Wong, the old adversary of the GMD left, was running the regime's Central News Agency English section by 1934. Poy Gum Lee, who had spent most of the 1920s working as an architect for the YMCA, started his own practice in Shanghai in 1928 and almost immediately received one of the most prestigious commissions in China: finishing the Sun Yat-sen Memorial Hall in nearby Nanjing, the new GMD capital.[70] Using his sudden renown as the Sun memorial's finishing architect, Lee also received a commission to design a Sun memorial in Guangzhou and by the early 1930s had become one of the most sought-after architects in China.[71]

For these older and more established immigrants, the 1930s were often the best years of their lives, a period in which skills, connections, and reputations

FIGURE 13. The 1932 Yenching University women's baseball team included several players from Honolulu. Most of the major missionary-founded colleges in China encouraged athletics, and American-born students, especially from Hawaii, often dominated sports teams. Reprinted with permission of the United Board for Christian Higher Education in Asia (archived at Special Collections, Yale Divinity School Library).

built over the previous decade finally yielded security, wealth, and prestige. Poy Gum Lee designed commercial buildings and houses for Europeans, Americans, and Chinese alike, lived with his family in a gracious Shanghai home with servants, and was elected president of the recently founded Chinese Architects Association.[72] A number of other middle-aged American immigrants enjoyed similar acclaim from their colleagues and stature in their communities. The government's Ministry of Justice invited well-known ophthalmologist Dr. T. M. Li to act as an advisor on medicine and forensics, the Shanghai Public Education Association elected Dr. John Woo a board member, and the Railroad Ministry appointed Lau Waan-wai to a commission of inquiry that traveled to Japan.[73]

However, American newcomers who dreamed of being the next Loy Chang or Poy Gum Lee found that the GMD regime offered recent American immigrants almost no comparable opportunities. The American-born people listed in a 1931 directory of well-known Chinese were men such as Lau Waan-wai, H.C. Mei, Samuel Young, Frank Lee, Tsai Yan Lum, and John Woo—all modernizers who had come to China between 1901 and 1915, when a mere handful of China-born people had ever studied abroad and an ethnic Chinese with a credential from a foreign university was a rarity.[74] By the 1930s, however, thousands of China-born people boasted degrees from schools in the United States, Britain, France, or Germany. These returned students were inevitably better connected and more culturally adept than the vast majority of Chinese American immigrants, including those fluent in some dialect of Chinese. A staff member of Shanghai's *China Press* newspaper pointed out in the mid-1930s that due to the Depression, even "returned students, once much sought after by society, are finding their 'rice bowl' problem unsolved."[75] Unsurprisingly, Chinese American citizens particularly struggled.

The immigrants who moved to Shanghai and other Chinese cities in the 1930s generally coped with this grim situation by seeking jobs with foreign institutions and companies in which their American upbringing gave them a cultural edge. The immigrants flocked in particular to English-language newspapers, foreign hospitals, firms that imported American technology, and Western schools. The *China Press*, a Chinese-owned newspaper that portrayed itself as an American-style publication, hired a series of Chinese Americans, including brothers Ernest, Herbert, and William Moy and the photographer Norman Soong.[76] Thomas Chinn, who had owned a small sporting goods store in San Francisco, came to China to work as a distributor for Wilson Sporting Goods, while Francis Yee took a job as an export manager for Ford Motor Company in central China.[77] Hawaiian Ruby Leong taught briefly in Guangzhou before accepting a position at the exclusive McTyeire School for Girls, a favorite of Shanghai's elite families who wanted an English-language education for their daughters.[78] Dentist George Owyang and physician Ellen Leong both moved from Hawaii to work in central China, Owyang as a dental surgeon in Hangzhou and Leong at the newly built Hungjao Sanatorium facility off the Great Western Road in Shanghai.[79] Dr. Stephen M.K. Hu, a Hawaiian malaria expert, came to China as a fellow of the Rockefeller Institute of Medicine attached to the central government in Nanjing and moved to the Henry Lester Institute in Shanghai after the fellowship ended.[80] Previous regimes almost certainly would have recruited at least the doctors in this group, but even Hu found the GMD government less supportive of his vital work than the Lester Institute.

The Depression also recast previous patterns of Chinese American immigration, since both educated and less skilled workers and men and women alike arrived in Shanghai in large numbers. In earlier decades, education and networks had shaped Chinese American choices, with highly educated, largely male university graduates taking jobs around China and Chinese American citizen students and merchants relying on family and native-place ties to study Chinese and enter business, almost always in the south. Chinese Americans without such ties or superior educational credentials traditionally stayed in America, where salaries for unskilled workers were much higher. Furthermore, before the 1930s, US-based Chinese parents almost never allowed their single daughters to immigrate to China, unless they were Christian missionaries. But the Depression left people of color, including Chinese Americans, even more disadvantaged in the US job market than they had been before the economic catastrophe. As white workers demanded jobs, the US government deported Mexican (and Mexican American) residents and tried to convince Filipino migrants to return to the Philippines.[81] At the same time, New Deal work programs discriminated against the same blacks and Asian Americans whom the segregated job market already disadvantaged.[82] Chinese American citizens desperate for employment now looked abroad, whether they possessed advanced university training or not. In Chinese American communities, views of working women also improved, and Chinese parents struggling to support their offspring now showed far more willingness to let their daughters seek employment in China than they had in the previous decades.[83]

The new arrivals worked in a wide range of fields, many of them largely unknown to the earlier immigrants. Clarence Wun Young came from Hawaii to help run his brother In Young's auto importing business.[84] Honolulu sisters Evelyn and Edna Goo arrived in Shanghai in 1933 and established the American Beauty Shop on Bubbling Well Road, where they offered an opening special of a "permanent wave with ringlets, shampoo, and one extra finger wave."[85] The next year, another Chinese Hawaiian woman, Edna Ahana, gave them some competition when she established the Ahana Beauty Salon a few blocks down.[86] While New Yorker Herbert Moy staged dramas and called boxing matches for the bilingual station XGRC, other Chinese Americans worked behind the scenes in Shanghai's booming radio world.[87] Two Chinese American brothers from San Francisco ran a restaurant together in the International Settlement, while other recent immigrants attempted to break into the city's entertainment industry.[88] By the mid-1930s, musician William K.

Lee played regularly at the Sun Sun Department Store's cabaret, while Anna Chang sang at the Paramount Ballroom and George Lee, the "Chinese Crooner," warbled standards with the Dixie Sisters at the Lido Ballroom on Medhurst Road.[89]

Such men and women moved to China not to modernize it but simply to work, and many of them felt disgust or at least dismay at what they found in the land of their ancestors. Before their arrival, they had understood in an abstract sense that major differences existed between life in China and America, but to many the reality was far worse than what they had anticipated. In particular, the standard of living in China was much lower than in the United States, particularly outside the major coastal cities. "Life in Kaifeng, whenever you contemplate it, is depressing," lamented Fresno native Flora Belle Jan, who followed her China-born husband to his Henan hometown. "Sanitary conditions are bad. One is exposed to a disease every minute. The servants are not clean. The kitchen is filthy."[90] Diseases rare in the United States, such as smallpox, yellow fever, typhoid, and cholera, were far more widespread in China and killed many Chinese American immigrants.[91] Some Chinese Americans thus preferred Shanghai not just for its employment opportunities but because it allowed them to live in China without sacrificing high living standards or physical safety.

But many in this newest generation of Chinese American immigrants struggled even in Shanghai to transcend cultural differences they had not anticipated and to come to terms with the fact that they were perhaps not as Chinese as they had always assumed. While their parents sought to instill in them a pride in their ancestry, being Chinese in America in these years usually meant first and foremost living in a Chinatown or on a skid row, working in a menial job, and using segregated public facilities. Because race defined the lives of ethnic Chinese in America, many Chinese Americans saw Chineseness as a racial designation above all. In terms of their cultural orientation, however, the vast majority by the 1920s were thoroughly American. In the public schools, they studied US democracy and, more informally, how to assert independence from their Chinese parents through clothing, attitudes, and slang.[92] The lessons they learned in a few hours of night or weekend Chinese school simply could not prepare them for lives in China. "I had spoken English all my life, and the upside-down Cantonese that I had learned in those afternoon classes on [San Francisco's] Stockton Street only evoked hilarity over there," a Chinese American engineer recalled.[93] Such people struggled just as much with the different attitudes and behavioral expectations they encountered in their new home. According to one Chinese leader, "in China we usually consider [the overseas Chinese] as too foreign," while an overseas Chinese carped about the "typical China-borns. . . . To them more or less must be attributed the backwardness China has been undergoing for four thousand long years."[94] Few of the Chinese American newcomers in the 1930s ever fully bridged this cultural gap during their years in China.

FIRST RUMBLINGS OF WAR

While young Chinese Americans in Shanghai struggled to adapt to cultural differences few had anticipated, political and social turbulence and tensions increasingly roiled the city. In the early 1930s, student activists and angry patriots in Shanghai expressed frustration at the Nationalist government's seeming inability or unwillingness to thwart the Japanese seizure of Manchuria. Japanese citizens made up the largest foreign group in Shanghai, and they complained loudly about mounting Chinese harassment, boycotts of Japanese products, and anti-Japanese student protests there. As tensions grew, the Japanese Navy slowly added ships to its standing fleet at Shanghai, and in late January 1932, the Japanese consul in the city warned Mayor Wu Tiecheng to suppress the anti-Japanese movement. Although Wu eventually complied with this demand, the Japanese nevertheless ordered all Chinese troops out of the Zhabei district and landed a force of marines there on January 28. The Chinese soldiers, part of General Cai Tingkai's Nineteenth Route Army, did not retreat but in fact stopped the Japanese marines in their tracks. The next day, Japanese planes bombed Zhabei, a crowded neighborhood and the location of numerous factories, causing immense damage and bloodshed. Cai and the Nineteenth Route Army became national heroes, holding out against the better armed and more numerous Japanese until March 2. The Japanese declared a unilateral armistice soon after and agreed with the Chinese to an internationally brokered armistice later that month.[95]

The "Shanghai Incident" began to erode Chinese Americans' belief that the city was a safe haven from China's disorder. More than two hundred thousand refugees from the battle poured into the foreign concessions in January and February. And while the combatants stayed out of the foreign-controlled areas—where Westerners in evening clothes drank cocktails and watched the fighting with detached amusement—bombs and shells occasionally hit the restricted zone.[96] More likely than other US citizens to live outside the foreign concessions, Chinese Americans also felt the effects of the Shanghai War far more directly. Several Chinese American citizen doctors worked at missionary-run hospitals, where they treated the wounded, while a number of Chinese American students at St. John's University fled the fighting for the safety of the United States.[97] H. C. Mei's home and everything in it was destroyed, and Andrew Zane discovered decapitated children's bodies in front of his house.[98] Young Chan Chun, a mining engineer from Hawaii, lost his wife and two of his five children during the two-month war, which occurred while he was traveling in the United States. "The house was hit by a bomb," he remembered. "We sent people to try to identify the bodies, but could find no trace."[99]

Like ethnic Chinese around the world, Chinese American citizens living in China donated money to support the anti-Japanese campaign and contributed their skills and energy as well.[100] Chinese American women in the country particularly stepped up. Ching Leong Young of Tianjin organized other Chinese American and Chinese women nationwide to send bandages and gauze to the Nineteenth Route Army.[101] Former nurse Ruth Koesun Moy, who lived in Shanghai with her husband, Ernest, and sons, Loring and Kenneth, trained and directed a group of nurses at a makeshift field hospital for wounded soldiers brought into the International Settlement.[102] She and her New York–born sister-in-law Alice Moy Lee also helped organize the Ladies' Aid for Chinese Soldiers to coordinate foreign donations with the Chinese Red Cross.[103]

At the same time, the war-inspired surge of sentiment revealed growing tension between the Nationalist state and Chinese American immigrants, even strong supporters of the GMD. Some American citizens openly questioned the Nationalists' competence. As the war started, GMD enthusiast Ernest Moy publicly wondered, "Has the Kuomintang collapsed?" and castigated its leaders for not being able to "agree among themselves upon a policy that will enable their country to meet and overcome the gravest menace it has encountered in a generation."[104] Concerned about the popularity of the Nineteenth Route Army, whose members and leaders criticized the lack of support they received from Nanjing, Chiang Kai-shek after the Shanghai War sent them to Fujian to fight communists there and also sought to downplay their heroism.[105] A handful of Chinese American citizens followed the unit, accepting official positions in the area the army controlled as it increasingly distanced itself from the Nanjing regime.[106] Inspired by the Shanghai War and angered by Japanese imperialism, a group of fourteen Chinese American aviators, including Virginia

FIGURE 14. Pilots Virginia Wong (left) and Hazel Ying Lee (right) shortly before their departure for China in 1933. Wong died of malaria the next year. When Chinese officials refused to allow Lee to join the national air force, she accepted an administrative position with a commercial airline in Guangzhou. Courtesy of Alan H. Rosenberg, Museum of Chinese in America (MOCA), Hazel Ying Lee/Frances M. Tong Collection.

Wong and Hazel Ying Lee, also arrived from Oregon in 1933 to help fight Japan—at the very moment that the Nationalist regime sought to suppress anti-Japanese sentiment across the country.[107] Party leaders who tried to channel and shape Chinese American patriotism simply could not control the way it developed as Sino-Japanese relations worsened. Indeed, the divide between Nationalist exhortations and Chinese American actions showed that the immigrants' loyalties focused on China in general, not on the regime.

POLITICAL REPRESSION AND CHINESE AMERICAN STUDENTS

Despite Japanese encroachment, Chiang Kai-shek focused far more during the Nanjing Decade on fighting the Chinese communists and rooting out Western decadence and political ideas than on resisting Japan. Chiang's obsession with crushing communism and asserting his own primacy resulted in an increasingly oppressive GMD regime, especially in areas under the government's direct control. Chinese American students discerned the party's growing influence as early as 1928, when the Guomindang issued regulations requiring all colleges to register with the government and to appoint Chinese presidents. Missionary colleges across the Yangzi delta complied, as did heavily overseas Chinese schools in the south. At Canton Christian College, President James M. Henry stepped down in favor of W. K. Chung, the school eliminated its once-compulsory religious instruction and chapel attendance, and the trustees changed the college's official name to Lingnan University, its longtime Chinese name. Only St. John's, the most prestigious Western college in central China, refused to comply with the registration law and thus lost its accreditation. This did little to hurt the school's popularity with the Shanghai business classes or Chinese Americans, however.[108]

The GMD's school registration policy was far more measured than the government's reaction to the intense activism that developed on college campuses beginning in 1931. That year, a massive student movement emerged to demand that the Nanjing government and the semi-independent Guangdong party faction work together to resist the Japanese seizure of Manchuria. Speaking in Washington, DC, in 1932, the New York–born Vice Minister of Foreign Affairs Frank Lee compared the student protesters to the Bonus Marchers who had demanded help from the US government that summer. The "USA is getting to be just like China," he joked, failing to mention either the US Army's tear-gassing and dispersal of the Bonus Marchers or his own government's even more repressive treatment of student protesters. By 1935 rival organizations in the Nanjing government specialized in infiltrating student organizations, arresting activists, and torturing or murdering them, all in the name of stamping out communism.[109] Although demonstrations continued to roil campuses, this extreme repression created a climate of frustration and despair at many Chinese colleges.[110]

Few Chinese Americans took part in or felt much kinship with the student movement, but their standoffishness reflected cultural differences and educational expectations rather than any deep attachment to the GMD's policies. Chinese American students tended to befriend each other rather than China-born classmates whose lives and experiences were often radically different from their own. At St. John's University in Shanghai, for example, Hawaiian students organized a large and active "Ilimokilani Club," all of whose members hailed from the islands.[111] This sorting process occurred even at Lingnan University, where Chinese American students generally spoke fluent Cantonese but where San Franciscan Doris Shoong Lee recalled that she and other American-born people "quickly found a group of friends from overseas, both male and female."[112] Historian Wen-hsin Yeh has argued that "disillusionment with the Nationalist Revolution depressed the atmosphere of university and college campuses.... [and led to] pessimism, passivity, and ... a sense of helplessness and meaninglessness" on Chinese campuses during the Nanjing Decade.[113] Having grown up in the United States, Chinese Americans who enrolled in these same colleges rarely expressed similar feelings about the revolution, which to most seemed an abstract, distant event.

However, Chinese American students also developed little common feeling with those on the right. By the mid-1930s, right-wing Guomindang activists were scathingly criticizing the Americans' campuses of choice (especially pricey St. John's) for the allegedly lavish, Westernized lifestyles of the students there. Nevertheless, most Chinese Americans threw themselves into campus social and extracurricular activities, just as they might have at an American college.[114]

IMMIGRANT ALIENATION

The Guomindang's ruthless anti-communist campaigns and its repression of dissent entangled other Chinese American immigrants after US government officials began withholding protection from these citizens in the late 1920s.

JOHN HEU

KAM YOU YUEN

EDWARD WONG

SHEREVIN S. ZANE

JAMES KAM

BUNG YUEN QUON

SUNG LIM YUAN

QUON SHEW FONG

JOHN GOO

QUON HIM FONG

WILLIAM YEE

PETER CHING

WILLIAM CHANG

THE ILIMOKILANI CLUB

EDMUND LEE

MISS BUDD, ADVISER

The Ilimokilani Club started off her second year with a bang. The neophytes were led out to the athletic field on a moonlight nite in October, blindfolded and set off on a cakewalk. They danced to the music which arose from the swishing of bamboo rods finely slitted. The tranquil atmosphere of the nite was suddenly erupted by outcries of "au-we! pau!" and "ho-lin!" As a final act of formality, the recruits were given a dose of castor oil, for all true kanakas must be able to take it at both ends.

The organization sponsored a Hallowe'en Masquerade Ball in Oct. The gala event was attended by "Shanghai lils" and girls from St. Mary's. The program consisted of vocal selections from the Hawaiian Quartette, instrumental renditions by the Hawaiian Trio, hula by Hawaiian-Chinese girls, native songs and displays of individual talent. The unmasking of masqueraders climaxed the evening.

In the line of sports, the Ilimokilani Club initiated the rigging up of an American football team. The Hawaiian eleven, uncoached and handicapped by lack of facilities faced almost insurmountable odds in their efforts to promote this "Monarch of American Sports" in China. In borrowed uniforms and shoes the Johaneans massacred the S. A S. in two consecutive games by overwhelming scores.

The successes of the organization were due to the close cooperation among the officers, adviser and members. The officers for the first and second semesters respectively were: Edward Wong, and Benjamin Char, president; David Yee and Wm. Chang, vice-pres.; Quon Hin Fong and John Goo, Sec.; Thomas Wong and Quon Shew Fong, treas.; Miss J. Budd has presided as adviser, through out the year.

The organization looks forward to an eventful year and a glorious wind-up.

JOHN GOO,
Secretary.

FRANK TONG

THOMAS WONG

STEVEN TYAU

RAYMOND YAP

DAVID YEE

LESLIE ZANE

FIGURE 15. The 1935 Ilimokilani Club, from the St. John's University *Johannean* yearbook. The many Chinese Hawaiians at St. John's organized the club in 1934. It disbanded after the Japanese occupied Shanghai in 1937, and the vast majority of its members left for the United States. Courtesy of the Archives of the Episcopal Church.

US authorities sought to placate the new Chinese regime without endangering the privileges white Americans enjoyed in China; sacrificing Chinese American rights proved especially effective for this purpose, because the Nationalists so relentlessly championed jus sanguinis. Party officials framed the question as one both of national prestige and of maintaining GMD influence over the overseas Chinese, and they portrayed any victory of jus soli as catastrophic for China's future. While British officials continued to push the GMD to be more flexible on the question, the US government remained aloof because its diplomats wished to avoid taking action on behalf of Chinese American citizens in China.[115]

Unchecked by US consular officials, different GMD factions and their allies suppressed Chinese American immigrant dissidents, whom they treated as Chinese citizens. San Francisco–born Wong Bock-yue, the publisher of a newspaper in Beijing, had lived peacefully and securely in the old capital for more than a decade by 1930. But when a GMD faction that opposed the paper alerted its allies in the north, they jailed Wong for allegedly carrying out "subversive activities." Although Wong's daughter contacted the State Department, American officials declined to intervene to help free him.[116] Chinese police also dragged another Chinese American newspaper editor from his ship when he arrived in Shanghai in 1931.[117] Journalists were not the only targets. After the GMD again extended its control to Guangdong, government officials arrested two Chinese American citizens for "anti-revolutionary activity," largely on the basis of anonymous accusations made against both men. While the US consul in Guangdong made inquiries about the status of the two, he did not demand their release, again citing their status as Chinese citizens due to local citizenship laws.[118]

The politically inactive majority of Chinese Americans found Nationalist repression far less frustrating than perceived GMD arrogance and tolerance of corruption, which alienated a wide array of overseas Chinese. After just a few months in China, many ethnic Chinese immigrants from across the globe came to resent the high-handed, tone-deaf actions of Guomindang officials. One Shanghai overseas Chinese resident complained that most Chinese officials seemed to live in the foreign concessions, when they should instead be living and paying taxes in Chinese-controlled territory. Another overseas Chinese man pointed out the widespread corruption of such officials. "Our feeling of patriotism needs no description, but many of us will not deny that that divine feeling turns into disappointment as soon as we return to this country where things are very far different from what we hoped them to be," he concluded. Ethnic Chinese from abroad most often encountered corruption in the "squeeze" (small bribes) that lubricated so many ordinary transactions. In Shanghai, an overseas Chinese man admitted getting into "a fight with one of the [tram] conductors because [I] was unwilling to have [my] money squeezed." A more well-connected Chinese American woman began to feel so bad about the free rides her Chinese friends secured for her on public trains and boats that she eventually sent a check to the Ministry of Transportation.[119]

GMD officials grappled with this simmering discontent in part by publicly accusing westernized Chinese of being effete, alien, and even unpatriotic, a tactic that did little to encourage overseas Chinese in China to identify with the regime. In mid-1931, as tensions grew between Chiang Kai-shek and Guangdong-based party dissidents like Sun Fo and Eugene Chen, a Nanjing-aligned Shanghai party branch loudly condemned the Trinidad-born Chen as a "mulatto scribe, a foreigner posing as a Chinese." The nasty accusation particularly stung because Chen's rightist critics also singled out his lack of Chinese language ability—a trait many Chinese Americans shared—as a major reason he was not a "real" Chinese.[120] Right-wing elements in the party also attacked the YMCA, an institution central to both Chinese American citizen immigrants and their returned student friends, as a bastion of "imperialistic cultural invasion."[121] Chang Hsin-hai, a Chinese diplomat, even blasted the returned students as petulant and soft, mocked their "undue self esteem," and criticized their "eager pursuance of western superficialities and luxuries."[122] Meanwhile, the government demanded that the World Overseas Chinese Federation fold, and officials ordered municipal authorities to close the group's vocal Shanghai branch, accusing it of "illegal actions." The head of the Overseas Chinese Affairs Commission also began lobbying for the power to register all overseas Chinese in the country.[123]

THE NEW LIFE MOVEMENT AND CHINESE AMERICANS

These GMD attacks on westernized Chinese were part of a larger shift in Chinese political and economic thought away from idealizing representative Western democracy and toward admiring fascism. During the 1910s and 1920s, China's students, intellectuals, and politicians often showed great interest in democratic political systems, especially during the May Fourth Movement.[124] But when Western representative democracies appeared to flounder because of the Depression, a wide spectrum of GMD leaders looked to various models of fascism, which many saw as at the cutting edge of modernity. Wang Jingwei embraced fascist Italy's model, which focused on economic self-sufficiency and rejected Western representative democracy, while his rival Chiang Kai-shek particularly admired Nazi Germany's militarism. In 1934 Chiang and his wife, Song Meiling, launched the fascist-inflected "New Life Movement" to inject what they saw as greater morality and discipline into Chinese life. The movement sought to teach citizens obedience, self-restraint, hygiene, and respect for authority, as well as to reintroduce aspects of Confucianism into their lives. At the heart of the movement were scores of rules for everyday behavior, including commands to button up one's clothing and not to spit or smoke. A deeply anti-foreign current crackled through the movement, with its most ardent practitioners organizing boycotts of foreign goods and even physically attacking Chinese who wore Western clothes or watched foreign movies.[125]

Longtime Chinese American residents of China tended to offer the least resistance to the New Life Movement or to even welcome it for personal or ideological reasons. Some of these immigrants saw the movement as China's salvation; far more sensed in it a chance to stake a claim to Chineseness despite their own foreign origins, or to gain social and political cachet. Once arrested for allegedly participating in the murder of Liao Zhongkai, college student Chu Shea Wai jumped at the chance to prove his loyalty to the regime by joining the student wing of the New Life Association Promotion Association and helping lobby for a ban on dancing.[126] Selma James Wong confirmed her social standing by accepting an invitation to join the board of the Women's New Life Movement Promotion Association, which the wife of Shanghai mayor Wu Tiecheng founded and chaired with the backing of Madame Chiang Kai-shek.[127] Not all American citizen old-timers celebrated the movement, of course. The US movie distributor Luther Jee and the tobacco broker Alfred Sy-hang Lee likely balked at its condemnations of public smoking, drinking alcohol, watching impure films, singing obscene songs, and using foreign rather than native goods. But they kept quiet and remained in Shanghai, where the presence of foreign concessions blunted the movement's power.[128]

In a tediously familiar move, conservative male leaders who sought to suppress political dissent and enforce cultural conformity used the movement to attack the consumption habits and westernized behaviors of China's "modern" urban women, including Americans. In the 1920s, an influx of Chinese American women found in China's coastal treaty ports and missionary colleges a small but growing feminist movement, new educational opportunities for women, and even suitors who, unlike in America, admired rather than mocked their Western habits. With the New Life Movement, however, Nationalist leaders pushed a conservative vision of Chinese womanhood that stigmatized and threatened the female immigrants from America.[129] Recently arrived in Beijing, Flora Belle Jan scrimped and saved part of her teaching salary for a new dress, a "striking black, red, and pink print on a background of white organdie"; within a month it violated the old capital's new female dress code.[130] In Guangzhou, a policeman seized Martha F. Law, who was wearing a dress he deemed too foreign and revealing, and took her to headquarters to wait until she could send for another garment. Officials then released her old dress, now stamped with indelible ink to indicate its inappropriate nature and to render it unwearable.[131] To Chinese American women like Jan and Law, the New Life Movement proved far more restrictive than the critical parents and communities they had left behind in the United States.

Regardless of their clothing, though, most Chinese American women unintentionally challenged the Nationalists' vision of acceptable womanhood from the moment they arrived in China. While the Nationalist state emphasized traditional gender roles and stigmatized "foreign" behaviors, a larger number of Chinese American citizen women moved to China in the 1930s than ever before.[132] While some were teenagers and young adults who came for school, or wives accompanying husbands, most were single women who hoped to find a job during the Depression. Some parents who might once have prohibited their daughters from traveling to China to seek work now even came to depend on these daughters' earnings. After her father's death, Honolulu native Ting Cho Goo supported herself and her four siblings on her salary as a typist for the foreign-run Chinese Customs Service in Shanghai.[133] Evelyn and Edna Goo's American Beauty Shop made enough money to sustain the pair as well as their mother and baby sister.[134] Chinese American married women now often worked outside the home as well to supplement the low wages their husbands earned. Jay Lai Wong, a married mother of six, supported her family by opening the Hollywood Beauty Shop in Shanghai.[135] Eleanor I. Chang ran the Eurasian Company import-export firm in Tianjin, while Honolulu-born Ah Huna Tong, the women's columnist for the *China Press*, continued her work at the paper after her marriage to Clarence Wun

Young.[136] Not all women aspired to be like Tong: Flora Belle Jan complained bitterly that her husband's low salary required her to keep teaching even after the birth of their second child.[137] But in working outside the home and providing crucial income to support their families, each of these immigrants defied the GMD's conservative construction of proper Chinese womanhood.

More obviously, younger Chinese Americans of both sexes in Shanghai openly flouted New Life dictums by rejecting the GMD's model of acceptable Chineseness and patriotic consumption. In 1934 movement leaders declared that permanent waves were "ugly and dangerous" and the next year barred them for all women. Nevertheless, Edna and Evelyn Goo specialized in perms at their salon inside the International Settlement and advertised at the height of the perm prohibition that "a permanent for Christmas is just the gift for her."[138] When New Life Movement leaders supported bans on large parties and mixed dancing in much of urban China, the St. John's University Ilimokilani Club sponsored a large Halloween masquerade ball, while the school's mostly American-citizen, tuxedo-clad "Blue Bird" jazz band routinely played at area weddings and dances.[139] The New Life Movement condemned foreign fabrics and styles and ornate clothing, but in 1935 Ah Huna Tong advised that furs were the season's indispensable material, because "bags and belts, hats and muffs and ascots and scarfs come in luxurious as well as inexpensive furs and do their part to turn extremely simple outfits into rather pretentious ensembles." St. John's student William Yukon Chang even pasted his tailor receipts into his scrapbook, alongside multiple attendance cards from Shanghai nightclubs such as the Paramount.[140] Tong, Chang, and most of their peers in China embraced consumption as a means of self-expression, sharing expectations and desires that reflected their upbringing in the United States. College life meant masquerade balls, football, and rushing a fraternity, while one of the rewards of a job in Shanghai was the ability to buy fashionable clothes and enjoy the city's social whirl.

Unsurprisingly, then, Chinese American men and women in these years often forged their closest relationships with each other, ethnic Chinese from Canada and Australia, and returned students who shared their values. The *China Press* of this era brims with accounts of parties, socials, and weddings that mixed overseas Chinese from across the English-speaking world and returned students.[141] Even older Chinese American professional men socialized primarily in US-style organizations, including the Rotary Club, the Y Men's Club, the Amity Lodge Masons, and the American University Club.[142]

FIGURE 16. The June 1941 marriage of ophthalmologists James Yee and Marian Li reflected the tendency of overseas Chinese and returned students to socialize and intermarry with each other during this era. Yee was a Stanford-educated Arizona native who came to Beijing to work at the Peking Union Medical College. Li, the Guangzhou-born daughter of renowned ophthalmologist and Honolulu native T. M. Li, graduated from Shanghai's Margaret Williamson Women's Medical College, an American missionary institution. The couple met while teaching at PUMC. Courtesy of Robert D. Yee.

Rejecting the patriarchal, anti-Western emphases of the Guomindang state, Chinese American women also sought companionship among like-minded people.[143] One US citizen woman helped revive and run the YWCA-affiliated Business and Professional Women's Association of Shanghai, whose members hailed from almost two dozen countries, while another organized Shanghai's "Chinese Business Girls Club," a group of mainly overseas Chinese whose common language was English.[144] Numerous Chinese American citizen women, from Ruth Moy to Edna Goo, also joined the influential Chinese Women's Club, whose members included so many Chinese Canadians, Australians, Americans, and returned students that it also conducted its meetings in English.[145] Other women chose their college alumni associations or the American Association of University Women.[146]

As the GMD state attempted to tighten its grip on the population as a whole, much of the new American immigrant generation essentially took refuge in Shanghai's foreign concessions and cosmopolitan social milieu, which offered them the benefits of life in China without much of its discomfort, disorientation, and repression. Scholars Jean C. Oi and Nara Dillon have labeled republican Shanghai as a "crossroads of Euro-American and Asian empires," while historian Jeffrey Wasserstrom describes those residents who helped create a cosmopolitan space at the crossroads as "border-crossers" and their importance as linked to the "transnational networks they were part of and helped to extend." The image these scholars create is of residents who, as they moved about Shanghai, ultimately belonged to and in many ways represented the interests of one of the city's foreign or Chinese "constituent groups," in Oi and Dillon's words.[147] But the generation of Chinese Americans who settled in Shanghai in the 1930s was not wholly connected to either the foreign or the Chinese communities of the city. Rather than border crossers, they were border dwellers. They implicitly understood that they were stranded at the crossroads, and that none of the paths leading away from it offered them the kind of acceptance or security that white Americans and China-born people expected in Shanghai.

MODERNIZERS AND THE RHETORIC OF "RETURNING" TO CHINA

Stateside Chinese Americans' idealism about their assumed "homeland" and their place in it help explain the alienation so many of them felt when they finally arrived in China. In 1936 the Ging Hawk Club of New York City sponsored a nationwide essay contest for Chinese American youths on the topic "Does My Future Lie in China or America?" By this point, the Guomindang had spent years working to instill patriotism and party loyalty in the overseas population. The winning essays, published in San Francisco's *Chinese Digest* newspaper, demonstrated that theoretically, at least, party efforts had proven quite successful. When Harvard University student Robert Dunn, who captured first place, envisioned a future in America, his essay prompted an avalanche of criticism and accusations that he lacked proper patriotism. In response, Dunn felt the need not only to publicly declare his loyalty to China but also to claim that he had picked the America option simply because it was the more "original" choice. He explained, "Ever since I can remember, I have been taught by my parents, by my Chinese friends, and by my teacher in Chinese school, that I must be patriotic to China." Second-place winner Kaye Hong, a University of Washington graduate and San Francisco resident, provoked no similar torrent of abuse for choosing a future in China. In fact, the China-born San Francisco social worker Jane Kwong Lee wrote to *Chinese Digest* to argue that while both Hong and Dunn's viewpoints were valid, "to hope that all second generation Chinese will go back to China is very satisfying."[148] The contest suggested that emigrants to China were an imagined and sanctioned majority, despite being an actual minority, of the Chinese American citizen population. But while the Nationalist regime succeeded in encouraging this kind of abstract patriotism, it never managed to instill in almost any young Chinese Americans complete acceptance of party authority or anything beyond the vaguest sense of GMD goals.

To Dunn, Hong, and their peers, the GMD regime's importance came mainly from the fact that it seemed to provide China needed unity and a stable government. Other than that, they had scant knowledge of its agenda and particularly its program for social and cultural transformation—or of the negative attitudes of its leaders toward Western cultural and political ideas. In fact, the youths' beliefs about China showed little difference from those of the generation that came of age in the twilight of the Qing. Dunn described the Chinese as possessing "utilitarian ideals, conservative attitudes, and . . . a fatalistic outlook upon life."[149] In the tradition of earlier modernizers, Kaye Hong saw his purpose as bringing his "American background, . . . American spirit of aggressiveness, [and] . . . American 'go-getter' enthusiasm" to his parents' native land, and he also argued that "it matters not whether capitalism, socialism, or communism provides the means of motivation" as long as "China's salvation is accomplished." His ambition, he concluded, was simply to "become a good citizen of the great Republic . . . [and] support the Nationalist government."[150] But in GMD leaders' worldview, Hong could never be a good citizen, because he failed to perceive that communism was the greatest threat to China and that his American "go getter" attitude reflected an insidious individualism and the baleful influence of Western liberalism.[151]

Given that so many Chinese Americans saw China in the same way as Kaye Hong, the ones who arrived in the country in the 1930s often struggled outside the treaty ports, Hong Kong, and the heavily overseas areas of the Pearl River Delta. Everywhere else, their ordinary behavior, habits, and clothing risked crossing a line into unpatriotic and even dangerous behavior. Though many of the Chinese Americans who arrived in China in the 1930s hoped to contribute to strengthening the beleaguered nation, they primarily came because they believed race would not be a handicap to finding work there; indeed, their sense of Chineseness generally revolved more around their racial identity than around any Chinese cultural fluency. They soon discovered that good intentions and a Chinese face were not the same as being Chinese. "As soon as we are old enough to learn our A.B.C.'s we were taught the lessons of democracy, equality and liberty . . . but as soon as we step on the soil of our ancestors, we feel and see the difference everywhere," wrote a Chinese American from Pennsylvania who lived in China during the Nanjing Decade. "Down deep in my heart I am an American and will remain one until I die."[152]

GMD social and cultural policies and cronyism made such people feel increasingly irrelevant to the future of a China moving ever further away from American ideals such as "democracy, equality, and liberty." A decade or two earlier, Chinese American modernizers had often felt culturally adrift in a strange land, yet the prestige and employment opportunities they received as "American returned students" in China helped compensate for such sentiments. Almost none of the newcomers in the 1930s shared this experience. Even graduates of top US programs struggled to find a place in GMD bureaus and agencies during the Nanjing Decade, while the government cast their clothing, activities, and ideas as detrimental to the state. The most successful gravitated instead to Western-owned private businesses and Western-run missionary institutions. Younger Chinese American citizens resisted the GMD's demands in part because growing up in the United States had so deeply shaped their ambitions, desires, and plans for the future. But they also did so because the party offered them no incentives to behave otherwise.

NO GOLDEN AGE

During the 1930s, people of Chinese ancestry were among the many Americans of different backgrounds living in limbo, having moved from their birth nation, which denied them full membership on racial grounds, to their parents' homelands, which snubbed them for cultural and linguistic reasons. The thousands of Mexican American citizens whom the US government deported to Mexico alongside their Mexican parents often struggled with Spanish and faced ridicule for their "foreign" behaviors. As scholars Francisco E. Balderrama and Raymond Rodríguez point out, "in the United States, Mexican American children were always referred to as Mexicans, but in Mexico they were commonly called *gringos*, *yanquis*, or worse."[153] Chinese American citizens would certainly have related to such treatment. But ironically, the

Americans whose experiences even more closely paralleled their own were the Nisei—the second-generation Japanese Americans—who worked and studied in Japan, an empire increasingly bent on dominating China. By the mid-1930s, Japan's government worked to teach such people "nationalistic ideology to make them stronger Japanese and to utilize them ... [for] spreading the national glory abroad," as one Japanese American complained.[154] Overall this effort failed, partly because Japanese authorities and many ordinary citizens saw most Nisei as uncultured, individualistic, licentious, potentially disruptive of the social order, and requiring tight control and even surveillance.[155] Chinese Americans faced similar attitudes in Guomindang China, which like 1930s Japan was increasingly suspicious of Western cultural imports and political ideas.[156]

Lacking full sovereignty over China, the Nationalists never wielded the kind of power over Chinese Americans that Japanese authorities routinely used with the Nisei, but they also did little to win Chinese American goodwill in positive ways. Most significantly, the GMD regime rejected the practice of earlier governments that had avidly sought the services of Western-educated Chinese Americans. Already well versed in nepotism and cronyism, many Guomindang leaders in the 1930s reserved positions in government bureaus and agencies for their friends and relatives.[157] The only Chinese American beneficiaries were a handful of already established men, such as Loy Chang and Jun-ke Choy, whose mentors were powerful within the Guomindang, or those Chinese American citizens like Anthony Leefong Ahlo and Art Lym who chose to serve Chen Jitang.

The rejection that Chinese American citizen newcomers felt as a result of GMD policies and cronyism easily grew into a sense of alienation. The New Life Movement further encouraged such feelings and eventually led a group already marginalized by cultural and linguistic differences to openly defy the campaign. Movement leaders who sought to police social mores, sexual expression, and clothing curbed what Chinese American citizens saw as basic rights. Like other GMD initiatives, the movement simply helped solidify the newest immigrants' sense of being irrelevant to the GMD's state-building project.

The GMD also gave Chinese Americans a stake in the preservation of the foreign-controlled areas of the country and the economy at the very moment the party was attempting to eliminate both. The GMD's tacit exclusion of most Chinese American citizens from government employment mattered so much because the GMD in the 1930s sought to extend state control over large parts of the economy, particularly areas requiring the type of Western expertise Chinese Americans often possessed.[158] By restricting educated Chinese Americans to jobs in a struggling private sphere that the regime hoped to shrink over time, the GMD inadvertently weakened its influence over such people. At the same time, the American immigrants usually lacked the language skills and cultural fluency to work in purely Chinese private firms. Instead, more and more of them sought jobs with foreign-owned companies, usually Western enterprises operating in the concession areas, or started their own businesses catering to overseas Chinese, non-Chinese foreigners, and returned students. The immigrants' frustration with China's low standard of living and the GMD regime's attempts to define and police appropriate Chineseness further reinforced their social and economic segregation as well as their interest in preserving spaces where they could comfortably live and work.

Because of this segregation and alienation, Chinese American citizen immigrants, while expressing a basic allegiance to the Nationalist state, never demonstrated the deeper devotion and obedience to party that GMD leaders demanded. In short, very few Chinese Americans equated the Guomindang with China. The failings of the Nationalist state and its intolerance of Chinese American values made that degree of fidelity impossible. In the years after the 1937 Japanese invasion of China, this difference—between passive allegiance and active devotion—became abundantly clear.

CHAPTER 5

Agonizing Choices

The War against Japan, 1937–1945

Seattle native and Lingnan University student Marjorie Lew Kay spent the first part of her 1937 summer vacation at her uncle's home in Qingdao and then headed to Beijing to enroll in a Yenching University course. Almost simultaneously, Chinese and Japanese soldiers near the old capital clashed at the Lugouqiao (known to Westerners as the "Marco Polo Bridge") in the incident that started the Second Sino-Japanese War. When Japanese troops attacked nearby Beijing and Tianjin, Marjorie Lew Kay was stranded, unable to reach Yenching University, return to Qingdao, or even contact her uncle, the American-born dentist Don Geate Lew. Finally, she used her remaining money to go to Shanghai, which remained accessible despite the conflict in the north. She arrived in the city in early August and was staying with some Chinese friends there when the Battle of Shanghai began. When the fighting neared the home in which she had taken refuge, Lew Kay fled to a hotel and finally to the International Settlement, where she watched Japanese planes bomb the Chinese sections of the city.[1] After evacuating again, this time to Hong Kong, Lew Kay finally returned to the United States. So did the vast majority of Chinese American citizens living in China when the war broke out in 1937. While such people largely supported and admired China's fight against Japan, the worsening war forced them to seriously contemplate the depth and nature of their attachment to the nation and its regime. For most, their ties to China and their identification with it remained far too abstract and tenuous to justify the sacrifice of remaining.

This chapter explores the choices and dilemmas that Chinese American citizens in war-torn China faced during the four years of American neutrality after the Marco Polo Bridge Incident and the three and a half years following Japan's attack on Pearl Harbor. Between 1937 and 1941, Chinese Americans who lived in Japanese-occupied areas had to decide whether or not to seek shelter in foreign concessions, flee to "Free China," live under Japanese rule, or leave for Hong Kong or the United States. Throughout the country, those who stayed in Japanese-occupied or neutral territory also gambled on whether relations between the United States and Japan would continue to worsen. The vast majority of Chinese Americans who made such choices found few of their options palatable. Professionals with successful careers in China pondered returning to an economically struggling country where racial discrimination usually confined Chinese Americans to menial work. Many Chinese Americans lacked the money to buy a ticket to the United States or the willingness to abandon noncitizen spouses and children inadmissible under American immigration law. Yet Chinese American citizens who did return to the United States before December 1941 ultimately fared far better than almost all of those stranded in occupied China after Pearl Harbor. In contrast to the anxious uncertainty of the period between 1937 and 1941, the outbreak of the Pacific War meant almost certain deprivation and terror, and sometimes death, for those Chinese Americans who stayed in China.

In the end, the war in China reaffirmed that Chinese Americans' loyalties and sense of identity were tied to an abstract "China" rather than to the Nationalist regime. During the Nanjing Decade, the GMD's repressive policies and cronyism marginalized Chinese American immigrants and gave them almost no sense of investment in the government's policies and priorities, a problem that became increasingly obvious after the Marco Polo Bridge Incident. A small number of the most prominent first-generation modernizers did follow the government into the interior and serve the Chiang regime for the entire war, but they were very much in the minority. Beginning in 1937, the vast majority of Chinese American citizens left occupied China not for service in Free China but for the safety of the United States. Even many of those who stayed in China showed a deep reluctance to follow the government to Chongqing, however much they loathed the Japanese. Despite criticism from the Chiang regime, well-educated Chinese Americans, like their Chinese colleagues, often remained in Shanghai's foreign concessions rather than join the retreat to the interior.[2] Hundreds of Chinese American students and merchants also continued to live with their families in Guangdong, and some immigrants even kept studying at colleges located in Japanese-held areas.

While a handful of Chinese Americans left the United States to enlist directly in the Nationalist army, almost none of the citizen men living in China when the war broke out joined the armed forces there.

Most Chinese American immigrants made subtle declarations of allegiance with such choices, but a significant number broadcast their fidelity—or lack of it—far more clearly and pointedly. Several immigrants chose to serve one of the puppet regimes that the Japanese formed in China between 1938 and 1945, while far more passively collaborated in order to save themselves from starvation after 1941. While opportunism and ambition motivated most of the active collaborators, at least a handful were enthusiastic about the "new order," and their decisions to serve in puppet regimes reflected their personal experiences in the United States and prewar China. These few saw in Japanese "pan-Asianism" more opportunities for influence and power than Chiang's government had ever offered.

China's long anti-Japanese war, which dragged on for eight years and cost close to twenty million lives, marked the end of the Chinese American exodus to China.[3] Like other immigrants, Chinese Americans in the prewar years left the land of their birth because of "push" and "pull" factors.[4] The former revolved around the deeply entrenched racial discrimination that operated in every area of American life; the latter included the opportunities that China offered to those who spoke English, possessed an advanced degree, or sought the kind of education that would enable them to move comfortably in ethnic Chinese merchant networks. But the war destroyed much of coastal urban China, decimating its economy and eliminating the jobs the region had once offered to immigrants from America.[5] The Chiang regime, whose policies had already alienated so many Chinese Americans during the Nanjing Decade, spiraled into new depths of corruption with each passing year.[6] The war also devastated the old colonial empires in Asia, undercutting Western imperialism, destroying the ambiguous borders and competing sovereignties of the treaty port world, sparking even greater nationalism in the region, and transforming overseas Chinese networks.[7] Meanwhile, wartime mobilization in the United States, the growing civil rights movement, and the 1943 repeal of exclusion offered Chinese Americans the possibility of new economic and political opportunities in their homeland, even though racism remained deep and persistent there.[8] By 1945, when immigration to China became physically possible for the first time since Pearl Harbor, the vast majority of Chinese American citizens finally had more reasons to stay in the United States than to leave it.

THE WAR OF RESISTANCE AGAINST JAPAN

The Marco Polo Bridge Incident and the battle for Shanghai showed the way Nationalist priorities had shifted since the anti-communist campaigns of the early and mid-1930s. Late in 1936, General Zhang Xueliang kidnapped Chiang Kai-shek at Xi'an and pressed him to stop fighting the Chinese Communists and focus on the Japanese threat instead. Chiang made no public promises but did offer private assurances to Zhang in order to gain freedom. The "Xi'an Incident" demonstrated the unpopularity of Chiang's anti-communist policy, but it simultaneously confirmed his national leadership. It also prompted the Communists and Nationalists to create a "Second United Front" (the first was the anti-warlord coalition that lasted from 1923 to 1927) against Japan. Chiang saw the Japanese capture of Tianjin and Beijing in July 1937 as intolerable, and he quickly massed his forces at Shanghai and besieged the Japanese marines there.[9] In the 1932 Shanghai War, stiff Chinese resistance and international pressure led to a Japanese ceasefire after two months, but the valor of Chinese troops in 1937 could not stop the better-trained and armed Japanese this time around. After weeks of bitter fighting, the last Chinese-governed areas of Shanghai fell to Japanese troops on November 12, 1937.[10]

Far worse was yet to come. After the Battle of Shanghai ended, Japanese soldiers moved up the Yangzi, captured Nanjing, and subjected the capital to six weeks of merciless torture and slaughter in what has since become known as the Rape of Nanjing. Other similar but smaller incidents occurred across central China, with Japanese troops at various times not only killing scores of civilians and laying waste to towns and cities but also using chemical and biological agents to subdue and punish the population.[11] Chinese resistance continued, but the war exacted a horrible price: untold numbers of civilians and 300,000 Chinese soldiers died in the first few months of the conflict, and the nation's armies were largely in retreat much of that time.[12] Patriotic Chinese hailed the Nationalists' spring 1938 victory in the Battle of Taierzhuang, but the celebration proved premature. Japanese forces captured both Wuhan and Guangzhou near the end of that year and extended their control of central China in 1939.[13]

After the Wuhan defeat, Chiang Kai-shek's government withdrew to remote Chongqing in Sichuan Province and remained there for the next seven years. Despite sporadic fighting, the war in China became one of attrition by 1940: the Japanese were overextended and the GMD forces bled almost dry since the Nationalists lost so much of their trained officer corps and most of their best troops in 1937 and 1938.[14] Representatives of Chiang and the Japanese secretly met on several occasions to negotiate an end to the war but could not come to terms, particularly since the Japanese also set up several puppet governments, including in 1940 a new Nanjing regime under the leadership of Wang Jingwei, Chiang's old rival.[15]

In refusing to accept Japan's terms, Chiang Kai-shek gambled that if Free China could persevere, it would eventually receive assistance from the United States when that nation went to war against the Japanese—a conflict the Chinese leader correctly predicted.[16] Even before the outbreak of the Pacific War in December 1941, the United States began to include China in its Lend-Lease program, and after Pearl Harbor the two countries became formal allies, along with Britain and the Soviet Union, in the war against the Axis powers.[17] Still, Chiang expressed constant frustration with President Franklin Roosevelt's decision to pursue a "Europe first" strategy for fighting the war even as Japan's planes rained bombs on Chongqing and other Nationalist-held cities, and as Japanese armies successfully cut off land links between Free China and Burma to the southwest. The United States did fly tons of supplies over the Himalayas to Nationalist-held areas, however, while US engineers helped build alternative land routes from Burma to the Chinese interior.[18]

CRISIS OF CONFIDENCE

More than three hundred Chinese American immigrants and close to four thousand other US citizens lived in Shanghai when the war broke out there, but as in 1932, the former often felt the war's impact more profoundly than the latter.[19] Chinese Americans were likelier than other US citizens to socialize with Chinese citizens and to live in the Chinese-controlled areas of the city. "At night . . . we'd sit up in bed and listen for the sound of firing," Marjorie Lew Kay recalled of the period she spent at the home of Chinese friends in the war zone. "We knew the Japanese were landing troops or trying to advance."[20] The husbands of Americans Mary Akwai Hoh and Lois Loi-tsin Chong were both injured when a Chinese plane accidentally bombed a busy shopping area.[21] Japanese soldiers also attacked and looted Chinese American homes and businesses, including Henry Loo Kong's rental house, which he complained "was destroyed by fire caused by the war."[22]

As the battle raged around them, alarmed Chinese American citizens participated in the relief effort, but they also showed a quiet unwillingness to sacrifice their larger interests for a GMD regime they viewed with mistrust. The government had spent the decade after the Northern Expedition portraying itself as the protector of the overseas Chinese and as the natural focus of their loyalty; now, the Chiang regime reiterated this theme, repeatedly praising "patriotic overseas Chinese who are whole-heartedly doing their share" in the war by donating money to the government.[23] Back in the United States, Chinese Americans contributed hundreds of thousands of dollars to the Chinese war effort, believing, in the words of one Chinese New Yorker, that "to give up your life fighting at the front and to contribute your money from behind—this is the only creed to follow for national salvation and defense against Japanese invasion."[24] In contrast, Chinese American immigrants in Shanghai and other Chinese cities volunteered their time to help refugees and soldiers, but almost none sought to fight for or donate large sums to the GMD.[25] With so many banks closed and communications in northern and central China disrupted, most Chinese Americans avoided giving away money that they might soon require for their own subsistence.[26] However enthusiastic they felt about China's cause, they did not wish to sacrifice for it to that degree. And after the corruption they had seen during the Nanjing Decade, including the disappearance of so many donations during the 1932 Shanghai War, few Chinese Americans wholly trusted the regime to use their funds well or wisely.[27]

The first months of the war offered little reassurance to the many Chinese Americans in China who desperately wanted to believe in the regime despite their past experiences with it. Although the Marco Polo Bridge Incident sparked anger across China, the commander in charge of defending Beijing appeared to offer little opposition to the Japanese attacks on the city.[28] In Shanghai, better-trained and more effectively led troops ferociously resisted the Japanese, yet the war there quickly caused food shortages and threatened electricity, gas, and water supplies. Chinese mobs in the city also attacked rice shops and suspected traitors with equal enthusiasm, while municipal authorities struggled, at times unsuccessfully, to maintain public order.[29] On August 14, a Chinese airplane mistakenly dropped bombs on the Sincere and Wing On department stores, the Cathay and Palace Hotels, the centrally located race course, and busy Nanjing Road, killing or injuring hundreds of civilians.[30] The same day, another Chinese plane discharged its cargo of bombs into the harbor, almost blowing up the USS *Augusta*; a week later, a Chinese shell hit the same ship's deck, killing one American sailor and injuring eighteen others.[31] None of these events built Chinese American confidence in the Chiang regime's competence.

EVACUATION

Like other US citizens in China, Chinese American immigrants weighed whether to stay as the war made life in Shanghai more dangerous and threatened other parts of the country as well. In the first few months of the conflict, 1.5 million Chinese refugees from the surrounding region and the GMD-governed parts of the city streamed into Shanghai's International Settlement and French Concession, doubling the area's population.[32] These refugees soon discovered that the "neutral" zone's safety was relative: between August and October, two thousand Chinese and sixteen foreigners died from bombs, bullets, and anti-aircraft shells that fell inside the concessions.[33] By mid-August 1937, the ferocity of the conflict had already convinced US Consul Clarence Gauss and Admiral Harry Yarnell of the US Asiatic Fleet to ask the US-owned Dollar Line to reroute its ships to Shanghai in order to evacuate American women and children to Manila. An alarmed Congress appropriated funds to make loans to American citizen residents of China who could not afford to pay for a ticket on one of the ships. Late in August, the State Department also began warning residents of other parts of China to evacuate, anticipating that the area under Japanese threat might quickly grow.[34]

By this point, hundreds of Chinese Americans had decided to return to the United States, including many of the young people who first arrived in China during the Nanjing Decade. Although most came to China for work, they still imagined themselves as part of a beneficial, even transformative, force, bringing what Kaye Hong once called their "American spirit of aggressiveness, [and] . . . American 'go-getter' enthusiasm" to a stagnant, benighted nation.[35] But living under the Nationalist regime forced them to grapple with its corruption, conservative cultural and social agenda, and lack of interest in their skills, and by 1937 most felt little sense of investment in the government or almost any obligation to it. Facing a brutal war and shrinking employment prospects, about half the Chinese American citizens in Shanghai fled the city in August and September 1937. Similarly, Beijing consular officials who took a survey of local American citizens there discovered that most of those who wished to leave that fall were Chinese Americans.[36] By evacuating, these US citizens were voting with their feet, revealing the Guomindang's failure to convince them that the party and the nation were the same and that the GMD's interests aligned with their own. Many ordinary urban Chinese were just as unconvinced, but they generally lacked the ability to flee to safety elsewhere.[37]

The growing war and the geography of American life in China quickly complicated the US government's evacuation task. In 1937 American citizens of all backgrounds lived scattered across China. Most diplomats and businesspeople resided in major cities, many of them on or near the coast, including Beijing, Qingdao, Tianjin, Shanghai, Hankou, and Guangzhou. A thousand or more Chinese American citizens, along with a few other Americans, were located in the Pearl River Delta of Guangdong.[38] Scores of missionaries also dwelled in remote inland areas or, during the summer, clustered in resort areas such as Moganshan and Kuling, where an international school operated.[39] Consular officials particularly struggled to arrange transportation for the missionaries living upriver in central China. Initially, the US government advised such people to evacuate via the Canton-Hankow railroad, but Japanese planes began to bomb the line and also to strafe automobiles.[40] Removing residents of Shanghai proved more straightforward at first, because evacuees could purchase berths on one of the Dollar Line ships calling at the port and sail to safety in Manila. But as the Battle of Shanghai escalated, ship companies began to reconsider the safety of docking there, particularly after Chinese planes mistakenly bombed the SS *President Hoover* of the Dollar Line.[41]

As the evacuation of US citizens became more difficult, the State Department demonstrated greater concern for white American citizens than for their Chinese American peers, a tendency that grew more pronounced over time. After the *Hoover* bombing, the ship's captain returned its passengers to Shanghai, while other inbound Dollar Liners avoided Shanghai altogether and proceeded directly south to Hong Kong.[42] Shanghai consular officials and their assistants at the newly organized American Emergency Committee now scrambled to transport hundreds of evacuating Americans to Hong Kong to meet the Dollar Line ships there. Staff at the Shanghai consulate arranged for most of these people to travel aboard US Navy ships and drew up a list of approved passengers, separating Chinese Americans from everyone else. Officials did not explain this move, but they appear to have been conforming to the racial practices of the US Navy, a starkly segregated service. The only two people of Chinese ancestry sent on the USS *Sacramento*, a small gunboat that carried about two dozen Americans from Shanghai to Hong Kong, were the young, mixed-race children of Dorothy Fischer Cheng.[43] Consular officials told Ruth Moy and her two teenage sons, whom the Emergency Committee originally booked on the *Sacramento*, that they could not take the ship because it lacked enough space for women, yet committee members publicly declared after the ship's departure that they could not find enough passengers of either sex to fill it.[44] After the *Sacramento* sailed, the consulate placed all Chinese Americans bound for Hong Kong on the USS *Chaumont*, a much larger transport ship whose facilities enabled easier segregation.[45] In addition, Shanghai consul Clarence Gauss orally approved grants of US$10 only to Chinese Americans in order to encourage them to find other, often risky, transportation to Hong Kong.[46] A ticket on a foreign-flag boat from Shanghai to Hong Kong at this time cost about US$25. In contrast, the cheapest train ticket between Shanghai and Guangzhou was about $9 without food or transport to Hong Kong included, although train travel was far less safe after the Japanese began bombing the lines.[47] Still, Gauss apparently hoped to push Chinese Americans with Dollar Line tickets to either buy a train ticket or take one of the cheaper Chinese boats down the coast to Hong Kong. He did not expect white Americans to take such risks or evacuate under similar conditions.

However they traveled, Chinese Americans arriving in Hong Kong struggled to find places to stay, to contact family and friends, and to secure funds either to remain in the city or to travel on to the United States. Life in the colony grew more difficult with each passing week: by early September, the *South China Morning Post* lamented the combined effects of "war tension, profiteering, a cholera epidemic, . . . a flood of refugees, [and a] typhoon."[48] Two weeks later, so many Chinese and foreign refugees from the war were pouring into the colony that US Navy ships transporting Americans out of China no longer stopped in Hong Kong but headed directly to Manila. Still, Chinese American citizens continued to arrive in the colony by rail and boat from neighboring Guangdong, which Japanese planes began to bomb with frightening regularity.[49] As Chinese Americans streamed into the colony, their families and friends around the world frantically sought any information about whether these loved ones were safe. When China-born scientist Thomas Wen-I Liao reached Hong Kong, he advertised in local newspapers and over radio stations to find his Chinese American citizen wife, Anna. Families in the United States contacted the State Department in Washington and the Hong Kong consulate, desperate for any news of lost children, siblings, and friends.[50] Meanwhile, American refugees who had spent all their savings just to reach Hong Kong also turned to the State Department to contact family members in the United States for help. As in Shanghai, at least some Chinese American citizens who reached Hong Kong in 1937 eventually received repatriation assistance from the US government.[51]

THE WIDENING WAR

In mid-November, Japanese forces finally crushed the last vestiges of Chinese resistance in Shanghai and began moving up the Yangzi toward the Nationalist capital at Nanjing. No foreign concessions existed there, and Chinese American citizens living in the capital showed little desire to endure the expected Japanese attack with the rest of the city's ordinary residents. Very quickly, the remaining Chinese American students at the American-founded University of Nanking returned to the United States, while other immigrants left for Hong Kong or Shanghai. With each month, the number of Chinese Americans in Nanjing dwindled, from more than two dozen in August to fifteen in September to seven in mid-October to three in late November.[52]

By the time the Japanese began their attack that December, the only Chinese American in Nanjing was Norman Soong, who had moved to the city to open a *China Press* office a few months before the Marco Polo Bridge Incident. Soong's wife, the Honolulu native and Yenching University graduate Irma Tam Soong, fled Nanjing shortly after the outbreak of war in August 1937. As the conflict continued, Norman Soong became a stringer for the *New York Times*, covering the war in Shanghai and then the wider Yangzi region. Together with a number of other foreign journalists, Soong watched the battle for Nanjing from the apparent safety of the USS *Panay*, a US Navy gunboat sent to evacuate the last American citizens from the Chinese capital. On December 12, 1937, Japanese planes bombed and strafed the neutral *Panay* despite its clear American markings, killing four passengers, wounding dozens more, and sinking the ship. Soong and the other *Panay* survivors spent the night huddled in the cold mud of the Yangzi as the battle continued in the city. The photographer eventually recovered his camera, and his photos of the "*Panay* Incident" became famous around the world. After a brief rest in Shanghai, he returned to Nanjing, where he and other reporters discovered the remains of the Japanese military's six week orgy of violence and rape in the fallen capital.[53]

By that point, the Japanese were moving south as well as west, occupying large swaths of China's heartland. Most foreign observers watching the Sino-

Japanese conflict focused their attention on the war in central China, including the Nationalist government's withdrawal first to Hankou (one of the three cities that made up the Wuhan metropolis) and then to Chongqing; Chiang Kai-shek's decision to blow up the dikes on the Yellow River in an effort to slow the Japanese; and the seizure of Wuhan after valiant Chinese resistance there. But the war in central China was intimately tied to the fate of Guangzhou, for the southern city and the Pearl River Delta were key transfer points for supplies and soldiers flowing north. Wuhan fell to the invaders just weeks after Guangzhou capitulated in October 1938.[54]

THE WAR IN THE SOUTH

The first Japanese air raids on Guangzhou began in August 1937, frightening residents so much that about a third of them left the city and thousands more unsuccessfully sought refuge in the small foreign concession of Shameen Island, to which foreign guards refused them entry. Within days, the US consulate began to warn Americans to evacuate the Tungshan district, a popular residential spot for foreigners and overseas Chinese but also the home of the city's airfield. Soon, the US consul started quietly advising all Americans in the city to leave if they could or, if that was not possible, to flee to Shameen at the first sign of trouble. Although some of Guangzhou's Chinese residents trickled back in, bombing continued at such a pace that about half of the city's population fled again in mid-October 1937. By this point, the Japanese were also dropping bombs in areas of the province with large Chinese American populations, including Shekki and Toisan, the ancestral county of more Chinese Americans than any other. That December, the Japanese bombed the Union Middle School, an institution where overseas Chinese had been sending their children for two generations. In June 1938, the Japanese dropped bombs on Lingnan University, still tremendously popular with overseas Chinese students from across the world.[55]

As in Shanghai, the Guangzhou US consulate's staff members treated the protection of white Americans as their paramount duty and Chinese Americans as only a secondary concern. Shortly after the Lingnan bombing, Guangzhou consul Irving Linnell reported to the State Department that "practically the only Americans in this district at present are those actively engaged as doctors, nurses, teachers, missionaries (many of whom assist in medical work), newspaper representatives and representatives of American companies." He counted 113 Americans in the area, but this total omitted the two hundred or so Chinese American citizen children studying in the district and the hundreds of citizen adults, both native-born and derivative, who also lived there.[56] Linnell simple left every person of Chinese ancestry off his roster of "Americans."

Linnell and the State Department also proved unwilling to use much diplomatic muscle to protect these Chinese American citizens as the situation in the province grew worse. In early October 1938, with the Japanese poised to attack Guangzhou, Linnell urged all Americans to leave the city via Shekki for Macao, one of the only safe routes out. By then, 82 white Americans and at least 79 Chinese Americans remained in and around Guangzhou, although the latter total included only those who had registered with the consulate. Evacuating the Chinese Americans proved particularly difficult. Many of them lived scattered in villages, and not only were Japanese planes bombing the rail lines in the area, but Chinese forces had also stopped traffic on the Pearl River. Linnell discovered that in case of a Japanese attack, Chinese American citizens who still lived in Guangzhou or managed to reach the city could not take refuge in the Shameen Island concession with other US nationals. The British controlled the concession, and they would not allow any Chinese except for servants to reside there. The citizenship of the people in question did not make a difference, even after Linnell assured the British consul that any Chinese American evacuees would not be permanent residents but simply temporary refugees. Secretary of State Cordell Hull eventually asked Nelson Johnson, the US ambassador to China, to take the matter up with the British ambassador, but only informally, and no evidence exists that Johnson bothered to comply. Either way, Hull proved unwilling to push the British, leaving Linnell to tell Chinese Americans to evacuate to Hong Kong—a route he no longer recommended to others—or to take refuge at Lingnan University, where much of the American faculty decided to remain.[57] Linnell planned to place any Chinese Americans who showed up at Shameen anyway on a barge alongside the island so that their presence would not violate the British racial prohibition. But by the time Japanese forces entered Guangzhou—whose fleeing Chinese defenders torched the city to deny it to the invaders—all remaining Chinese Americans had fled to Hong Kong, Macao, or one of the villages of the Pearl River Delta.[58]

Like their predecessors the year before, the Chinese American refugees who crossed into Hong Kong in 1938 grappled with the continuing cholera epidemic, intense overcrowding, and difficulties contacting family and friends for help. Worse yet, some of the newest arrivals had actually been in almost constant motion since the beginning of the war. When the Japanese began bombing Guangzhou in 1937, the six California-born Fong siblings fled the city, taking refuge in their grandfather's village. Once the war widened in 1938, they again took to the road, crossing into Hong Kong and crowding into a friend's flat before finally boarding a ship back to the United States.[59] They were among the luckier refugees. One anxious Chinese American father from Pennsylvania appealed to the Red Cross to find his US citizen children, who had been separated from each other while fleeing into Hong Kong from Guangdong.[60] Charles and Kelley Wong's mother in Butte, Montana, eventually located her sons, who had also escaped to Hong Kong, but she lacked the money to bring them home.[61] The seven American-born Low siblings left Hokshan with their Chinese citizen mother and found a room at a Hong Kong hotel, but like the Wong brothers, they lacked the funds to return to the United States.[62] Such stories were typical.

These newest American refugees languished in the colony because the State Department did not consider them a priority and because they lacked the political clout to change that. In 1937 the department asked Congress for an appropriation to enable it to make loans to hundreds of US citizens attempting to evacuate from China but lacking the money to do so.[63] While this group included some Chinese Americans, most were white citizens, often with vocal friends and family members in America. The department did not ask for more funds in 1938, when the majority of the US citizen refugees were Americans of Chinese ancestry whose stateside relatives wielded almost no political power.[64] Sadly, some Chinese Americans in the United States wrongly assumed that the US government felt a degree of concern for their relatives. In 1940 a St. Louis father read a story in his local Chinese-language newspaper contending that Chinese American citizens who did not return to the United States by January 1941 would expatriate but that President Roosevelt was sending ships to retrieve them all from China before then. He managed to contact his three American daughters in Toisan and told them to make the dangerous trip to Hong Kong for their free tickets; they did so, only to discover that the president had sent no ships. They then undertook the perilous journey back to the village, where they remained until 1946.[65]

Despite such tales of desperation, far fewer Chinese American citizens tried to leave Guangdong in 1938 than attempted to flee Shanghai in 1937. While almost no Chinese Americans stayed in Guangzhou when it fell to the

Japanese, some eventually trickled back, far more remained in the Pearl River Delta villages, and a surprising number actually traveled from the United States to China between 1938 and 1941.[66] Many of these returnees seemed secure in the knowledge that as Americans, they were relatively safe from the Japanese, although Guangzhou US consular officials offered them no support when the occupiers harassed them.[67]

Unlike their peers in Shanghai and elsewhere in the country, significant numbers of the immigrants in the south had developed a durable and concrete attachment to the China they knew. That China was closely linked to their extended families, it was tied to broader overseas networks through nearby Hong Kong, and its villages showed the impact of such networks through architecture, institutions, entertainment options, and products for sale in stores. Western cultural influences were pervasive in many Pearl River Delta villages, helping Chinese identity there remain relatively fluid and inclusive. In contrast, Shanghai's Chinese Americans, who experienced GMD rule much more directly and for far longer than their southern peers, formed part of a population that the regime decried as undesirable, unpatriotic, and decadent. Culturally alienated, many of them came to rely on the foreign concessions for social and recreational outlets and, in the summer and fall of 1937, for physical protection. Unsurprisingly, they showed far less willingness to remain in China as conditions deteriorated there than did their counterparts in the south.

THE LONG HAUL

By late 1938, the remaining Chinese American immigrants in northern and central China increasingly relied on their US citizenship to protect them because the Japanese government continued to recognize many foreign-controlled institutions and spaces until 1941. Most of the Chinese American citizens who stayed in occupied north China were thus employees or students at US-affiliated institutions such as the Peking Union Medical College (PUMC) and Yenching University. Farther south, Shanghai's foreign concession area—which became known as the *gudao*, or solitary island, because of its position as a neutral place in a sea of Japanese occupation—not only seemed like the safest outpost in coastal China but was also newly full of potential. When the war began, numerous industrialists, publishers, and Chinese government-owned banks shifted operations to the concession area, and

Shanghai's 1937 economic worries soon gave way to a refugee-driven boom. A burst of prosperity largely confined to the *gudao*, the surge drove up the prices of already scarce goods, pushed down wages, and made housing increasingly overcrowded.[68]

After 1937 dozens of Chinese Americans, many of them longtime modernizers from other parts of China, took refuge in the *gudao* in a tacit rejection of the GMD government's call for patriots to relocate to Free China. Not affiliated with protective American institutions in the occupied north, such people chose Shanghai's constricted concessions over life in remote Chongqing. The new residents included Marjorie Lew Kaye's uncle Don Geate Lew, who finally left Qingdao with his family when life in the occupied north grew intolerable. Another arrival was Tin Chong Goo, a Hawaiian-born Yenching University graduate and *Peiping Chronicle* editor whom Japanese soldiers briefly kidnapped after the Marco Polo Bridge Incident.[69] Mon Yin Chung, who managed the Central Mint in Nanjing before the war, also debarked for Shanghai after the capital fell to the Japanese.[70] Chung had flourished under the patronage of GMD finance official T. V. Soong, but such ties were not enough to convince him to decamp to the far west. Similarly, government railroad manager Lau Waan-wai also stayed in Shanghai, taking a position as a professor in the civil engineering department at St. John's University, now relocated to the safety of the International Settlement.[71]

Japanese mistreatment and harassment of Chinese outside the concession areas encouraged almost all of these immigrants, whether old timers or newcomers, to both live and work within the *gudao*.[72] Chinese Americans residing in Chinese-controlled areas of Shanghai when the war broke out now retreated into the foreign-controlled spaces, squeezing into tiny apartments and friends' homes as housing grew scarce. Some who had run businesses outside of the protected zone tried to relocate the enterprises to the International Settlement or the French Concession. Others simply sold them or, like thirty-eight-year-old George K. T. Wong of Majestic Motors and the Sino-American Syndicate, "retired."[73]

As an artificial calm settled over Shanghai, some of the citizens who had left for America in 1937 returned, seeking work, excitement, or the familiarity of their old lives. Ruth Moy, who fled to the United States with her two children when the war broke out, now came back to the city with her younger son Loring to resume their lives there. Her in-laws, tobacco broker Alfred S. Lee and Alice Moy Lee, also returned to Shanghai after a brief stint in New York.[74] William Yukon Chang, a 1937 St. John's graduate, could not stay away either.

FIGURE 17. Honolulu native and St. John's University graduate William Yukon Chang in front of Jimmy's Kitchen, a Shanghai restaurant popular with American expatriates. Although Chang evacuated from Shanghai in 1937, he missed its excitement and dynamism and returned in 1940, soon becoming a sportswriter for the *China Press*. Copyright Dallas Chang/William Y. Chang Collection.

After sailing home to Hawaii when the war broke out, he enrolled briefly in the University of Hawaii's teacher education program, but "working at Dole's pineapple cannery during vacations and lolling on the Manoa Valley campus or at Waikiki Beach between classes became boring after more than a year," he later recalled. "I took a ship back to turbulent, stimulating Shanghai . . . [and] after a few wild months . . . a job in the sports department of the English-language *China Press*."[75]

By staying in Shanghai or returning there after 1937, Americans like these signaled their belief in the durability of the city's semicolonial order and, at the same time, their lack of faith in the GMD regime. Few put their assessment so bluntly and in fact often broadcast their Chinese patriotism instead. At the Chinese Women's Club, Alice Moy Lee and other citizen women spoke glowingly of China's war effort.[76] Chinese American citizen businessmen and professionals did their part, helping manage and raise money for the many war refugee organizations based in the concessions.[77] Yet these Chinese American residents of Shanghai chose to ignore the Nationalist government's call for patriotic Chinese, particularly businesspeople, doctors, and industrialists, to move to Free China.[78] Like many of their citizen peers in the south, these people stayed in Shanghai because they had developed durable and concrete attachments to the China they knew: the China of treaty ports, foreign concessions, and Western institutions, all of which the GMD rejected.

COLLABORATORS

Scores of Chinese Americans after 1937 talked about patriotism while putting their trust in *gudao* Shanghai, but others openly abandoned the Chiang regime. In March 1938, the Japanese government appointed the "Reformed Government of the Republic of China" to act as its puppet regime in Shanghai and Nanjing as well as the provinces of Jiangsu, Zhejiang, and Anhui. The chairman of the new regime was Liang Hongzhi, an old member of the warlord-era Anfu Clique, and in this he resembled many of the men who served with him in the Reformed Government and its successor, Wang Jingwei's Reorganized Government of the Republic of China: large numbers were old warlord or Beiyang officials sidelined by the GMD after 1927.[79] The members of Liang's "government," which exercised almost no power but simply functioned to legitimate Japanese rule, lived for their own safety in Shanghai's New Asia Hotel under military police protection. Most avoided going out, knowing that Chiang Kai-shek's undercover agents in Shanghai sought to kill Chinese collaborators.[80] But on September 23, 1938, puppet legislator Chen Zitang made the mistake of leaving the New Asia Hotel, after which three Chongqing agents beat him so savagely that he was hospitalized.[81] The incident received no coverage in the city's English-language press, and indeed, no one in the foreign community seemed to realize that the injured man was Russell Bates Shue Chen, the Boston-born lawyer and second-generation US citizen who had immigrated to China in the early 1920s. The highest-ranking Chinese American in any of the puppet regimes, Chen managed somehow to avoid attracting the attention of Shanghai's Western residents while serving as chairman of the foreign relations committee of the Reformed Government's Legislative Yuan. His beating at the hands of Chongqing agents signaled that the Chiang regime certainly knew of his activities, but the Reformed Government was so powerless that only its very top leaders attracted any attention from non-Japanese foreign residents.[82]

Chen's friends and family members likely played a key role in his decision to join the Reformed Government. Chen's wife, Julia Tong Chen, was the daughter of Tong Kai-cho, a Shanghai sharebroker who had worked as former Beiyang president Xu Shichang's English secretary years earlier. Xu, like Liang Hongzhi, was affiliated with the Anfu Clique during the height of the warlord period, and Tong likely remained close to those in the group who went on to serve the Japanese. One of Tong Kai-cho's friends (and a possible relative) was Tong Shao-yi, who also knew Russell and Julia Chen. In 1937 agents of the Chiang regime assassinated Tong Shao-yi after rumors swirled in Shanghai that he would accept the presidency of a puppet regime there.[83]

Equally important, by the late 1930s Russell Chen had been friends with Lawrence Klindt Kentwell, an enthusiastic Japanese collaborator, for close to fifteen years. After his 1927 disbarment from the Shanghai Provisional Court, the embittered Kentwell struggled to make a living as a journalist, also teaching law at National Sun Yat-sen University in Guangdong while Chen Jitang was in power. Although Kentwell publicly supported the GMD and the cause of Chinese nationalism, the Chiang regime appears to never have trusted him very much. Perhaps officials had heard the rumor that Kentwell secretly offered to sell his services as a journalist to the British government despite his professed Chinese patriotism. In any case, Kentwell was editing a journal called the *Chinese Outlook* when the war broke out, and he quickly changed the publication's name to the *Voice of New China* to please his new sponsor, Japan.[84] From the renamed publication, he continued to excoriate Britain but also contended that "a New China will arise under new leadership in close co-operation with Japan to preserve Oriental civilization and culture as the destiny of China and Japan are interdependent and closely linked." Two months later, the *Voice* also carried an advertisement for the new Nanjing-based law firm of "Kentwell, Chen & Cheng," whose partners included Russell Chen.[85]

上より法制委員長
潘承鍔、外交委員會委員長陳子棠、財政委員會委員長揚
景斌、經濟委員會委員長張韜、治安委員會委員長溫慶彪

FIGURE 18. Boston-born lawyer Russell Bates Shue Chen, second from the top, in 1940, while serving as a member of the collaborationist Reformed Government of the Republic of China's Legislative Yuan and the chairman of its foreign relations committee. Later that year, Chen chose to accept a position in the Legislative Yuan of Wang Jingwei's new Reorganized Government of the Republic of China. Reprinted from *Zhonghua minguo weixinzhengfu gai shi* (Record and history of the Reformed Government of the Republic of China), Nanjing: Executive Yuan Propaganda Department, 1940.

Similar ties of friendship and kinship also ensnared Chinese American women, with those married to collaborators struggling to reconcile their allegiance to Nationalist China and the United States with their loyalty to their husbands. San Francisco–born Lily Soo-hoo Sung coped by simply ignoring the actions of her husband, William Z. L. Sung. The president of St. John's University, Sung remained at the college despite the occupation and accepted low-level positions in the puppet regime after 1940.[86] Regardless, Soohoo Sung complained right after the war that "our middle class, especially teachers and those who *did not work for* the Japs have had a very hard time. We have sold all of our possessions which anyone was willing to buy to pay for food which reached such fantastic prices."[87] California native Lillian Loo Kiang, who was married to the China-born Socialist Party leader Jiang Kang-hu, escaped the Japanese-controlled north with the help of American officials in Beijing and returned to the United States in 1939. Months later, Jiang Kang-hu met with his old friend Wang Jingwei in Shanghai and agreed to join Wang's new collaborationist regime.[88] Lillian Loo Kiang never publicly condemned her husband's actions, but after Pearl Harbor, she sought to prove her patriotism by volunteering for the American Red Cross, while her son joined the US Army. Privately, she described "humiliation" as a constant part of her new American life.[89]

Chinese Americans' motives for collaboration included not just the politics of their friends and families but, unsurprisingly, their own career ambitions.[90] Another old friend of Kentwell, Anthony Leefong Ahlo, was in early 1938 working for the mayor of doomed Guangzhou, but he had little stomach for a fight. That August, as the Japanese began to prepare for their assault on the city, Ahlo suddenly resigned from his position and left for Hong Kong to enter business, although without much apparent success. The next year, he found his way to Shanghai, where he told the British consul that Wang Jingwei had signed a secret agreement with the Japanese. He noted, too, that Wang offered him a job. As the consul reported to his superiors, "my impression is that [Ahlo] is hoping to get some employment by British authorities either here or in Hongkong, but I have made it clear that H.M. Embassy are not interested in that aspect." Returning to Hong Kong, a disappointed Ahlo quietly created a new firm called the Asiatic Phosphate Corporation, which focused on an agricultural chemical coveted by the Japanese. Significant phosphate deposits existed in French Indochina, a colony in which Ahlo also began to show great interest.[91] After the fall of France, the Japanese signed a treaty with the Vichy regime and sent soldiers and technicians to Lao Cai, Vietnam, specifically to exploit the large phosphate deposits there. Soon after, Ahlo followed.[92]

While frustration and disillusionment motivated Ahlo's choices, Herbert Moy acted out of a desire to preserve the opportunities that the unique world of the concessions had created for him. The youngest brother of Ernest and William Moy and Alice Moy Lee, Herbert Moy was the target of a failed June 1938 assassination attempt for his anti-Japanese broadcasts over American-owned XMHC.[93] When the manager of the new Nazi radio station XGRS offered Moy a position in late 1940, he jumped at the chance to earn a handsome salary, gain local stardom, and win protection from Japanese threats without having to directly serve Japan's occupation forces or the puppet government in central China. Moy knew that returning to the United States would end his radio career; indirect collaboration, on the other hand, ensured that he could continue broadcasting. Moy received the highest salary of any announcer at XGRS, a fact that likely helped soothe any qualms he had about serving an overtly racist regime.[94]

The previous China experiences and expectations of each of these immigrants shaped the degree and nature of their collaboration. Anticipating acceptance and opportunity, many younger Chinese Americans who arrived in China during the Nanjing Decade grappled instead with culture shock, social isolation, and a sense of estrangement from an increasingly corrupt government that veered toward fascist models and condemned liberal democracy and individualism. Herbert Moy's work for Nazi Germany revealed the results: professions of loyalty to the Chinese people, mixed with basic opportunism born of economic necessity and cynicism.[95] In contrast, those Chinese Americans who responded with the greatest enthusiasm to the puppet regimes and Japan's pan-Asian rhetoric often remembered the pre-GMD days, when American diplomas and ideas stirred envy and respect rather than suspicion or apathy. Anthony Leefong Ahlo, one of the first modernizers, had served on the Qing Supreme Court and as a Beiyang ambassador to Samoa and North Borneo, but he received only a low-level position in the GMD regime's foreign ministry and never rose higher. Russell Chen's China-born friends were returned students and people pushed out of power during the Nanjing Decade, and he moved in the kinds of cosmopolitan circles that the Nationalists increasingly critiqued.[96] Moy chose an indirect method of collaboration, siding with a Japanese ally that had not yet declared war on China. Chen and Ahlo more openly defied the GMD government, suggesting that they rejected it as a legitimate focus for Chinese patriotism.

THE END OF NEUTRALITY

The war in China and Japanese expansion in Southeast Asia increasingly poisoned the relationship between Japan and the United States and threatened the ability of American citizens to remain in China indefinitely. Between 1939 and 1941, the Japanese announced their intention to abrogate their commerce treaty with the United States, the American government discussed including China in its new Lend-Lease program, and the Roosevelt administration began to limit the materials it allowed Japan to buy from the United States. American officials warned Japan against further expansion into Southeast Asia, while Japanese ships carrying scrap metal purchased in America faced growing lines of protestors at West Coast docks.[97]

In Shanghai, the US consulate quietly gathered the names and addresses of American citizens in the city and monitored new arrivals and departures, while the American Emergency Committee, originally formed in 1937, resumed its meetings. In early October 1940, the State Department finally advised American women and children, and any men whose presence in China was not "essential or urgent," to evacuate to the United States.[98] The announcement quickened the already substantial flow of US citizens out of Shanghai, but almost no Chinese Americans left in response. The Shanghai consulate noted that about 750 Americans departed from the city in 1940. Fewer than twenty were Chinese Americans. More than four hundred US citizens left Shanghai in the month after the evacuation advisory, but only three of these repatriates were ethnic Chinese.[99]

The cost and availability of transportation influenced the decisions of many Americans who wished to leave. Once the State Department called for nonessential US citizens to evacuate China, local consular officials pointed out that more than a thousand people who wished to repatriate could not find space on US-bound ships. The American President Lines' October 1940 announcement that it would send extra ships provoked widespread anger when the company declared its intention to charge first-, second-, and third-class tickets at the first-class rate, with only a small discount for improvised dormitories. The ticket prices varied from $395 to $450, or around $8,000 in 2019 dollars. Every career officer at the US consulate in Shanghai endorsed a protest message to the State Department, reminding officials there that local US citizens were selling their belongings and preparing to leave at the government's urging. "Americans here are loyal and patriotic. . . . [and] their Government over a period of years has encouraged them to come to China in the furtherance of American export trade and American missionary and philanthropic enterprises," wrote the officers. "Local Americans . . . resent being charged high fares at a time when they feel they are assisting the National policy and their personal fortunes are being jeopardized." The next day, the career officers at the Beijing legation concurred.[100]

Meanwhile, potential Chinese American evacuees grappled not only with the high cost of ship tickets but also with racially discriminatory American immigration laws. In 1925 the Supreme Court had interpreted the new 1924 immigration law to mean that Chinese citizen wives of US citizens were not entitled to enter the United States, even though China-born merchants could bring in their own Chinese citizen wives indefinitely.[101] Six years later, Congress amended the 1924 Immigration Act to give China-born wives of US citizens the right to enter the United States, but only if the couples had married before 1924. US law disadvantaged Chinese American citizen women even more than their male peers, despite Congressional tinkering meant to make the immigration statutes somewhat equitable. One change in 1931 allowed Chinese American women who had previously lost their US citizenship by marrying China-born men to regain it through naturalization. Another amendment gave Chinese American citizen women the right to pass their citizenship to any of their children born after May 1934. However, the 1931 amendment did not give China-born husbands of Chinese American citizen women the right to enter America, even if they had married before 1924. Furthermore, many women who had lost their citizenship did not possess the means to travel to the United States, and they could not petition from China for naturalization as US citizens. Finally, the amendment that allowed Chinese American women married to foreign men to pass citizenship to their offspring was not retroactive: their children born before May 1934 remained aliens.[102]

The State Department showed no inclination to bend such laws, even as officials sought a solution for the problem of cash-strapped white citizens trying to flee China. After hemming and hawing, the Department in late October finally responded to US expatriates' and consular officials' outrage by agreeing to again provide financial assistance to citizens who lacked the money to evacuate to the United States. If necessary, government funds would also cover alien spouses and children, but only in cases where "such alien relatives are properly documented for admission into the United States after having been found admissible under the Immigration laws." Secretary of State Cordell Hull further clarified that US officials should make no loans to "American citizens of alien extraction who are bound by family ties to aliens ineligible to citizenship or otherwise inadmissible under the Immigration law . . . [if doing so] would constitute virtual desertions of their family obligations."[103] In other words, the State Department would not make loans to evacuate the alien spouses and children of Chinese American citizens, since such people were inadmissible to the United States because of the Chinese exclusion law, nor would the Department assist Chinese Americans who wished to leave alone if they had non-citizen dependents.

US policy thus trapped numerous Chinese Americans and their families in China, even as white citizens fled to safety with government assistance. Some of those who would not abandon alien spouses were middle-aged professional men, such as the architect Poy G. Lee and the dentist Don Lew, who in the 1920s and early 1930s had married into the Chinese coastal elite.[104] Even more of the stranded were Chinese American women unable to extend the protection of their citizenship to their spouses and any children born before 1934. A few Chinese citizen husbands might have resisted leaving China themselves, but their American wives never had the chance to consider the option. Some couples did act to protect their children when they could. Lois Loi-tsin Chong whose China-born husband was injured in 1937 when Nationalist planes mistakenly bombed the Sincere Department Store, never lost her own citizenship and was able to register her three children as US citizens as well because of their birth after May 1934. She received American government assistance to repatriate with them to Hawaii but did not see her husband again until 1946. In contrast, Flora Belle Jan, almost broke in Beijing, was marooned there with her Chinese citizen husband and children; one of her girls was a Chinese citizen because of her birth before 1934, and Jan had neither the money nor the will to leave the child behind.[105]

THE VISE TIGHTENS

As the US-Japan relationship worsened, Chinese Americans in south China struggled not just with American immigration law but also with the Japanese, who began to harass US citizens and especially people of Chinese ancestry. "The Japanese will avail themselves of every possible opportunity to interfere with the interests and work of Americans out here," complained the superintendent of the missionary-run Canton Hospital in 1940, but at least he managed to persist.[106] Japanese pressure on Lynne Lee Shew's overseas Chinese–funded and locally run Heungshan Benevolent Hospital eventually became intolerable, forcing her to shutter the facility and return to the United States in 1939.[107] With each month, the harassment of individual Chinese American citizens also increased. In late 1940, almost three dozen Chinese Americans attempted to reach Hong Kong from Toisan after hearing rumors that they needed to return to the United States immediately to protect their citizenship rights.[108] The rush to the colony reaffirmed the value that many such people placed on their formal citizenship but also showed how little Japanese military personnel respected their status as neutral foreign nationals. Japanese sailors intercepted the various junks on which the immigrants were traveling, confiscated many of the American passengers' documents and valuables, and assaulted some of the travelers as well. As one of the Chinese American victims recalled, "when the Japanese noticed that I was an American, they shouted at me, 'You American, eh' and then tore up and threw away all my papers and slapped my face."[109]

Despite the crisis across the border, Hong Kong-based Chinese Americans until 1941 continued to trust in the city's insulation from the nearby conflict and to assume that the prewar colonial order would hold indefinitely. Louey Shuck and his son Edward Louie both traveled to the United States for business in 1940 under the assumption that their Hong Kong–based families would be perfectly safe.[110] Father and son had each weathered the warlord decades in the south and probably believed that the most recent crisis would eventually end, but in December 1941 they became involuntary exiles. So did Harry Hong Sling and his wife, Francis Yee, who traveled with their three children to the United States and were stranded there until 1945. Jun-ke Choy's son, who left Hong Kong for school in America in 1941, did not see his father again for three years.[111]

As in Shanghai, scores of Chinese Americans in Hong Kong pondered their dim economic prospects in the United States and the inflexibility of the country's immigration laws and eventually decided to stay in the colony, even as the news from China grew more ominous. Some, like Bill Hong Sling and Frances Lui Au, were married to Chinese citizens who could not necessarily join them if they evacuated to the United States.[112] Other immigrants kept in touch with friends who told sobering tales of unemployment or underemployment in America. Beautician Edna Goo, who lived in Hong Kong after leaving Shanghai in 1937, eventually sailed home to Hawaii, where the only job she could find was working as a maid for a white family. Once Norman Soong's short-term job with the *New York Times* ended, he also returned to Hawaii, where, as his wife, Irma Tam Soong, recalled, he "received warm acclaim, but could find no work." By 1941 he was back in Asia as an employee of the GMD Central News Agency's Hong Kong office.[113] Hearing about such experiences discouraged other Chinese American citizens with jobs in the colony from leaving.

Even more Chinese American citizens in the south simply could not afford tickets to the United States, and the US government did not offer Chinese Americans in Guangdong and Hong Kong the financial assistance it made available to Shanghai's residents. This discriminatory treatment meant that in early 1941, more than seven hundred Chinese American citizens, including about two hundred children, were still living in Hong Kong, a number that did not include recent refugees from the mainland. Only about sixty of these Chinese Americans managed to leave the colony for the United States between March and December 1941.[114] Far more of them, especially young people, lacked the money to buy tickets, including Alfred and Charles Poy, whose mother in Detroit could not send them enough for return passage, and twelve year-old orphan Clara Chin, whose widowed mother had died in 1940.[115] The Hong Kong consul ignored these young Americans in the colony, just as his Guangzhou counterpart in 1938 neglected the hundreds of Chinese American citizens in his district.

By 1941, then, a combination of American government policy and Chinese American penury and sanguinity meant hundreds of US citizens of Chinese ancestry in the south and Hong Kong were eventually trapped without any means of escape. As late as February of that year, Hong Kong US consul Addison Southard reassured citizens in the colony, "There are American ships calling here every few days" and "I do not think there is any immediate crisis in view."[116] Almost simultaneously, the Japanese occupied Toisan and other heavily overseas Chinese areas of Guangdong and blockaded routes out to Macao and Hong Kong. Chinese Americans who finally arrived in Hong Kong after the Japanese lifted the blockade in mid-1941 learned that the US government's Lend-Lease program had unexpectedly requisitioned almost every ship in the American President Lines, the main service linking Hong Kong to the United States. The liners previously called at Hong Kong about four to five times a month on their way to Manila, Honolulu, and San Francisco; now, despite

Southard's reassurances, the number of sailings fell to just one a month.[117] Desperate Chinese Americans who rushed to buy tickets found that they could not be had at any price. Wong Yee-bong of Detroit paid dearly for his faith in the consul: after traveling into occupied Guangdong in February to visit his dying wife, he escaped to Hong Kong that July but could not book any passage home. Lacking other options, he returned to his ancestral village and, during the war, sold everything he owned in order to stay alive.[118] The fact that he survived at all made him one of the luckier people in the Pearl River Delta.

AFTER PEARL HARBOR

On the morning of December 8, 1941, a group of fifteen Japanese airplanes bombed the Hong Kong airport at Kaitak in Kowloon, ending the illusion that the colony could remain aloof from the war in China. The Japanese, who had attacked Pearl Harbor just hours earlier, also raided Singapore, sank two battleships off Malaya, and landed troops in the Philippines that same day.[119] Less than two weeks later, Japanese troops overwhelmed Hong Kong's British garrison and crossed into the colony, shelling the downtown apartment building where Jun-ke Choy and his wife, Pei-tsung Wu, were then living. A marked man because of his work for the Nationalist government, Choy took cover in an opium den in the city's slums before fleeing with his wife to the Portuguese colony of Macao, where they lived in hiding for the next two years. Across the harbor in Kowloon Tong, Norman Soong raced to his office, later calling his wife, Irma Tam Soong, and instructing her to burn all his newspaper clippings and letters. Once the Japanese captured the colony, the couple fled, splitting up for safety and only reuniting in Chongqing.[120]

Like the Soongs and the Choys, Chinese Americans of all backgrounds rushed to escape from Hong Kong when the Japanese crossed the border. Customs chief Loy Chang, who turned down the offer of a seat on US consul Clarence Gauss's departing plane, later fled with his wife through Guangdong into Free China. Chu Shea Wai, now manager of Look Poong Shan's old Bank of Canton in Hong Kong, escaped by boat and eventually reached Guilin in Free China. California native Elsie Chin Yuen Seetoo, a Pooi To graduate doing her nurse training at Hong Kong Island's Queen Mary Hospital, slipped back to her ancestral village in Toisan with two friends and her US citizen brother, a Hong Kong government immigration officer.[121] Several other Chinese American citizen students also sought shelter in their parents' ancestral villages in the Pearl River Delta, while one young man walked all the way to unoccupied Hunan.[122]

Chinese Americans who chose to stay in Hong Kong became easy prey for local collaborators knowledgeable about the compact colony.[123] In November 1942, the Japanese secret police seized Bill Hong Sling and imprisoned him on suspicion of spying for the Allies. Held in jail for a hellish six months, Hong Sling lived in a tiny, filthy cell crammed with more than a dozen other men, and he watched helplessly as the Japanese beat, tortured, and allowed their dogs to maul prisoners, including his nephew, who did not survive.[124] After a collaborator claimed that another American, Wong Pui, was a spy, Japanese gendarmes arrested, tortured, and killed him too.[125]

In Shanghai, Japanese forces on December 8 occupied the International Settlement and exerted more control over the Vichy-run French Concession, ending the *gudao* period and forcing Chinese Americans to decide whether to flee, try to blend in with the Chinese population, or announce themselves as US citizens. In Young, who had sold Nash automobiles in the city for more than a decade, now lost his business to confiscation and made his way with his wife and children to Chongqing. Aviator Tom Gunn's sister Mae Tom Owyang and her husband, George Owyang, also fled Shanghai, eventually finding their way to unoccupied Yunnan.[126] Most other Chinese Americans stayed put, uncertain about the future in Shanghai yet unwilling to make the tremendously risky trip into Free China.

Japanese officials in Shanghai viewed ethnic Chinese as less threatening than white US citizens, who more visibly represented the enemy, so the occupiers imposed fewer restrictions on Chinese Americans. After Pearl Harbor, Andrew Zane and William Yukon Chang both turned themselves in to the occupiers, who "city interned" them. "I was taken to the Camp because of the fact that I was not afraid to recognize myself as an American citizen," Zane explained. "I was subsequently released on the grounds of my Chinese knowledge [but] during the entire period of the war I had to report to the Police Station each month, wearing [an] air raid arm band [and] was regarded wherever I went as an enemy." The "air raid arm band" was red, with a black "A" for "American." Although this system left Chinese Americans free to move about Shanghai, they lived a hand-to-mouth existence, unable to access money in US banks and forced to compete with the rest of the population for increasingly scarce food, clothing, and fuel. "Those were years of cold winters and scanty meals," Chang recalled a few years later. "I eked out a living buying and selling on the black-market everything that had a value and demand including firewood, rice, quinine, bicycle tires, moth balls and woolen yarn." Zane and Chang were among the luckier US citizens.[127] Between 1942 and 1943, the Japanese interned not only all the white civilian enemy aliens in Shanghai but also a handful of Chinese Americans.[128]

Elsewhere in China, the Japanese took a similar view of Chinese Americans, whose citizenship status made them enemy aliens but whose ancestry now protected them to a certain degree. Dr. James Yee was still living in Beijing and working at the American-controlled PUMC when the Japanese attacked Pearl Harbor. He glanced out the window of his operating suite on December 8 and saw Japanese troops marching up to the gate of the hospital, his first indication that it was no longer a protected space. Yee's younger son, Robert, who was born during the occupation, notes that the Japanese did not imprison his father or his mother, Marian, also a doctor at PUMC and a derivative US citizen. After all, the rhetoric of fighting white colonialism under Japanese leadership in the "Greater East Asia Co-Prosperity Sphere" meant that the occupiers "did not want the populace to see Chinese being marched down the streets to concentration camps." Still, Japanese officials pressured the Yees to renounce their US citizenship, and when the couple refused, they lost their jobs and only made due with loans from the neutral Swiss Embassy, a last resort for destitute Americans in occupied China. Like Chinese American citizens in Shanghai, the Yees wore armbands denoting their enemy alien status and could move about Beijing during the day. Still, the Japanese required them to live in a detention center at night. James delivered both of the couple's sons, who were born in the center during the war.[129]

RESISTANCE OR COLLABORATION

Chinese Americans who had once taken refuge from American racism and GMD repression in the treaty port world now struggled to decide just how much they would accommodate or resist Japanese demands. In particular, they weighed immediate survival needs against the potential consequences of acting against not just one but two governments with claims on them: the Nationalist regime and the United States. Many of the immigrants felt considerable ambivalence about both nations, which had long denied them full membership. Nevertheless, the very nature of the war—of war in general—made fence sitting almost impossible.

Despite Japanese vigilance, a handful of Chinese American citizens actively resisted the occupation. During the conflict, the Chinese American explorer Jack T. Young returned to Shanghai as an Office of Strategic Services (OSS) agent in an attempt to collect information about Japanese positions, communications, and officials.[130] As he surveyed the occupied city, Young came to depend on his wife's aunt Ruth Moy, who had stayed in Shanghai to protect her family's house in the French Concession after her husband, Ernest, fled to Chongqing in 1940. At great personal risk, Moy made the home a safe house for Young and a small group of agents working with him. Moy's son Loring, still a teenager, also surreptitiously took valuable photographs for OSS reports.[131] Few Chinese Americans followed the Moys' example, however. Active resistance required not only great courage but also a deep enough faith in the American or Nationalist cause—and the belief that it would prevail—to make such tremendous risks seem worthwhile.

More often, Chinese Americans who remained "free" in occupied China negotiated the extent to which they would collaborate or curry favor with the representatives of the new order or their allies. In other words, the immigrants made the same calculations as millions of other Chinese hoping to survive the war.[132] Aviation instructor Henry K. Chan quit his job when Japan attacked the United States, after which Japanese officials jailed and slowly starved him. Finally, he broke down and agreed to teach English, but not flying, to civilian Japanese in Shanghai—a degree of accommodation, but not full capitulation. Similarly, Flora Belle Jan scrambled to help pay her family's bills by writing a social column for the *Peking Chronicle* while facing "the insults of God knows whom because the *Chronicle* is controlled by the Regime." Poy Gum Lee, attempting to support his wife, children, and grown siblings, accepted a position teaching architecture to Japanese and Chinese students at St. John's University. During the occupation, an OSS informant contended that Ruth Moy's in-laws, Alfred Lee and Alice Moy Lee, who had proclaimed their patriotism before Pearl Harbor, "are cunning fence sitters, have glib tongues. . . . are for whoever happens to win, and also they were seen constantly with the Japanese in public." Similarly, Samuel Orne Moy (no relation), who was trapped in China when the war began, survived by socializing with Nazi officials and some collaborators but did not collaborate himself.[133] Already accustomed to living between two nations, many Chinese Americans showed considerable skill at balancing the various forces now demanding their acquiescence.

FIGURE 19. After Pearl Harbor, Illinois native Ruth K. Moy remained in her family's Shanghai residence, which she turned into a safe house for undercover American intelligence agents. National Archives and Records Administration, San Bruno regional facility.

Like active resistance, active collaboration required a level of commitment that most Chinese Americans lacked. In demonstrating such commitment, however, Herbert Moy, the star broadcaster for Nazi radio station XGRS, showed that the Japanese occupiers and the regimes they sponsored were even less adept at wooing Chinese Americans than their GMD predecessors had been. After Pearl Harbor, Moy preferred to remain with the German station, despite Japanese attempts to convince him to broadcast for Tokyo.[134] Moy's service to the Nazis provided him a handsome income but also enabled him to walk a tightrope between acknowledging Japanese power and refusing to directly support it. The FCC's Foreign Broadcast Intelligence Service monitors reported that Moy was critical of the US-backed Chongqing regime of Chiang Kai-shek but at the same time "will have no part of Wang Ching-wei or the Nanking crowd, refusing to be associated with any propaganda for them. His sympathies are with the Chinese people, and he claims to be one of them."[135] Fear now drove Moy's behavior, but so did the sentiments that so many Chinese Americans who arrived during the Nanjing Decade felt: an affinity for an imaginary, denationalized China and a deep dislike of the actual governments that claimed it.

If Herbert Moy symbolized the disaffection of the 1930s immigrants, Russell Chen embodied the disillusionment of the previous generation of modernizers. A third-generation American, he had attended some of the nation's finest universities, yet in the midst of the booming 1920s, he still had to emigrate to China to find work. Chen originally joined the Reformed Government of China in 1938, a period of US neutrality, but he stayed in the Legislative Yuan after the 1940 establishment of Wang Jingwei's "Reorganized Government of the Republic of China," the Japanese attack on Pearl Harbor, and the Wang regime's 1943 declaration of war on the United States.[136] Historian Timothy Brook argues that "the leaders of the occupation state did indeed make statements expressing support for Japan's pan-Asianist pitch, but it is very difficult to find any genuine evidence that more than a few took Japanese war aims seriously."[137] Chen may have been one of the few true believers, at least in the early years of the war. The Japanese actively recruited him and those in his wife's family's circle, including men like Tong Shao-yi, whom the GMD had largely sidelined. The puppet government also found a place for his longtime friend Kentwell, a man whom both the Nationalists and the British disdained and even mocked.[138] Whatever regrets he may eventually have felt, Russell Chen wholeheartedly and voluntarily collaborated for several years because the puppet government was the first he ever encountered that valued him, his family, and his friends.

DESPERATION IN THE VILLAGES

In the south, far more Chinese Americans experienced the Japanese occupation as a seemingly unending series of natural disasters and manmade calamities than as an opportunity for wealth and power. By 1942 remittances from abroad stopped, Japanese forces routinely seized farmers' produce, and a drought parched the Pearl River Delta. Together, these developments proved catastrophic for thousands of overseas Chinese families in the delta counties, including Chinese American citizens of all ages. As historian Madeline Hsu has shown, the residents of areas such as Toisan had over the decades grown tremendously dependent on relatives working overseas. Many had no idea how to farm their own land, which they had long since leased to tenants anyway. "Their resources were ones that could not be eaten: education, houses, and gold jewelry," Hsu explains.[139] By late 1942, Chinese Constitutionalist Party leader and overseas activist Dai-ming Lee agonized, "The means of sustenance have almost been cut . . . [and] the people of the so-called 'Four Districts,' particularly Toy-shan, have died because of hunger by more than one-half of their number." A missionary in Toisan reported, "It is a common sight to see a whole village desolate and overrun with long grass" because all the residents had died or fled.[140] In 1942 a handful of desperate Chinese American citizens managed to cross into neutral Macao, but the situation there grew increasingly dire, too, because of the nearby famine. One Chinese American youth who spent much of the war in the Portuguese colony contracted such bad dysentery—a common famine disease—that he later recalled being "laid up . . . for almost a year." Jun-ke Choy lived in hiding in Macao until mid-1943 and secretly wrote to the colonial governor that without official action, "the class who cannot leave Macao . . . will all die of starvation (for it is reported that about 100 are dying daily)."[141]

Chinese American citizens in the nearby Pearl River Delta villages struggled both to feed themselves and to comprehend the horrors around them. US citizen students dropped out of school when remittances from America dried up, and many who could not farm sold their possessions to pay for food.[142] American siblings who had traveled to the south to study together in their ancestral villages frequently became separated after attempting to flee Japanese troops.[143] One Chinese American, whom the Japanese briefly detained, later lamented that during his imprisonment "all my clothes and belongings were looted, [and] I had a hard time all through the war."[144] Worst of all, Chinese American citizens watched parents and friends die of starvation because of the famine that gripped the overseas districts between 1942 and 1944.[145] Lee Yow-Lim's experience was common: his father died during the Japanese bombing of Guangzhou in 1938, and he lost his mother in 1944 when she and many other residents of her village starved.[146] Fear, hunger, and despair eventually prompted numerous Chinese American citizens in the south to try to escape to Free China.

END OF THE ROAD: FREE CHINA

Chinese Americans who fled to unoccupied China after 1941 came to understand more than almost any other group the extent of the war's destruction, the pervasive corruption in both the legitimate and the collaborationist Chinese regimes, and the potential power of their US citizenship. Those who slipped out of Shanghai, Hong Kong, the Pearl River Delta, and other parts of coastal China passed through areas that had, even before the war, been some of the country's least developed regions. Most also traveled at a time when the conflict between the Japanese and the Nationalists had turned into a war of attrition in which smugglers and corrupt officials on both sides barely hid their activities and interactions. A few months after the war began, the veteran Chinese American journalist Hin Wong extolled life in Free China, contending that "both the people and the government have passed the 1938 New Year holidays without any pessimism; and in a way, cheerfully, while realizing that this would be the hardest and the darkest in physical and material sufferings, it would also be most glorious and brightest in history and the future."[147] However, Wong died of cancer a year later, and by 1943 other Americans who followed his path into the Nationalist-controlled areas merely saw corruption, venality, and grinding poverty as well as the "steady and quite open [smuggling] traffic across . . . the boundary between occupied and Free China" that US consular officials described with dismay.[148] In addition to such activity and widespread social disintegration, those who passed through northern and central China also noticed the unmistakable signs of the deep, terrible famine that was strangling the life out of Henan.[149]

For Chinese American students from Guangdong, life in Free China was often their first extended exposure to the Nationalist regime, and it proved a disillusioning experience that left many determined to return to the United States if and when escape became possible. The GMD government appeared incompetent or simply absent in many of the places it supposedly controlled. A Chinese American Pui Ching student who followed the school into Free China remembered frequently going without food while robbers targeted him with impunity because of the lack of any law enforcement.[150] Immense inflation constantly ate away at the value of the money Chinese American citizens could scrape together. Making matters even worse, the GMD government forced families abroad to remit funds to unoccupied China at an artificially low exchange rate. This reduced the value of remittances by three-quarters while enriching the government-controlled banks.[151]

Even Chinese American refugees who had wholeheartedly supported the GMD after 1937 found conditions in the interior shocking enough to make them question the basic honesty of the Nationalist regime. Displaced people clogged the roads, creating an unending flow of exhaustion and despair. As before the war, however, those with connections to the right officials were able to move far more quickly and easily. When Irma Tam Soong traveled inland, she noted with relief that her husband's "contacts got us transportation on an ammunition truck Chungking [Chongqing]-bound," a luxury most refugees did not enjoy.[152] Ettie Toy-Len Chin, an American teaching at Ginling College, informed friends back home that the well-connected president of her institution had booked passage for her and her students on a boat to Chongqing. "We are lucky indeed because I understand that there are about 20,000 people waiting at Ichang [Yichang] for passage up the river," she said.[153]

Chinese American immigrants who reached Free China's major cities and sought work there discovered that even in wartime, politics, factionalism, and connections remained more important to the GMD leadership than competence, experience, and ability. In 1940, after members of the New York GMD branch scathingly critiqued Minister to Brazil Samuel S. Young, party leaders cashiered him and recalled him to Chongqing; he spent the rest of the war there with no discernable occupation, despite his English fluency, education, experience with infrastructure development, and years of diplomatic service.[154] Party leaders also ignored former general Moy Quong-poy, who died in Hong Kong in 1940, and they kept trained military engineer George Bow at arm's length for the entire war, placing him at the head of the Salt Administration in a remote area of unoccupied Guangdong.[155] After Art Lym and his wife, Sarah Chuck, made their way to Chongqing, the only agency willing to hire the veteran pilot was the US government's Foreign Economic Administration, where Lym helped coordinate supply transport with the China National Aviation Corporation.[156] None of these longtime supporters of the government enjoyed ties to a powerful faction or the assistance of a patron in the party's inner circle. Younger Chinese Americans with even fewer connections had no chance to serve the GMD government in Chongqing, regardless of their training.

While living conditions in Free China depressed the immigrant refugees, many of them also perceived a general social, military, and political breakdown there that more deeply shook their faith in the regime's future. Now with the Chinese Red Cross in Guiyang, the former Hong Kong nurse trainee Elsie Chin Yuen Seetoo noticed that in the face of Japanese advances, the Nationalist soldiers "were not putting up a defense. . . . They just [kept] on retreating, that's all." Her acquaintanceship with a former classmate in the Communist base areas also caught the government's attention, and she began to fear for her life.[157] In Chongqing, vermin, heat, lack of dependable transportation, and inflation exhausted Flora Belle Jan, who arrived there from Beijing in 1944. After a burglar broke into her home, though, she described the experience not just as frustrating but as reflective of the pitiless and unprincipled culture of Free China, which seemed to lack a crucial sense of common purpose. "Robberies of this kind are very common in this city," she wrote resignedly. "Even secondhand goods are worth so much that many people prefer to steal and sell rather than to hold a legitimate job."[158] Jun-ke Choy shared Jan's opinion of the moral rot in the wartime capital. In 1943 an acquaintance's threat to expose him to the Japanese convinced him to finally leave Macao, despite the fact that his dying wife could not accompany him. Choy made his way to Chongqing, but what he observed there profoundly disheartened him. "There was no coordinated command; one order from one department countermanded that of the other, and Chiang could cancel them all," he recalled. "The general inefficiency and political corruption in Chungking did not provide bright hopes for the future."[159]

The practices of many of the white Americans who worked in Free China also discouraged Chinese American refugees seeking to contribute to the war effort there. In Chongqing, Flora Belle Jan found a job with the US Office of War Information, but her boss paid her and the other Chinese American citizen employee the same low wages as Chinese citizen employees rather than at the US citizen staff rate. "It is hard to be born a woman, but hopeless to have been born Chinese!" she declared. Irma Tam Soong worked for an American missionary office in Chongqing, where, "though other American offices were paying their secretaries high, comfortable salaries, my salary remained the same as when I first started," despite galloping inflation.[160] Ernest Moy helped manage a unit of the War Area Service Corps, a Chinese organization for welcoming US soldiers, but constantly contended with a stream of often petty and demeaning complaints from American military personnel about sanitary conditions and food.[161] These US refugees realized with great frustration that the war had not changed the negative attitudes of many white Americans about all people of Chinese ancestry.

At the same time, Chinese American refugees noticed that certain ethnic Chinese, most of them sent directly from the United States, filled positions unimaginable in prewar years. In Chongqing, General Joseph Stilwell, commander of the China-Burma-India Theater, relied heavily on his Chinese Hawaiian aide, Lieutenant Richard Ming-Tong Young, while OSS Major Jack Young became a well-known presence in the capital after his return from Shanghai.[162] During the war, Kunming also emerged as a major center for Chinese American servicemen and servicewomen. Posted in the city with her Chinese Red Cross unit, Elsie Chin Yuen Seetoo eventually worked out a way to get a commission with the US Army Nurse Corps. One of her fellow

Chinese American officers was Captain Emily Ying Wee Lee Shek, a New York native, onetime Hong Kong resident, and Women's Army Corps and OSS officer. She made target studies of the occupied British colony while hoping that her husband and children were still alive there.[163] The pilots and support staff of the largely Chinese American Fourteenth Air Service Group also thronged the streets of Kunming.[164] Immigrant refugees envied all these Chinese Americans, who wore US uniforms and enjoyed steady salaries, status, and, best of all, guaranteed access to food, clothing, and shelter.

THE IMMIGRANTS RETURN

Worn down by living conditions and demoralized by the Nationalist government, most Chinese American citizen refugees who managed to reach Free China tried to leave for the United States as soon as possible. Only those with positions in one of the regime's agencies, such as Ernest Moy, Chu Shea Wai, and Loy Chang, chose to remain, while ordinary immigrants and modernizers alike sought to flee. Flora Belle Jan tried almost immediately to find a way to get herself and her children back to America after her 1944 arrival in Chongqing. When Irma Tam Soong's war correspondent husband, Norman, transferred to the Pacific theater, she jumped at the opportunity to leave the Chinese wartime capital. Engineer Michael Foon Ching arrived in Kunming in 1940, and his wife, the dental surgeon Nancy Ngan Sin Loo Ching, joined him there after the fall of Hong Kong; in 1943, however, the two boarded a plane bound for India with the United States their final destination. Former Shanghai car dealer In Young tried to get himself and his family out of Chongqing, too, but they had to wait until the end of the war to leave for the United States. George Taikin Owyang and Maye Tom Owyang were more fortunate, escaping Yunnan for America in 1944. Even Nationalist official Jun-ke Choy, who had served China in one capacity or another since 1912, applied for temporary home leave in 1944 and, after receiving it, left Chongqing for America without telling Chinese officials that he had no plans ever to return.[165]

For scores of Chinese Americans refugees, the reality of life in Free China undermined whatever remaining faith they still had in the stability, competence, and integrity of the GMD regime. Students from the south probably felt the greatest sense of disillusionment; most had lived under Nationalist rule for only a brief period between the fall of Chen Jitang in 1936 and the

Japanese occupation of Guangdong in 1938. Such people's experiences with the regime before arriving in Free China were limited to a few New Life Movement slogans and some largely unimplemented policies. Now, they realized that the party leaders whom they believed would bravely lead China against Japan seemed more adept at lining their own pockets than at running an efficient government. In contrast, the many Chinese Americans who had lived in Nationalist-controlled areas of central and northern China before the war were already familiar with the cronyism and corruption that characterized the government.

Still, the degree to which these problems worsened during the war, despite the pressing need for national unity and common purpose, made a profound impression on almost all of the Chinese American citizens who once dreamed of playing some role in building a stronger China. Of course, many Chinese American immigrants in Free China rediscovered the racist attitudes of white Americans, yet they were also impressed by the sight of ethnic Chinese serving as officers in the US military and specialists in American agencies. Forced to contemplate where their futures would now be, the vast majority of the immigrants gambled on this vision of incremental progress. China's future under GMD rule simply seemed far too bleak.

As many of the immigrants in Free China sensed, the United States to which they wished to return was slowly becoming a more hospitable place for Chinese Americans than the nation they had left behind years before. In its wartime propaganda, Japan used racist American immigration laws to remind the Chinese and other people of color that the United States refused to admit Asians or grant them citizenship.[166] In response, the US Congress in 1943 reluctantly passed the Chinese Exclusion Repeal Act, which also allowed Chinese to naturalize and created a tiny token quota for Chinese immigrants. In addition, America's need for manpower pushed employers, the military, and the US government to recruit significant numbers of women and people of color for the first time. Chinese Americans, both alien and citizen, now streamed into the US military, the defense industry, and the mainstream economy, and they also participated in wartime coalitions for civil rights. Entrenched, systematic racial discrimination continued to limit their opportunities long after the war, but never again were their horizons quite as narrow as they had been in previous decades.[167]

Conclusion

For almost forty years, Chinese American immigrants in China managed to exist simultaneously in the American state and in the Chinese nation. In part, this reflected their recognitions of the benefits of US citizenship, but like other immigrants' children, they also felt both an affinity for their parents' homeland and an admiration for the United States' professed ideals of liberty, democracy, and equality. While the racism and discrimination they faced in the land of their birth left them deeply disillusioned, so did the corruption, nepotism, and anti-Westernism they encountered in China. As a result, few Chinese American citizens in China expressed exclusive or racialized views of nationalism. And while they often described their Chineseness as an unchanging essence, it was in fact a dynamic ethnic, racial, and cultural identity forged both in diverse urban America and in China's treaty ports, concession areas, overseas counties, and warlord states. Most modernizers were professed Chinese patriots who simultaneously acted as evangelists for American science, law, education, systems of government, and technology. Their citizen merchant and student peers often identified more closely with treaty port society and other overseas Chinese than with ordinary Chinese citizens.

Officials in either country might have resolved the issues that dual citizenship created by treating Chinese Americans as full citizens, but instead, the two nations never bothered to create a truly satisfying place in their respective societies for such people. Racial discrimination in the United States meant that full membership in the American nation remained exclusive of all but white citizens. Full membership in the Chinese nation also eluded Chinese

American citizen immigrants for cultural, social, and, eventually, political reasons. While the Guomindang claimed from the early 1920s that all overseas Chinese belonged to the Chinese nation, one significant way in which party leaders built that nation was by casting overseas Chinese as potentially seditious agents of Western cultural values and imperialism.

What enabled Chinese Americans in China to withstand the resulting pressure from both the US and Chinese governments for so long was the existence of the colonies, foreign concessions, quasi-independent warlord territories, and overlapping and often conflicting citizenship statuses that created economic, social, and educational opportunities for them while protecting their often ambiguous identities. The Pacific War eliminated such protections and in the process helped end the Chinese American exodus to China. Of course, the war made travel between the two countries almost impossible, but it also destroyed much of the overseas Chinese world in which thousands of US citizen emigrants had once moved and thrived. During the Nanjing Decade, the Nationalists did their best to change the terms of that world, attacking extraterritoriality, upholding jus sanguinis citizenship, and seeking to influence and control the overseas Chinese populations inside and outside of China. The Japanese invasion and occupation of China and Southeast Asia and attack on Pearl Harbor reshaped the overseas Chinese world far more radically, however. Out of consideration for ally China, Britain and the United States in 1943 repudiated extraterritoriality and agreed to accept Chinese control of the old concession areas.[1] Elsewhere in Asia, the Japanese fanned the flames of existing anti-colonialism, undercutting the position of the ethnic Chinese who often served as intermediaries between European colonizers and their subject peoples. Such moves helped topple the pillars of the prewar overseas Chinese world, with its vague boundaries, overlapping jurisdictions, and complicated citizenship and nationality statuses. The Chinese civil war and its aftermath then eliminated what was left of that world's economic foundations.[2]

After World War II, the US government, which had for decades stringently policed immigration *from* China, also moved to restrict for the first time the emigration of Chinese American citizens *to* China. As the United States grew more involved in East and Southeast Asia, the possibility that some Chinese American citizens might choose the People's Republic of China (PRC) over the land of their birth threatened to provide valuable propaganda for the new communist regime. US authorities also felt particular concern that Chinese

Americans who visited family in China by slipping across the border at Hong Kong might become indoctrinated with communist ideas and return to the United States to spread them.[3]

Ironically, the prewar US government had actually supported and encouraged Chinese government policies intended to assert control over America's ethnic Chinese citizens. While imperial powers such as Britain, France, and Holland sought to maintain jurisdiction over their ethnic Chinese subjects in China, the United States happily ceded control over its dual citizens to a series of prewar Chinese regimes. US consular officials ostensibly based this decision, solidified in the Chu Shea Wai case, on international law, but the choice largely reflected American racial nationalism. After all, the US government never even tried to preserve its authority over Chinese American citizens in China by negotiating a treaty with that country, as officials had done with "white" nations such as Germany and France.[4]

Instead, State Department officials in China actively undermined the meaning and value of Chinese American citizenship there. American diplomats routinely denied protection to Chinese Americans but not to their white counterparts by interpreting the same behaviors and decisions—marriage to a foreigner, the decision to wear certain clothing, the ability to speak English, the desire to start a business—in dramatically different ways based on the race of the citizen in question. In some cases, consular staff and State Department employees relied on discriminatory immigration policies to justify their actions, while at other points, they defied US law and neglected their own jobs, violating the 1907 Expatriation Act's clear protections of the native born.

The State Department did so in part because it had learned that Chinese governments cared about US mistreatment of ethnic Chinese only when it took place abroad. In dealing with Chinese Americans in China, Department officials discovered that treating them with disrespect—even outright contempt—and ignoring their citizenship rights actually made the US government seem more sympathetic to Chinese nationalism. More to the point, it gave consuls a bargaining chip that enabled them to protect the special privileges of white Americans—and to maintain white supremacy in China while claiming to support Chinese nationalism and sovereignty. American officials routinely congratulated themselves for the supposed fairness of their country's "Open Door Policy" in China, but their treatment of Chinese American citizens showed that they had the same goal as their British, French, Dutch, and Japanese colleagues: maintaining their nation's privileges and power in China.[5]

Chinese American immigrants' struggle to avoid becoming pawns in the Sino-American relationship meant that by the 1930s, their China had come to consist largely of the liminal spaces in which they could define Chineseness and Americanness for themselves. This China included American-run institutions, Shanghai's foreign concessions, the Pearl River Delta, and Hong Kong, in-between zones where the immigrants rejected both the GMD regime's exclusive model of citizenship and the US government's racialized one. But war, an extreme expression of nationalism, compels people to pick sides even if they do not genuinely wish to do so, and the war in China was no different. It forced Chinese Americans to make excruciating choices that reflected their deeper feelings not just about loyalty and identity, but about safety and survival. In the end, most chose America.

Epilogue

After a two-month journey from Chongqing by plane, train, and ship, Jun-ke Choy finally arrived at the port of Los Angeles in February 1945. Now 54, he had spent his entire adult life working for various Chinese regimes, but he wondered what his efforts had accomplished. His wife, who was too sick to flee to Free China with him, had died in Macao in 1944. He had not seen any of his children since 1941. And he had lost faith in both the Nationalist regime and in his ability to improve China's future. "My wife had been needlessly sacrificed to help China win the war," he lamented, "and I had wasted the best part of my life trying to help and serve the people of my ancestors." Now he just wanted to go back to America and start what he called his "second life."[1] Choy was hardly alone. Almost every Chinese American citizen who stayed in China during the war returned to the United States after the conflict ended, while very few who fled the country between 1937 and 1941 ever returned to rebuild.

By 1946 Chinese American citizens were pouring out of China. The first group to leave consisted mainly of Chinese Americans from the south who had emigrated to Guangdong and Hong Kong in the prewar years. In the first months of 1946, the reopened US consulate in Guangzhou finally offered repatriation assistance to such people, if they could establish in some way their right to return to the United States. By fall of that year, about fifteen hundred Chinese American citizens had left, including scores of young adults whose parents sent them to China during the Depression.[2] Survivors of war and famine, most had lost touch with their families in the United States after Pearl

Harbor. They often struggled to speak or write in English or to recall the American names they had once used, like Mabel, Loretta, and Billie. Some had started families of their own, but far more had watched friends and relatives die of starvation. Whatever their experiences, they were now united in a common goal: to return to the United States, with its safety, comfort, and plenty.

Even the handful of modernizers who chose to stay after 1945 eventually left China for good after the Chinese civil war began again. Paul Ball Young and Ching Leong Young, Ruth Moy, Dr. John Y. T. Woo, Luther Jee, Ernest K. Moy, Andrew Fong Zane, and Lau Waan-wai all remained in China after 1945 but departed between 1946 and 1950.[3] Women's Army Corps and OSS officer Emily Lee Shek managed to reach Hong Kong in 1945, only to discover that a bomb had fallen on her family home, killing her mother-in-law, father-in-law, and husband. Her son survived because the Japanese sent him to a labor camp elsewhere, and now she took him back to America for good.[4] H. C. Mei finally retired to the United States in 1947 after trying without success to rebuild his law practice in Shanghai.[5] Frank Lee, who had renounced his US citizenship in 1913, was serving as a special advisor to China's United Nations delegation when the Communists took over the Chinese mainland. He died in 1956 not far from the place he had grown up in New York City and where his three children also now lived.[6]

Age and career status often determined how well Chinese Americans readjusted to life in the land of their birth. Many of the young, single people who came back to the United States between 1937 and 1941 initially struggled but eventually started careers when World War II created labor shortages and broke down some of the old racial barriers in the job market.[7] The Cold War continued this process, especially for younger Chinese American returnees. Like other people of color, they often took jobs in the public sector, where they encountered less racial discrimination than in private business.[8] Many of the young Hawaiians who attended St. John's University in the 1930s found jobs in the expanding postwar civil service, working as civil engineers, Veterans Administration (VA) doctors, and postal service employees.[9] Scores of other Chinese Americans used college credits and degrees earned in China to enter US universities and workplaces during and after the war. Marjorie Lew Kay returned to the University of Washington, graduated in 1940, worked as a dance instructor in New York and Boston, and earned a master's degree from Wellesley.[10] Dr. Flora Liu entered private practice in Fresno, California, after returning to the United States with a St. John's medical degree.[11] Former Lingnan University student Monroe Jang, who lived through the Japanese attack on Shanghai while waiting to leave the country in late 1937, founded the Monroe's clothing stores in the California Central Valley.[12] Tin Chong Goo, the former St. John's and Yenching University student whom the Japanese briefly kidnapped in 1937, eventually attended the University of Michigan Law School and practiced immigration law in Honolulu, where one of his colleagues was Nick Char.[13] St. John's graduate and *China Press* reporter William Yukon Chang finally settled in New York, where he worked in community development and, in the 1950s, began publishing the first English-language Chinese American newspaper in the city, the *Chinese-American Times*.[14]

Education and language divided the generations who emigrated to China and then returned during and after the war. Overall, modernizers tended to possess far more valuable credentials than their student and merchant peers, particularly as the US job market slowly opened to Chinese Americans. Dr. Stephen Hu, who once studied malaria at the Henry Lester Institute in prewar Shanghai, worked in mosquito control in postwar Hawaii before taking a position with the US Agency for International Development and eventually retiring as a research associate at Walter Reed Medical Center and Johns Hopkins.[15] Sau Ung Loo Chan, the lawyer who helped Jun-ke Choy save part of the China Merchants Steamship Company fleet before leaving Hong Kong in 1940, became the first Asian American woman to practice law in Hawaii, where she earned a reputation as a legal reformer and an expert in small estates.[16] Michael Foon Ching, once an engineer for the Shing Mun Dam in Hong Kong, became an engineer for the Department of the Interior in Washington, DC.[17] When James and Marian Yee returned to the United States, they had to repeat their residencies and internships, only completing their training when they were in their forties. But they, too, bounced back, with Marian Yee opening the first ophthalmology office in San Francisco's Chinatown and James Yee working for the VA.[18]

In contrast, many Chinese American citizen students returned to occupational choices that proved little different than their parents' had been. Stanley Chin Din, who came back to the United States in 1939, found work as a waiter in a New York Chinatown restaurant and later invested in a tiki lounge.[19] Kay Keong Woo joined the merchant marine, Jackson Woon clerked at a Chinese American grocery in Sacramento, and Charles Hong Wong waited tables and cooked at Chinese restaurants in Montana and Wyoming.[20] Tong Quong

FIGURE 20. Dr. James Yee with his sons, Robert and James, after World War II, while Dr. Yee was serving as a United Nations Refugee and Resettlement Agency officer in China. His wife, Marian, gave birth to the two boys during the Japanese occupation, when the couple was living in an enemy alien detention center in Beijing. Courtesy of Robert D. Yee.

Wong, whose merchant father Wong Fee Lee prospered in Deadwood, South Dakota, in the late nineteenth century, became well known as magician "Wan Wan San" in overseas Chinese communities across Southeast Asia. After the war, he finally returned to the United States with his wife, Sue Woon, and their children, but while he occasionally picked up gigs, Sue Woon supported the family by working in garment factories and a bakery.[21] Girls and women faced both racial and gender discrimination in the United States and experienced less social and economic mobility than many male student and merchant returnees. Lucille Poy cut her education short to come back to the United States in 1940 and marry the China-born Lem Fong Chan, with whom she ran a restaurant.[22] Lily and Annie Seid, who survived the war and famine in Toisan, married brothers from Arkansas, where the vast majority of Chinese Americans traditionally ran small provisions stores. Lily and her husband opened a hardware store in one tiny Mississippi Delta town, while Annie and her husband started a grocery in another one.[23]

In contrast, some young men who retained their English and came back to the United States early enough often benefited from postwar economic growth and opportunities. When brothers Omar and James Wing returned to the United States in 1946, they were eighteen and twenty years old, with no dependents. After completing college at the University of Tennessee, near where their father ran a grocery, James earned a PhD at Purdue and became a research chemist, while Omar did his graduate work in electrical engineering at MIT and Columbia and joined the faculty of the latter.[24] Many returnees who arrived in the United States before Pearl Harbor also served in the military and gained access to veterans' benefits afterward. After receiving a Bronze Star for his service in World War II, Kelly Hong Wong used his GI Bill to earn a graphic arts degree from Montana State University and became a successful interior designer.[25] Herbert K. Luke left China in 1940 and finished secondary school in Hawaii. After serving in the army at the end of World War II, he used the GI Bill to study architecture at the University of Michigan.[26] Army nurse Elsie Chin Yuen Seetoo arrived back in the United States in 1946 and used her GI Bill to earn a degree in nursing from the University of North Carolina at Greensboro.[27] Hazel Ying Lee was not as fortunate. Returning to America in 1938, she finally achieved her goal of serving as a military aviator after Pearl Harbor. The first Chinese American to fly for the Women Airforce Service Pilots (WASP), Lee died while trying to land at her Montana base in 1944.[28]

Many well-educated middle-aged professionals who had already established careers in China before the war never achieved the same degree of success and renown in America. Because of the Chinese civil war, social worker Lynne Lee Shew could not return to the Heungshan Benevolent Hospital, which she had founded in the early 1930s. Instead, she settled in San Francisco and lived quietly with her relatives there until her death while in Japan on vacation.[29] Jun-ke Choy—onetime mayor of Hangzhou, finance authority in Shanghai and Guangzhou, railroad official, and head of the China Merchants Steamship Company—traveled briefly to Nanjing in the late 1940s to represent the overseas Chinese–dominated Chinese Democratic Constitutionalist Party during talks to end the civil war. With another onetime immigrant, the Hawaiian journalist Dai-ming Lee, he also helped run the San Francisco *Chinese World* newspaper, which loathed both the Chiang regime and the Communists. Choy later worked as a banker and became active in local Democratic Party politics, but he never again wielded the kind of municipal or financial authority he had enjoyed during the 1920s and 1930s.[30] Poy Gum Lee, one of China's most famous architects in the 1930s, finally returned to the United States with his family in 1946. He was determined to rebuild his practice in China, but the civil war there changed his plans. Instead, Lee found work as an architect with the New York City Housing Authority, a position he held until his retirement in the early 1960s. A modest brick bungalow in Mineola, Long Island, replaced the gracious home the Lees had once occupied in Shanghai's French Concession.[31] Celebrated translator and drama critic George Kin Leung, who came back in 1937, volunteered for the US Army in 1942 and served for two years before working briefly as a wartime Chinese language instructor at Yale. The college let him go after the war, so he moved to New York's Lower East Side, where he worked as a court translator and moonlighted as a lecturer on Chinese topics and as a Chinese folk singer.[32]

Some returnees had lived so long in China that American immigration officials attempted to bar them from reentering the United States. Dr. John Woo spent his entire career in China until he and his family left in 1949. Prevented from entering the United States, he had to fight exclusion proceedings before being allowed to land in Hawaii, his birthplace.[33] Another Hawaii native, Kenneth Young, was a graduate of both St. John's University and its medical school and owned his own practice in Shanghai and Tianjin for many years. In 1949 he left his diplomas and all his papers behind when he fled from the communists to Hong Kong, where he spent the next four years establishing his US citizenship and right to return to America. When he finally arrived in New York, he confessed to a former teacher, "I now find myself with nothing to prove that I am a graduate of St. John's and the School of Medicine; and [am thus] a doctor without a license!"[34]

While most Chinese American citizen immigrants returned to the United States, a handful stayed in Asia, especially in Hong Kong, which remained central to the remnants of the Cantonese-speaking overseas Chinese world. The Hong Sling brothers never went back to the United States except to visit. Once Harry Hong Sling was able to return to Hong Kong, he continued his career as a successful real estate investor, while his brother Bill Hong Sling remained a cricket and lawn bowling champion in the colony for decades.[35] In early 1949, Louey Shuck's son James Jung Yan Louie served in W. W. Yen's non-partisan peace delegation, which unsuccessfully attempted to end the Chinese civil war.[36] After the failure of these negotiations, Louie fled to Hong Kong, where he appears to have remained for the rest of his life.[37] His sister Francis Lui Au also stayed in Hong Kong until after her husband's death in 1959 and then returned to the San Francisco Bay Area, where her daughter, Aida, lived. She died there in 1966. Her sons Lincoln and Duncan, who both worked for Asian airlines, eventually retired to the United States as well.[38]

Chinese American Guomindang loyalists who stayed in Asia usually chose Hong Kong over Taiwan, hinting at the unpopularity of Chiang Kai-shek with a group of people mostly loyal to the long dead Sun Yat-sen. While Chu Shea Wai never bothered to go back to the United States, the country that abandoned him in 1925, he also chose not to follow the GMD to Taiwan. The man who had once lived on "Overseas Merchant Street" in Guangzhou now settled in Hong Kong, where he became well known for his involvement with the Daxia University Alumni Association.[39] Similarly, Sun Yat-sen's old bodyguard George Y. S. Bow also chose not to follow the GMD to Taiwan, despite his long service to the party. Resettling in Timor, he worked as an engineer until the climate affected his health, and he died as he was planning his return to Hong Kong.[40] Although Nationalist customs official Loy Chang did follow the ROC regime to Taiwan, his children settled in America, and after his retirement, he and his wife joined them there.[41]

Whatever their politics, most of the modernizers who returned to or remained in Hong Kong never fully regained their economic footing there, or the kind of social status they had enjoyed in prewar China. Samuel Sung Young, the former diplomat for both the Beiyang and Nationalist regimes, found a position as a bursar at St. Paul's Co-educational College in Hong Kong and worked there until his retirement in 1954. At the time of his death in 1957, two of his five children lived in the United States, while two were in the PRC.[42] Art Lym and his family fled to Hong Kong just ahead of the communist takeover. Lym, who was 59, had spent most of his adult life in China and was in failing health due to stress-related high blood pressure. Without the funds to afford anything better, his family crowded into a tiny flat in Hong Kong and lived off the salary of his older daughter, who worked at the new Civil Air Transport company and moonlighted as a piano teacher. Lym attempted to regain his US citizenship in 1953, but the State Department rejected him because of his work for the Nationalist Air Force. He died in Hong Kong in 1962.[43]

As Art Lym discovered, the war often destroyed health as well as careers. Flora Belle Jan left Chongqing in 1945 and found work as a newspaper editor in Shanghai, but she still struggled to earn enough to help support her family, and she continued to dream of returning to the United States. "I cannot say when I am coming back to America, but I shall come, if it is just to die," she wrote to her childhood best friend in 1947. "Everything in China is revolting to me." In early 1949, Jan finally reached the United States with her two daughters, but the hardships of the war in Beijing and Chongqing had prematurely aged her. She died from high blood pressure at age 43, succumbing less than a year after her return to the United States.[44] In Young also lived barely long enough to get back to America with his family, dying in 1948.[45] Louey Shuck, the onetime comprador and wealthy merchant, never returned to Asia after his last trip to America in 1940. Already in poor health at that time, he died in California in 1953.[46]

The stress of those years destroyed marriages too. Norman Soong's work as a war correspondent kept him away from his family for months at a time, and he and Irma Tam Soong divorced just a few years after the conflict.[47] Anna Faith Lee Liao, whose husband, Thomas Wen-I Liao, led the postwar Taiwan Independence League, sold black market medicine to support herself and her children in postwar Hong Kong. She managed to pay for their return to the United States in 1951, but Thomas stayed in Asia. According to her granddaughter, after her return to New York, she "never spoke of her husband or Taiwan again."[48] The war also broke up Ernest and Ruth Moy; she had survived in occupied Shanghai while her husband stayed in Free China, and the distance seems to have undermined their marriage. Ruth Moy went back to the United States in 1948, settling near Fort Ord with her new husband, Lt. Peter Kim. In 1951 the US government awarded her the Medal of Freedom, its highest civilian honor, for her bravery in gathering intelligence during the Japanese occupation of Shanghai.[49] Ernest Moy left China in 1950, but he struggled to reestablish himself in New York as an anti-communist journalist. Although he helped found the organization Aid Refugee Chinese Intellectuals to relocate educated Chinese refugees from Hong Kong, the group eventually pushed him out.[50]

Ernest Moy could never escape the shadow of Herbert Moy's disloyalty, even though he had publicly condemned his now-dead brother.[51] On August 15, 1945, the day the Japanese surrendered, Herbert Moy came to work as usual but drank heavily throughout the evening. According to the police who investigated his death, a deeply inebriated Moy eventually locked himself in a colleague's empty third-floor office, slashed his own throat with his late father's razor, and flung himself out the window to his death.[52] Given the unlikely nature of this scenario, rumors swirled around Shanghai that Japanese military officers had held a macabre farewell banquet for the broadcaster before murdering him and dumping his body in the garden of the German Embassy.[53] Regardless of the truth, for the next decade, American officials confused Ernest with Herbert; they also mistakenly linked the anti-communist Ernest to Eugene Moy, the former editor of the *China Daily News*, a communist-backed New York newspaper under investigation by the Federal Bureau of Investigation (FBI). Frustrated with his life and increasingly feeling his age, Ernest Moy committed suicide in Taipei, Taiwan, in 1958.[54]

Collaboration hampered the lives and careers of other Chinese American immigrants in the years after the war. While Samuel Orne Moy socialized with Nazis in wartime Shanghai, he likely never met Herbert Moy. Still, because of his surname and former associates, he struggled to escape from Herbert Moy's reputation, and after he returned to the United States and secured a job at Wright-Patterson Air Force Base, the FBI spent several years investigating his wartime actions.[55] He arguably fared better than Henry K. Chan, the young aviation instructor whom Nationalist officials imprisoned for collaboration after the war.[56] Lily Soo-hoo Sung's husband, William Z. L. Sung, stood trial for treason after the conflict and received an eighteen-month prison sentence from the GMD regime for accepting a position in Wang Jingwei's puppet government. After his release, the couple emigrated to America, where Soohoo regained her citizenship and Sung became a US citizen too.[57] In contrast, Lillian Loo Kiang never again saw her husband, Jiang Kang-hu, after he left the United States in 1939. Like Sung, Jiang stood trial for treason after the war, but the Chiang regime considered his actions far worse than Sung's. Left behind when the Nationalists fled to Taiwan, Jiang became a prisoner of the communists and died in their custody in 1954. His wife took the autobiography he had written and sent to her while in prison in 1948 and put it in a safe-deposit box. She did not look at it again for more than forty years.[58]

Not all collaborators faced punishment, however. In 1947 Anthony Leefong Ahlo's wife and children inserted a small item in the *South China Morning Post* in memory of the former diplomat, who had died in 1943 near Haiphong in Japanese-occupied Indochina.[59] He did not live to face the consequences of doing business with the Japanese, although the Nationalist regime found his friend Lawrence Klindt Kentwell guilty of treason.[60] Russell Chen, another friend of Kentwell's and an official in two Japanese puppet governments in wartime China, avoided Kentwell's fate entirely. At some point in 1945, he and his family slipped over the border into Hong Kong, which after the war became known to at least some critics as the "Paradise of Collaborators."[61] Having resumed the use of his English name, Chen by the mid-1950s worked for the shipping firm Ralli Brothers and may even have visited the United States in 1962.[62] Despite committing treason against both the Nationalist regime and the United States government, Russell Chen died of old age in Hong Kong in 1982. A few years earlier, his daughter Gladys and her husband had emigrated to the United States.[63]

NOTES ABBREVIATIONS

AH.	Institute of Modern History, Academia Historica, Taipei, Taiwan
ARCGI.	*Annual Report of the Commissioner-General of Immigration to the Secretary of Commerce and Labor* (Washington, DC: USGPO)
BFO.	British Foreign Office Files for China, Archives Direct (Adam Matthew database)
CP.	*China Press* (Shanghai)
CT.	*Canton Times* (Guangzhou)
CWR.	*China Weekly Review* (Shanghai)
DGB.	*Da Gong Bao* (city varies by date)
FRUS.	*Papers Relating to the Foreign Relations of the United States* (Washington, DC: USGPO)
MR.	*Millard's Review/Millard's Review of the Far East* (Shanghai)
NARA-CP.	National Archives and Records Administration facility, College Park, Maryland
NARA-NY.	National Archives and Records Administration regional office, New York, New York
NARA-SB.	National Archives and Records Administration regional office, San Bruno, California
NARA-SEA.	National Archives and Records Administration regional office, Seattle, Washington
NCH.	*North-China Herald and Supreme Court & Consular Gazette* (Shanghai)

NYT.	*New York Times*
PCA.	*Pacific Commercial Advertiser* (Honolulu)
SB.	*Shen Bao* (Shanghai)
SCMP.	*South China Morning Post* (Hong Kong)
SFC.	*San Francisco Chronicle*
SMP.	"Policing the Shanghai International Settlement" collection, Shanghai Municipal Police Files, 1894–1945 (Gale Group Archives Unbound database)
SRRPC.	Survey of Race Relations on the Pacific Coast, Hoover Institution, Stanford, California
ST.	*Shanghai Times*
TLU.	Archives of the Trustees of Lingnan University, Yale Divinity School Library, New Haven, Connecticut
United Board.	Archives of the United Board for Christian Higher Education in Asia, Yale Divinity School Library, New Haven, Connecticut
USCRA.	US Consular Registration Applications, 1916–1925 (Provo: Ancestry.com Operations, Inc., 2012)
USPA.	US Passport Applications, 1795–1925 (Provo: Ancestry.com Operations, Inc., 2007)
WR.	*The Weekly Review* (Shanghai)
ZGMD.	*Zhongguo guomindang* records, Hoover Institution, Stanford, California

NOTES

INTRODUCTION

1. Detlef Hanson testimony, June 20, 1910, p. 1, Louey Shuck file (9170/3528), NARA-SB; Wah Shuck and Louey Shuck passport applications, 1900, 1904, USPA; Louey Shuck or Wah Shuck, Certificate of Registration of American Citizen, Oct. 26, 1908, p. 7, Hong Kong consulate vol. 513, RG 84, NARA-CP.

2. Yen-p'ing Hao, "A 'New Class' in China's Treaty Ports: The Rise of the Comprador-Merchants," *Business History Review* 44, no. 4 (1970): 447–48; Josephine Fox, "Common Sense in Shanghai: The Shanghai General Chamber of Commerce and Political Legitimacy in Republican China," *History Workshop Journal* 50 (2000): 39.

3. As Beth Lew Williams argues in *The Chinese Must Go: Violence, Exclusion, and the Making of the Alien in America* (Cambridge: Harvard University Press, 2018), the 1882 Act, originally called the Chinese Restriction Act, proved fairly ineffective for its first few years until Congress essentially revised it into a law bent on exclusion rather than restriction. Still, the Chinese population of the United States did begin to shrink considerably after this point, despite the continued immigration of laborers unlawfully and merchants lawfully. US Bureau of the Census, *Census Bulletin 127: Chinese and Japanese in the United States* (Washington, DC: USGPO, 1914), 7. Federal court decisions before 1882 had declared that Chinese aliens were ineligible for citizenship, but the Exclusion Act codified this.

4. United States v. Wong Kim Ark, 169 U.S. 649 (1898).

5. Yucheng Qin, *The Diplomacy of Nationalism: The Six Companies and China's Policy Toward Exclusion* (Honolulu: University of Hawaii Press, 2009), 134–38; Erika Lee, *At America's Gates: Chinese Immigration during the Exclusion Era, 1882–1943* (Chapel Hill: University of North Carolina Press, 2003), 89–91; Yong Chen, *Chinese San Francisco, 1850–1943: A Trans-Pacific Community* (Stanford: Stanford University Press, 2000), 151–52.

6. US Bureau of the Census, *Compendium of the Tenth Census, Part I* (Washington, DC: USGPO, 1885), 557; US Bureau of the Census, *Census Bulletin 127*, 7, 10,16, 21; US Bureau of the Census, *Census Reports, Vol. I, Twelfth Census of the United States, Taken in the Year 1900* (Washington, DC: USGPO, 1901), xvii.

7. 1910 *ARCGI*, 110, 112; 1911 *ARCGI*, 114; 1912 *ARCGI*, 164, 166; 191; 1913 *ARCGI*, 144, 148; 1914 *ARCGI*, 152, 156; 1915 *ARCGI*, 173, 176; 1916 *ARCGI*, 134, 140.

8. John Higham, *Strangers in the Land: Patterns of American Nativism, 1860–1925* (New York: Athaneum, 1963), 165–75; Mae M. Ngai, "The Architecture of Race in American Immigration Law: A Reexamination of the Immigration Act of 1924," *Journal of American History* 86, no. 1 (June 1999): 70.

9. James D. Phelan, "Why the Chinese Should Be Excluded," *North American Review* 173, no. 540 (1901): 673.

10. Sarah E. Simons, "Social Assimilation. V." *American Journal of Sociology* 7, no. 4 (1902): 542.

11. Prasenjit Duara, "Transnationalism and the Predicament of Sovereignty in China," *American Historical Review* 104, no. 4 (Oct. 1997): 1043–48.

12. For a more in-depth discussion of many of these ideas, see Frank Dikotter, *The Discourse of Race in Modern China* (Stanford: Stanford University Press, 1992).

13. Qin, *The Diplomacy of Nationalism*, 19; Philip A. Kuhn, *Chinese among Others: Emigration in Modern Times* (New York: Rowman and Littlefield, 2009), 22–30.

14. Tsai Chutung, "The Chinese Nationality Law, 1909," *American Journal of International Law* 4, no. 2 (1910): 405–11.

15. Shao Dan, "Chinese by Definition: Nationality Law, Jus Sanguinis, and State Succession, 1909–1980," *Twentieth Century China* 35, no. 1 (2009): 19–26.

16. Soon Keong Ong, "Chinese but Not Quite: Huaqiao and the Marginalization of the Overseas Chinese," *Journal of Chinese Overseas* 9 (2013): 4. See also John Fitzgerald, "The Misconceived Revolution: State and Society in China's Nationalist Revolution, 1923–26," *Journal of Asian Studies* 49, no. 2 (1990): 329.

17. Scholars of Asian American history who mention the exodus invariably do so briefly, relying on part of a chapter from Gloria Heyung Chun, *Of Orphans and Warriors: Inventing Chinese American Culture and Identity* (New Brunswick: Rutgers University Press, 1999), 21–33, which discusses the *debate* about emigrating rather than the ongoing emigration. Two exceptions are Haiming Liu, *The Transnational History of a Chinese Family: Immigrant Letters, Family Business, and Reverse Migration* (New Brunswick: Rutgers University Press, 2005), which devotes part of one chapter to some of the members of a Chinese American family who "returned" to China; and K. Scott Wong, *Americans First: Chinese Americans and the Second World War* (Philadelphia: Temple University Press, 2005), 11–17, which also discusses the emigration briefly.

18. Richard Alba and Nancy Foner, *Strangers No More: Immigration and the Challenges of Integration in North America and Western Europe* (Princeton: Princeton University Press, 2015), 12.

19. See, for example, Donna R. Gabaccia, "Is Everywhere Nowhere? Nomads, Nations, and the Immigrant Paradigm of United States History," *Journal of American*

History 86, no. 3 (1999): 1115–17; Günter Moltmann, "American-German Return Migration in the Nineteenth and Early Twentieth Centuries," *Central European History* 13, no. 4 (1980): 378–80; Neil Larry Shumsky, "'Let No Man Stop to Plunder!' American Hostility to Return Migration, 1890–1924," *Journal of American Ethnic History* 11, no. 2 (1992): 56; Nancy Foner, *From Ellis Island to JFK: New York's Two Great Waves of Immigration* (New Haven: Yale University Press, 2000), 10, 172–75; Thomas A. Guglielmo, *White on Arrival: Italians, Race, Color, and Power in Chicago, 1890–1945* (New York: Oxford University Press, 2003), 15–16; Robert L. Fleegler, *Ellis Island Nation: Immigration Policy and American Identity in the Twentieth Century* (Philadelphia: University of Pennsylvania Press, 2013), 4–5; and, tellingly, Mark Wyman, *Round-Trip to America: The Immigrants Return to Europe, 1880–1930* (Ithaca: Cornell University Press, 1993), 4–14. Among others, the Oxford American Dictionary and Merriam Webster's Dictionary define the term *immigrant* this way.

20. See, for example, Melissa R. Klapper, *Small Strangers: The Experiences of Immigrant Children in America, 1880–1925* (New York: Ivan Dee, 2007), 16; John Radziłowski, "Born a Gypsy: Secondary Migration and Spatial Change in Two Polish Immigrant Communities, 1880–1925," *Polish American Studies* 66, no. 2 (2009): 74; Andrew Rolle, "The Immigrant Experience: Reflections of a Lifetime," *Italian Americana* 19, no. 1 (2001): 38.

21. Edith C. Wong, Eileen French, and Rose Estep Fosha, "Deadwood's Pioneer Merchant: Wong Fee Lee and His Wing Tsue Bazaar," *South Dakota History* 39, no. 4 (2009): 283–300; Edward and Nancy Wong family history website, accessed May 23, 2016, imedwong.yolasite.com/grandparents.php; Liping Zhu, "Ethnic Oasis: Chinese Immigrants in the Frontier Black Hills," in *Ethnic Oasis: The Chinese in the Black Hills*, ed. Liping Zhu and Rose Estep Fosha (Pierre, SD: South Dakota State Historical Society Press, 2004), 7–9, 20–21, 38; Wong Tom Quong, "Certificate of Registration of American Citizen," Oct. 10, 1908, p. 1, and Wong King Sowe, Wong King Que, Wong Faye King, Wong Faye Jucks, Wong Tong Quong, Wong Faye Launde, "Certificate of Registration of American Citizen," Nov. 15, 1908, p. 1, all in Canton consulate volume 670, RG 84, NARA-CP. The children's father, Wong Fee Lee, accompanied them, returning to the United States in 1904 with only his infant child.

22. *SFC*, "Will Refund Special Tax," Sept. 27, 1904, 11; *SFC*, "Chinese Boy Is Running an Undertaking Establishment to Keep Himself in School," Aug. 16, 1903, 3; Judy Yung, *Unbound Feet: A Social History of Chinese Women in San Francisco* (Berkeley: University of California Press, 1995), 125–30. Despite some expansion of course offerings in the 1910s, a Chinese American graduate of the school criticized it in 1921 for the "insufficient" education it offered and for producing many students for whom high school "is difficult . . . in every way." Mary Bo-tze Lee, "Problems of the Segregated School for Asiatics in San Francisco" (master's thesis, University of California, Berkeley, 1921), 34.

23. "List of American Citizens Residing in the Canton Consulate District," Dec. 31, 1914, p. 6, Canton consulate vol. 358, RG 84, NARA-CP; Lee Yuk Sue, "Cer-

tificate of Registration of American Citizen," Nov. 20, 1912, Hong Kong vol. 513, NARA-CP.

24. A number of financially successful China-born people who participated in the 1924 Survey of Race Relations on the Pacific Coast complained about the issue of social status. See, for example, C. H. Burnett, "Life History as a Social Document of Chin Cheung," Aug. 21, 1924, p. 6, file 187, box 27, and C. H. Burnett, "Social Document of Pany Lowe," July 5, 1924, p. 3, file 242, box 28, both in SRRPC.

25. Willie Hong Sling, Harry Hong Sling, and Jennie Hong Sling, "Certificate of Registration of American Citizen," Nov. 5, 1915, Hong Kong vol. 513.

26. Adam McKeown, "Conceptualizing Chinese Diasporas, 1842–1949," *Journal of Asian Studies* 58, no. 2 (1999): 307. This is a tendency that dates back to the Nanjing Decade. See, for example, Huang Jingchu, *Huaqiao mingren gushi lu* [Record of the stories of famous overseas Chinese] (Shanghai: Commercial Press, 1940); *Qishier lieshi zhong de huaqiao* [The seventy-two overseas Chinese martyrs] (Hong Kong: Haichao Publishing, c.1950s); *Guiqiao qiaojuan guiguo huaqiao xuesheng xianjin shiji huibian* [A compilation of the meritorious deeds of the returned overseas Chinese, overseas dependents, and overseas Chinese students] (Beijing: All China Returned Overseas Chinese Federation, 1959); Liu Boji (Pei Chi Liu), *Meiguo huaqiao shi, xubian* [History of the American overseas Chinese, sequel] (Taipei: Li Ming Cultural Enterprises, Ltd., 1981); Chen Min, *Minguo huaqiao mingren zhuanlüe* [Biography of prominent overseas Chinese of the republican era] (Beijing: China Overseas Chinese Publishing Company, 1991); Gong Bohong, ed., *Guangfu huaqiao huaren shi* [History of overseas Chinese from Guangdong] (Guangzhou: Guangdong Higher Education Publishing, 2003); Wang Yixin, *Women huijia: Xin zhongguo chuqi huaqiao guiguo ji* [We returned home: Overseas Chinese memories of returning to the nation in the early years of New China] (Jinan: Shandong People's Publishing House, 2013).

27. Among other scholars who have discussed these networks at length are Madeline Hsu, Elizabeth Sinn, and Adam McKeown. See also Henry Yu, "The Intermittent Rhythms of the Cantonese Pacific," in Donna R. Gabaccia, ed., *Connecting Seas and Connected Ocean Rims: Indian, Atlantic, and Pacific Oceans and China Seas Migrations from the 1830s to the 1930s* (Leiden: Brill, 2011), 395–96.

28. Elizabeth Sinn, *Pacific Crossing: California Gold, Chinese Migration, and the Making of Hong Kong* (Hong Kong: University of Hong Kong Press, 2013), 300.

29. Lizabeth Cohen, *A Consumers' Republic: The Politics of Mass Consumption in Postwar America* (New York: Vintage Books, 2003), 125; Elaine Tyler May, *Homeward Bound: American Families in the Cold War Era* (New York: Basic Books, 1988), 12–18; Chen Jian, *Mao's China and the Cold War* (Chapel Hill: University of North Carolina Press, 2001), 241–42; Denny Roy, *Taiwan: A Political History* (Ithaca: Cornell University Press, 2003), 88–90.

30. Ellen D. Wu, *The Color of Success: Asian Americans and the Origins of the Model Minority* (Princeton: Princeton University Press, 2014), 113, 123–26; Madeline Y. Hsu, *The Good Immigrants: How the Yellow Peril Became the Model Minority* (Princeton: Princeton University Press, 2015), 128–29; Mary L. Dudziak, *Cold War Civil Rights:*

Race and the Image of American Democracy (Princeton: Princeton University Press, 2000), 48–56.

31. James T. Campbell, *Middle Passages: African American Journeys to Africa, 1787–2005* (New York: Penguin, 2007), 103, 235–36, passim.

32. H.R. 10384; Pub. L. 301; 39 Stat. 874.

33. 1921 *ARCGI*, 26, 56.

34. See, for example, 1925 *ARCGI*, 33, 55, 82; 1926 *ARCGI*, 29, 76, 90; 1927 *ARCGI*, 29, 57, 75; 1928 *ARCGI*, 35, 59, 85; 1929 *ARCGI*, 35, 60–61, 77. Candice Lewis Bredbenner, in *A Nationality of Her Own: Women, Marriage, and the Law of Citizenship* (Berkeley: University of California Press, 1998), 225, discusses the way some (but not all) of those who departed permanently were American-born minors accompanying alien parents.

35. See, for example, Isabel Wilkerson, *The Warmth of Other Suns: The Epic Story of America's Great Migration* (New York: Vintage, 2011), 266; James N. Gregory, *The Southern Diaspora: How the Great Migrations of Black and White Southerners Transformed America* (Chapel Hill: University of North Carolina Press, 2005), 53–54; Nicholas Lemann, *The Promised Land: The Great Black Migration and How It Changed America* (New York: Vintage, 1992), 16; and Leah Platt Bouston, *Competition in the Promised Land: Black Migrants in Northern Cities and Labor Markets* (Princeton: Princeton University Press, 2017), 15. I use here the traditional periodization of the Great Migration, dividing it from the Second Great Migration (about 1940–1965).

36. Gary Gerstle discusses a similar but not identical phenomenon, the difference between racial nationalism and civic nationalism, in *American Crucible: Race and Nation in the Twentieth Century* (Princeton: Princeton University Press, 2001).

37. Yuzun Liu, Dehua Zheng, and Larry Lam, eds., *Hu Jingnan Wenji* [The collected works of Gilbert Woo] (Hong Kong: Xiangjiang Publishing Company, 1991), 558. Whiteness was and is a shifting category, as Woo acknowledged in other columns, but he and many other Chinese Americans suspected that however much it shifted, it would continue to exclude them.

CHAPTER 1

1. Ng Ah Tye, "Certificate of Registration of American Citizen," c. 1908, Hong Kong consulate vol. 513, RG 84, NARA-CP; *Crook County Journal* (Prineville, Oregon), "Japanese Bazaar," Jan. 2, 1901, 28; Cynthia A. Brandimarte, "Japanese Novelty Stores," *Winterthur Portfolio* 26, no. 1 (1991): 1–2. The "Tye" family's Chinese surname was Ng (Wu): 吳.

2. K. Scott Wong, *Americans First: Chinese Americans and the Second World War* (Philadelphia: Temple University Press, 2005), 11.

3. Erika Lee and Judy Yung, *Angel Island: Immigrant Gateway to America* (New York: Oxford University Press, 2010), 8–9; Lucy Salyer, *Laws Harsh as Tigers: Chinese Immigrants and the Shaping of Modern Immigration Law* (Chapel Hill: University of North Carolina Press, 1995), 58–68.

4. Craig Robertson, in *The Passport in America: The History of a Document* (New York: Oxford University Press, 2010), 178–81, describes the clash between the State Department and the Bureau of Immigration, which viewed Chinese American passports skeptically and relied on the Form 430, which its agents trusted, as evidence of citizenship. The form was also known as the "Native's Return Certificate."

5. Erika Lee, *At America's Gates: Chinese Immigration During the Exclusion Era, 1882–1943* (Chapel Hill: University of North Carolina Press, 2003), 91–92, 107; Salyer, *Laws Harsh as Tigers*, 57–68; Lee and Yung, *Angel Island*, 84.

6. John Higham, *Strangers in the Land: Patterns of American Nativism, 1860–1925* (New York: Atheneum, 1963), 77, 170.

7. See, for example, Man-Houng Lin, "Overseas Chinese Merchants and Multiple Nationality: A Means for Reducing Commercial Risk (1895–1935)," *Modern Asian Studies* 35, no. 4 (2001); Lisa Rose Mar, *Brokering Belonging: Chinese Canada's Exclusion Era, 1885–1945* (New York: Oxford University Press, 2010), 12–16, 71; Elliott Young, *Alien Nation: Chinese Migration in the Americas from the Coolie Era through World War II* (Chapel Hill: University of North Carolina Press, 2014), 118. The Spanish and Portuguese governments became infamous in Shanghai for selling certificates of protection to Chinese attempting to avoid their own government's reach. Sir Miles Lampson, "Chinese Nationality," Nov. 4, 1927, p. 1, file 371/12459, BFO.

8. Jung-Fang Tsai, *Hong Kong in Chinese History: Community and Social Unrest in the British Colony, 1842–1913* (New York: Columbia University Press, 1993), 23–34.

9. John M. Carroll, *Edge of Empires: Chinese Elites and British Colonials in Hong Kong* (Cambridge: Harvard University Press, 2005), 50, 100.

10. Elizabeth Sinn, *Pacific Crossing: California Gold, Chinese Migration, and the Making of Hong Kong* (Hong Kong: Hong Kong University Press, 2015), 302.

11. Carroll, *Edge of Empires*, 84.

12. Peter Zarrow, *After Empire: The Conceptual Transformation of the Chinese State, 1885–1924* (Stanford: Stanford University Press, 2012), 11. Despite reforms to the exam system between 1901 and 1905, it continued to emphasize the Confucian classics.

13. Denise Austin, *"Kingdom-Minded" People: Christian Identity and the Contributions of Chinese Business Christians* (Leiden: Brill, 2011), 39.

14. Carroll, *Edge of Empires*, 34, 86–88.

15. Madeline Hsu, *Dreaming of Gold, Dreaming of Home: Transnationalism and Migration between the United States and South China, 1882–1943* (Stanford: Stanford University Press, 2000), 9, 167–68.

16. Him Mark Lai, *Chinese American Transnational Politics*, ed. Madeline Y. Hsu (Urbana: University of Illinois Press, 2010), 10–13.

17. Historian Prasenjit Duara has shown that the Qing government in its last years sold titles and bestowed honors on Chinese abroad who donated to China, essentially providing an alternative route to prestige. However, the regime seems to have done this only in Southeast Asia and not in the United States. Prasenjit Duara, "Nationalists among Transnationals: Overseas Chinese and the Idea of China, 1900–1911," in

Aihwa Ong and Donald M. Nonini, eds., *Ungrounded Empires: The Cultural Politics of Modern Chinese Transnationalism* (New York: Routledge, 1996), 42–46.

18. Madeline Hsu, "Trading with Gold Mountain: *Jinshanzhuang* and Networks of Kinship and Native Place," in *Chinese American Transnationalism: The Flow of People, Resources, and Ideas between China and America during the Exclusion Era*, ed. Sucheng Chan (Philadelphia: Temple University Press, 2006), 27–33.

19. The US romanization of the characters for the firm was "Tsue Chong Wing." Chinese often called San Francisco, and sometimes California as a whole, "Gold Mountain" (*jinshan*) because of its association with the 1849 Gold Rush.

20. Zheng Zican, ed., *Xianggang shangyeren minglu* [Hong Kong business directory] (Hong Kong, 1910), 1; Zheng Zican, ed., *Xianggang shangyeren minglu*, v. 1 [Hong Kong business directory, v. 1] (Hong Kong, 1915), 16–78.

21. Hong Kong Census Office, "Report on the Census of the Colony for 1911" (Hong Kong: Hong Kong Legislative Council, 1911), 103.

22. The average male Chinese laborer ("coolie" in the terminology of the time) in Hong Kong earned about US$4.50 per month, at a time when the average male wage-earner in the United States earned about $50 per month. Even assuming higher living costs in the United States and lower wages for Chinese American men there because of racial discrimination, the disparity is still quite stark. William F. Spalding, *Eastern Exchange, Currency and Finance* (London: Pitman, 1918), 278–80; *Hong Kong Legislative Council Hansard/Votes and Proceedings, 1911*, Mar. 23, 1911, p. 46, accessed May 18, 2016, www.legco.gov.hk/1911/h110323.pdf; U.S. Bureau of the Census, *Census of Manufacturers: 1905—Earnings of Wage-Earners* (Washington, DC: USGPO, 1908), 11; 1910 exchange rates from the *SCMP*.

23. *SCMP*, "Out of Jurisdiction," Sept. 17, 1909, 2; *SCMP*, "Local and General," July 28, 1921, 2; Louey Shuck passport application, May 29, 1918, USPA.

24. Dong Wing, "Certificate of Registration of American Citizen," Aug. 5, 1909, Hong Kong vol. 513; Chin Hien Lee, "Application for Registration—Native Citizen," May 16, 1918, p. 1, USCRA Hong Kong; Lee Goon, "Application for Registration—Native Citizen," Dec. 9, 1919, p. 1, USCRA Hong Kong.

25. Wong Sun On, "Certificate of Registration of American Citizen," 1908, Hong Kong vol. 513; Wong Sun On, "Application for Registration—Native Citizen," Sept. 17, 1917, p. 1, USCRG, Hong Kong; N. A. Tye and Brothers advertisement, *SCMP*, May 3, 1913, 15; Ng Ah Tye, "Certificate of Registration of American Citizen," c. 1908, Hong Kong vol. 513.

26. *SCMP*, "Western Banking Methods," Mar. 25, 1912, 3.

27. Look Poong Shan, "Company Report," *SCMP*, Mar. 25, 1914, 11.

28. Jun-ke Choy, *My China Years: Practical Politics in China after the 1911 Revolution* (San Francisco: East/West Publishing, 1974), 68–71.

29. *SCMP*, "New Chinese Bank," Aug. 23, 1918, 6.

30. Chen Fulin, *Liao Zhongkai Nianpu* [Chronicle of Liao Zhongkai] (Changsha: Hunan Publishing House, 1991), 1–9. Sun Yat-sen also attended Queen's a few years earlier.

31. Willie Hong Sling, Harry Hong Sling, and Jennie Hong Sling, "Certificate of Registration of American Citizen," Nov. 5, 1915, Hong Kong vol. 513; *SCMP*, "Speech Day," Feb. 12, 1923, 12; *SCMP*, "Cricket," Oct. 26, 1925, 10; *SCMP*, "Local Baseball," Oct. 25, 1929, 6; *SCMP*, "Late Mr. Hong Sling," Jan. 28, 1937, 9; *SCMP*, "Mrs. Hong Sling," Nov. 18, 1948, 8; *Xianggang Gongshang Ribao* [Hong Kong Industry and Commerce Daily], "Tong Rongyao shishi" [Harry Hong Sling passes away], Dec. 8, 1969, 6.

32. *SCMP*, "School's Speech Day," Oct. 5, 1935, 9; *SCMP*, "Wedding Bells," July 2, 1934, 9.

33. *SCMP*, "The Bishop's Fall," Feb. 13, 1922, 3; *SCMP*, "Diocesan Girls School," Mar. 12, 1923, 3; *SCMP*, "Italian Convent School," Jan. 21, 1919, 10; *SCMP*, "Big Estate Settled," Oct. 12, 1928, 14; *SCMP*, "Help the Refugees," Feb. 16, 1915, 6.

34. Thom Y. Deck testimony, May 11, 1912, p. 2, Thom Wing Get file (56/988), NARA-NY; Chu Gum Fie, Mon Fie Chu, and Arthur Chu, "Certificate of Registration of American Citizen," 1907, pp. 92–94, Canton consulate vol. 670 RG 84, NARA-CP.

35. See, for example, Wat Gum, Wat Kum Lin, Wat Ging Hung, and Wat Kam Hung, "Certificate of Registration of American Citizen," 1907; Liu Ah Yee and Liu Ah Sam, "Certificate of Registration of American Citizen," 1907; Lee Young Fon, "Certificate of Registration of American Citizen," 1907, all in Canton vol. 670.

36. C. H. Burnett, "Life History and Social Document of Albert King," July 31, 1924, n.p., file 193, box 27, SRRPC.

37. Him Mark Lai, "Retention of the Chinese Heritage: Chinese Schools in America before World War II," *Chinese America: History and Perspectives* 14 (2000): 10–14.

38. Adam McKeown, "Transnational Chinese Families and Chinese Exclusion, 1875–1943," *Journal of American Ethnic History* 18, no. 2 (1999): 76.

39. Catharine Holt, "Interview with Mr. George Lem," Aug. 4, 1924, p. 3, file 298(7), box 30, SRRPC.

40. McKeown, "Transnational Chinese Families," 76.

41. William C. Smith interview with Louise Leung, Aug. 13, 1924, p. 1, file 63, box 34, SRRPC.

42. Untitled interview, Oct. 13, 1924, p. 10, file 233, box 28, SRRPC.

43. C. H. Burnett, "Life History as a Social Document of Mr. Chin Cheung," Aug. 21, 1924, pp. 4–5, file 187, box 27, SRRPC. See also Holt, "Interview with Mr. George Lem," p. 3; C. H. Burnett, "Life History and Social Document of Ying Foy," Aug. 11, 1924, p. 3, file 184, box 27, SRRPC; C. H. Burnett, "Life History of Mr. Woo Gen," July 29, 1924, n.p., file 183, box 27, SRRPC; C. H. Burnett, "Social Document of Pany Lowe," July 5, 1924, p. 3, file 242, box 28, SRRPC.

44. He Guohua, *Minguo Shiqi de Jiaoyu* [Education in the Republican Period] (Chaoguan, Guangdong: Guangdong People's Publishing House, 1996), 359–61.

45. Xiaoping Cong, *Teachers' Schools and the Making of the Modern Nation-State, 1897–1937* (Vancouver: University of British Columbia Press, 2007), 29–31, 38–39, 52–56, 63–70; Chi-Pao Cheng and W. T. Tao, "China's New System of Schools," *The Annals of the American Academy of Political and Social Science* 122 (1925): 104.

46. Edward Wong, "Magic Man," accessed Mar. 29, 2016, imedwong.yolasite.com/parents.php.

47. Eloise Fong, interview by Robin Li, 2011, p. 4, Regional Oral History Office, University of California, Berkeley, accessed Nov. 16, 2017, digitalassets.lib.berkeley.edu/roho/ucb/text/fong_eloise_2013.pdf.

48. Trustees of the Canton Christian College, *Canton Christian College, 1919–1924: Report of the President* (New York: Trustees of Canton Christian College, 1924), 25, file 1, box 67, TLU.

49. *Jiaoyu Zazhi* [Education Magazine] (Shanghai), "Diqijie quanguo jiaoyuhui lianhehui jilue" [A brief record of the seventh National Education Federation Conference], 14, no. 1 (1922): 24.

50. *Xinwen Zhoubao* [News Weekly], "Huaqiao zidi huiguo jiu xue banfa" [Handling the children of the overseas Chinese who return to the nation for education], 8, no. 31 (1931): 4.

51. Wen-hsin Yeh, *The Alienated Academy: Culture and Politics in Republican China, 1919–1937* (Cambridge: Council on East Asian Studies, 1999), 66–77.

52. Statement of Kong Yin Tet, Jan. 23, 1913, Kong Tet En file (C-512), NARA-SB.

53. Mary Lamberton, *St. John's University Shanghai, 1879–1951* (New York: United Board for Christian Colleges in China, 1955), 162; *Honolulu Evening Bulletin*, "Graduates with Honor," June 19, 1907, 1; Francis H. Woo, *Johanneans of Hawaii* (Honolulu: Hawaii Chinese History Center, 1981), 19–23; *China Weekly Review, Who's Who in China*, 4th ed. (Shanghai: China Weekly Review, 1931), 230.

54. Yeh, *The Alienated Academy*, 59–65.

55. For a more thorough discussion of the 1911 revolution, see Frederic Wakeman Jr., *The Fall of Imperial China* (New York: The Free Press, 1975), 248–51.

56. Marie-Claire Bergère, *Sun Yat-sen*, trans. Janet Lloyd (Stanford: Stanford University Press, 1998), 202–09.

57. Jerome Ch'en, *Yuan Shih-k'ai*, 2nd ed. (Stanford: Stanford University Press, 1972), 140–212.

58. Wakeman, *The Fall of Imperial China*, 248–51; Peter Zarrow, "Historical Trauma: Anti-Manchuism and Memories of Atrocity in Late Qing China," *History and Memory* 16, no. 2 (2004): 94.

59. F. L. Hawkes Pott, *St. John's University, 1879–1929* (Shanghai: Kelly and Walsh, 1929), 23.

60. Woo, *Johanneans of Hawaii*, 22–23.

61. Lee Young Fon, "Application for Registration as Native Citizen," USCRA Canton, Nov. 18, 1924; Lee Yuk Sue, "Certificate of Registration of American Citizen," 1913; Lau Lem, "Certificate of Registration of American Citizen," 1913; Low Qui Yuen, "Certificate of Registration of American Citizen," 1914; Foo Buck Hing, "Certificate of Registration of American Citizen," 1912; Louey Shuck, "Certificate of Registration of American Citizen," 1912, all in Canton vol. 670; *Huiyuan timinglu* [Membership roster], *Minyi* [Public Opinion] 4, no. 1, 1913.

62. Michael Tsin, *Nation, Governance, and Modernity in China: Canton, 1900–1927* (Stanford: Stanford University Press, 1999), 45–57.

63. Bergère, *Sun Yat-sen*, 246–99.

64. Lee Gee to US consulate, Canton, Jan. 30, 1916, pp. 1–2, Canton consulate vol. 367, RG 84, NARA-CP; Consul P. S. Heintzleman to Chu Ching Lan, May 26, 1917, pp. 1–2, Canton consulate vol. 397, RG 84, NARA-CP; *SCMP*, "Canton News," Oct. 28, 1916, 6; unsigned memo, Nov. 30, 1917, p. 1, Canton vol. 397.

65. Ho Tak Chiu to US consul, Feb. 27, 1918, pp. 1–2, Canton consulate vol. 403, RG 84, NARA-CP; Mo Yung Hsin to Albert Pontius, Dec. 28, 1918, p. 1, Canton vol. 403; Chang Chin Fang to Leo Bergholz, Jan. 8, 1920, p. 1, Canton consulate vol. 417, RG 84, NARA-CP; Leo Bergholz to Chang Chin Fang, Dec. 29, 1919, p. 1, Canton consulate vol. 409, RG 84, NARA-CP; Chan Sowe Tai to C. B. Meinhardt, Sept. 25, 1919, p. 1, Canton vol. 409.

66. 1916 *ARCGI*, 134, 140; 1917 *ARCGI*, 138, 141; 1918 *ARCGI*, 219, 222.

67. Robertson, *The Passport in America*, 187–88.

68. Lee Gee Shun to consul, Sept. 21, 1918, p. 1, Canton vol. 367.

69. Choy, *My China Years*, 83.

70. Bergère, *Sun Yat-sen*, 296; Hin Wong, "The Return of Kuomintang Rule in Kuangtung," *CWR*, Feb. 19, 1921, 641.

71. Kwok Min to US Consul, Aug. 28, 1916, p. 1, Canton vol. 367.

72. See, for example, Paul Josselyn to Chang Ming Chi, Feb. 29, 1916, p. 1, Canton vol. 367; Wei Pang Ping to P. S. Heintzleman, Dec. 26, 1917, p. 1, Canton vol. 397; F. B. Cheshire to Li Kai Shen, May 15, 1914, p. 1, Canton consulate vol. 350, RG 84, NARA-CP; Albert W. Pontius to the Fa Yuen Magistrate, Mar. 6, 1919, p. 1, Canton vol. 409.

73. For a contemporary understanding and definition of "extraterritoriality," see F. E. Hinckley, "Extraterritoriality in China," *Annals of the American Academy of Political and Social Science* 39 (1912).

74. See, for example, Chang Chin Fang to C. D. Meinhardt, Sept. 10, 1919, pp. 1–2, Canton vol. 409; R. P. Tenney to Eddie Jung, Mar. 14, 1923, p. 1, Canton consulate vol. 455, RG 84, NARA-CP; Frank W. Lee to US Vice Consul, June 15, 1922, pp. 1–2, Canton consulate vol. 442, RG 84, NARA-CP. That last case is particularly interesting because the Chinese official seeking to deny the validity of Chinese American citizenship claims was Frank William Lee Chinglun, a Chinese American born in New York who (as I will discuss in chapter 2) renounced his American citizenship in 1913.

75. Lin, "Overseas Chinese Merchants and Multiple Nationality," 995–96.

76. *American Journal of International Law*, "Dual Citizenship," 9, no. 4 (1915): 944–48.

77. Albert Pontius to the Secretary of State, Mar. 28, 1919, p. 1, Canton vol. 409.

78. F. D. Cheshire to George E. Anderson, Dec. 26, 1914, p. 1, Canton vol. 350.

79. Pontius to Secretary of State, p. 1; "Chin Wee Kok Protection Case," Nov. 3, 1924, p. 1, Canton consulate vol. 484, RG 84, NARA-CP; handwritten note on Louie Young to US consul, Aug. 2, 1920, p. 1, Canton vol. 417.

80. One famous example was Wai Yuen Nicholas Char, a Shanghai lawyer who served the Chinese government. I discuss this in depth in chapter 3.

81. See, for example, Chu Ching Lan to P.S. Heintzleman, Jan. 5, 1917, pp. 1–2, Canton vol. 397; Carl D. Meinhardt to US Attorney, Honolulu, Nov. 21, 1919, p. 2, Canton vol. 397; Albert W. Pontius to Frank Hennessy, Mar. 27, 1919, p. 1, Canton vol. 409. "Treaty ports" were the cities in which, by Sino-foreign treaty, foreign citizens could reside and do business.

82. Chinese Americans who participated in Chinese political parties included Daiming Lee (Chinese Constitutionalist Party); Mei Guangbei, a.k.a. Moy Quong-poy, a.k.a. Mei Kuang-bi (GMD); and Frank Lee Chinglun (GMD). Members of the military and related forces included Arthur F. Lym, Tom Gunn, and George Y. S. Bow; officials in various governments included Anthony Leefong Ahlo, Charles Wong Afook, Jun-ke Choy, and Mon Yin Chung.

83. Sir Shouson Chou and Dr. R.H. Kotewall, "Memorandum on the Status of British Subjects of Chinese Race," Oct. 1, 1927, p. 4, file FO 371/13203, BFO.

84. Eileen P. Scully, *Bargaining with the State from Afar: American Citizenship in Treaty Port China, 1844–1942* (New York: Columbia University Press, 2001), 86–107, 143–56.

85. Wilbur J. Carr to George E. Anderson, May 9, 1914, p. 1, Canton consulate vol. 349, RG 84, NARA-CP; Wilbur J. Carr to F.D. Cheshire, Mar. 2, 1914, p. 1, Canton vol. 349; "Lew Shee Protection Case," Oct. 17, 1924, p. 1, Canton vol. 484; C.D. Meinhardt to Yim Choy, Sept. 16, 1919, p. 1, Canton vol. 409.

86. "An Act in Reference to the Expatriation of Citizens and Their Protection Abroad," Mar. 1907, Office of the Law Revision Counsel, accessed Jan. 31, 2017, uscode.house.gov/statviewer.htm?volume=34&page=1228#. For more on the 1907 act, see Ben Herzog, *Revoking Citizenship: Expatriation in America from the Colonial Era to the War on Terror* (New York: New York University Press, 2015), 43.

87. In several cases, the Chinese Americans in question had emigrated to China before the regular issuance of the Form 430, meaning they had no travel documents available when denied a passport, unless they had returned previously and obtained a writ of habeas corpus. This made the purchase of a ship ticket to America almost impossible because ship companies feared paying potential deportation expenses.

88. Paul Monroe, *A Report on Education in China (for American Educational Authorities)* (New York: Institute of International Education, 1922), 9–10, 21–22; Ping-wen Kuo, *The Chinese System of Public Education* (New York: Columbia University Teachers College, 1915), 167–68.

89. See, for example, Mae Yuit Leu, "Application for Registration as Native Citizen," May 16, 1924, USCRA Canton.

90. See, for example, Oscar Lee, "Application for Registration as Native Citizen," Apr. 21, 1920, USCRA Canton.

91. Burnett, "Chin Cheung," 4.

92. For instance, the postwar repatriation files of the US consulate in Guangzhou (Canton consulate vols. 697–700, RG 84, NARA-CP) contain about 150 records of Chinese Americans sent to China for education, some as late as 1940.

93. Gum Fie Chu, "Emergency Passport Application," Peking Legation, July 15, 1919, USPA.

94. Canton Christian College, *Catalogue of the College of Arts and Sciences, 1921–1922* (Guangzhou: Canton Christian College, 1921), 102.

95. Soon Keong Ong, "Chinese but Not Quite: *Huaqiao* and the Marginalization of the Overseas Chinese," *Journal of Chinese Overseas* 9 (2013): 24.

96. In the Boxer Protocol of 1901, which ended the anti-foreign Boxer Uprising, the Qing government promised to pay 450 million silver taels (plus interest) in reparations to the foreign powers. The US percentage of this was larger than what the country had demanded of China. In 1907 the US pledged to use the overage to support Chinese students who wanted to study in the United States; some of the funds helped establish Tsing Hua as a preparatory academy for these students.

97. *Educational Directory and Yearbook of China, 1917* (Shanghai: Educational Directory of China Publishing, 1917), 5.

98. Dong Wang, *Managing God's Higher Learning: U.S.-China Cultural Encounter and Canton Christian College (Lingnan University), 1888–1952* (Lanham, MD: Lexington Books, 2007), 35; Trustees of the Canton Christian College, *Canton Christian College, 1919–1924: Report of the President*, 21.

99. Presbyterian Church in the USA, *85th Annual Report of the Board of Foreign Missions of the Presbyterian Church in the U.S.A.* (New York: Presbyterian Church in the USA, 1922), 180.

100. He, *Minguo Shiqi de Jiaoyu*, 368.

101. Ong, "Chinese but Not Quite," 23, 28.

102. Yeh, *The Alienated Academy*, 10–12; St. John's University Shanghai, *Catalogue, 1919/1920* (Shanghai: St. John's University, 1919), 80, 82; Canton Christian College, *Catalogue of the College of Arts and Sciences, 1921–1922* (Guangzhou: Canton Christian College, 1921), 24, 36.

103. John Israel, "The Beida-Tsinghua Connection: Yenching in the World of Beijing's Elite Universities," *Journal of American-East Asian Relations*, 14 (2007), 64–66.

104. Jun Xing, "The American Social Gospel and the Chinese YMCA," *The Journal of American-East Asian Relations* 5, nos. 3/4 (1996): 280–81; Tsou Mingteh, "Christian Missionary as Confucian Intellectual: Gilbert Reid (1857–1927) and the Reform Movement in the Late Qing," in *Christianity in China: From the Eighteenth Century to the Present*, ed. Daniel Bays (Stanford: Stanford University Press, 1996), 87; Terrill V. Lautz, "The SVM and Transformation of the Protestant Mission to China," in *China's Christian Colleges: Cross-Cultural Connections, 1900–1950*, ed. Daniel H. Bays and Ellen Widmer (Stanford: Stanford University Press, 2009), 3–22.

105. Fong F. Sec, "Government and Mission Education in China," *Chinese Recorder*, Mar. 1, 1915, 158.

106. Herbert E. House, "English in Education in China," *Chinese Recorder*, Feb. 1, 1916, 98.

107. *Canton Christian College, 1919–1924: Report of the President*, 25.

108. "Canton Christian College: Girl Students," c. 1927, pp. 1–3, file 181:3252, RG 11, United Board; Canton Christian College, *Catalogue of the College of Arts and Sciences, 1921–1922*, 99–104.

109. "Canton Christian College: Girl Students," 3.

110. Canton Christian College, *Catalogue of the College of Arts and Sciences, 1921–1922*, 99–104; Canton Christian College, *Catalogue of the College of Arts and Sciences, 1917–1918* (Guangzhou: Canton Christian College, 1917), 28; "Canton Christian College: Girl Students," 1–3.

111. Charles Hodge Corbett, *Lingnan University: A Short History Based Primarily on the Records of the University's American Trustees* (New York: Trustees of Lingnan University, 1963), 68–71.

112. Hung Tak Shin and Hung Tak Sang, "Application for Registration—Native Citizen," Apr. 5, 1923; Edward Fook Leung, "Application for Registration—Native Citizen," Dec. 6, 1923; Lew Foot Jung, "Application for Registration—Native Citizen," Jan. 31, 1925, all in USCRA Canton.

113. Tsin, *Nation, Governance, and Modernity in China*, 58; *SCMP*, "Canton News," Feb. 6, 1920, 7; *SCMP*, "Canton News Letter," Dec. 20, 1921, 5; Shui on Shareholders' List, 1918, Canton vol. 403; Corbett, *Lingnan University*, 68–71.

114. Gee Ah Bow, "Application for Registration as Native Citizen," Dec. 30, 1918, USCRA Shanghai. A number of Chinese American citizens of this era gave China Agency and Trading as their address in Hong Kong, suggesting that it undertook several *jinshanzhuang* functions.

115. Hsu, *Dreaming of Gold, Dreaming of Home*, 41–49; Hsu, "Trading with Gold Mountain," 33.

116. H. A. Start to US Consul General, Apr. 1, 1918, p. 1, Canton vol. 403; Leo Bergholz to Li Chik-nam, Aug. 16, 1920, p. 1, Canton vol. 417; Lew Toy to Leo Bergholz, Aug. 29, 1920, pp. 1–2, Canton vol. 417; *CT*, "Dr. Andrew Wu Gayson," Oct. 3, 1919, 5; *CT*, "Shool [*sic*] for Chauffeurs," July 7, 1920, 8; Lew Toy, "Application for Registration as Native Citizen," Apr. 28, 1920, USCRA Canton.

117. Ong, "Chinese but Not Quite," 23, 28.

118. *NCH*, "Wedding," Aug. 6, 1921, 408; *SCMP*, "Mrs. S. H. Yeung," June 18, 1937, 3.

119. *SCMP*, "Local and General," July 28, 1921, 2. Theodora Yen appears to have been an orphan raised by her uncles.

120. Tungwah Hospital Group, "Board of Directors, 1919/1920," accessed Jan. 31, 2017, www.tungwah.org.hk/upload/CH/organization/bd/bd1919.pdf; Hong Kong YMCA, *Qingnianhui shiye gai yao* [An outline of the purpose of the YMCA] (Hong Kong: YMCA, 1918), 58; Carroll, *Edge of Empires*, 106.

121. William C. Smith, "Interview with Lillie Leung," Aug. 12, 1924, p. 1, file 76, box 25, SRRPC.

122. Yung, *Unbound Feet*, 108–16.

123. Lynne Lee Shew, "The Modern Chinese Girl," *China Review* I, no. 2 (August 1921): 80.

124. Kay Ann Johnson, *Women, the Family, and Peasant Revolution in China* (Chicago: University of Chicago Press, 1983), 27–29; Christine K. Gilmartin, *Engendering the Chinese Revolution: Radical Women, Communist Politics, and Mass Movements in the 1920s* (Berkeley: University of California Press, 1995), 19–24.

125. *NCH*, "Wu-Feng," Nov. 3, 1928, 189; *SCMP*, "Registry Wedding," Feb. 26, 1938, 5; *SCMP*, "Journalist Weds," Jan. 20, 1940, 5; *Directory and Chronicle for China, Japan, Corea, Indo-China, Straits Settlements, Malay States, Siam, Netherlands Indies, Borneo, the Philippines, and etc.* (Hong Kong: Hong Kong Daily Press, 1905), 348.

126. Jonathan D. Spence, *The Gate of Heavenly Peace: The Chinese and Their Revolution, 1895–1980* (New York: Penguin, 1981), 151–87; Tse-tung Chow, *The May Fourth Movement: Intellectual Revolution in Modern China* (Cambridge: Harvard University Press, 1960); Jeffrey Wasserstrom, *Student Protests in Twentieth-Century China: The View from Shanghai* (Stanford: Stanford University Press, 1991), 51–71.

127. Tsin, *Nation, Governance, and Modernity in China*, 73–74; *SCMP*, "Kiaochou Decision," May 13, 1919, 6.

128. He, *Minguo Shiqi de Jiaoyu*, 328.

129. "Daxue yuke" [College preparatory], *The Lingnaam Magazine*, III, no. 4 (December 1919): 111; *SCMP*, "Canton News," May 20, 1919, 7; *SCMP*, "Suppressing the Boycott," Sept. 25, 1919, 3.

130. *SCMP*, "Local and General," June 26, 1919, 2; *SCMP*, "Canton News," May 29, 1919, 6.

131. *SCMP*, "Canton News," June 10, 1919, 6.

132. *SCMP*, "The Boycott," June 2, 1919, 6.

133. Corbett, *Lingnan University*, 70–71; *SCMP*, "Canton News," Nov. 18, 1919, 6.

134. *SCMP*, "Canton Students Riot," Nov. 11, 1919, 6; *SCMP*, "The Students Parade," Dec. 11, 1919, 3; *SCMP*, "Canton Students and Tact," Dec. 11, 1919, 3.

135. Wen-Hsin Yeh, *Shanghai Splendor: A Cultural History* (Berkeley: University of California Press, 2007), 71–72; Sherman Cochran, *Big Business in China: Sino-Foreign Rivalry in the Cigarette Industry, 1890–1930* (Cambridge, Harvard University Press, 1980), 114–17.

136. US Bureau of the Census, *Fifteenth Census of the United States: 1930. Population, Vol. II: General Report, Statistics by Subject* (Washington, DC: USGPO, 1933), 34; 1920 *ARCGI*, 273, 276; 1921 *ARCGI*, 153, 156; 1922 *ARCGI*, 53, 145, 148; 1923 *ARCGI*, 70, 160, 161; 1924 *ARCGI*, 64, 157, 158; 1925 *ARCGI*, 55, 179; 1926 *ARCGI*, 54, 161; 1927 *ARCGI*, 57, 182; 1928 *ARCGI*, 59, 182; 1929 *ARCGI*, 60, 176; 1930 *ARCGI*, 93, 192.

CHAPTER 2

1. *SCPM*, "A Chinese Aviator's Romance," July 19, 1913, 12; Paddy Gully, *Shiguang feishi: zhongguo kongjun xianqu linfuyuan zhuan* [Time flies: The biography of Chinese

aviation pioneer Art Lym], trans. Zhang Chaoxia (Guangzhou: Huacheng Publishing, 2013), 47; Edward J. M. Rhoads, *China's Republican Revolution: The Case of Kwangtung, 1895–1913* (Cambridge: Harvard University Press, 1975), 259–60; Albert A. Altman and Harold Z. Schiffrin, "Sun Yat-sen and the Japanese, 1914–1916," *Modern Asian Studies* 6, no. 4 (1972): 387.

2. *SCMP*, "Chinese Aviator," Apr. 10, 1914, 2; *Maui News*, "First Aviation Meet Was Big Success," Nov. 1, 1913, 1; *The Garden Island* (Hawaii), "Grand Airship Carnival on Plains Near Koloa," Jan. 6, 1914, 3; *Singapore Free Press and Mercantile Advertiser*, "Aviation at Manila," July 3, 1914, 7; *Straits Times* (Singapore), "Chinese Aviator," July 22, 1915, 10; Chu Cheng letter, 1915, file 6629, series HUAN, reel 43, ZGMD; *MR*, "News from Canton," Sept. 20, 1919, 105; *SCMP*, "Today's Flying," Aug. 7, 1915, 3; *SCMP*, "Aviation at Macao," Aug. 31, 1915, 7; *SCMP*, "Flood Relief Fund," Aug. 20, 1915, 5; advertisement for Asiatic Petroleum Company Ltd., *SCMP*, Aug. 9, 1915, 3; *CT*, "Tom Gunn Returning with Horses, Dogs, and Aeroplanes," June 30, 1920, 8; *SCMP*, "For Sale," Aug. 11, 1920, 4; *CT*, "Country Correspondence," Sept. 22, 1919, 2; *Xianggang Huazi Ribao* [Chinese Mail, Hong Kong], "Tan gen hui yue xu wen" [More on Tom Gunn's return to Canton], Jan. 22, 1920, 3.

3. White Europeans and Americans could and did provide such expertise, yet their assistance came with a high price tag and rankled many patriotic Chinese. Shellen Wu, *Empires of Coal: Fueling China's Entry into the Modern World Order, 1860–1920* (Stanford: Stanford University Press, 2015), 122–23; Benjamin A. Elman, "Naval Warfare and the Refraction of China's Self-Strengthening Reforms into Scientific and Technological Failure, 1865–1895," *Modern Asian Studies* 38, no. 2 (2004): 292–301.

4. The same was the case for ethnic Chinese from Southeast Asia.

5. Jonathan D. Spence, *The Gate of Heavenly Peace: The Chinese and Their Revolution, 1895–1980* (New York: Penguin, 1981), 142–47, 159–69; Vera Schwarcz, *The Chinese Enlightenment: Intellectuals and the Legacy of the May Fourth Movement of 1919* (Berkeley: University of California Press, 1986), 59–127.

6. Lu Xun, "What Is Required of Us as Fathers Today," in *Lu Xun: Selected Works, Vol. II*, trans. Yang Xiangyi and Gladys Yang (Beijing: Foreign Languages Press, 1985), 64.

7. Rana Mitter, *Modern China: A Very Short Introduction* (New York: Oxford University Press, 2008), 15.

8. US Bureau of the Census, *Census Bulletin 127: Chinese and Japanese in the United States, 1910* (Washington, DC: USGPO, 1914), 11–12, 17–18, 25–29, 31–35.

9. Erika Lee, in *At America's Gates: Chinese Immigration during the Exclusion Era, 1882–1943* (Chapel Hill: University of North Carolina Press, 2003), 200–2, discusses the slippery definition of "merchant" status.

10. US Bureau of the Census, *Census Bulletin 127*, 11, 12, 21–24; Weili Ye, *Seeking Modernity in China's Name: Chinese Students in the United States, 1900–1927* (Stanford: Stanford University Press, 2001), 9; US Bureau of the Census, *Fourteenth Census of the United States, 1920: Population, Vol. IV: Occupations* (Washington, USGPO, 1923), 885, 1002, 1037, 1278; US Bureau of the Census, *Fifteenth Census of the United States, 1930: Population, Vol II: General Report* (Washington, DC: USGPO, 1933), 34.

11. *PCA*, "Leading Chinese Merchant Dead," July 4, 1906, 8; *Hawaiian Star*, "Ahlo's Estate," July 10, 1906, 5. Overseas Chinese merchants often formed families abroad while maintaining their primary wives in China. Lee Ahlo does not appear to have married more than once, however. His marriage would have placed him squarely in the mainstream in Hawaii, where many Chinese immigrant men married Hawaiian women.

12. *Evening Bulletin* (Honolulu), "Exercises at Punahou," June 25, 1897, 1; *Hawaiian Gazette*, "Yellow Dragon Flag Waves for the Emperor," Aug. 1, 1902, 6.

13. *Hawaiian Star*, "Ahlo on Chinese Reform," Sept. 20, 1901, 6; *Evening Bulletin*, "Ahlo Talks Reform," Sept. 18, 1901, 4.

14. *PCA*, "Island Boy a Reformer," Sept. 20, 1901, 3; *San Francisco Call*, "Chinese Nation under Misrule," Sept. 12, 1901, 9; *Hawaiian Star*, "Mystery of the Baggage," Sept. 19, 1901, 3.

15. The famous Malaya-born physician Wu Lien-teh, who attended Cambridge with Ahlo, remembered scrimping and saving to make his scholarship cover his expenses, while Ahlo spent his time outside of class playing the mandolin. Wu Lien-teh, *Plague Fighter: The Autobiography of a Modern Chinese Physician* (Cambridge: W. Heffer and Sons, Ltd., 1959), 169.

16. William Michael Morgan, *Pacific Gibraltar: U.S.-Japanese Rivalry over the Annexation of Hawai'i, 1885–1898* (Annapolis: Naval Institute Press, 2011), 145; *SFC*, "Died at Ninety-Eight," Feb. 15, 1905, 3; *Hawaiian Star*, "Ahlo on Chinese Reform," 6.

17. Shelley Lee, *A New History of Asian America* (New York: Routledge, 2013), 126; *PCA*, "Insurance Money Won," May 12, 1905, 8.

18. *Hawaiian Gazette*, "Young Chinese Licensed in Law," Jan. 22, 1904, 8; Beth L. Bailey and David Farber, *The First Strange Place: Race and Sex in World War II Hawaii* (Baltimore: Johns Hopkins Press, 1994), 24–27; Gary Y. Okihiro, *Cane Fires: The Anti-Japanese Movement in Hawaii, 1865–1945* (Philadelphia: Temple University Press, 1992), 13–15.

19. Mary Ting Yi Lui, *The Chinatown Trunk Mystery: Murder, Miscegenation, and Other Dangerous Encounters in Turn-of-the-Century New York City* (Princeton: Princeton University Press, 2007), 27–34.

20. Frank William Lee passport application, Feb. 6, 1908, USPA.

21. Charlotte Brooks, *Between Mao and McCarthy: Chinese American Politics in the Cold War Years* (Chicago: University of Chicago Press, 2015), 21; Scott D. Seligman, *Tong Wars: The Untold Story of Vice, Money, and Murder in New York's Chinatown* (New York: Viking, 2016), 1–77.

22. *CP*, "Prof. F. W. Lee Is Named Vice President of College," Dec. 15, 1926, 7.

23. *SFC*, "A Chinese Wedding," Nov. 4, 1881, 2; *Who's Who of American Returned Students* (Beijing: Tsing Hua College, 1917), 173–74; Mary Lockwood, "The Celestial Goes to School," *Potter's American Monthly* XV, no. 108 (December 1880): 446; Rev. D.O. Kelley, *History of the Diocese of California, from 1849 to 1914* (San Francisco: Bureau of Information and Supply, 1915), 85.

24. *SCMP*, "Sudden Death of Dr. Samuel S. Young," Jan. 9, 1958, 8.

25. Paul A. Cohen, *History in Three Keys: The Boxers in Event, Experience, and Myth* (New York: Columbia University Press, 1997), 16–56. See also Joseph Esherick, *The Origins of the Boxer Uprising* (Berkeley: University of California Press, 1988).

26. Zhongping Chen, *Modern China's Network Revolution: Chambers of Commerce and Sociopolitical Change in the Early Twentieth Century* (Stanford: Stanford University Press, 2011), 1–2, 56; Ya-pei Kuo, "'The Emperor and the People in One Body': The Worship of Confucius and Ritual Planning in the Xinzheng Reforms, 1902–1911," *Modern China*, 35, no. 2 (2009): 123–24; Mary Backus Rankin, "Nationalistic Contestation and Mobilization Politics: Practice and Rhetoric of Railway-Rights," *Modern China*, 28, no. 3 (2002): 317.

27. Rhoads, *China's Republican Revolution*, 65–70.

28. Yong Chen, *Chinese San Francisco, 1850–1943: A Trans-Pacific Community* (Stanford: Stanford University Press, 2000), 148–61.

29. Julia C. Strauss, "Creating 'Virtuous and Talented' Officials for the Twentieth Century: Discourse and Practice in Xinzheng China," *Modern Asian Studies*, 37, no. 4 (2003): 838–41; Xiaoqun Xu, *Chinese Professionals and the Republican State: The Rise of Professional Associations in Shanghai, 1912–1937* (Cambridge: Cambridge University Press, 2001), 4–5.

30. Him Mark Lai, "Retention of the Chinese Heritage: Chinese Schools in America before World War II," *Chinese America: History and Perspectives* 14 (2000): 10–13.

31. Most China-born people who attended university in the United States during the late Qing and early republican years were required to study such subjects. Madeline Hsu, *The Good Immigrants: How the Yellow Peril Became the Model Minority* (Princeton: Princeton University Press, 2015), 47–48.

32. US Bureau of the Census, *Twelfth Census of the United States—1900, Volume I: Population Part I* (Washington, DC: USGPO, 1901), xciii; US Bureau of the Census, *Census Bulletin 127*, 11, 18.

33. US Office of Education, 1909 Bulletin, no. 2 (Washington, DC: USGPO, 1909), 180.

34. Jun-ke Choy, *My China Years: Practical Politics in China after the 1911 Revolution* (San Francisco: East/West Publishing, 1974), 31, 43.

35. Yung Wing, *My Life in China and America* (New York: Henry Holt and Co., 1909), 249.

36. *Achievements of the Class of 1902, Yale College* (New Haven: Yale University Press, 1908), 619; *Hartford Courant*, "Yung Wing's Son Tortured in Pekin," Sept. 16, 1913, 1.

37. *Who's Who of American Returned Students*, 113, 169; William A. Wong, "Application for Registration—Native Citizen," Feb. 5, 1921, p. 1, USCRA Hankow; "List of American Citizens Residing in the Canton Consular District on December 31, 1915," Dec. 31, 1915, p. 7, Canton, China vol. 367, RG 84, NARA-CP; Pond Shuck Wu "Application for Registration—Native Citizen," Nov. 23, 1917, p. 1, USCRA Changsha; Coon Ai Yee, "Application for Registration—Native Citizen," May 4, 1918, p. 1, USCRA Hong Kong.

38. Hung Yau Ching, "A Word to Those Intending to Take Up Mining," *First Annual Journal of the Chinese Students' Alliance of Hawaii*, Honolulu, 1909, 14–16.

39. *University of Illinois Directory for 1929* (Urbana-Champaign: University of Illinois, 1929), 1061; *The Miami Bulletin* IV, no. 12 (Feb. 1906): 182; *CP*, "Prof. F. W. Lee Frank Is Named Vice President of College," 7; *Christian China*, "Personal News," VII, nos. 2/3 (Dec. 1920/Jan. 1921): 119. Frank Lee graduated from New York Law School but appears to have completed coursework at one of the seminaries attached to the University of Chicago, although he is not listed in its directories.

40. Ching Leong, "Application for Registration—Native Citizen," Dec. 11, 1918, p. 1, USCRA Changsha; Grace Young, "Certificate of Registration of American Citizen," July 11, 1916, p. 1, USCRA Tientsin. Leong and Young both taught at missionary institutions.

41. *NCH*, "Canton Memorial to Robert Morrison," Nov. 18, 1916, 361; *CT*, "Wedding Bells," Sept. 10, 1919, 1; *Who's Who of American Returned Students*, 42.

42. Henry Loo Kong, "Certificate of Registration of American Citizen," 1909, Canton consulate vol. 670, RG 84, NARA-CP.

43. Ernest K. Moy testimony, Sept. 9, 1920, p. 2, Ernest K. Moy file (3625/225), NARA-SEA; Ernest K. Moy to Paul Linebarger, Oct. 17, 1930, pp. 1–2, file 38, box 11, Paul M. W. Linebarger papers, Hoover Institution, Stanford, CA. According to the *State of Illinois Official Register of Legally Qualified Other Practitioners* (Springfield: Illinois State Board of Health, 1917), 29, Ernest Moy possessed a "legally qualified other practitioner" license in 1917, but bribery and fraud tainted the licensing process during this period.

44. *FRUS, 1930, Vol. II*, 522–23; *NCH*, "At the Mixed Court," Aug. 30, 1919, 554. Moy, a friend of Sun Yat-sen, later served as Commissioner of Finance in the southern government. As chapter 3 notes, he was one of two Chinese Americans charged with participating in the murder of another American-born Chinese, Liao Zhongkai. Shao Yong, *Jindai huidang yu minjian xinyang yanjiu* [Research on modern anti-Qing societies and folklore] (Taipei: Xiuwei Science and Technology Ltd., 2011), 72; *SB*, "Yuesheng zhengbu jubian ji" [Record of the violent developments in the Guangdong political situation], Sept. 4, 1925, 10.

45. Gully, *Shiguang feishi*, 7–10, 20–57; Tom Gunn statement, Feb. 12, 1918, p. 1, Tom Gunn file (18976/101-1), NARA-SB.

46. See, for example, L. Eve Armentrout Ma, *Revolutionaries, Monarchists, and Chinatowns* (Honolulu: University of Hawaii Press, 1990) 71–124, and Him Mark Lai, *Chinese American Transnational Politics*, ed. Madeline Y. Hsu (Urbana: University of Illinois Press, 2010) 9–12.

47. See, for example, Chinese Students' Alliance, *Meizhou Liuxue Baogao* [Report of the American Returned Students] (California: Chinese Students Alliance, 1905), 1–2.

48. Charles Ahfook Wong, "Our Duty," *First Annual Journal of the Chinese Students' Alliance of Hawaii*, 24.

49. Weili Ye, *Seeking Modernity in China's Name: Chinese Students in the United States, 1900–1927* (Stanford: Stanford University Press, 2001), 21–22.

50. Strauss, "Creating 'Virtuous and Talented' Officials for the Twentieth Century," 318.

51. *Who's Who of American Returned Students*, 174; *SB*, "Kaoshi youxue biyesheng dengdi bang" [Results of returned student exam posted], Oct. 20, 1907, 4.

52. *Baptist Missionary Magazine*, "From Exchanges," May 1905, 239; Fong F. Sec, "American Educated Chinese at Work," *Chinese Students Monthly* VI, no. 5 (Mar. 1911): 440–49; Y. T. Tzur, "A Supplement," *Chinese Students Monthly* VI, no. 5: 449–52.

53. Samuel Sung Young, "Application for Registration—Native Citizen," Apr. 2, 1919, p. 1, USCRA Tientsin; *Who's Who of American Returned Students*, 174.

54. *PCA*, "Ahlo Exploiting Mines in China," June 25, 1904, 3; Mary Backus Rankin, "Nationalistic Contestation and Mobilization Politics: Practice and Rhetoric of Railway Rights Recovery at the End of the Qing," *Modern China* 28, no. 3 (2002): 317; W. W. Yen, "The Recent Imperial Metropolitan Exams," *NCH*, Jan. 18, 1907, 125; *PCA*, "Former Honolulan's Responsible Charge," Sept. 29, 1910, 8; *SB*, "Kaoshi youxue biyesheng dengdi bang," 4.

55. *Who's Who of American Returned Students*, 151–52.

56. Chinese Inspector to Chinese Inspector in Charge at Angel Island, June 20, 1910, p. 1, Shin Min Benton Jee file (12376/13), NARA-SB; *Who's Who of American Returned Students*, 23.

57. *Who's Who of American Returned Students*, 23, 174.

58. *Who's Who of American Returned Students*, 23.

59. Chee Soo Lowe, "Application for Registration—Native Citizen," Nov. 9, 1917, p. 1, USCRA Canton; *The Directory & Chronicle for China, Japan, Corea, Indo-China, Straits Settlements, Malay States, Sian, Netherlands India, Borneo, the Philippines, &c* (Hong Kong: Hong Kong Daily Press, 1914), 1067.

60. Jerome Ch'en, *Yuan Shih-k'ai*, 2nd ed. (Stanford: Stanford University Press, 1972), 118, 123–37, 147–50; *SCMP*, "Loan of Fifteen Millions," Feb. 7, 1912, 7.

61. *Who's Who of American Returned Students*, 191; *Peking Gazette*, "The Departure of a Returned Student," Jan. 17, 1916, 7.

62. Frank Lee, "Certificate of Registration of American Citizen," c. 1908, Canton vol. 670, RG 84, NARA-CP.

63. *CP*, "Prof. F. W. Lee Is Named Vice President of College," 7.

64. *NCH*, "Question of Citizenship," May 10, 1913, 418.

65. Ch'en, *Yuan Shih-k'ai*, 135; *Who's Who in China*, 4th ed. (Shanghai: *China Weekly Review*, 1931), 229; *Northwestern Christian Advocate*, "Chicago's First Chinese Church," LXIII, no. 44 (Oct. 27, 1915): 1040.

66. *Zhonghuaminguo shishi jiyao, chugao, minguo ernian qi zhi shieryue fen* [Summary of historical events of the Republic of China, first draft, July–December 1913] (Taipei: Academica Historica, 1981), 194; Kurt Werner Radtke, *China's Relations with Japan, 1945–83: The Rise of Liao Chengzhi* (New York: Manchester University Press, 1990), 26.

67. *NCH*, "Hong Kong Ready to Make Munitions," Aug. 21, 1915, 487; *SCMP*, "Flying at Shatin," Nov. 22, 1915, 5; Chen Cungong, "Zhongguo hangkong de faren:

min qian liunian zhi minguo shiqinian" [The origins of Chinese aviation: From 1905 to 1928], *Bulletin of the Institute of Modern History, Academia Sinica* 7 (1978): 383.

68. *SCMP*, "Canton Newsletter," Nov. 19, 1915, 6.

69. *ST*, "M.A.P.," Sept. 20, 1917, 7; Chen, "Zhongguo hangkong de faren," 383.

70. *ST*, "Southern News," Nov. 9, 1916, 8; *ST*, untitled, July 20, 1918, 12; *NCH*, "Tom Gun [*sic*] Detained in Hong Kong," Aug. 5, 1916, 59; Edward White to Annette A. Adams, Jan. 23, 1920, p. 1, Tom Gunn file (18652/103-1), NARA-SB; *ST*, "Southern News," Sept. 17, 1918, 12; *CT*, "Country Correspondence," Sept. 22, 1919, 2; Jerome Ch'en, "Defining Chinese Warlords and Their Factions," *Bulletin of the School of Oriental and African Studies* 31, no. 3 (1968): 598; *ST*, untitled, June 22, 1920, 2; *SCMP*, "Old Brass: Consignment of Empty Shells at Canton," Apr. 27, 1923, 1; *CT*, "Tom Gunn Returning with Horses, Dogs, and Aeroplanes," 8; *SCMP*, "New Advertisements," Aug. 10, 1920, 4; advertisement for Asiatic Petroleum Company Ltd., *SCMP*, 3; Liu Xibo to Sun Yat-sen, Jan. 2, 1917, p. 1, file 1824, series HUAN, reel 12, ZGMD; Hin Wong, "News from South China," *MR*, Feb. 19, 1921, 680; Hin Wong, "News from South China," *WR*, Sept. 9, 1922, 64; *NCH*, untitled, Nov. 24, 1923, 521.

71. Edward A. McCord, *The Power of the Gun: The Emergence of Modern Chinese Warlordism* (Berkeley: University of California Press, 1993), 245–309.

72. *Who's Who of American Returned Students*, 169; McCord, *The Power of the Gun*, 271–72.

73. Pond Shuck Wu "Application for Registration—Native Citizen," p. 1; Pond Shuck Wu "Application for Registration—Native Citizen," Sept. 17, 1917, p. 1, USCRA Hankow; Pond Shuck Wu "Affidavit to Explain Protracted Foreign Residence and to Overcome Presumption of Expatriation," Oct. 20, 1921, in Pond Shuck Wu "Application for Registration—Native Citizen," Dec. 3, 1924, USCRA Shanghai; *ST*, "Engineers Captured," Apr. 5, 1918, 3; Choy, *My China Years*, 108.

74. *Who's Who of American Returned Students*, 42; Chin Meu Li passport application, Apr. 10, 1920, USPA; Chin Leong Li, "Application for Registration—Native Citizen," June 20, 1918, p. 1, USCRA Changsha; Edward A. McCord, "Burn, Kill, Rape, and Rob: Military Atrocities, Warlordism, and Anti-Warlordism in Republican China," in *Scars of War: The Impact of Warfare on Modern China*, ed. Diana Lary and Stephen McKinnon (Vancouver: University of British Columbia Press, 2001), 20–21.

75. Yansheng Ma Lum and Raymond Mun Kong Lum, *Sun Yat-sen in Hawaii: Activities and Supporters* (Honolulu: University of Hawaii Press, 1999), 88.

76. Gully, *Shiguang feishi*, 97; *SB*, "Minsheng zuijin zhi junshi tan" [Discussion of the latest military affairs in Fujian], Dec. 13, 1918, 7.

77. *Peking Leader*, "American Engineers Here to Rebuild Grand Canal," Sept. 26, 1919, 3; *NCH*, "The Grand Canal Scheme," Mat 31, 1919, 564; O. J. Todd, "The Yellow River Reharnessed," *Geographical Review* 39, no. 1 (1949): 55.

78. Reginald F. Johnston, *Twilight in the Forbidden City* (London: Victor Gollancz Ltd., 1934), 272–73.

79. *CWR*, "Who's Who in China," Jan. 26, 1924, 307; *MR*, "*Canton Times* Begins Publication," Oct. 5, 1918, 192.

80. *CWR*, "Who's Who in China," Apr. 26, 1930, 336. The appointment put Young in an ambiguous position, for Daye was a major part of the Hanyeping iron mining and smelting complex that supplied pig iron to Japan. Hanyeping's status played a significant role in Japan's infamous 21 Demands and thus represented to many Chinese nationalists Japan's encroachment upon China. Albert Feuerwerker, "China's Nineteenth Century Industrialization: The Case of the Hanyehping Coal and Iron Company Limited," in *The Economic Development of China and Japan*, ed. C. D. Cowan (New York: Routledge, 1964), 92; William D. Wray, "Japan's Big-Three Service Enterprises in China, 1896–1936," in *The Japanese Informal Empire in China, 1895–1937*, ed. Peter Duus, Ramon H. Myers, and Mark R. Peattie (Princeton: Princeton University Press, 1989), 48–51.

81. *SCMP*, "Modern Hospitals for Canton," Sept. 7, 1915, 6; *SCMP*, "Chinese Medicines," Apr. 8, 1919, 8.

82. Y. T. Tong, "A Word for the Returned-Students-to-Be," *The Chinese Students' Monthly* (May 1915): 556.

83. Sao-ke Alfred Sze, "What the Returned Students Are Doing for China," *Young China* (Urbana, IL) 5 (August 1920): 5.

84. Stacey Bieler, *"Patriots" or "Traitors"? A History of American-Educated Chinese Students* (Armonk: M. E. Sharpe, 2004), 15.

85. *CWR*, "News from South China," Jan. 15, 1927, 187; *China Daily* (Beijing), "President Encourages Students to Come Back," Oct. 9, 2003; *Chinese Students' Monthly*, "American Returned Students' Association of East China," vol. 10 (1914–1915), 462; *Peking Daily News*, "European-American Returned Students Meeting," Aug. 23, 1915, 4; *MR*, "Men and Events," May 18, 1918, 430; *MR*, "Returned Chinese Women's Club," Jan. 8, 1921, 312.

86. *A Report of the Proceedings of the First North China Returned Student Conference Held at Peking* (Beijing: Peking Leader Press, 1918); *ST*, "Returned Students," Aug. 30, 1919, 7.

87. *CT*, "The Euro-American Returned Students Association," Mar. 29, 1920, 1; *CT*, "110 Members in Euro-American Returned Students Ass'n," July 14, 1920, 1.

88. *MR*, "News from North China," Dec. 6, 1919, 22; *Peking Gazette*, "The University of California," Oct. 23, 1915, 6; *NCH*, "Columbia Alumni," Feb. 7, 1920, 372; *CP*, "N.Y. University Alumni Elect New Officers," Jan. 15, 1925, 6; *CP*, "Roster of Univ. of California in China Completed," Nov. 14, 1930, 1; C. L. Boynton, "The Club's History in Outline," in American University Club of China, *American University Men in China* (Shanghai: Commercial Press, 1936), 19; *NCH*, "The Rights of Chinese Girl Graduates," Feb. 3, 1923, 313.

89. Wen-Hsin Yeh, *Shanghai Splendor: Economic Sentiments and the Making of Modern China, 1843–1949* (Berkeley: University of California Press, 2007), 30.

90. See, for example, *SB*, "Wangqiu dandu bisai ji" [Record of the tennis singles competition], Sept. 2, 1919, 11; *SB*, "Tianjin tiyu xiejinhui chengli" [Tianjin Association for the Promotion of Sports established], Nov. 1, 1927, 10; *CP*, "Chinese Baseball Team Completes Fine Season Here," Sept. 13, 1925, A1; *NCH*, "Shanghai American Football," Nov. 27, 1926, 411.

91. See, for example, *SB*, "Zhonghua yixue hui kaihui richeng" [Agenda of the Chinese Medical Education Association], Feb. 7, 1916, 10; *SB*, "Jiangsu xiaoyuhuiyi dierci jiangyanhui xiangji" [Detailed record of the speeches at the Jiangsu Educational Association's second meeting], Sept. 3, 1915, 6; *SB*, "Yishe gonghui zhiweihui ji" [Record of the medical association executive committee], Jan. 8, 1930, 14; *CP*, "Becomes President," Jan. 8, 1930, 2. For more on new professional associations, see Xu, *Chinese Professionals and the Republican State*, 133, 169.

92. *CT*, "Social and Personal," Aug. 2, 1920, 8; *CT*, "Tungshan No Mean Place Now," Sept. 4, 1919, 4; Hin Wong, "Chinese in Canton Take Steps to Rival Hong Kong as South China Seaport," *CWR*, Nov. 1, 1925, 29; Edward Bing-Shuey Lee, *Modern Canton* (Shanghai: The Mercury Press, 1936), 26, 29. Chinese other than servants were not allowed to live in Shameen, whatever their citizenship.

93. List of American residents of Shanghai, 1937, in Shanghai consulate vol. 2721, RG 84, NARA-CP; Yeh, *Shanghai Splendor*, 119.

94. Michael Gibbs Hill, "Between English and Guoyu: 'The English Student, English Weekly,' and the Commercial Press's Correspondence Schools," *Modern Chinese Literature and Culture* 23, no. 2 (2011): 100–1; Liping Feng, "Democracy and Elitism: The May Fourth Ideal of Literature," *Modern China* 92, no. 2 (1996): 171–75; Leo Ou-fan Lee, *Shanghai Modern: The Flowering of a New Urban Culture in China, 1930–1945* (Cambridge: Harvard University Press, 1999), 53–54; W. K. Cheng, "Enlightenment and Unity: Language Reformism in Late Qing China," *Modern Asian Studies* 35, no. 2 (2001), 479–83.

95. Vera Schwarcz, *The Chinese Enlightenment: Intellectuals and the Legacy of the May Fourth Movement of 1919* (Berkeley: University of California Press, 1986), 83–115.

96. Marie-Claire Bergère, *Sun Yat-sen*, trans. Janet Lloyd (Stanford: Stanford University Press, 1998), 371–73.

97. Wen-Hsin Yeh, *The Alienated Academy: Culture and Politics in Republican China, 1919–1937* (Cambridge: Council on East Asian Studies, 1990), 97–102; Arif Dirlik, *The Origins of Chinese Communism* (New York: Oxford University Press, 1989), 60–120; Jerome B. Grieder, *Hu Shih and the Chinese Renaissance: Liberalism in the Chinese Revolution, 1917–1937* (Cambridge: Harvard University Press, 1970), 45–50.

98. Lee, *Shanghai Modern*, 3–4.

99. Marie-Claire Bergère, *The Golden Age of the Chinese Bourgeoisie, 1911–1937*, trans. Janet Lloyd (Cambridge: Cambridge University Press, 1989), 64.

100. Debin Ma, "Economic Growth in the Lower Yangzi Region of China in 1911–1937: A Quantitative and Historical Analysis," *Journal of Economic History* 68, no. 2 (2008): 361–62; Yeh, *Shanghai Splendor*, 56–57; *Jindai zhongguo baihuoye xianqu—shanghai sida gongsi dang'an huibian* [Modern China's department store pioneers—an archival compilation on Shanghai's big four companies] (Shanghai: Shanghai Municipal Archives, 2010), 1–9.

101. Mao Dun quoted in Lee, *Shanghai Modern*, 1.

102. Yeh, *Shanghai Splendor*, 53–54.

103. Hanchao Lu, *Beyond the Neon Lights: Everyday Shanghai in the Early Twentieth Century* (Berkeley: University of California Press, 1999), 25–43; Robert Bickers, *Empire*

Made Me: An Englishman Adrift in Shanghai (New York: Columbia University Press, 2003), 50–60.

104. Bickers, *Empire Made Me*, 103; Sir J. Jordon to Mr. Balfour, Dec. 23, 1918, p. 33, file FO371/6630, BFO; "American Propaganda," 1921, pp. 132–36, file FO671/437, BFO. As they feared, US investment in China increased steadily between 1900 and 1930, though it never matched that of Britain or Japan. Michael H. Hunt, "Americans in the China Market: Economic Opportunities and Economic Nationalism, 1890s–1931," *Business History Review* 51, no. 3 (1977): 278.

105. Bergère, *Golden Age of the Chinese Bourgeoisie*, 209–27; Parks M. Coble, *The Shanghai Capitalists and the Nationalist Government, 1927–1937* (Cambridge: Council on East Asian Studies, Harvard University, 1980), 25–27; Yeh, *Shanghai Splendor*, 71–72.

106. Russell Bates Chen statement, Sept. 20, 1922, pp. 1–2, Russell Bates Shue Chen file (2500/5014), National Archives and Records Administration regional office, Boston, MA; *WR*, "In the United States Court for China," June 2, 1923, A1; *NCH*, untitled, Aug. 19, 1922, 554; Statement of Char Wai Yuen, Sept. 23, 1922, p. 1, Nicholas Wai Yuen Char file (1302/6761), NARA-SB.

107. Kim Tong Ho, "Application for Registration—Native Citizen," May 4, 1920, p. 1, USCRA Shanghai; "Report of Birth of Children Born to American Parents," Apr. 4, 1932, p. 1, Hong Kong consulate vol. 450, RG 84, NARA-CP; *CP*, "Counterfeit Note Case up in US Court," Aug. 11, 1925, 6; Koon Chong Loo and Lau Chu Ngo, "Certificate of Marriage, American Consular Service," July 14, 1927, Shanghai consulate vol. 1853, RG 84, NARA-CP; Alfred Sy-hang Lee, passport application, May 31, 1922, p. 1, USPA; *Who's Who in China*, 4th ed., 230; *NCH*, "Chinese Girl's Business Venture," May 12, 1923, 418.

108. *WR*, "Men and Events," Aug. 27, 1921, 674. Of course, not all of these people were citizens, but in 1921 at least 1,300 more Chinese American citizens left the United States than returned from China.

109. Judy Yung, *Unbound Feet: A Social History of Chinese Women in San Francisco* (Berkeley: University of California Press, 1995), 108–16; Penina Migdal Glazer and Miriam Slater, *Unequal Colleagues: The Entrance of Women into the Professions, 1890–1940* (New Brunswick: Rutgers University Press, 1987).

110. Yung, *Unbound Feet*, 133.

111. Huie Kin, *Reminiscences* (Peiping: San Yu Press, 1932), 85–86.

112. Marguerite Chiu James, "Application for Registration—Native Citizen," Nov. 2, 1921, p. 1, USCRA Shanghai; Lilly Dong, testimony, Aug. 23, 1929, pp. 3–4, Gertrude Chew Wu file (125/1130), NARA-NY.

113. Hin Wong, "News from South China," *CWR*, Sept. 29, 1923, 185; *Evening Bulletin* (Honolulu), "Havana Cigars Cheap," Dec. 27, 1901, 1; *Missionary Review*, "A Chinese Christian Teaches Japanese," 34, no. 3 (1912): 226; *Chinese Students' Monthly*, "Club Activities," 8, no. 4 (1913): 283.

114. *NCH*, "Chinese Girl's Business Venture," May 12, 1923, 418.

115. Dora Kam Tom, "Application for Registration—Native Citizen," Mar. 23, 1923, p. 1, USCRA; *CWR*, "In the United States Court for China," Jan. 26, 1924, 340.

116. Gertrude Chew Wu testimony, Sept. 12, 1929, p. 3, Gertrude Chew Wu file (125/1130), NARA-NY; Mabel S. Dill testimony, Oct. 30, 1929, p. 5, Gertrude Chew Wu file (125/1130), NARA-NY.

117. Michael G. Chang, "The Good, the Bad, and the Beautiful: Movie Actresses and Public Discourse in Shanghai, 1920s–1930s," in *Cinema and Urban Culture in Shanghai, 1922–1943*, ed. Yingjin Zhang (Stanford: Stanford University Press, 1999), 129–39.

118. See, for example, *CP*, "Prominent Chinese Women Bidden to Meet Dame Crowdy," Oct. 25, 1931, 12; *CP*, "Tsing Hua Alumni Association Will Hold Reunion Here," May 31, 1929, 2; *CP*, "Fourth Club Institute Gets Enthusiastic Start Today," May 15, 1931, 5; *NCH*, "Reception," Feb. 17, 1931, 247; *Weekly Review of the Far East*, "Chinese Women to Help in Mosquito Campaign," July 1, 1922, 182; *CP*, "Chinese Women Leaders Greet Foreign Club Women," May 16, 1926, 1; *NCH*, "The Old and the New in Chinese Dresses," Dec. 18, 1926, 544.

119. Jeffrey Wasserstrom, "Cosmopolitan Connections and Transnational Networks," in *At the Crossroads of Empire: Middlemen, Social Networks, and State-Building in Republican Shanghai*, ed. Nara Dillon and Jean C. Oi (Stanford: Stanford University Press, 2007), 223.

120. Francis Zia, "How They Mastered English," *The English Student* (Shanghai) 7, no. 4 (1921): 253; Hua Chuan Mei, "Guomin duiyu sifa zhi guannian" [The people's concept of the court], lecture trans. into Chinese by Cai Liucheng, *Faxue Jikan* [Legal Quarterly, Shanghai] 1, no. 1 (1922): 25–30; Hua Chuan Mei, "Some Pressing Problems in China," *American Bar Association Journal* 8, no. 4 (Apr. 1921); Hua Chuan Mei, "Our Book Table," *Chinese Recorder*, June 1, 1926, 432; *NCH*, "Shanghai Civic League," June 19, 1920, 735.

121. *Who's Who of American Returned Students*, 151–52; *SB*, "Guo huo weichi hui kaihui jishi" [Chronicle of the national products preservation meeting], Oct. 10, 1915, 10; *SB*, "Guo huo weichi hui chuxuan jiexiao" [Preliminary election results announced for the national products preservation society], Nov. 27, 1927, 15; *SB*, "Jiandehui ken qin youyihui ji" [Record of the Moral and Frugal Society's reception], May 28, 1923, 18.

122. *NCH*, "Society of Chinese Architects," Feb. 12, 1936, 269.

123. Betty Wong, "Business and Professional Women's Association Grows into Modern Shanghai Colossus with a Membership of 12,000 and More to Come," *CP*, May 13, 1932, 9.

124. *NCH*, "Far Eastern Olympic Games," Mar. 27, 1915, 910; *SB*, "Huazhong yundonghui zhi diyiri" [First day of the central China sport meet], May 8, 1923, 7.

125. *SB*, "Zhonghua yixuehui kaihui ji" [Report on the National Medical Association meeting], Mar. 17, 1923, 10; *Who's Who in China*, 4th ed., 230.

126. Choy, *My China Years*, 175; *SB*, "Guangdong tongxianghui gaixuan dong jianshi" [Cantonese Residents Association elects director and board], Feb. 20, 1934, 14; *SB*, "Qun zhi zheng weiyuanhuiyi ji" [Record of the organizational consolidation committee], July 20, 1931, 12.

127. Lu, *Beyond the Neon Lights*, 57–58; Bryna Goodman, *Native Place, City, and Nation: Regional Networks and Identities in Shanghai, 1853–1937* (Berkeley: University of California Press, 1995), 62, 107.

128. Yeh, *Shanghai Splendor*, 30.

129. *Who's Who in China*, 4th ed. 313–14; Claire Wolford, New York University archives, email to author, Dec. 10, 2012; Thomas Whittaker, University of Chicago Special Collections, email to author, Dec. 7, 2012.

130. Hal Mills quoted in William James Burke, "Herbert Erasmus Moy," Mar. 5, 1943, p. 2, file "100155291 sec. 1, 2 of 3," box 72, and Glenn W. Wilson, "Herbert Erasmus Moy," Mar. 3, 1943, p. 1, file "100155291 sec. 1, 3 of 3," box 72, both in classification 100, RG 65, NARA-CP.

131. *China Press*, "Popular Pair Wed at Canton Union Church," May 7, 1933, 3; *Who's Who of American Returned Students*, 193; *North China Herald*, "Marriages," Apr. 21, 1923, 207; Choy, *My China Years*, 8, 80; *SCMP*, "Obituary," Sept. 6, 1932, 10; *CP*, "Yinson Lee and Daughter Are Shower Hosts," July 1, 1933, 13; Mary Lamberton, *St. John's University, Shanghai, 1879–1951* (New York: United Board for Christian Colleges in China, 1955), 134; *CP*, untitled, July 22, 1934, A4.

132. *Boston Daily Globe*, "Shue Hopes to Redeem Ward 7," Sept. 26, 1912, 4. Shue was a Republican in a heavily Democratic district.

133. *CWR*, "Prominent Wedding Announced," May 15, 1926, 284; *NCH*, "Tong-Chen," Dec. 24, 1927, 532.

134. Yung, *Unbound Feet*, 108–16.

135. K. L. Chau, "Present Weaknesses Found in the Life of the Returned Students," *A Report of the Proceedings of the First North China Returned Student Conference Held at Peking*, 5.

136. Flora Belle Jan, *Unbound Spirit: Letters of Flora Belle Jan*, ed. Fleur Yano and Saralyn Daly (Champaign: University of Illinois Press, 2009), 18, 41.

137. Lily Soo-hoo, "The Why and the Wherefore of the Chinese Students Abroad," *Young China* (Urbana, IL), 6 (Nov. 1920), 14; *NCH*, "Impressive Consecration," May 8, 1940, 212; handwritten note on Marguerite Chiu James, "Application for Registration—Native Citizen," Nov. 2, 1921, p. 1, USCRA Shanghai; Hin Wong, "News from South China," *CWR*, Sept. 29, 1923, 185; *Christian China*, "Personal Notes," VIII, no. 1 (1922): 92; Mary Kui Fa Kong Tsang, "Petition for Citizenship," Mar. 1, 1931, in New York Naturalization Records, 1882–1944, online database (Provo: Ancestry.com Operations, Inc., 2012); Alice Moy Kee-ging Lee, "Application for Nonimmigrant Visa," Aug. 30, 1937, p. 1, Alfred Sy-hang Lee file (132/672), NARA-SB. Alice Moy Lee, Mary Kong Tsang, and Caroline Huie petitioned to regain their citizenship after 1931.

138. Y. S. Tsao, "A Challenge to Western Learning: The Chinese Student Trained Abroad—What He Has Accomplished—His Problems," *News Bulletin (Institute of Pacific Relations)*, Dec. 1927, 15. Capitalization in the original.

139. "Supplement No. 18: Summaries from the Chinese Press," *Bulletin of International News* 6, no. 9 (Nov. 7, 1929): 2.

140. Mei, "Some Pressing Problems in China," 180.

141. Y. C. Yang, "Making Patriotism Count Most," *Chinese Students' Monthly* XIII, no. 2 (Dec. 1917): 111.

142. *Chinese Students' Monthly*, "Editorial," XIV, no. 7 (May 1919): 464.

143. Dorothy Gee to Mr. Mason, June 23, 1923, pp. 1–2, file 128, box 26, SRRPC.

144. William C. Smith, "The Life History of a Hawaiian-born Chinese Girl," c. 1924, p. 11, file 310, box 31, SRRPC.

145. Tse-Tung Chow, *The May Fourth Movement: Intellectual Revolution in Modern China* (Cambridge: Harvard University Press, 1960), 5–7.

146. Hu Xiansu, "Shuo xinri jiaoyu zhi weiji" [Speaking of the crisis in education today], *The Critical Review* 4 (Apr. 1922): 474.

147. Chen Duxiu, "Xinwenhuayundong shi shenme?" [What is the New Culture Movement?], *New Youth* 7, no. 5 (1920): 175.

148. Lung-Kee See, "To Be or Not to Be 'Eaten': Lu Xun's Dilemma of Political Engagement," *Modern China* 12, no. 4 (1986): 459.

149. Lu, *Beyond the Neon Lights*, 11; Lucian W. Pye, "How China's Nationalism Was Shanghaied," *Australian Journal of Chinese Affairs* 29 (1993): 121–22.

150. Ye, *Seeking Modernity in China's Name*, 40–43.

151. Margherita Zanasi, *Saving the Nation: Economic Modernity in Republican China* (Chicago: University of Chicago Press, 2006), 60–61; Parks M. Coble, *The Shanghai Capitalists and the Nationalist Government, 1927–1937*, 32–46.

152. Pye, "How China's Nationalism Was Shanghaied," 115.

153. Moy Dip Poy, "Application for Registration—Native Citizen," Sept. 8, 1917, p. 2, Shanghai consulate vol. 3068, RG 84, NARA-CP; Charles Wyman Chun, "Application for Registration—Native Citizen," Jan. 10, 1919, p. 1, USCRA Canton; Shum Yuen Moy, "Certificate of Registration of American Citizen," 1916, p. 1, USCRA Shanghai; Yeh, *Shanghai Splendor*, 71; Sherman Cochran, *Big Business in China: Sino-Foreign Rivalry in the Cigarette Industry, 1890–1930* (Cambridge, Harvard University Press, 1980), 114–15; David A. Wilson, "Principles and Profits: Standard Oil Responds to Chinese Nationalism, 1925–1927," *Pacific Historical Review* 46, no. 4 (1977): 631–38.

154. Jessie G. Lutz, "Chinese Nationalism and the Anti-Christian Campaigns of the 1920s," *Modern Asian Studies* 10, no. 3 (1976): 397–410.

155. Say Chock Lee, "Application for Registration—Native Citizen," July 14, 1920, p. 1, USCRA Shanghai; Tin Loo, "Application for Registration—Native Citizen," Dec. 21, 1917, p. 1, USCRA Shanghai; *Weekly Review*, "Men and Events," Mar. 3, 1923, 24; *CP*, "'Ways of Youth' Compares East, West Marriage," Nov. 3, 1926, A4; *CP*, "Lurton Fines Chinese G.$30 on 3 Charges," Mar. 21, 1926, 1; *CP*, "History of Cantonese Banking Institution Traced to California," Jan. 29, 1935, 11; *The Sincere Co., Ltd., Twenty-fifth Anniversary, 1900–1924* (Shanghai: The Sincere Co., 1924).

156. Bergère, *The Golden Age of the Chinese Bourgeoisie*, 28–29.

157. Lu, *Beyond the Neon Lights*, 11.

158. Soon Keong Ong, "Chinese but Not Quite: *Huaqiao* and the Marginalization of the Overseas Chinese," *Journal of Chinese Overseas* 9 (2013): 25; John Fitzgerald, *Awakening China: Politics, Culture, and Class in the Nationalist Revolution* (Stanford: Stanford University Press, 1996), 169–70.

159. Washington and Lee College, *The Callyx XXXII* (Lexington, VA: Students of Washington and Lee, 1926), 192; Lynn W. Franklin, "Memorandum," Dec. 29, 1926, p. 1, Hong Kong consulate vol. 371, RG 84, NARA-CP; S.S. Talthybius, Apr. 1940, "List 1: List or Manifest of Alien Passengers for the United States," and S.S. President Jefferson, Mar. 29, 1929, "List 27: List or Manifest of Alien Passengers for the United States," in Washington, Passenger and Crew Lists, 1882–1965, online database (Provo, Utah: Ancestry.com Operations, Inc., 2006); *SCMP*, "Passengers Arrived," Jan. 30, 1928, 18.

160. *NCH*, "Wedding," Aug. 6, 1921, 408.

161. *SCMP*, "Sportsman's Sudden Death," July 20, 1972, 14; Yale University, *Alumni Directory of Yale University Living Graduates and Non-Graduates* (New Haven: Yale University, 1926), 237; *Hong Kong Dollar Directory 1930* (Hong Kong: Local Printing Press, Ltd., 1930), 122.

162. Prasenjit Duara, *Rescuing History from the Nation: Questioning Narratives of Modern China* (Chicago: University of Chicago Press, 1995), 158–59.

163. Sun Yat-sen quoted in Wm. Theodore de Bary, Wing-tsit Chan, and Chester Tan, *Sources of Chinese Tradition, Vol II* (New York: Columbia University Press, 1960), 106, 110.

164. See, for example, Hollington K. Tong, "The Western Returned Students' Conference," *MR*, Apr. 12, 1919, 239; and *CT*, "Euro-American Returned Students Association Supporting Sun Yat-sen and Wu Ting-fang," Feb. 19, 1919, 1.

CHAPTER 3

1. Although Liao was born in San Francisco and lived in the United States until his teens, he never claimed American citizenship.

2. Marie-Claire Bergère, *Sun Yat-sen*, trans. Janet Lloyd (Stanford: Stanford University Press, 1998), 309–15.

3. Sun Yat-sen, "Guanyu minshengzhuyi zhi shuoming" [Regarding an explanation of people's livelihood], Jan. 21, 1924, "Collected Works of Sun Yat-sen Online Full Text Retrieval System," accessed Mar. 15, 2017, sunology.culture.tw/cgi-bin/gs32/s1gsweb.cgi?o=dcorpus&s=id=%22SP0000000791%22.&searchmode=basic.

4. John Fitzgerald, *Awakening China: Politics, Culture, and Class in the Nationalist Revolution* (Stanford: Stanford University Press, 1996), 169, Bergère, *Sun Yat-sen*, 346.

5. *SB*, "Guonei zhuandian" [Domestic special dispatches], Sept. 2, 1925, 7.

6. Fitzgerald, *Awakening China*, 168–73.

7. Warren I. Cohen, *America's Response to China: A History of Sino-American Relations*, 4th ed. (New York: Columbia University Press, 1990), 41–43.

8. Mae M. Ngai, *Impossible Subjects: Illegal Aliens and the Making of Modern America* (Princeton: Princeton University Press, 2004), 21–55; *New York Times*,

"Congress to Tighten Immigration Curb," Jan. 27, 1924, El; James O'Donnell Bennett, "House Bars Out Japanese," *Chicago Daily Tribune*, Apr. 13, 1924, 1.

9. Bergère, *Sun Yat-sen*, 294–304; *NCH*, "Mrs. Sun Yat-sen in Shanghai," July 1, 1922, 31.

10. Bergère, *Sun Yat-sen*, 302–05, 311–12.

11. Fitzgerald, *Awakening China*, 169.

12. *NCH*, "Question of Citizenship," May 10, 1913, 418.

13. R. P. Tenney to Eddie Jung, Mar. 14, 1923, p. 1, Canton consulate vol. 455, RG 84, NARA-CP.

14. See, for example, Sue Chue Yet to American Consul, Aug. 17, 1922, p. 1, Canton vol. 442, RG 84, NARA-CP; Leo Bergholz to Chen Jiongming, Feb. 4, 1922, p. 1, Canton vol. 442; "Wong Sun On," Feb. 16, 1922, p. 1, Canton vol. 442; Chan Hong Quong to American Consul, June 26, 1922, pp. 1–2, Canton vol. 442.

15. See, for example, Frank Lee to Leo Bergholz, Feb. 18, 1922, p. 1, Canton vol. 442; Leo Bergholz to Frank Lee, Feb. 22, 1922, p. 1, Canton vol. 442; Frank Lee to Leo Bergholz, Feb. 25, 1922, p. 1, Canton vol. 442; Wong Sun On to US Consul General, Mar. 24, 1922, p. 1, Canton vol. 442.

16. Michael Tsin, *Nation, Governance, and Modernity in China: Canton, 1900–1927* (Stanford: Stanford University Press, 1999), 91–98; Hin Wong, "News from South China," *CWR*, June 2, 1923, 20; Hin Wong, "News from South China," *CWR*, June 23, 1923, 110; Hin Wong, "News from South China," *CWR*, May 19, 1923, 426; Elizabeth J. Remnick, *Regulating Prostitution in China: Gender and Local Statebuilding, 1900–1937* (Stanford: Stanford University Press, 2014), 109–10, 113–24; *NCH*, "An Opium Monopoly in Kuangtung," May 26, 1923, 513; *WR*, "The Week in the Far East," Apr. 14, 1923, 253.

17. Chin Gee Hee to William H. Gale, Oct. 4, 1923, pp. 1–2, Canton vol. 455; *WR*, "Weekly Review's Correspondent Arrested in Canton," Feb. 10, 1923, 439; *WR*, "Review's Canton Correspondent Released," Feb. 24, 1923, 524.

18. Tsin, *Nation, Governance, and Modernity in China*, 91–94; Bergère, *Sun Yat-sen*, 346–47; Fitzgerald, *Awakening China*, 294–95.

19. Shi Lingju to Wu Xianzi, Aug. 28, 1923, n.p., file 12, carton 13, Records of the Chinese World, Asian American Studies Library, University of California, Berkeley.

20. C. Martin Wilbur, *The Nationalist Revolution in China, 1923–1928* (New York: Cambridge University Press, 1983), 4; Bergère, *Sun Yat-sen*, 317–18.

21. Hin Wong, "The Anti-Foreign Agitation in Canton," *CWR*, Jan. 19, 1924, 268.

22. Wong, "The Anti-Foreign Agitation in Canton," 268.

23. Sun Yat-sen, "Guanyu minshengzhuyi zhi shuoming"; Sun Yat-sen, "Wei guangzhou shangtuan shijian duiwai xuanyan" [Manifesto regarding the Guangzhou Merchant Corps Incident], Sept. 1, 1924, "Collected Works of Sun Yat-sen Online Full Text Retrieval System," accessed Mar. 15, 2017, sunology.culture.tw/cgi-bin/gs32/s1gsweb.cgi/ccd=rx8RPX/record?r1=39&h1=1.

24. Hin Wong, "Canton Situation Darkest Spot in China Today," *CWR*, Nov. 3, 1923, 350; *CWR*, "Why Sun Yat-sen Fails," May 24, 1924, 446; J. B. Powell to US Consul, May 19, 1924, pp. 1–2, Canton consulate vol. 484, RG 84, NARA-CP; J. W. Creighton to Douglas Jenkins, May 17, 1924, p. 1, Canton vol. 484; J. C. Thomson to Consul General, May 17, 1924, p. 1, Canton vol. 484; Douglas Jenkins to Edwin Cunningham, May 20, 1924, p. 1, Canton vol. 484; M. M. Hamilton, "Case of Hin Wong," May 26, 1924, p. 1, Canton vol. 484; Hin Wong to Douglas Jenkins, May 31, 1924, p. 1, Canton vol. 484. After Sun's death and the Northern Expedition, Wong was able to return to Guangdong.

25. Wilbur, *The Nationalist Revolution in China*, 10–13; Fitzgerald, *Awakening China*, 170.

26. *NCH*, "The Volunteers of Kuangtung," Aug. 23, 1924, 287; Tsin, *Nation, Governance, and Modernity in China*, 83–91, 103–5.

27. Wilbur, *The Nationalist Revolution in China*, 19–20.

28. Hin Wong, "Red Sun Over Canton," *CWR*, Nov. 1, 1924, 269.

29. Tsin, *Nation, Governance, and Modernity in China*, 83–88.

30. Tsin, *Nation, Governance, and Modernity in China*, 84, 111.

31. Sun Yat-sen, "Zhongguo neiluan zhi yin" [The cause of internal strife in China], Nov. 25, 1924, "Collected Works of Sun Yat-sen Online Full Text Retrieval System," accessed Mar. 15, 2017, sunology.culture.tw/cgi-bin/gs32/s1gsweb.cgi/ccd=rx8RPX/record?r1=1&h1=7.

32. Fitzgerald, *Awakening China*, 374n88.

33. Tsin, *Nation, Governance, and Modernity in China*, 96–97.

34. See "Memoranda of Protection Cases: Merchants Volunteer Trouble," Oct. 1924, in Canton vol. 484.

35. M. M. Hamilton, "Chew Sue Pong Protection Case," Oct. 17, 1924, p. 1, and M. M. Hamilton, "Memorandum: Yee Jew Siu," Oct. 17, 1924, p. 1, both in Canton vol. 484.

36. M. M. Hamilton, "Memorandum: Thom Wing Get," Oct. 21, 1924, p. 1, and M. M. Hamilton, "Memorandum: A Certain Chinese," Nov. 4, 1924, p. 1, both in Canton vol. 484.

37. Sun, "Zhongguo neiluan zhi yin"; Tsin, *Nation, Governance, and Modernity in China*, 83–84, 86, 89–90, 109–110; Sherman Cochran, *Big Business in China: Sino-Foreign Rivalry in the Cigarette Industry, 1890–1930* (Cambridge: Harvard University Press, 1980), 55–77.

38. Jun-ke Choy, *My China Years: Practical Politics in China after the 1911 Revolution* (San Francisco: East/West Publishing, 1974), 83–85; *Industrial and Commercial Directory of Shanghai* (Shanghai: General Chamber of Commerce, 1927), 413; *CT*, "Marriage Announcement," Jan. 23, 1919, 8; *CP*, "Chinese Baseball Club Will Meet at 12 Noon Today," Apr. 22, 1926, 4; "List of American Citizens Residing in the Shanghai Consular District," Dec. 31, 1930, p. 13, Shanghai consulate vol. 2072, RG 84, NARA-CP; Hin Wong, "News from South China," Dec. 2, 1922, 30; Paddy Gully, *Shiguang feishi: zhongguo kongjun xianqu linfuyuan zhuan [Time flies: The fiography of Chinese aviation*

pioneer Art Lym], trans. Zhang Chaoxia (Guangzhou: Huacheng Publishing, 2013), 139–41.

39. George Kin Leung passport application, Dec. 6, 1923, p. 1, USPA; *SCMP*, "Chinese Literature," Dec. 24, 1926, 14; *CWR*, "Who's Who in China," Nov. 4, 1933, 416; *SCMP*, "Passengers Departed," July 14, 1924, 17; *NCH*, "Obituary," July 5, 1939, 24; "List of American Citizens Residing in the Shanghai Consular District," 13, 33, 34, 40, 41; *CWR*, "Who's Who in China," Apr. 26, 1930, 336.

40. Chester G. Fuson to Douglas Jenkins, Oct. 22, 1925, pp. 1–2, Canton consulate vol. 488, RG 84, NARA-CP; M. M. Hamilton to A. E. Carleton, Dec. 9, 1924, p. 1, Hong Kong consulate vol. 347, RG 84, NARA-CP.

41. Hong Kong Census Office, *Report on the Census of the Colony for 1921* (Hong Kong, BCC: Hong Kong Legislative Council, 1921), 188, 191, 205; Hong Kong Census Office, *Report on the Census of the Colony for 1931* (Hong Kong, BCC: Hong Kong Legislative Council, 1931), 128.

42. 1923 *ARCGI*, 70, 160, 161; 1924 *ARCGI*, 64, 157, 158; 1925 *ARCGI*, 55, 179; 1926 *ARCGI*, 54, 161.

43. Catharine Holt, "Interview with Mr. George Lem," Aug. 4, 1924, p. 3, file 298(7), box 30, SRRPC.

44. Tsin, *Nation, Governance, and Modernity in China*, 149.

45. Emily Honig, *Sisters and Strangers: Women in the Shanghai Cotton Mills, 1919–1949* (Stanford: Stanford University Press, 1992), 26–28; Cochran, *Big Business in China*, 154–55.

46. Robert Bickers, *Empire Made Me: An Englishman Adrift in Shanghai* (New York: Penguin, 2003), 163–70.

47. John M. Carroll, *Edge of Empires: Chinese Elites and British Colonials in Hong Kong* (Cambridge: Harvard University Press, 2005), 132–34; Tsin, *Nation, Governance, and Modernity in China*, 146–64.

48. Carroll, *Edge of Empires*, 134-135, 149-152, 158; *NCH*, "Chinese Red's Cash on British Soil," Sept. 5, 1925, 291.

49. Hong Kong Legislative Council, "Jurors List for 1924," *1924 Sessional Papers* (Hong Kong BCC: Hong Kong Legislative Council, 1924), 47.

50. *SCMP*, "Sino-European Medical Dinner," Jan. 21, 1926, 6; *SCMP*, "Local Wedding," April 19, 1926, 10.

51. Carroll, *Edge of Empires*, 132; *SCMP*, "Hongkong Students," Dec. 25, 1925, 3.

52. Tsai-Yan Lum [sic] to editor, *SCMP*, July 11, 1925, 6.

53. Carroll, *Edge of Empires*, 133, 140-141.

54. *SCMP*, "A Canton Panic," Sept. 26, 1925, 7.

55. Carroll, *Edge of Empires*, 133; *SCMP*, "The Boomerang," July 2, 1926, 8; *SCMP*, "High Cost of Food," May 19, 1926, 10. Merchant Quan Tong of Blue Bird apparently coped with the strike in part by using his second wife as low-wage labor in his shop. Judy Yung, *Unbound Feet: A Social History of Chinese Women in San Francisco* (Berkeley: University of California Press, 1995), 171.

56. "Report of Birth of Children Born to American Parents: Wong Pui King," Mar. 9, 1932, p. 1, Hong Kong consulate vol. 450, RG 84, NARA-CP; "Report of Birth of Children Born to American Parents: Sai Wing Chinn and Sai Yeu Chinn," June 9, 1932, p. 1, Hong Kong vol. 450.

57. Fitzgerald, *Awakening China*, 304–13; Wilbur, *The Nationalist Revolution in China*, 37–40.

58. Tsin, *Nation, Governance, and Modernity in China*, 158–60; W.H. Chen, "Canton as Seen by a Cantonese," *NCH*, May 29, 1926, 422.

59. *FRUS 1926, Vol. I*, 691-693.

60. Gastao Fidelino da Rosa to American Consulate, Hong Kong, June 1926, p. 1, Canton consulate vol. 486, RG 84, NARA-CP.

61. Cheung Shee to Consul General, Canton, May 27, 1926, p. 1, Canton vol. 486.

62. Memorandum, Dec. 28, 1926, p. 1, Canton vol. 486; Louey Shuck to Douglas Jenkins, Dec. 11, 1926, pp. 1-2, Canton vol. 486.

63. Wilbur, *The Nationalist Revolution in China*, 70; *FRUS 1926, Volume I*, 695–97, 700–1.

64. *FRUS 1926, Volume I*, 698–99.

65. *NCH*, "Trouble at Canton Christian Coll.," Apr. 24, 1926, 154.

66. Chen Anren, *Lingnan daxue nianjian* [An almanac of Canton Christian College] (Guangzhou: Canton Christian College, 1925), 97–98; Wy Lee passport application, Jan. 7, 1925, p. 1, USPA; William Noyes to P.L. Heintzleman, Apr. 23, 1917, p. 1, Canton consulate vol. 397, RG 84, NARA-CP; Baldwin Lee passport application, Feb. 9, 1924, USPA; Alice Lee passport application, Feb. 9, 1924, p. 1, and Alice Lee, application for passport extension, Mar. 18, 1924, p. 1, USPA. Pui Ching was actually Chinese founded and controlled, but some anti-imperialist activists attacked it because of its ties to a foreign religion—Christianity.

67. Tsin, *Nation, Governance, and Modernity*, 118.

68. Chen, *Lingnan daxue nianjian*, 97, 99; *SCMP*, "Canton Unrest," Mar. 19, 1926, 8.

69. See, for example, Albert Hing, "Application for Registration—Native Citizen," Sept. 3, 1924, p. 1, USCRA Canton; Eugene Chun, "Application for Registration—Native Citizen," Sept. 12, 1923, p. 1, USCRA Canton; Henry Chun, "Application for Registration—Native Citizen," Sept. 12, 1923, p. 1, USCRA Canton; Willie Wong, "Application for Registration—Native Citizen," Apr. 30, 1923, p. 1, USCRA Canton; Alice Lee passport application, Feb. 9, 1924, p. 1, and Alice Lee, application for passport extension, Mar. 18, 1924, p. 1, USPA; *SCMP*, "Passengers: Departed," Aug. 26, 1926, 15; *SCMP*, "Passengers: Departed," Mar. 29, 1926, 16; *SCMP*, "Passengers: Departed," June 29, 1927, 17; *SCMP*, "Passengers: Departed," Oct. 12, 1927, 17; Hong Kong Legislative Council, "Jurors List for 1928," *1928 Sessional Papers* (Hong Kong BCC: Hong Kong Legislative Council, 1928), 31.

70. Lingnan University, *Bulletin No. 38: Catalogue of College of Arts and Sciences and Lingnan Agricultural College* (Guangzhou: Knipp Memorial Press, 1926), 117–25, box 181, RG 11, United Board; *SCMP*, "Canton Christian College," Apr. 1, 1925, 9.

71. *CP*, "Students' Sires Uphold Rights of the Faculty," Apr. 27, 1926, 7.

72. Chan K. Wong, "An Appeal to Lingnan Alumni," in *Lingnan: Our Alma Mater* (New York: Lingnan University Board of Trustees, 1927), file 1, box 68, TLU.

73. Tsin, *Nation, Governance, and Modernity in China*, 91–97.

74. "Memorandum of a Conversation Held with Joe Nom Wing," Aug. 25, 1925, p. 1, Canton vol. 488; Joe Wing [Jo Nom Wing] to Douglas Jenkins, Mar. 25, 1926, p. 1, Canton vol. 486. Chu Shea Wai's family shared a surname, Chu (Pinyin Zhao, 趙), but many family members used different romanizations of it or versions of their names. Siblings Chu Shea Wai, Chu Su Gunn, Laurand Chu, and Ow Wing Chu all used Chu. Henry Joe Young's Chinese name was Zhao Shiyang (Chu Shea Young), but he used Young, not Chu or Joe, as his surname. Jo Nom Wing's Chinese name was Zhao Nan (probably Zhao Nanrong), but he used a variety of names and spellings in English, including Joe Nom Wing, Joe Wing, Jo Nom Wing, George Joe Nam Wing, and Chu S. Nam.

75. Warner M. Van Norden, *Who's Who of the Chinese in New York* (New York: Warner Van Norden, 1918), 31–32; Henry Joe Young testimony, Aug. 15, 1917, pp. 1–2, Henry Joe Young file (3225/43), NARA-NY.

76. Chu Fung Wing testimony, June 11, 1918, p. 1, Joe Wing (Joe Nom Wing) file (3225/428), NARA-NY; Jo Nom Wing testimony, Apr. 29, 1918, pp. 1–2, Jo Nom Wing file (3225/389), NARA-NY.

77. Van Norden, *Who's Who of the Chinese in New York*, 31–32, 35–36; *Zhonghuaminguo shishi jiyao, chugao, minguo liunian* [Summary of historical events of the Republic of China, first draft, 1917] (Taipei: Academica Historica, 1976), 296.

78. *Chinese Mail* (Hong Kong), "Yuejing gongting zheng pang ji" [Record of the disorderly palace disputes in Guangzhou], May 1, 1924, 3; *Xianggang Gongshang Ribao* [Hong Kong Keungsheng Daily], "Zhao shiguan linghui guominxinwen she" [Chu Su Gunn brings back the *Guomin News* organization], July 30, 1928, 6.

79. Chu Su Gunn was acquainted with but hardly friendly toward Sun Yat-sen's old comrade Moy Quong-poy, an American-born conservative also arrested for Liao Zhongkai's assassination. Moy hated the communists but also clashed both verbally and physically with Hu Hanmin's party faction while serving as head of the military's general affairs department and working as Canton's finance commissioner. *SB*, "Sun zhongshan chuxun gui bian" [Sun Yat-sen travels to Guilin], Oct. 20, 1921, 11; *Chinese Times* (Vancouver), "Yuanlao pai da ma ti mei" [Elders faction hits Ma and kicks Moy], Nov. 7, 1924, 7; *SCMP*, "Canton News," Feb. 13, 1924, 9.

80. Frank Lee, "Communism and the Anti-Christian Movement," *Chinese Recorder*, Apr. 1, 1925, 232.

81. Chu Shea Wai testimony, June 3, 1918, p. 1, Chu Shea Wai file (3225/430), NARA-NY; Chu Shea Wai, "Application for Registration—Native Citizen," Sept. 15, 1921, p. 1, USCRA Canton.

82. *SCMP*, "Political Murder," June 7, 1926, 1; *SCMP*, "Death Sentence," July 16, 1926, 1.

83. Suisheng Zhao, *Power by Design: Constitution-Making in Nationalist China* (Honolulu: University of Hawaii Press, 1996), 91–92.

84. *CP*, "Correspondent Describes Situation in Canton," July 22, 1926, 7; *SB*, "Hu hanmin beibu xiangqing" [Detailed information about the arrest of Hu Hanmin], Sept. 3, 1925, 10.

85. Joe Nom Wing to Consul General, Sept. 23, 1925, p. 1, Canton vol. 488; *Nanyang Shangbao* (Singapore), "Liao an zhi gongpan qingqiu shu" [Judge in Liao case requests document], Mar. 23, 1926, 4.

86. Henry Joe Young to American Consul General, Aug. 26, 1925, p. 2, Canton vol. 488.

87. *NCH*, news briefs, Aug. 30, 1919, 554.

88. Douglas Jenkins to Foo Bing-chang (Fu Bingchang), Aug. 27, 1925, p. 1, Canton vol. 488.

89. Roger Culver Treadwell to Douglas Jenkins, Nov. 10, 1925, pp. 1–3, Canton vol. 488; Treadwell to Jenkins, Nov. 12, 1925, p. 1, Canton vol. 488.

90. Douglas Jenkins to J. V. A. MacMurray, Nov. 5, 1925, pp. 1–2, Canton vol. 488.

91. *Boston Globe*, "Full Text of President Coolidge's Message," Dec. 7, 1923, 19. For more on Coolidge's racial views, see Eric S. Yellin, *Racism in the Nation's Service: Government Workers and the Color Line in Woodrow Wilson's America* (Chapel Hill: University of North Carolina Press, 2013), 185; Nancy Foner, *From Ellis Island to JFK: New York's Two Great Waves of Immigration* (New Haven: Yale University Press, 2002), 165.

92. Mae M. Ngai, "The Architecture of Race in American Immigration Law: A Reexamination of the Immigration Act of 1924," *Journal of American History* 86, no. 1 (June 1999): 70.

93. James S. Pacy, "British Views of American Diplomats in China," *Asian Affairs* 8, no. 4 (1981): 252; Kerry W. Buckley, "A President for the 'Great Silent Majority': Bruce Barton's Construction of Calvin Coolidge," *New England Quarterly* 76, no. 4 (2003): 602; Jon Thares Davidann, "'Colossal Illusions': U.S.-Japanese Relations in the Institute of Pacific Relations, 1919–1938," *Journal of World History* 12, no. 1 (2001): 169; Kristofer Allerfeldt, "'And We Got Here First': Albert Johnson, National Origins and Self-Interest in the Immigration Debate of the 1920s," *Journal of Contemporary History* 45, no. 1 (2010): 21; *FRUS 1925, Vol. I*, 800.

94. *FRUS 1926, Vol. I*, 1102.

95. John V. A. MacMurray, "Opening Remarks," *Proceedings of the American Society of International Law at Its Annual Meeting*, Apr. 1932, 37–45.

96. Jenkins to MacMurray, Nov. 5, 1925, p. 1, Canton vol. 488.

97. Jenkins to MacMurray, Dec. 9, 1925, p. 2, Canton vol. 488.

98. Stuart J. Fuller quoted in MacMurray to Jenkins, Nov. 30, 1925, p. 2, Canton vol. 488.

99. "An Act in Reference to the Expatriation of Citizens and Their Protection Abroad," *American Journal of International Law* I, no. 2 (1907): 258–59.

100. MacMurray to Jenkins, Nov. 30, 1925, p. 2.

101. MacMurray to Jenkins, Nov. 30, 1925, p. 2.

102. *FRUS 1902*, 2–3.

103. *FRUS 1910*, 2–3.

104. Jenkins to Treadwell, June 11, 1926, p. 1, Hong Kong consulate vol. 371, RG 84, NARA-CP; W. Leonard Parker, "Memorandum," June 29, 1936, p. 2, Canton consulate vol. 606, RG 84, NARA-CP.

105. Cohen, *America's Response to China*, 92–97.

106. *FRUS 1925 Volume I*, 754; *FRUS 1926, Volume I*, 691–93.

107. David A. Wilson, "Principles and Profits: Standard Oil Responds to Chinese Nationalism, 1925–1927," *Pacific Historical Review* 46, no. 4 (1977): 632; *FRUS 1926, Volume I*, 719–21.

108. Mrs. Chu Fong Wing to Roger Culver Treadwell, Jan. 23, 1926, p. 1, Hong Kong vol. 371.

109. *FRUS 1926, Volume I*, 731–32.

110. Louey Shuck to Douglas Jenkins, Dec. 10, 1926, pp. 1–2, Canton vol. 486; Douglas Jenkins to Louey Shuck, Dec. 4, 1923, Canton vol. 486.

111. Jenkins to Treadwell, Dec. 22, 1926, pp. 1–3, Canton vol. 486; Louey Shuck to Douglas Jenkins, Dec. 17, 1926, pp. 1–2, Canton vol. 486; Louey Shuck, "Application for Registration—Native Citizen," Feb. 7, 1917, pp. 1–4 (including subsequent renewals), Canton vol. 486.

112. Memorandum, Dec. 28, 1926, p. 1, Canton vol. 486.

113. J. T. Pratt, "Memorandum: The Protection of Anglo-Chinese in China," Feb. 4, 1928, pp. 1–43, in file FO 371/13203, BFO.

114. See, for example, Jim English, "Empire Day in Britain, 1904–1958," *The Historical Journal* 49, no. 1 (2006): 248–49, 258–60; G. Alex Bremmer, "Nation and Empire in the Government Architecture of Mid-Victorian London: The Foreign and India Office Reconsidered," *The Historical Journal* 48, no. 3 (2005): 723–24; Ian J. Barrow, "India for the Working Classes: The Maps of the Society for the Diffusion of Useful Knowledge," *Modern Asian Studies* 38, no. 3 (2004): 678. For the impact of empire on British identity in an earlier period, see Linda Colley, *Britons: Forging the Nation, 1707–1837* (New Haven: Yale University Press, 1992).

115. John Darwin, "Orphans of Empire," in *Settlers and Expatriates: Britons over the Seas*, ed. Robert Bickers (New York: Oxford University Press, 2010), 338–40.

116. J.P. Brenan, "Procedure Whereby Chinese May Renounce Their Chinese Nationality," pp. 2–3, file FO 371/12511, BFO.

117. Foreign Office to Miles Lampson, Jan. 17, 1927, p. 7, file FO 371/12459, BFO; Brenan, "Procedure Whereby Chinese May Renounce Their Chinese Nationality," 3.

118. Grindle to Mounsey, Apr. 9, 1927, pp. 1–2, file FO 371/12459, BFO.

119. Herbert Phillips to British Consulate General for Nanking, July 18, 1927, p. 2, file FO 371/12511; J. F. Brenan to Lampson, July 4, 1927, p. 1, file FO 371/12511, BFO.

120. Enclosure no. 3, "Shanghai Despatch No. 42 to Peking," Mar. 2, 1928, p. 1, file FO 371/13203, BFO.

121. Brenan to Lampson, July 4, 1927, p. 1.

122. Hallett Abend, *My Life in China, 1926–1941* (New York: Harcourt, Brace and Company, 1943), 29–33; Wilbur, *The Nationalist Revolution in China*, 40–55; Tsin, *Nation, Governance, and Modernity*, 165–68.

123. *CP*, "Chinese Baseball Club Selects Its Officers for '26," May 18, 1926, A1; *CP*, "S.A.B.C. Will Play All-Star Nine On Race Course Today," June 26, 1926, A1; *CP*, "Lurton Fines Chinese G$30 on 3 Charges," Mar. 21, 1926, 1; advertisement, *CP*, Sept. 23, 1926, 4; *CP*, "A Cantonese Wedding," Sept. 26, 1926, B1; *CP*, "In the U.S. Court for China," Feb. 22, 1925, 15; *CP*, "Peeping through the Window," Apr. 11, 1926, C4; Geraldine Sartain, "'On the Lot,' or the Making of Movies," *CP*, July 18, 1926, 2; *NCH*, "U.S. Court for China: Moon vs. Moon," Dec. 31, 1926, 639.

124. Jun Xing, "The American Social Gospel and the Chinese YMCA," *Journal of American-East Asian Relations* 5, nos. 3/4 (1996): 300–1; Nicholas Clifford, "A Revolution Is Not a Tea Party: The 'Shanghai Mind(s)' Reconsidered," *Pacific Historical Review* 59, no. 4 (1990): 515–21; Wen-Hsin Yeh, *The Alienated Academy: Culture and Politics in Republican China, 1919–1937* (Cambridge: Council on East Asian Studies, 1990), 76–77.

125. H. C. Mei letter to the editor, *Chinese Recorder*, Feb. 1, 1925, 124.

126. Lee, "Communism and the Anti-Christian Movement," 232.

127. *SB*, "Guonei yaowen er" [Important domestic news, part 2], June 18, 1926, 9.

128. For more on the new professional organizations, see Xiaoqun Xu, *Chinese Professionals and the Republican State: The Rise of Professional Associations in Shanghai* (New York: Cambridge University Press, 2001), 3–9.

129. Jeffrey Wasserstrom, "Cosmopolitan Connections and Transnational Networks," in *At the Crossroads of Empire: Middlemen, Social Networks, and State-Building in Republican Shanghai*, ed. Nara Dillon and Jean C. Oi (Stanford: Stanford University Press, 2007), 217–20.

130. *SB*, "Shanghai xuesheng lianhehui choukuanbu shoudao" [Shanghai Student Union fundraising arm receipts], July 10, 1925, 5; Jeffrey N. Wasserstrom, *Student Protests in Twentieth-Century China: The View from Shanghai* (Stanford: Stanford University Press, 1991), 109–23; *NCH*, "Communists Executed," July 9, 1927, 49.

131. *CWR*, "Chinese Bankers Want Tariff Autonomy," Sept. 19, 1925, 57.

132. Testimony of Russell Bates Shue Chen, Sept. 20, 1922, pp. 1–2, in Russell Chen file (2500/5014), National Archives and Records Administration regional office, Boston, MA.

133. See, for example, *WR*, "In the United States Court for China," June 2, 1923, A1; *SB*, "Luxuechen jianshi kaishi zhixing zhiwu" [Russell Chen begins his work], Apr. 1, 1924; *NCH*, "Kidnapping Ringleader on Trial," Aug. 1, 1925, 97.

134. Erika Lee, *At America's Gates: Chinese Immigration During the Exclusion Era, 1882–1943* (Chapel Hill: University of North Carolina Press, 2003), 79–80; *Hawaiian Star* (Honolulu), "Starting Maturity," Nov. 19, 1907, 8. Both men graduated from Oahu College (Punahou School) in 1897.

135. *NCH*, untitled, Oct. 11, 1919, 103; *CWR*, "The Case of Francis Zia and L. K. Kentwell," Feb. 12, 1927, 275.

136. *CP*, H. A. Thompson to editor, Sept. 8, 1925, 12; *NCH*, "Until Chinese Are on the Council," Aug. 29, 1925, 268; *CP*, "Prosecutor Is Anti-Chinese, Lawyer Says," Aug. 25, 1925, 5; *CP*, L. K. Kentwell to editor, Sept. 5, 1925, 12.

137. *CP*, "Ratepayers Unanimous in Inviting Chinese," Apr. 15, 1926, 1; *Shanghai Municipal Gazette*, "Report of the Annual Meeting of Ratepayers," XIX: 1019, Apr. 15, 1926, 130–31.

138. *Shanghai Municipal Gazette*, "Report of the Annual Meeting of Ratepayers," 120. H. C. Mei also had voting rights.

139. *Shanghai Municipal Gazette*, "Report of the Annual Meeting of Ratepayers," 130–31.

140. *NCH*, "Ratepayers Fully in Favour of Chinese on Council," Apr. 17, 1926, 109.

141. *CP*, "Ratepayers Unanimous in Inviting Chinese," 1.

142. *CWR*, "The Case of Francis Zia and L. K. Kentwell," 275; *CP*, "Kentwell Now Chinese Subject, He Tells Court," Jan. 25, 1927, 1; *CP*, "Crowd Jams British Court to Hear Kentwell's Version of Snobbery," Feb. 2, 1927, 1.

143. *CP*, "New Drink Introduced to Shanghai People," July 24, 1936, 11; *CP*, "Broker's Daughter to Wed Young Lawyer," May 9, 1926, 4; *NCH*, "Ling-Tong," Apr. 7, 1928, 15.

144. *CWR*, "The Case of Francis Zia and L. K. Kentwell," 275; D. I. Yorke, "Report on Staff of *China Courier*," June 15, 1927, p. 1, file "Reports Made 1916–1929: Extracts From D. S. I. Robertson's Report re: L. K. Kentwell, July 1, 1927," SMP.

145. Confirming the US abandonment of its citizens, a Sino-foreign commission set up to adjudicate foreign citizens' property claims after the Nanjing incident dismissed the ones that Chinese American citizens filed, accepting the Nationalists' argument that such people were Chinese citizens. *FRUS 1929, Vol. II*, 859, 868.

146. Wilbur, *The Nationalist Revolution in China*, 70; *FRUS* 1927, *Vol. II* 236–60; Michael G. Murdock, "Exploiting Anti-Imperialism: Popular Forces and Nation-State-Building during China's Northern Expedition, 1926–1927," *Modern China* 35, no. 1 (2009): 73–75, 82–88.

147. Wilbur, *The Nationalist Revolution in China*, 104–80; Charles D. Musgrove, *China's Contested Capital: Architecture, Ritual, and Response in Nanjing* (Honolulu: University of Hawaii Press, 2013), 37–40; Margherita Zanasi, *Saving the Nation: Economic Modernity in Republican China* (Chicago: University of Chicago Press, 2006), 7.

148. Frederic Wakeman Jr., *Spymaster: Dai Li and the Chinese Secret Service* (Berkeley: University of California Press, 2003), 27, 67.

149. Zanasi, *Saving the Nation*, 88–89.

150. Choy, *My China Years*, 86.

151. "Qingli dang'anchu" [Organization archiving], *Zhiyuanlu* [Staff roster] (Beijing: Printing Bureau, 1920); *SB*, "Guonei zhuandian" [Domestic special dispatches], Apr. 9, 1922, 3; Lo Koon-lai, "Application for Registration—Native Citizen," May 27, 1918, p. 1, USCRA Tientsin; *CP*, "Passengers Departed," Jan. 17, 1929, 15.

152. Choy, *My China Years*, 108; Young Chan Chun, "Application for Registration—Naturalized Citizen," June 18, 1917, p. 1, USCRA Changsha; Young Chan Chun testimony, May 25, 1936, p. 2, Young Chan Chun file (4382/811), NARA-SB. Wong Achuck eventually decamped to Macao, where he ran the waterworks. *SCMP*, "Interest in Macao's Waterworks," Oct. 26, 1932, 9.

153. Ernest K. Moy to Paul Linebarger, Oct. 17, 1930, p. 1, file 38, box 11, Paul M. W. Linebarger papers, Hoover Institution, Stanford, CA.

154. Bergère, *Sun Yat-sen*, 312; Choy, *My China Years*, 113–36.

155. *SB*, "Kuoda zuzhi jingguo" [Organization undergoes expansion], July 28, 1933, 12; Mon Yin Chung to T. V. Soong, Sept. 22, 1943, p. 1, file 35, box 6, T. V. Soong papers, Hoover Institution; Mon Yin Chung testimony, June 19, 1935, p. 1, Mon Yin Chung file (4500/2695), NARA-SB.

156. Harvard University, *Quadrennial Catalogue of the Officers and Graduates, 1636–1920* (Cambridge: Harvard University, 1920), 482, 498; Abend, *My Life in China*, 123; *SB*, "*Caibu cui jie shuishou*" [Finance ministry expedites tax collection], Feb. 5, 1928, 5; *CP*, "State Lottery Is Inaugurated at Meet Here," Apr. 27, 1933, 11; *SB*, "Zheng lai zuori jiuzhi" [Loy Chang assumes office], Dec. 12, 1935, 13.

157. *SB*, "Liu huanwei bei wei hui liang diwu kezhang" [Lau Waan-wai appointed head of two railroads], Nov. 22, 1927, 15; *NCH*, "Outside Meddling with Railways," Aug. 18, 1928, 265; *Cornell Alumni Directory* (Ithaca: Cornell University, 1922), 187, 189.

158. Cohen, *America's Response to China*, 101; Wilbur, *The Nationalist Revolution in China*, 170–90.

159. *CP*, "Frank Lee on Way to U.S. as Nanking Envoy," Aug. 11, 1927, 3; *CP*, "Nanking Council Orders Removal of Minister of Health," Oct. 26, 1929, 1; *SCMP*, "Death in U.S. of Mr. Frank Lee," Feb. 24, 1956, 7.

160. A. W. Brough to Commissioner of Immigration, Seattle, Jan. 19, 1925, p. 1, Samuel S. Young file (61/526), NARA-NY; I. F. Wixon to District Director, Ellis Island, Feb. 10, 1938, p. 1, Samuel S. Young file; *CWR*, "Samuel S. Young, First Cantonese Consul General in N.Y.," Apr. 21, 1928, 232; *SCMP*, "Sudden Death of Dr. Samuel S. Young," Jan. 9, 1958, 8.

161. Hin Wong, "News from South China," *WR*, Oct. 7, 1922, 206; *NCH*, untitled, Sept. 22, 1928, 493; telegram to Mr. Ingram, Jan. 9, 1934, p. 1, file 371/18116, BFO; *SCMP*, "Canton Portfolio," Dec. 16, 1932, 14.

162. American University Club of China, *American University Men in China* (Shanghai: Commercial Press, 1936), 211, 212; Julia C. Strauss, "The Evolution of Republican Government," *China Quarterly* 150 (1997): 337–39.

163. *CWR*, Hsiu Shu-cheng to editor, Sept. 14, 1940, 37.

164. *NCH*, "China's Railway Administration," Jan. 26, 1929, 139; *SB*, "Yunshu lei" [Transport], Aug. 20, 1928, 11; *SCMP*, "Canton Changes," Jan. 10, 1929, 12; *SB*, "*Songjiang*" [Songjiang district], Aug. 2, 1932, 10; *SCMP*, "Kwangtung Money," Feb. 14, 1928, 10. Bow's next position of real significance within the government was, unsurprisingly, in Guangxi under the patronage of Li Zongren, a Chiang rival, in 1937.

165. Zanasi, *Saving the Nation*, 109–10.

166. Parks M. Coble, *The Shanghai Capitalists and the Nationalist Government, 1927–1937* (Cambridge: Council on East Asian Studies, Harvard University, 1980), 31–33.

167. Frederic Wakeman Jr., *Policing Shanghai, 1927–1937* (Berkeley: University of California Press, 1995), 122–27.

168. Coble, *The Shanghai Capitalists*, 34–35.

169. *CWR*, "Men and Events," June 11, 1927, 42; Coble, *The Shanghai Capitalists*, 34–35.

170. *CWR*, "Dr. Sun's Principles and Some Current Practices," June 25, 1927, 77.

171. Christian Henriot, *Shanghai, 1927–1937: Municipal Power, Locality, and Modernization*, trans. Noel Castelino (Berkeley: University of California Press, 1993), 63–64; Marie-Claire Bergère, *The Golden Age of the Chinese Bourgeoisie, 1911–1937*, trans. Janet Lloyd (Cambridge: Cambridge University Press, 1989), 280–88.

172. Henriot, *Shanghai, 1927–1937*, 236.

173. Robert Dunn, "Does My Future Lie in China or America?" *Chinese Digest* (San Francisco), May 15, 1936, 3.

174. *NCH*, "Sensational Case of Mr. Char," July 20, 1929, 24; *FRUS 1929, Vol. II*, 514.

175. *CP*, "Commissioner of Foreign Affairs Arrests Mr. Nick Char, Well-Known Lawyer," July 13, 1929, 1; *CP*, "Mr. Char in Jail," Aug. 12, 1929, 17.

176. *CP*, "Commissioner of Foreign Affairs Arrests Mr. Nick Char," 1; *FRUS 1929, Vol. II*, 513–17.

177. Eileen P. Scully, *Bargaining with the State from Afar: American Citizenship in Treaty Port China, 1844–1942* (New York: Columbia University Press, 2001), 168–70; Cohen, *America's Response to China*, 94-101.

178. *FRUS 1929, Vol. II*, 518.

179. *China Critic* (Shanghai), "The Case of Mr. W. Y. Char," Feb. 21, 1929, file "D-62: Reports of Special Branch Made between 1929–1949: Newspaper Articles—Sentence of 'Nick' Char," SMP.

180. *FRUS 1929, Vol. II*, 639–42; *CWR*, "Nationalists Demand Revision of Treaties," July 14, 1928, 225.

181. *FRUS 1929, Vol. II*, 514, 517; *CP*, "Commissioner of Foreign Affairs Arrests Mr. Nick Char," 1.

182. *NCH*, "Nick Char Freed by Chinese," Sept. 28, 1929, 488.

183. Nicholas Wai Yuen Char testimony, May 4, 1939, p. 1, Nicholas Wai Yuen Char file (1302/6761), NARA-SB.

184. Soon Keong Ong, "Chinese but Not Quite: Huaqiao and the Marginalization of the Overseas Chinese," *Journal of Chinese Overseas* 9 (2013): 4; John Fitzgerald, "The Misconceived Revolution: State and Society in China's Nationalist Revolution, 1923–26," *Journal of Asian Studies* 49, no. 2 (1990): 329.

185. *Yishibao* (Tianjin), "Qiaobao xiang zuguo tou zi re" [Overseas compatriots enthusiastic about investing in the homeland], Oct. 27, 1932, 2; *Jiaoyu Zazhi* [Education Magazine], "Zhongguo daxueyuan huaqiaojiao weihui zhi zuzhi dagang" [Outline of the China university committee overseas Chinese education committee], 19, no. 12

(1927): 8; *Xingzhengyuan Gongbao* [Executive Yuan Gazette], "Huaqiao huiguo xingban shiye jiangli fa" [A law to encourage the undertakings of overseas Chinese who return to the nation], 27 (1929): 4–5.

CHAPTER 4

1. Jin Gun Oy testimony, Aug. 30, 1933, p. 5, Pheto Yee file (7030/5951), NARA-SEA.

2. Bureau of the Census, *Fifteenth Census of the United States, 1930: Population Number and Distribution of Inhabitants* (Washington, D.C.: USGPO, 1931), 266.

3. Erika Lee, *At America's Gates: Chinese Immigration During the Exclusion Era, 1882–1943* (Chapel Hill: University of North Carolina Press, 2003), 26–27; Renqiu Yu, *To Save China, To Save Ourselves: The Chinese Hand Laundry Alliance of New York* (Philadelphia: Temple University Press, 1992), 32; Charlotte Brooks, *Alien Neighbors, Foreign Friends: Asian Americans, Housing, and the Transformation of Urban California* (Chicago: University of Chicago Press, 2009), 87–88.

4. Adam McKeown, *Chinese Migrant Networks and Cultural Change* (Chicago: University of Chicago Press, 2001), 268–69.

5. Parks M. Coble, *The Shanghai Capitalists and the Nationalist Government, 1927–1937* (Cambridge: Council on East Asian Studies, Harvard University, 1980), 85, 141–42.

6. Some likely found work as "lower cost" replacements for white workers in the racialized treaty port economy. Robert Bickers, *Empire Made Me: An Englishman Adrift in Shanghai* (New York: Penguin, 2003), 234.

7. "Huaqiao xuexiao li'an tiaoli" [Overseas Chinese school registration regulations], 0574, Feb. 22, 1928, pp. 1–4, "Huaqiao xuexiao li'an zanxing tiaoli," file 001-012550-00001-00, Guominzhengfu records, AH; *Zhongyang Dangwu Yuekan* [Central Party Affairs Monthly], "Huaqiao fasheng xinwenzhi zazhi dengji banfa" [Means for the registration of newspapers and magazines published by overseas Chinese], 24 (1930): 256–57; *Yishibao* (Tianjin), "Qiaobao xiang zuguo tou zi re" [Overseas compatriots enthusiastic about investing in the homeland], Oct. 27, 1932, 2; *Gongshang Banyuekan* [Industry Bimonthly], "Huaqiao huiguo xingban shiye jiangli tiaoli" [Regulations to encourage and reward overseas Chinese who return to the nation to set up industries and businesses], 1, no. 5 (1929): 3–4; *CWR*, "League of Overseas Chinese in Shanghai Issues Prospectus," May 26, 1928, 416; *CWR*, "Construction Work Is Under Way on New Nanking Hotel," July 12, 1930, 229.

8. Margherita Zanasi, *Saving the Nation: Economic Modernity in Republican China* (Chicago: University of Chicago Press, 2006), 2–5, 7–8; Frederic Wakeman Jr., *Spymaster: Dai Li and the Chinese Secret Service* (Berkeley: University of California Press, 2003), 95–97; Lloyd E. Eastman, *The Abortive Revolution: China Under Nationalist Rule, 1927–1937* (Cambridge: Harvard University Press, 1975), 5–7, 208–39; Prasenjit Duara, *Culture, Power, and the State: Rural North China, 1900–1942* (Stanford: Stanford University Press, 234–42.

9. Rana Mitter, *Forgotten Ally: China's World War II, 1937–1949* (New York: Mariner Books, 2014), 61–67; Jeffrey N. Wasserstrom, *Student Protests in Twentieth-Century China: The View from Shanghai* (Stanford: Stanford University Press, 1991), 157–64; Diana Lary, *Region and Nation: The Kwangsi Clique in Chinese Politics, 1925–1937* (New York: Cambridge University Press, 1974), 18–19.

10. See, for example, Charles D. Musgrove, *China's Contested Capital: Architecture, Ritual, and Response in Nanjing* (Honolulu: University of Hawaii Press, 2014), 144; *CP*, "Overseas Group Due on Trade Mission Soon," Mar. 25, 1931, 8; *CP*, "Straits Chinese Warmly Received in Capital City," May 19, 1931, 2; P.S. Cheng, "Chinese Group Will Tour China," *CWR*, Mar. 21, 1936, 94.

11. *Xingzhengyuan Gongbao* [Executive Yuan Gazette], "Huaqiao huiguo xingban shiye jiangli fa" [Law to encourage and reward returned overseas Chinese for setting up businesses], no. 27 (1929): 4–6.

12. *CP*, "Membership of Siam Inquiry Group Filled," Mar. 15, 1936, 3; *CP*, "Chinese Quit Mexico," Apr. 16, 1933, 4; *Huaqiao Banyuekan* [Overseas Chinese semi-monthly], "Heyin yimin tiaoli huaqiao zuishou yingxiang" [Overseas Chinese greatly affected by Dutch East Indies immigration regulations], no. 33 (1933): 27.

13. *Zhongyang Dangwu Yuekan*, "Huaqiao jiaoyu huiyi xuanyan" [Manifesto of the overseas Chinese educational conference], 9, no. 22 (1931): 44–45.

14. Lin Shiheng, "Zhengdun meizhou huaqiao jiaoyu zhi chuyi" [My humble ideas for rectifying overseas Chinese education in the Americas], *Huaqiao Yuekan* [Overseas Chinese Monthly], Sept. 1936, 3.

15. *Waijiao Pinglun* [Foreign Affairs Review], "Minzu jingshen yu huaqiao jiaoxue" [Racial spirit and overseas Chinese education], no. 2 (1930): 3.

16. "*Huaqiao xuexiao li'an tiaoli,*" 1–4; Wu Xiren, "Huaqiao jiaoyu de jiben yuanze" [The basic principles of overseas Chinese education], *Haiwai Yuekan* [Overseas Monthly] 13 (1933): 30–36; Statement of the Ministry of Education, Jan. 13, 1930, pp. 1–2, file FO 371/14716, BFO; Xiao Jishan, "Huaqiao jiaoyu" [Overseas Chinese education], *Shishi Yuebao* [Current Affairs Monthly], 1930, 235.

17. Liu Shimu and Xu Zhigui, eds., *Huaqiao Gaiguan* [General Survey of the Overseas Chinese] (Shanghai: Chunghwa Book Co., 1935), 50–52.

18. *Daxueyuan Gongbao* [University Gazette], "Huaqiao zidi huiguo jiu xue banfa" [Measures for the children of the overseas Chinese who are attending college], I, no. 4 (1928): 12–13; *Guoli Daxue Lianhehui Yuekan* [National University Federation Monthly], "Zhongshan daxue youdai huaqiao xuesheng tiaoli" [Sun Yat-sen University regulations giving special preference to overseas Chinese students], I, no. 6 (1928): 110; *Xinwen Zhoubao* (Shanghai), "Huaqiao zidi huiguo jiu xue banfa" [Handling the children of the overseas Chinese who return to the nation for education], 8, no. 31 (1931): 4; K. Kaiser Wang, "The Mission of the Central Military Academy," *CWR*, May 20, 1933, 474.

19. *NCH*, "Agitation Practically Confined to Students," May 19, 1928, 265; *CWR*, "Student Rioters Quiet Down in Nanking and Shanghai," Apr. 19, 1930, 285; *CP*, "Chinan Middle School Students Suspend Studies," Dec. 3, 1930, 2; *CWR*, "1,400

Chinan University Students Go on Strike," Dec. 13, 1930, 67; *CP*, "Students Hold Mayor Prisoner Following Tangpu Arrest of Visiting Fellows Here," Dec. 10, 1931, 1; *CP*, "Students at Chenju Fired on by Mob," May 26, 1934, 1.

20. *Yishibao* "Qiaobao zidi" [The sons and younger brothers of the overseas compatriots], Aug. 8, 1934, 3.

21. Central Executive Committee collective letter 1427, Feb. 12, 1931, pp. 1–2, file 001-096000-00002-000, Guominzhengfu records, AH; *CP*, "Kwangtung to Help Returned Chinese," Nov. 15, 1933, 9. The Nanjing government eventually created an "Overseas Happy Village" for destitute overseas Chinese returning to China, but it was in Anhui, a province with almost no history of overseas migration. Most returnees were from Guangdong and Fujian.

22. Herbert Yee testimony, Dec. 12, 1935, pp. 1–5, Katie King So Yee file (7030/8272), NARA-SEA.

23. Sarah T. Phillips, *This Land, This Nation: Conservation, Rural America, and the New Deal* (Cambridge University Press, 2007), 114, 232–33.

24. Seung-Joon Lee, *Gourmets in the Land of Famine: The Culture and Politics of Rice in Modern Canton* (Stanford: Stanford University Press, 2011), 138–40; Alfred H. Y. Lin, "Building and Funding a Warlord Regime: The Experience of Chen Jitang in Guangdong, 1929–1936," *Modern China*, 28, no. 2 (2002): 181–83.

25. Lin, "Building and Funding a Warlord Regime," 179.

26. 1930 *ARCGI*, 75, 192; 1931 *ARCGI*, 95, 112, 210; 1932 *ARCGI*, 81, 185.

27. Seid Fook Gee testimony, Sept. 23, 1930, pp. 1–2, Annie Seid file (7030/722), NARA-SEA; Chin Kin Gung testimony, June 15, 1931, pp. 1–5, Chin Fook Hing file (7030/2338), NARA-SEA; Chin Fook Hing, "Affidavit by Native American to Explain Protracted Foreign Residence," June 14, 1946, p. 1, Canton consulate vol. 697, RG 84, NARA-CP; Lam Sit testimony, July 2, 1935, pp. 1–2, Ernest Lam Wah Cip file (7030/7748), NARA-SEA; Lam Wah-cip, "Affidavit by Native American to Explain Protracted Foreign Residence," July 22, 1946, p. 1, Canton consulate vol. 698, RG 84, NARA-CP; Jennie Wong Yick-yung, "Affidavit by Native American to Explain Protracted Foreign Residence," July 29, 1946, p. 1, Canton consulate vol. 700, RG 84, NARA-CP; Betty Lou Woon, "Affidavit by Native American to Explain Protracted Foreign Residence," Aug. 20, 1946, p. 1, Canton vol. 700; Mee Ling Johnson, "Affidavit by Native American to Explain Protracted Foreign Residence," Sept. 25, 1946, p. 1, Canton vol. 698.

28. A. R. S. Major to US Consul General, Hong Kong, May 6, 1933, p. 1, Canton consulate vol. 559, RG 84, NARA-CP; Charles Shepherd to US Consul General, Hong Kong, Jan. 18, 1938, p. 1, General Records of the Hong Kong Consulate, 1936–49, box 38, RG 84, NARA-CP; Carolyn Chinn, "Affidavit by Native American to Explain Protracted Foreign Residence," May 19, 1946, p. 1, Canton vol. 697; Albert Fong to Alice Fong, Jan. 10, 1933, p. 1, file 3, box 17, Alice Fong Yu Papers, Stanford University Library Special Collections, Stanford, CA; *SCMP*, "Doctor of Pedagogy," Sept. 2, 1933, 12.

29. Howard V. Ross to American Consul, Hong Kong, June 18, 1934, p. 1, Canton consulate vol. 534, RG 84, NARA-CP.

30. John Hedge, "Yam Yau Sing states," Mar. 17, 1932, p. 1, Canton consulate vol. 549G, RG 84, NARA-CP.

31. Albert Ling to US Consul, Canton, July 9, 1933, p. 1, Canton vol. 559.

32. H. Loo Kong to US Consul General, Shanghai, Oct. 28, 1937, p. 1, Shanghai consulate vol. 2668, RG 84, NARA-CP; Yuen Ah Quan, "Affidavit to Be Executed by a Person Born in the United States (of Alien Parents) Who Is Applying for the First Time for a Passport or Registration," June 12, 1946, p. 2, Canton vol. 700.

33. Madeline Y. Hsu, *Dreaming of Gold, Dreaming of Home: Transnationalism and Migration between the United States and South China, 1882–1943* (Stanford: Stanford University Press, 2000), 40–54.

34. *CWR*, "Marked Diminution in Remittances from Overseas Chinese," Feb. 17, 1934, 451; *SCMP*, "American Chinese," Apr. 21, 1936, 14.

35. Roberto Chao Romero, *The Chinese in Mexico, 1882–1940* (Tucson: University of Arizona Press, 2010), 172–75; *CWR*, "Chinese Laborers Being Deported from Japan and Mexico," Feb. 7, 1931, 358; *CP*, "Bank Head Sees Small Hope for Restoration of Normal Conditions," May 17, 1931, 13.

36. Guangdong Provincial Archives *Huaqiao yu qiaowu shiliao xuanbian (guangdong)* [Selected historical materials on overseas Chinese and overseas Chinese matters (Guangdong)], vol. 1 (Guangzhou: Guangdong People's Publishing House, 1991), 112.

37. Hollington K. Tong, "Economic Depression Reaches South as Chinese Come Home," *CP*, Oct. 1, 1933, 15.

38. John Fitzgerald, "Increased Disunity: The Politics and Finance of Guangdong Separatism, 1926–1936," *Modern Asian Studies* 24, no. 4 (Oct. 1990): 767.

39. Fitzgerald, "Increased Disunity," 757, 758–73.

40. Lary, *Region and Nation*, 18–19.

41. Stephen G. Mark to Mr. Penfield, Dec. 14, 1932, p. 1, Canton vol. 549G; Irving N. Linnell to Howard Donovan, Oct. 1, 1937, p. 1, General Records of the Hong Kong Consulate, 1936–49, box 22 (1937), RG 84, NARA-CP; *SCMP*, "Rural Welfare," Jan. 19, 1939, 16; Richard Kam Yee Lam, "Affidavit by Native American to Explain Protracted Foreign Residence," 1946, p. 1, Canton vol. 698; Bruno Lasker, "Gray Gloves," *CP*, Aug. 27, 1938, 10; Lynne Lee Shew testimony, Sept. 25, 1939, p. 1, Lynne Lee Shew file (7030/12446), NARA-SEA.

42. *SCMP*, "Chemistry and Its Many Applications," Apr. 20, 1932, 9; "Report of Birth of Children Born to American Parents: Chow (Tseu) Kum Wing," June 23, 1932, p. 1, Hong Kong consulate vol. 450, RG 84, NARA-CP; *SCMP*, "Local and General," Mar. 23, 1931, 2.

43. Chinn, "Affidavit by Native American to Explain Protracted Foreign Residence," p. 1; *1938 Business Directory of Hong Kong, Canton, and Macao* (Hong Kong: Far Eastern Corporation, 1938), Canton section 11–12. Shim had taught at Lingnan before the Northern Expedition but fled when the GMD moved left.

44. Reprinted in *CWR*, "China Should Encourage Help from Over-Seas Chinese," Apr. 1, 1933, 193.

45. Lin, "Building and Funding a Warlord Regime," 183–86.

46. *SCMP*, "History of Centuries Ago," Sept. 30, 1931, 14; *SCMP*, "Canton Portfolio," Dec. 16, 1932, 14; Foreign Office Telegram No. 1, Jan. 9, 1934, p. 1, file 371/18116, BFO; G. C. Pelham to E. B. M. Ingram, Jan. 16, 1934, p. 1, file 371/18116, BFO; Lee Fong to V. M. Grayburn, Jan. 14, 1934, p. 1, file 371/18116, BFO.

47. Lin, "Building and Funding a Warlord Regime," 185–86.

48. Paddy Gully, *Shiguang feishi: zhongguo kongjun xianqu linfuyuan zhuan* [Time flies: The biography of Chinese aviation pioneer Art Lym], trans. Zhang Chaoxia (Guangzhou: Huacheng Publishing, 2013), 164, 173, 176–77, 182–83.

49. R. Keith Schoppa, *In a Sea of Bitterness: Refugees during the Sino-Japanese War* (Cambridge: Harvard University Press, 2011), 309–11.

50. "Report of Birth of Children Born to American Parents: Chow (Tseu) Kum Wing," June 23, 1932, p. 1.

51. *Report of the Commission Appointed by His Excellency the Governor of Hong Kong to Enquire into the Causes and Effects of the Present Trade Depression in Hong Kong* (Hong Kong: Noronha & Co. Government Printers, 1935), 75–81; *SCMP*, "Hong Kong as Haven," May 30, 1932, 10.

52. *Hongkong & Canton Business Guide, 1934 Issue* (Hong Kong: The Publicity and Information Bureau, 1934), 186; Ng Leland Stanford Tye, "Registration Card," Sept. 12, 1918, p. 1, U.S., World War I Draft Registration Cards, 1917–1918, online database (Provo: Ancestry.com Operations Inc, 2005).

53. Look King testimony, Sept. 14, 1920, pp. 1–2, Look King file (38025/3-3), NARA-SEA; *SCMP*, "Bank of Canton Meeting," Mar. 27, 1930, 14.

54. Edward H. T. Louie testimony, Apr. 22, 1927, p. 1, Louie Hong How (Edward H. T. Louie) file (7030/13026), NARA-SEA; *Hong Kong Dollar Directory 1930* (Hong Kong: Local Printing Press, Ltd., 1930), 122.

55. The party did little to convince many of Hong Kong's Chinese American citizen merchants, either, particularly the Cantonese bankers. T. V. Soong essentially took over Look's Bank of Canton on the mainland.

56. *SCMP*, "Local and General," Aug. 15, 1935, 2; Ethel Chun by Hiram Fong to the American Consul General at Hong Kong, Dec. 7, 1937, p. 1, Hong Kong consulate box 22.

57. McKeown, *Chinese Migrant Networks and Cultural Change*, 268–69.

58. See, for example, *Gongshang Wanbao* (Hong Kong), "Baoliangju xin zongli xuanchu" [New Po Leung Kuk president elected], Mar. 27, 1935, 4; "Report of Birth of Children Born to American Parents: Ching Chui Moi," June 26, 1932, p. 1, Hong Kong vol. 450; Chun by Hiram Fong to the American Consul General at Hong Kong, p. 1; *SCMP*, advertisement, June 27, 1936, 5.

59. Blossom Y. Tyau, "Sau Ung Loo Chan," in *Called from Within: Early Women Lawyers of Hawai'i*, ed. Mari J. Masuda (Honolulu: University of Hawaii Press, 1992), 173–76; Hong Kong Executive Council, "Jurors List for 1936," *Hong Kong Government Gazette* 262 (Mar. 20, 1936): 270; *SCMP*, "Local and General," May 7, 1934, 2; *SCMP*, "President Lincoln," July 6, 1934, 2.

60. *SCMP*, "Samuel B. Luke," Aug. 25, 1936, 10; *SCMP*, advertisement, June 27, 1936, 5.

61. See, for example, *SCMP*, "Positions Wanted," July 12, 1934, 5; *SCMP*, "Personal," Oct. 1, 1936, 5; *SCMP*, "Positions Wanted," Dec. 24, 1936, 5; *SCMP*, "Positions Wanted," Mar. 17, 1937, 5.

62. John Fitzgerald, *Awakening China: Politics, Culture, and Class in the Nationalist Revolution* (Stanford: Stanford University Press, 1996), 103–46.

63. "List of American Citizens Residing in the Shanghai Consular District," Dec. 31, 1930, pp. 1–73, Shanghai consulate vol. 2072, RG 84, NARA-CP. I use "native-born" here to distinguish that group from derivative citizens born in China of American citizen parents.

64. "Memorandum Regarding Estimated Number of Chinese Americans in the Shanghai Consular District," Jan. 1, 1937, p. 1, Shanghai consulate vol. 2667, RG 84, NARA-CP.

65. For instance, St. John's charged $120 for tuition and $100 for board and lodging per year in 1921, but school officials speculated that they would soon need to raise tuition (I had difficulty obtaining tuition rates for the 1930s). The "$" here almost certainly refers to Mexican silver dollars, the standard currency in Shanghai. The exchange rate for Mexican dollars in the early 1920s varied between US$0.50 and US$0.90, meaning that the University of Hawaii's tuition in 1930 was far less than St. John's in 1921. Julean Arnold, *Commercial Handbook of China, Vol. I* (Washington, DC: USGPO, 1919), 437; *Catalogue of the Officers and Students of St. John's University, September 1921–June 1922* (Shanghai: Presbyterian Mission Press, 1921), 95; Hawaiian Department and Territory of Hawaii, *Digest of Information* (Honolulu: US Army, 1930), 16.

66. Francis Woo, *Johanneans in Hawaii: Highlights of Activities and Events of Former Hawaii Students at St. John's University Shanghai* (Honolulu: Hawaii Chinese History Center, 1981), 15–23.

67. Samuel M. Chao, "Yenching University Carries on Tradition of Early Founders," *CP*, July 4, 1934, B20.

68. *SB*, "Daxuesheng fuxing yundong cujinhui fazhan yantai wenti xuanyan fabiao yan wu wenti xuanyan" [Student Revitalization Movement Promotion Association issues a manifesto on the question of prohibiting dancing], Nov. 24, 1934, 14. Daxia University had a right-wing reputation, which fit with the politics of the Chu family.

69. Wen-Hsin Yeh, *Shanghai Splendor: Economic Sentiments and the Making of Modern China, 1843–1949* (Berkeley: University of California Press, 2007), 59–65.

70. *SB*, untitled, Mar. 28, 1933, 7; *CP*, "Loy Chang Is Named New Customs Directory, Succeeding Shen Shu-yu," Jan. 31, 1935, 1; *CP*, "Hin Wong Takes Over English Central News," Sept. 29, 1934, 3; Poy Gum Lee, "Questionnaire for Architects' Roster and/or Register of Architects Eligible for Federal Public Works," Oct. 24, 1946, p. 1, Poy Gum Lee papers, collection of Kerri Culhane. Charles D. Musgrove, in *China's Contested Capital: Architecture, Ritual, and Response in Nanjing* (Honolulu: University of Hawaii Press, 2013), 138, argues that Y. C. Lu (Lu Yanzhi), the American-trained

Chinese architect who created the design, died of overwork trying to construct it in the tight timeframe the GMD leadership demanded.

71. Lee, "Questionnaire," 1; *NCH*, "Mr. Murphy in New Connection," Jan. 7, 1933, 372. In 1921, fresh out of Pratt Institute, Poy Gum Lee found a position with the same architect (Henry Murphy) who employed Lu in New York and who eventually moved to China to design a new city plan for Nanjing in the late 1920s.

72. *CP*, "Becomes President," Jan. 8, 1930, 2.

73. *SB*, "Sifabu pin ding fayixuehui guwen weiyuan" [Ministry of Justice appoints forensic medicine experts to committee], June 23, 1936, 6; *SB*, "Shanghai xian gongjiaohui zuo kai nian erjie huiyuandahui" [Shanghai county public education association opens second general assembly], May 11, 1935, 12; *SB*, "Tiedaobu pu ri kaochatuan" [Railroad Ministry sends commission of inquiry to Japan], Apr. 14, 1931, 9.

74. *DGB* (Tianjin), "Dangdai zhongguo mingren lu" [A directory of famous people in contemporary China], Oct. 3, 1931, 3.

75. *CP*, "Unemployment Faces Many China Seniors Graduating in June," May 26, 1936, 9

76. See, for example, *CP*, "School of Commerce to Expand Work," Jan. 20, 1933, 5; Herbert E. Moy, "Shanghai Show World," *CP*, Jan. 20, 1933, 5; William T. Moy testimony, Oct. 19, 1932, p. 3, William Taft Moy file (166/137), NARA-NYC; *NCH*, "Young-Tong," Mar. 7, 1934, 369; James D. Hammond, "Workers behind the Front Page," *CP*, Oct. 10, 1936, C76; Chu War Lee, "Application for Financial Assistance," 1937, Shanghai vol. 2668. Honolulu native William Yukon Chang worked for the paper before and after World War II as well.

77. Thomas Chinn, interview by Ruth Teiser, "A Historian's Reflections on Chinese-American Life in San Francisco, 1919–1991," 1990–1991, pp. 46–47, Regional Oral History Office, University of California, Berkeley, accessed July 21, 2017, content.cdlib.org/view?docId=hb5779n97v&brand=calisphere; *CP*, "Yee Leaves Soon," June 25, 1931, 13.

78. *CP*, "Chu-Leong Wedding Is Surprise to Friends," Jan. 5, 1936, 4.

79. *CP*, "Two Well Known Doctors to Arrive in Shanghai," Sept. 6, 1935, 4; *NCH*, "Personal Notes," May 20, 1936, 328.

80. *Washington Post*, "Dr. Stephen Hu Dies, Noted Scientist," Sept. 1, 1977, C8; Lester Institute of Medical Research, *Annual Report, 1934* (Shanghai: Lester Institute, 1934), 52, 55.

81. Francisco E. Balderrama and Raymond Rodriguez, *Decade of Betrayal: Mexican Repatriation in the 1930s* (Albuquerque: University of New Mexico Press, 2006), 119–51; Rick Baldoz, *The Third Asiatic Invasion: Empire and Migration in Filipino America, 1898–1946* (New York: New York University Press, 2011), 186–93.

82. Lauren Rebecca Sklaroff, *Black Culture and the New Deal: The Quest for Civil Rights in the Roosevelt Era* (Chapel Hill: University of North Carolina Press, 2014), 19–20; Brooks, *Alien Neighbors, Foreign Friends*, 70–85, 92.

83. Judy Yung, *Unbound Feet: A Social History of Chinese Women in San Francisco* (Berkeley: University of California Press, 1995), 195.

84. *NCH*, "Young-Tong," 369.

85. *CP*, American Beauty Shop advertisement, Apr. 1, 1934, 11.

86. *CP*, "Fine New Beauty Shop Opening Today," Aug. 1, 1935, 5.

87. Hal P. Mills, "Sidelights from the Press Row," *CP*, Oct. 2, 1936, 6; Herbert Moy, "Application for Registration," Mar. 1939, p. 1, file "100155291 sec. 1, 1 of 3," box 72, classification 100, RG 65, NARA-CP; Hal P. Mills, "Sidelights," *CP*, Oct. 25, 1936, B4; Hal P. Mills, "Sidelights," *CP*, Jan. 24, 1937, B1; *CP*, "Novel Radio Skit to Be Broadcast by XMHC," Nov. 27, 1936, 5; "Report of Birth: Nina Alwayne Chinn," Nov. 20, 1933, p. 1, Shanghai consulate vol. 2327, RG 84, NARA-CP; Michael A. Krysko, *American Radio in China: International Encounters with Technology and Communications, 1919–41* (New York: Palgrave Macmillan, 2011), 79–80.

88. Shanghai Municipal Council, "Medical Certificate of Birth: Louie How Tsing," May 14, 1937, p. 1, Shanghai consulate vol. 2657, RG 84, NARA-CP; Shanghai Municipal Council, "Medical Certificate of Birth: Kwok Toy Louis," Feb. 3, 1937, p. 1, Shanghai vol. 2657.

89. William Lee, "Application for Financial Assistance," 1937, p. 1, Shanghai vol. 2668; *CP*, "Chinese Girl Singer Popular at Paramount," Dec. 14, 1935, 5; *CP*, "Lido Ballroom Offers Patrons Two Programs," July 31, 1937, 13.

90. Flora Belle Jan, *Unbound Spirit: Letters of Flora Belle Jan*, ed. Fleur Yano and Saralyn Daly (Bloomington: University of Illinois Press, 2006), 112.

91. See, for example, *CP*, "News Brevities," Feb. 27, 1925, 6; *NCH*, "Deaths," June 28, 1939, 533; *CP*, "Death," June 19, 1934, 10; *Honolulu Star Bulletin*, "Honolulu Youth Dies in Shanghai," Apr. 17, 1935, clipping in Ben Tin Kong Char file (4500/2410), NARA-SB; *CP*, "Tom Gunn's Widow Dies in Shanghai," July 8, 1933, 9; Major to Consul General, 1.

92. Lizabeth Cohen, in *Making a New Deal: Industrial Workers in Chicago, 1919–1939* (New York: Cambridge University Press, 1990), 144–47, discusses this process among European immigrants' children in Chicago. See chapter 1 for more discussion of the way China-born people disparaged Chinese American women for their consumption habits.

93. Ernest O. Hauser, "Chinaman's Chance," *Saturday Evening Post*, Dec. 7, 1940, 87.

94. *Chinese Digest* (San Francisco), "Famine Relief Executive Pays Respects of Overseas Chinese," Nov. 27, 1936, 4; "An Overseas Chinese" to editor, *CP*, June 21, 1931, 20.

95. Frederic Wakeman Jr., *Policing Shanghai, 1927–1937* (Berkeley: University of California Press, 1995), 182–96.

96. Wakeman, *Policing Shanghai*, 190; Frances Wood, *No Dogs and Not Many Chinese: Treaty Port Life in China, 1843–1943* (London: John Murray, 1998), 274.

97. *NCH*, "Stubborn Resistance in Chapei," Feb. 9, 1932, 192; *NCH*, "St. John's University Commencement," July 20, 1932, 96; Woo, *Johanneans in Hawaii*, 18–19.

98. *The Recorder* (Port Pirie, Australia), "In War Ravaged China," June 23, 1938, 4; *Boston Globe*, "Mrs. Kwoh Tells of Japanese Army Atrocities at Shanghai," Mar. 20, 1932, A21.

99. Young Chan Chun testimony, May 25, 1936, pp. 1–2, Young Chan Chun file (4382/811), NARA-SB.

100. Chen Lifu to Chiang Kai-shek, Nov. 29, 1932, pp. 1–3, file 002-080200-00064-001, Jiang zhongzheng zongtong wenwu, AH; *CP*, "Peace Role of Rotary Reviewed at Noon," Mar. 4, 1932, 9; *CP*, "Ladies' Aid Fund," Mar. 11, 1932, 13; *SB*, donor list, Feb. 24, 1932, 3.

101. *CP*, "Brevities," Mar. 10, 1932, 10.

102. *CP*, "They Saved Hundreds in Sino-Japanese Hostilities," May 27, 1932, 13.

103. *CP*, "Foreign Women Organize to Aid Chinese Troops," Feb. 5, 1932, 3.

104. *CP*, "Has Kuomintang Collapsed?" Jan. 29, 1932, 11.

105. Eastman, *The Abortive Revolution*, 91–92.

106. Wilbur Burton, "Ominous Maneuvers in Southwest China," *CWR*, Oct. 28, 1933, 360.

107. *CP*, "U.S.-Chinese Soldiers of Fortune Arrive," Apr. 19, 1933, 9; *SCMP*, "Girl Flier," Feb. 15, 1939, 5; Wakeman, *Spymaster*, 55–61, 120–21.

108. Wen-Hsin Yeh, *The Alienated Academy: Culture and Politics in Republican China, 1919–1937* (Cambridge: Council on East Asian Studies, 1990), 86–88, 172–83.

109. *CP*, "U.S.A. Like China," Aug. 25, 1932, 13; Todd DePastino, *Citizen Hobo: How a Century of Homelessness Shaped America* (Chicago: University of Chicago Press, 2014), 195–98; Eastman, *The Abortive Revolution*, 248; Wakeman, *Spymaster*, 51, 132–56, 166; Wasserstrom, *Student Protests in Twentieth-Century China*, 171–99.

110. Yeh, *The Alienated Academy*, 231–33.

111. Frank N. Tseu, receipt, Jan. 26, 1936, William Y. Chang papers.

112. Doris Shoong Lee, interview by Elizabeth A. Castle, 2006, 35, Regional Oral History Office, Bancroft Library, accessed Nov. 6, 2017, digitalassets.lib.berkeley.edu/roho/ucb/text/lee_doris.pdf.

113. Yeh, *The Alienated Academy*, 191, 228, 231.

114. Yeh, *The Alienated Academy*, 191, 228, 231.

115. Chen Shuren, et al., "Huaqia guojie wenti" [Overseas Chinese citizenship problems], Jan. 2, 1935, pp. 119–22, file 001-067122-00001-000, Guominzhengfu records, AH; Miles Lampson, "Protection of Anglo-Chinese in China," Sept. 20, 1929, pp. 74–76, reg. no. 4782/55/10, file 371/13907, BFO; J. F. Brenan to Sir Miles Lampson, July 4, 1927, p. 1, file FO 371/12511, BFO.

116. *FRUS 1930, Vol. II*, 522–26.

117. *NCH*, "Canton's War on Nanking," May 26, 1931, 254.

118. W. Leonard Parker, "Memorandum," June 29, 1936, pp. 1–3, Canton consulate vol. 606, RG 84, NARA-CP.

119. "An Oversea Chinese" to editor, *CP*, July 11, 1934, 10; "Another Oversea Chinese" to editor, *CP*, July 26, 1934, 10; "An Overseas Chinese" to editor, *CP*, July 25, 1931, 18; *CWR*, "Men and Events," Jan. 25, 1936, 286.

120. *CWR*, "What Nanking Thinks of Chen," June 27, 1931, 128. The statement was issued on June 17.

121. Miles Lampson to A. Henderson, June 23, 1930, p. 1, file 371/14703, BFO.

122. H.H. Chang, "Criticising the Returned Students," *The Chinese Republic*, Dec. 17, 1932, 132, box 21, P.M.W. Linebarger Collection, Hoover Institution.

123. *Shishi Yuebao* [Current Affairs Monthly], "Yuesheng chuguo qiaomin" [Guangdong Province overseas people who have left the country], 1931, 73; *CP*, "Local News Brevities," Oct. 10, 1933, 11; *CP*, "Overseas Registration Bureau Is Discussed," Mar. 19, 1934, 1.

124. Xu Guoqi, *Chinese and Americans: A Shared History* (Cambridge: Harvard University Press, 2014), 207–08, 227.

125. Eastman, *The Abortive Revolution*, 39–41; Zanasi, *Saving the Nation*, 12–15, 26–27; Ruth Rogaski, *Hygienic Modernity: Meanings of Health and Disease in Treaty-Port China* (Berkeley: University of California Press, 2004), 314; Wakeman, *Spymaster*, 105.

126. *SB*, "Daxuesheng fuxing yundong cujinhui fazhan yantai wenti xuanyan fabiao yan wu wenti xuanyan," 14.

127. Carol Benedict, *Golden-Silk Smoke: A History of Tobacco in China, 1550–2010* (Berkeley: University of California Press, 2011), 220–21; *CP*, "Women to Start New Movement," June 21, 1936, 11; *Chinese News* (San Francisco), "Y Woman-of-Month," May 9, 1953, 5.

128. *NCH*, "Shanghai and the New Life," Feb. 27, 1935, 333; *CP*, "Composition, Singing of Obscene Songs Hit Here," Aug. 22, 1934, 2; *NCH*, "Film Censorship Assailed," Jan. 22, 1936, 137; *CP*, "Officials Visit New Tobacco Company," Aug. 20, 1935, 11.

129. Louise Edwards, "Policing the Modern Woman in Republican China," *Modern China* 26, no. 2 (2000): 119–20.

130. Jan, *Unbound Spirit*, 144–45; *CP*, "Strict Rules to Govern Peiping Female Dress," Oct. 31, 1934, 14.

131. C.J. Spiker to Charles Hoover, June 30, 1936, pp. 1–6, Canton vol. 606.

132. Pan Yihong, "Feminism and Nationalism in China's War of Resistance against Japan," *International History Review* 19, no. 1 (1997): 117. In 1924, forty-four Chinese American women declared that they were permanently departing the United States for China; by the late 1920s, that number was rising each year, and by 1932, the last year such statistics were collected, it had reached 123. 1924 *ARCGI*, 51; 1932 *ARCGI*, 81.

133. Ting Cho Goo, "Application for Financial Assistance," 1937, p. 1, Shanghai vol. 2667.

134. *CP*, "American Beauty Parlor Experts Highly Qualified," Apr. 1, 1934, A1; *CP*, "Dollar Liners Sail for East and South," Nov. 11, 1933, A1.

135. "List of American Firms and Organizations Registered at the Shanghai Consulate General," Mar. 1, 1941, p. 23, Shanghai consulate vol. 2960, RG 84, NARA-CP.

136. "List of American Firms and Organizations Registered at the Tientsin Consulate General," Jan. 1, 1941, p. 3, Shanghai vol. 2960; Ah Huna Tong, "Changing Status of Women," *CP*, Oct. 10, 1936, C151.

137. Jan, *Unbound Spirit*, 139–43.

138. *CWR*, "Settlement Becomes Naughtier as China Goes Puritanical," Feb 9, 1935, 347; *CWR*, "Women's Fashions and Politics," Nov. 24, 1934, 444; *CP*, "Schoolgirls Growing Long Hair for General," Jan. 24, 1935, 9; *SCMP*, "Permanent Waves," Feb. 26, 1936, 9; *CP*, American Beauty Shop advertisement, Dec. 22 1936, 11.

139. Paul K. Whang, "The Purity Drive," *CWR*, Aug. 25, 1934, 504; *The Johannean 1935* (Shanghai: The Johannean Board, 1935).

140. Ah Huna Tong, "Parisian Designer Is in Town," *CP*, Jan. 9, 1935, 5; *CP*, "Aspiration for a New Life," Mar. 16, 1934, 10; *CP*, "Chiang's New Life Crusade Inaugurated in Shanghai," Apr. 2, 1934, 1; scrapbooks in William Yukon Chang collection.

141. See, for example, *CP*, "Popular Pair Wed at Canton Union Church," May 7, 1933, 3; *CP*, "Chong, Wang Wedding Held at Chinese Y," July 2, 1933, 9; *NCH*, "Personal Notes," May 20, 1936, 328; *CP*, "Miss Eleanor Moo Weds Dr. Kau in Church," Dec. 5, 1935, 4.

142. *CP*, "A. Lodge Enjoys Outing," July 2, 1935, 5; *CP*, "University Club Prom Draws Large Crowd," May 22, 1937, 11; *CP*, "Rotary Club in Nanking Gets Underway," Apr. 8, 1934, 20.

143. Norma Diamond, "Women under Kuomintang Rule: Variations on the Feminine Mystique," *Modern China* 1, no. 1 (1975): 8–9; Edwards, "Policing the Modern Woman in Republican China," 119–20.

144. Betty Wang, "Business and Professional Women's Association Grows into Modem Shanghai Colossus with a Membership of 12,000 and More to Come," *CP*, May 13, 1932, 9; *CP*, "Business Girls Have Picnic on Sunday," Feb. 2, 1936, 11.

145. Sophie Loy-Wilson, *Australians in Shanghai: Race, Rights and Nation in Treaty Port China* (New York: Routledge, 2017), 26.

146. Herbert Day Lamson, "The American Community in Shanghai," Ph.D. diss., Harvard University, 1935, 684.

147. Nara Dillon and Jean C. Oi, "Middlemen, Social Networks, and State-Building in Republican Shanghai," 10–11, and Jeffrey Wasserstrom, "Cosmopolitan Connections and Transnational Networks," 223, in *At the Crossroads of Empires: Middlemen, Social Networks, and State-Building in Republican Shanghai*, ed. Nara Dillon and Jean C. Oi, (Stanford: Stanford University Press, 2007).

148. Robert Dunn, "Does My Future Lie in China or America?," *Chinese Digest* (San Francisco) 2, no. 20 (May 15, 1936): 3–13; Kaye Hong, "Does My Future Lie in China or America?," *Chinese Digest* 2, no. 21 (May 22, 1936): 3–14; Chinese Students Club of Stanford University to Robert Dunn, *Chinese Digest* 2, no. 22 (May 29, 1936): 11–15; Jane Kwong Lee to editor, *Chinese Digest* 2, no. 23 (June 5, 1936): 5; Robert Dunn to the Chinese Students Club of Stanford, *Chinese Digest* 2, no. 24 (June 12, 1936): 5–14. The letters and controversy continued through July 1936.

149. Dunn, "Does My Future Lie in China or America?," 13.

150. Hong, "Does My Future Lie in China or America?," 3, 14.

151. Lloyd E. Eastman, "Fascism in Kuomintang China: The Blue Shirts," *China Quarterly* 49 (1972): 7–8, 20–22.

152. "A Pennsylvanian" to the editor, *CP*, May 18, 1929, 4.

153. Balderrama and Rodríguez, *Decade of Betrayal*, 243.

154. Quoted in Eiichiro Azuma, *Between Two Empires: Race, History, and Transnationalism in Japanese America* (New York: Oxford University Press, 2005), 150.

155. Azuma, *Between Two Empires*, 151–56.

156. Michael Lucken, *The Japanese and the War: Expectation, Perception, and the Shaping of Memory* (New York: Columbia University Press, 2013), 10–16.

157. Eastman, *The Abortive Revolution*, 9–11.

158. Zanasi, *Saving the Nation*, 109–10.

CHAPTER 5

1. Abigail, "Stranded in Shanghai," *SCMP*, Nov. 22, 1937, 3. Beijing in these years was known as "Beiping" because it was no longer the capital.

2. Parks M. Coble, *Chinese Capitalists in Japan's New Order: The Occupied Lower Yangzi, 1937–1945* (Berkeley: University of California Press, 2003), 24–25, 206.

3. Rana Mitter, *Forgotten Ally: China's World War II, 1937–1949* (New York: Mariner Books, 2014), 363

4. Alejandro Portes and Ruben G. Rumbaut, in *Immigrant America: A Portrait* (Berkeley: University of California Press, 2014), 100–8, discuss the push-pull paradigm and other ways of looking at immigrants' motives.

5. R. Keith Schoppa, *In a Sea of Bitterness: Refugees during the Sino-Japanese War* (Cambridge: Harvard University Press, 2011), 239–60.

6. Lloyd E. Eastman, *Seeds of Destruction: Nationalist China in War and Revolution, 1937–1949* (Stanford: Stanford University Press, 1984), 27–28, 132–46.

7. Kenton Clymer, *A Delicate Relationship: The United States and Burma/Myanmar since 1945* (Ithaca: Cornell University Press, 2015), 21–24.

8. Charlotte Brooks, *Between Mao and McCarthy: Chinese American Politics in the Cold War Years* (Chicago: University of Chicago Press, 2015), 51–88.

9. Parks M. Coble, "Debating War in China: The Decision to Go to War, July-August 1937," in *Debating War in Chinese History*, ed. Peter A. Lorge (Leiden: Brill, 2013), 247–48; Mitter, *Forgotten Ally*, 72–74.

10. Poshek Fu, *Passivity, Resistance, and Collaboration: Intellectual Choices in Occupied Shanghai, 1937–1945* (Stanford: Stanford University Press, 1993), 2–5.

11. Schoppa, *In a Sea of Bitterness*, 2, 214, 285–86, 301, passim.

12. Coble, *Chinese Capitalists in Japan's New Order*, 12.

13. Mitter, *Forgotten Ally*, 151–53; Stephen R. MacKinnon, *Wuhan 1938: War, Refugees, and the Making of Modern China* (Berkeley: University of California Press, 2008), 39–43.

14. Eastman, *Seeds of Destruction*, 27–28.

15. Huang Meizhen and Yang Hanqing, "Nationalist China's Negotiating Position during the Stalemate," trans. David P. Barrett, in *Chinese Collaboration with Japan, 1932–1945: The Limits of Accommodation*, ed. David P. Barrett and Larry N. Shyu (Stanford: Stanford University Press, 2001), 57–72.

16. Jay Taylor, *The Generalissimo: Chiang Kai-shek and the Struggle for Modern China* (Cambridge: Belknap Press, 2011), 174–82.

17. The Soviet Union did not declare war on Japan until 1945, however.

18. Mitter, *Forgotten Ally*, 235–43.

19. *FRUS, 1937: Volume IV, The Far East*, 307–8; "Memorandum Regarding Estimated Number of Chinese Americans in the Shanghai Consular District on Jan. 1, 1937," Sept. 9, 1937, p. 1, Shanghai consulate vol. 2667, RG 84, NARA-CP.

20. Abigail, "Stranded in Shanghai," 3.

21. *CP*, "Injured Y's Men Are All Recovered," Aug. 28, 1937, 4.

22. Henry Loo Kong, "Application for Financial Assistance," Oct. 1937, p. 1, and Henry Loo Kong to American Consul General, Oct. 28, 1937, pp. 1–2, Shanghai consulate vol. 2668, RG 84, NARA-CP. See also "Bartlett Young and Company," Nov. 16, 1938, p. 1, "Alphabetical Indices to American Citizens, Schools & Companies Which Suffered Losses from Bombing, Looting," Tokyo Embassy General Records, 1937–1940, box 1, RG 84, NARA-CP.

23. *CP*, "Chinese Abroad Maintain Bonds with Homeland," Oct. 25, 1937, 8.

24. *CP*, "Chinese in United States Contribute to War Fund," Sept. 13, 1937, 2.

25. *CP*, "Elsie Lee Soong Makes Trip to Front Line with Gifts," Oct. 10, 1937, 7; *CP*, "New Hospital Being Used for Refugees," Aug. 15, 1937, 9; Abigail, "Stranded in Shanghai," 3.

26. *FRUS 1937: Volume IV*, 266, 406.

27. The disappearance of funds that overseas Chinese donated in 1932 received widespread attention in the years afterward. See, for example, Hoh Chih-hsiang, "Reflections on the 'Missing Millions' of Patriotic Contributions," *CWR*, Aug. 19, 1933, 489; Renqiu Yu, *To Save China, to Save Ourselves: The Chinese Hand Laundry Alliance of New York* (Philadelphia: Temple University Press, 1992), 91–92; *New York Times*, "Leakage in Funds for China Alleged," June 18, 1933; *SCMP*, "China Abroad," Mar. 2, 1934, 12.

28. Marjorie Dryburgh, "Regional Office and the National Interest: Song Zheyuan in North China, 1933–1937," in *Chinese Collaboration with Japan, 1932-1945*, ed. Barrett and Shyu, 51–52.

29. *FRUS, 1937: Volume III: The Far East* (Washington, DC: USGPO, 1954), 443.

30. Wen-hsin Yeh, "Introduction: The Struggle to Survive," in *Wartime Shanghai*, ed. Wen-hsin Yeh (New York: Routledge, 1998), 3, 6.

31. *FRUS, 1937: Volume IV*, 255, 273.

32. Yeh, "Introduction," 4.

33. *FRUS, 1937: Volume IV*, 368.

34. *FRUS, 1937: Volume IV*, 259–60, 266, 321–24.

35. Kaye Hong, "Does My Future Lie in China or America?" *Chinese Digest* 2, no. 21 (May 22, 1936): 3.

36. *FRUS, 1937: Volume IV*, 296.

37. Schoppa, *In a Sea of Bitterness*, 308–11.

38. This is my estimate based on US consular records of repatriates from after the war, including Canton consulate vols. 697, 698, 699, 700, and 740, RG 84, NARA-CP, and *South China Morning Post* accounts of postwar repatriation ships.

39. *FRUS 1937: Volume IV*, 267–68, 307–8.

40. *FRUS 1937: Volume IV*, 268–69, 290–93; *FRUS 1937: Volume III*, 521.

41. *FRUS 1937: Volume IV*, 473; *NCH*, "200 Students Charter SS Tjinegara," Sept. 8, 1937, 373.

42. *NCH*, "*President Hoover* Is Bombed," Sept. 1, 1937, 348; *CP*, "Evacuation by Foreigners Is Still Feasible," Sept. 2, 1937, 1.

43. American Consulate General, Shanghai, "Confidential List Prepared by the American Consulate General of Persons Scheduled to Travel from Shanghai to Manila or Hongkong on the United States Naval Transport *Chaumont*," Sept. 22, 1937, p. 1, and "Final List of American Citizens Sailing aboard U.S.S. *Sacramento*," Sept. 13, 1937, p. 1, Shanghai consulate vol. 2665, RG 84, NARA-CP.

44. Ernest K. Moy to Clarence E. Gauss, Oct. 7, 1937, pp. 1–2, Shanghai vol. 2668; *CP*, "U.S.S. *Sacramento* Takes 1st Americans Evacuated by Navy," Sept. 14, 1937, 1.

45. "Final List of American Citizens Sailing aboard U.S.S. *Sacramento*," p. 1.

46. Handwritten note on Clarence Kim, "Application for Financial Assistance," Sept. 5, 1937, p. 2, Shanghai vol. 2668.

47. *NCH*, "Shanghai-Kowloon by Train," Apr. 21, 1937, 107; *SCMP*, ship advertisements, Jan. 5, 1937, 19; *FRUS 1937: Volume IV*, 325–26.

48. *SCMP*, "Hong Kong's Woes," Sept. 3, 1937, 8.

49. *FRUS 1937: Volume IV*, 261, 324; Irving N. Linnell, "Circular to American Citizens in the Canton Consular District," Sept. 18, 1937, p. 1, box 38, General Records of the Hong Kong Consulate, 1936–49, RG 84, NARA-CP.

50. Howard Donovan to Editor, *SCMP*, Sept. 3, 1937, p. 1; Mrs. Joshua Liao and Mrs. Thomas Liao to American Consulate, Hong Kong, Sept. 6, 1937, p. 1; A. T. Rowe to American Consulate, Hong Kong, Sept. 2, 1937, p. 1; Howard Donovan to Sarah Elaine Lee, Oct. 3, 1937, p. 1; and Donovan to State Department, Oct. 9, 1937, p. 1, all in box 22, General Records of the Hong Kong Consulate, RG 84, NARA-CP; Dick Wong to American Consul, Hong Kong, Oct. 6, 1937, p. 1, box 23, General Records of the Hong Kong Consulate, RG 84, NARA-CP.

51. Addison E. Southard to Dollar Steamship Line, Dec. 2, 1937, p. 1; Cross-Reference Sheet Document File Note, Aug. 23, 1937, p. 1; Sumner Welles to American Consul, Hong Kong, Oct. 21, 1937, p. 1; and Howard Donovan to American Consul, Shanghai, Sept. 4, 1937, p. 1, all in box 22, 1937, General Records of the Hong Kong Consulate.

52. Nelson T. Johnson to American Consulate, Hong Kong, Aug. 20, 1937, p. 1, box 1, Classified General Records, 1937–1948, General Records of the Canton Consulate, RG 84; Harold D. Pease, "Outport Emergency Lists," c. 1937, pp. 1–3, Shanghai consulate vol. 2721, RG 84, NARA-CP; Irma Tam Soong, *Chinese American Refugee: A World War II Memoir* (Honolulu: Hawaii Chinese History Center, 1984), x–xi, xiii; "List of American Citizens Reported to be Resident in Nanking," Oct. 6, 1937, pp. 1–18,

Shanghai consulate vol. 2664, RG 84, NARA-CP; George Atcheson Jr. to State Department, Nov. 23, 1937, p. 1, Shanghai consulate vol. 2666, RG 84, NARA-CP.

53. Soong, *Chinese American Refugee*, xi–xii; Hallett Abend, *My Life in China, 1926–1941* (New York: Harcourt, Brace and Company, 1943), 268–78.

54. MacKinnon, *Wuhan 1938*, 97–99; Mitter, *Forgotten Ally*, 149–63, 200–1.

55. Irving N. Linnell to State Department, Aug. 19, 1937, p. 1, file "Canton, 1937, 110.2-800 (Aug.)," box 1, General Records of the Canton Consulate, RG 84, NARA-CP; Linnell to State Department, Aug. 21, 1937, p. 1; Linnell to State Department, Aug. 30, 1937, p. 1; Linnell to State Department, Sept. 1, 1937, pp. 1–2; and Linnell to State Department, Sept. 25, 1937, p. 1, all in file "Canton, 1937, 800 (Aug.–Sept.)," box 1, General Records of the Canton Consulate; Linnell to State Department, Oct. 22, 1937, p. 1; and Linnell to State Department, Dec. 31, 1937, p. 1, file "Canton, 1937, 800 (Oct.)–877," both in box 1, General Records of the Canton Consulate; *FRUS 1937: Volume IV*, 403; *FRUS 1938: The Far East, Volume IV*, 344–45, 356–57.

56. *FRUS 1938: The Far East, Volume IV*, 356–57.

57. I could not find any evidence of Johnson's intervention in the Foreign Office papers; the memo discussing it was also not included in the *Foreign Relations of the United States* volume covering this period.

58. *FRUS 1938: The Far East, Volume IV*, 494, 497–99, 502, 504, 508–9; John Hunter Boyle, *China and Japan at War, 1937–1945: The Politics of Collaboration* (Stanford: Stanford University Press, 1972), 186–88.

59. Eloise Fong, interview by Robin Li, p. 6, 2011, Regional Oral History Office, University of California, Berkeley, accessed Nov. 16, 2017, digitalassets.lib.berkeley.edu/roho/ucb/text/fong_eloise_2013.pdf.

60. State Department to American Consul Hong Kong, Dec. 2, 1938, p. 1; American Consulate General, "Memorandum," Dec. 2, 1938, p. 1; American Consulate General, "Memorandum," Dec. 7, 1938, p. 1; Addison E. Southard to State Department, Dec. 3, 1938, p. 1; and Addison E. Southard to State Department, Dec. 12, 1938, p. 1, all in box 40, General Records of the Hong Kong Consulate, RG 84, NARA-CP.

61. Addison E. Southard to Que Wong, Jan. 26, 1939, p. 1; Robert C. Coudray, "Memorandum for Mr. Southard," Mar. 24, 1939, p. 1; and Charles Hong Wong to "Mr. Consulate of America," Aug. 28, 1939, p. 1, all in box 57, General Records of the Hong Kong Consulate.

62. M. S. Myers to Cordell Hull, Feb. 25, 1939, pp. 1–2, box 56, General Records of the Canton Consulate, RG 84, NARA-CP.

63. *FRUS, 1937, Vol. IV: The Far East*, 266–67.

64. Brooks, *Between Mao and McCarthy*, 13–14.

65. *SCMP*, "American Chinese," Dec. 21, 1940, 16; Leong Choi to American Consul General, Hong Kong, Oct. 14, 1940, p. 1, box 74, General Records of the Hong Kong Consulate, RG 84, NARA-CP; Anna Suey-Linn Leong, "Application for Repatriation," pp. 1–4, Oct. 5, 1946, Canton consulate vol. 698, RG 84, NARA-CP.

66. Ten percent of the applicants for repatriation in Canton consulate vols. 697–700 left the United States for China between 1938 and 1941.

67. Shum Ah-sin and Leung Kai-bun to M.S. Myers, May 22, 1940, p. 1, box 74, General Records of the Hong Kong Consulate. See, for example, the Canton consulate's utter lack of response to Francis E. Lee, affidavit, Nov. 20, 1940, p. 1, box 74, General Records of the Hong Kong Consulate.

68. Yeh, "Prologue: Shanghai Besieged, 1937–1945," in *Wartime Shanghai*, 4–5.

69. *SCMP*, "American Kidnapped," Sept. 14, 1937, 10.

70. American Consulate General, Shanghai, "Supplementary List of Americans Residing in City of Shanghai," Jan. 31, 1940, p. 1; "Supplementary List of Americans Residing in City of Shanghai," June 30, 1940, p. 1; and "Supplementary List of Americans Residing in City of Shanghai," Dec. 31, 1940, p. 2, Shanghai consulate vol. 2881, RG 84, NARA-CP; Pease, "Outport Emergency Lists," 1.

71. St. John's University Shanghai, *The Johannean 1939* (Shanghai: China Press, 1939).

72. John B. Powell, *My Twenty-Five Years in China* (New York: Macmillan, 1945), 325; Abend, *My Life in China*, 276.

73. "Area No. 6," c. 1937, pp. 6 and 16, Shanghai vol. 2721; *CP*, "Merger of Five Big Movie Theaters Announced," Jun 24, 1938, 1; Poshek Fu, "Projecting Ambivalence: Chinese Cinema in Semi-Occupied Shanghai, 1937–41," in *Wartime Shanghai*, 89–92; American Consulate General, "Supplementary List of Americans Residing in City of Shanghai," Jan. 31, 1940, p. 1; *NCH*, "From Daily News Ads," Apr. 24, 1940, 160.

74. Anna Koe testimony, May 5, 1938, pp. 1–2, Anna Koe file (170/676), NARA-NY; Stella Dong, email to the author, Nov. 7, 2015; Moy Kee Ging Lee testimony, Jan. 15, 1938, pp. 3–5, Moy Kee Ging Lee file (170–452), NARA-NY. See also American Consulate General, Shanghai, "Supplementary List of Americans Residing in City of Shanghai," Jan. 31, 1940, p. 1.

75. William Y. Chang to William Grove, May 2, 1951, p. 1, William Y. Chang collection, in the possession of Dallas Chang.

76. *CP*, "Officers Named for Chinese Women's Club," May 11, 1938, 10.

77. *SB*, "Jiuji xiehui lishihuiyi" [Relief association board of directors meeting], Feb. 5, 1939, 15; *SB*, "*Jieyue jiunanhui*" [Organization to save for refugees], May 27, 1939, 12; *SB*, "Nanmin jiuji xiehui" [Refugee relief society], July 20, 1941, 10.

78. Coble, *Chinese Capitalists in Japan's New Order*, 24–25.

79. Boyle, *China and Japan at War*, 85–86, 113–14.

80. Frederic Wakeman Jr., *The Shanghai Badlands: Wartime Terrorism and Urban Crime, 1937–1941* (New York: Cambridge University Press, 1996), 11, 25; Coble, *Chinese Capitalists in Japan's New Order*, 68.

81. *DGB* (Hong Kong), "Hu yi hanjian bei ji zhongshang" [Traitor beaten severely in Shanghai], Sept. 24, 1938, 3.

82. *Zhonghua minguo weixinzhengfu gai shi* [Record and history of the Reformed Government of the Republic of China] (Nanjing: Executive Yuan Propaganda Department, 1940), 89–91.

83. Hollington K. Tong, "Industrial Development Can Save China, Says President Hsu," *MR*, Mar. 8, 1919, 47; Boyle, *China and Japan at War*, 112–14, 163–64; *CWR*, "Prominent Wedding Announced," May 15, 1926, 284.

84. William Yinson Lee, *World Chinese Biographies* (Shanghai: Globe Publishing Company, 1944), 105–6; G. S. Moss to Sir Miles Lampson, Oct. 26, 1929, pp. 1–3, file 371/14716, BFO; D. B. Ku, "Report," Oct. 12, 1932, p. 1, file "Reports Made 1916–1929: Extracts from D. S. I. Robertson's Report Re L. K Kentwell, July 1, 1927"; and "Translation of French Police Report 2454/S dated May 9, 1938," p. 1, May 1938, file "On Noulens Associates: Publication of an Article in the 'Voice of New China,'" SMP; FB to Dr. A. D. Wall, July 13, 1939, p. 1, file "On Noulens Associates: Publication of an Article in the 'Voice of New China,'" SMP; "Foreword," *Voice of New China* (Shanghai) I, no. 1 (Aug. 13, 1938): 1.

85. *Voice of New China*, "China and Japan Are Not at War," Aug. 15, 1938, 2–3; *Voice of New China*, "Announcement," Oct. 15, 1938, 5.

86. *SCMP*, "Educator Gaoled," Apr. 11, 1947, 1.

87. Eva Edwards, "News of Dr. Sung and Family," *Covina Argus* (Covina, California), Nov. 23, 1945, 10.

88. *SCMP*, "Socialist Party," Oct. 1, 1939, 14; *CWR*, "Personnel of the Puppet Government," Mar. 30, 1940, 163; Kiang Kang-hu, *Such a Life: Autobiography of Kiang Kang-hu*, 1948, pp. 40–55, 69, Rare and Special Collections, University of California, Berkeley, East Asian Library, Berkeley, CA.

89. Leonard Kiang, "Synopsis and Epilogue," in *Such a Life*, 139.

90. See, for example, Paxton to Drumright, "Additional Details in Regard to Imprisonment of Mr. Henry K. Chan in China," June 17, 1946, pp. 1–2, "War Crimes and Criminals" file, Records of the Office of Chinese Affairs, Gale Group Archives Unbound database.

91. Frank S. Gibbs, "Canton Intelligence Report for September Half Year 1936," p. 4, file 371/20256, BFO; *SCMP*, "Adviser to Mayor," Aug. 30, 1938, 12; *SCMP*, "Visit to Indo-China," Sept. 14, 1938, 8; Sir Hughe Knatchbull-Hugessen, "Reconstruction and Railway Projects in China," June 28, 1937, p. 1, file 371/20973, BFO; statements of Col. Li-fang, June 17, 1939, pp. 1–3 and June 20, 1939, pp. 1–2, file 676/410, BFO; Philip Broadhead to Foreign Office, May 27, 1939, p. 1, file 676/410, BFO; *Hong Kong Dollar Directory 1940* (Hong Kong: Hong Kong Dollar Directory Company, 1940), 686.

92. *SCMP*, "Japanese Designs," Dec. 30, 1940, 14.

93. D. S. I. Laurier, "Report," Nov. 1, 1937, p. 1, file D-8113, and D. S. I. Laurier, "Report," Oct. 24, 1937, p. 1, file "On Noulens Associates: Overseas Broadcasting Company 23/1729 Avenue Road: Believed Sold to Shanghai Evening Post & Mercury," SMP; *CP*, "Police Working on Theory Sunday Night Bombings Work of Pro-Japan Group," June 14, 1938, 8.

94. Astrid Freyeisen, *Shanghai und die Politik des Dritten Reiches* [Shanghai and the Politics of the Third Reich] (Würzburg: Königshausen und Neumann, 2000), 340–46; "Information Concerning the Death of Herbert Moy," Nov. 3, 1945, p. 1, WN24213, box 22, RG 226, NARA-CP.

95. See, for example, Foreign Broadcast Intelligence Service, "Special Report #90: Radio Tokyo Commentators and Features," Aug. 16, 1943, p. 9, file "100155291 sec 5, 3 of 3," box 74, classification 100, RG 65, NARA-CP.

96. *CP*, "Broker's Daughter to Wed Young Lawyer," May 9, 1926, 4; Parks M. Coble, *The Shanghai Capitalists and the Nationalist Government, 1927–1937* (Cambridge: Council on East Asian Studies, Harvard University, 1980), 197–205.

97. John A. Thomson, *A Sense of Power: The Roots of America's World Role* (Ithaca: Cornell University Press, 2015), 186–90; *FRUS 1940, Vol. IV: The Far East*, 985; Lim P. Lee, "Chinatown Goes Picketing," *Chinese Digest* (San Francisco), Jan. 1939, 10–11.

98. "Meeting of American Emergency Committee," May 20, 1940, pp. 1–3, Shanghai vol. 2881; *FRUS Vol. IV: The Far East*, 934–35.

99. American Consulate General, "Supplementary List of Americans Residing in City of Shanghai," Jan. 31, 1940, p. 1; Feb. 29, 1940, p. 1; Mar. 30, 1940, p. 1; Apr. 30, 1940, pp. 1–2; May 31, 1940, p. 1; June 30, 1940, p. 1; July 31, 1940, p. 1; Aug. 31, 1940, p. 1; Sept. 30, 1940, p. 1; Oct. 31, 1940, pp. 1–2; Nov. 30, 1940, pp. 1–10; Dec. 31, 1940, pp. 1–2, all in Shanghai vol. 2881. The lack of Chinese American evacuees did not indicate that the immigrants had long since gone, because during 1940 the consulate recorded that more than fifty Chinese Americans moved within Shanghai itself.

100. Richard P. Butrick to State Department, Oct. 14, 1940, p. 1, and F. R. Engdahl, "Memorandum," Oct. 22, 1940, pp. 1–2, Shanghai vol. 2881; Butrick to State Department, Oct. 21, 1940, pp. 1–2, and Robert L. Smyth to State Department, Oct. 22, 1940, p. 1, Shanghai consulate vol. 2882, RG 84, NARA-CP.

101. Chang Chan v. Nagle 268 U.S. 346 (1925).

102. Sucheng Chan, "The Exclusion of Chinese Women, 1870–1943," *Chinese America: History and Perspectives* 8 (1994): 108; Candice Lewis Bredbenner, *A Nationality of Her Own: Women, Marriage, and the Law of Citizenship* (Berkeley: University of California Press, 1998), 241. According to Green Haywood Hackworth, *Digest of International Law, Vol. III, Chapters IX–XI* (Washington, DC: USGPO, 1942), 34–35, the Minister for China recommended in 1916 that the US Court for China gain the right to naturalize prospective citizens, but the State Department rejected this advice.

103. Cordell Hull to embassies and consulates in China and Japan, Oct. 30, 1940, pp. 2–3, Shanghai vol. 2882.

104. See, for example, *CP*, photo section, Sept. 26, 1926, B1; Ellen Lee, repatriation certificate, Oct. 7, 1945, p. 1, file "Repatriation Certificate, Oct. 10. 45," container 45, RG 493, NARA-CP; Sally Wong, repatriation certificate, Oct. 8, 1945, p. 1, file "Repatriation Certificate, Oct. 10. 45."

105. F. Russell Engdahl to American President Lines, Nov. 27, 1940, p. 1, Shanghai vol. 2882; Flora Belle Jan, *Unbound Spirit: Letters of Flora Belle Jan*, ed. Fleur Yano and Saralyn Daly (Bloomington: University of Illinois Press, 2006), 159–73.

106. J. O. Thompson to American Consul General, Hong Kong, Sept. 12, 1940, p. 1, box 74, General Records of the Hong Kong Consulate.

107. Lynne Lee Shew testimony, Sept. 25, 1939, p. 1, Lynne Lee Shew file (7030/12446), NARA-SEA. On its website, the government of Shew's ancestral district (formerly Heungshan/Xiangshan, now Zhongshan) claims she resigned after her marriage and returned to the United States. In her 1939 immigration testimony, however, Shew said she was unmarried.

108. The Nationality Act of 1940 caused considerable confusion among Chinese Americans—Flora Belle Jan also believed she would lose her citizenship until the Beijing consulate corrected her misunderstanding. Essentially, the law laid out the conditions for expatriation, and a confusing section of the act seemed to imply that more than six months of residence abroad for dual citizens would result in expatriation.

109. *SCMP*, "American Chinese," 16; Francis E. Lee, affidavit, Nov. 20, 1940, p. 1, box 74, General Records of the Hong Kong Consulate.

110. Luey Shuck, testimony, July 30, 1940, pp. 1–2, Louey Shuck file (7030/3061), NARA-SEA; Louie Hong How testimony, May 8, 1940, p. 1, Louie Hong How file (7030/13026), NARA-SEA.

111. *SCMP*, "Hong Kong Man in USA," Dec. 11, 1945, 6; List or Manifest of Alien Passengers for the United States, SS President Cleveland, Aug. 6, 1940, list 6, in "California, Passenger and Crew Lists, 1882–1959," online database (Provo: Ancestry.com Operations, Inc., 2008); Jun-ke Choy, *My China Years: Practical Politics in China after the 1911 Revolution* (San Francisco: East/West Publishing, 1974), 188–89, 237.

112. Although alien spouses could gain temporary entry as Section 6 immigrants, they were not guaranteed it as a right. At a time when China was engulfed in war, US immigration officials might also have barred the entry of alien spouses, given the likelihood that the war would make their return to Asia impossible.

113. Sheet 11-B, Honolulu 2-65, 1940 United States Federal Census, online database (Provo: Ancestry.com Operations, Inc., 2012); Soong, *Chinese American Refugee*, xii.

114. *SCMP*, "Americans in Colony," Feb. 17, 1941, 13.

115. Carolyn Chinn, "Affidavit by Native American to Explain Protracted Foreign Residence," May 19, 1946, p. 1; Russell Chinn, "Affidavit by Native American to Explain Protracted Foreign Residence," Jan. 2, 1945, p. 1; and Bong Clara Chin, "Application for Financial Assistance and Repatriation," June 1946, p. 1, all in Canton vol. 697; Alfred Poy, "Affidavit by Native American to Explain Protracted Foreign Residence," July 30, 1946, p. 1, Canton vol. 699.

116. *SCMP*, "Americans in Colony," 13.

117. *SCMP*, "U.S. Foreign Trade," June 11, 1941, 15; *SCMP*, "American President Line Sailings," June 10, 1941, 13; *SCMP*, "American President Line Sailings," June 16, 1941, 17; *SCMP*, "Japanese Blockade," Feb. 17, 1941, 14; *SCMP*, "Base at Chungshan?" Apr. 27, 1941, 14; *SCMP*, "Chungshan Barrier," May 23, 1941, 12; *SCMP*, "Road to Macao Open," June 2, 1941, 15.

118. Yee Wing, "Affidavit by Native American to Explain Protracted Foreign Residence," Apr. 12, 1946, p. 1, and Wong Yee-bong, "Affidavit by Native American to Explain Protracted Foreign Residence," May 9, 1946, p. 1, in Canton vol. 700.

119. *FRUS 1941: Vol V, The Far East*, 374–80.

120. Choy, *My China Years*, 183–91; Soong, *Chinese American Refugee*, 7, 20.

121. Elsie Chin Yuen Seetoo, interview by Herman J. Trojanowski, Sept. 9, 2005, p. 11, Women Veterans Historical Project, University of North Carolina, Greensboro, accessed Aug. 27, 2018, libcdm1.uncg.edu/cdm/singleitem/collection/WVHP/id/10300/rec/1.

122. Subcommittee to Investigate the Administration of the Internal Security Act and Other Internal Security Laws of the Committee on the Judiciary, *Morgenthau Diary (China), Vol. 1* (Washington, DC: USGPO, 1965), 622–23; *DGB* (Guilin), "Guishi diandi" [Guilin droplets], Apr. 28, 1942, 3; *DGB* (Guilin), "Guishi diandi" [Guilin droplets], Jan. 27, 1942, 3; Kay Keong Woo, "Affidavit by Native American to Explain Protracted Foreign Residence," Apr. 19, 1946, p. 1; Omar Wing, "Affidavit by Native American to Explain Protracted Foreign Residence," Apr. 17, 1946, p. 1, Canton vol. 699; Poy, "Affidavit by Native American to Explain Protracted Foreign Residence," 1.

123. Chan Sui-jeung, *East River Column: Hong Kong Guerrillas in the Second World War and After* (Hong Kong: Hong Kong University Press, 2009), 36–37; Stanley S. K. Kwan and Nicole Kwan, *The Dragon and the Crown: Hong Kong Memoirs* (Hong Kong: Hong Kong University Press, 2008), 37–38.

124. *SCMP*, "Hong Kong Man in USA," 6; *SCMP*, "Treated Like Animals," Jan. 3, 1947, 1.

125. *SCMP*, "Scenes at Treason Trial," Apr. 6, 1946, 2; *SCMP*, "More Tales of Torture at George Wong Trial," Apr. 5, 1946, 1.

126. In Young testimony, Jan. 31, 1947, p. 2, In Young file (1300-47188), NARA-SB; W. Nelson Brown, "George Taikin Owyang," Mar. 22, 1949, p. 1, George Taikin Owyang file (125/181), NARA-NY.

127. Andrew Fong Zane, Application for "Certificate of Citizenship—Hawaiian Island," Dec. 14, 1948, p. 2, Andrew Zane file (1302/10981), NARA-SB; Chang to Grove, 1.

128. Robert Bickers, "Settlers and Diplomats: The End of British Hegemony in the International Settlement, 1937–1945," in *In the Shadow of the Rising Sun: Shanghai under Japanese Occupation*, ed. Christian Henriot and Wen-hsin Yeh (New York: Cambridge University Press, 2004), 253; Florence Woo Chan, certificate of repatriation, Sept, 22, 1945, p. 1, and Joseph F. Chu, certificate of repatriation, Sept. 23, 1945, p. 1, file "Repatriation Certificates, Sept. 1945," box 44, RG 493, NARA-CP.

129. Robert D. Yee emails to the author, Dec. 11, 2017, and Dec. 12, 2017.

130. Shun Shih, "Height of Mountains in Sikong Sought," *CP*, Aug. 4, 1932, 11; Mrs. Jack T. Young, "Young Sikong Expedition to West China Wilds Bags Takin," *CP*, June 29, 1934, 9.

131. Jack Theodore Young, *Yinshuisiyuan* [Never forget where you came from] (Taipei: Central Daily News, 1989), 258–59.

132. David P. Barrett, "Introduction: Occupied China and the Limits of Accommodation," in *Chinese Collaboration with Japan, 1932–1945: The Limits of Accommodation*, ed. David P. Barrett and Larry N. Shyu, 8; Timothy Brook, *Collaboration: Japanese Agents and Local Elites in Wartime China* (Cambridge: Harvard University Press, 2005), 12–13.

133. Paxton to Drumright, 1; Jan, *Unbound Spirit*, 171; *American Architects Directory, First Edition* (New York City: R.R. Bowker LLC, 1956), 324; "Herbert Moy, Espionage," Jan. 12, 1945, p. 2, document 112812, CIA FOIA Collection, accessed Sept. 20, 2017, www.cia.gov/library/readingroom/docs/DOC_0000112812.pdf; "Results of Investigation," Jan. 16, 1951, pp. 1–2, Samuel Orne Moy FBI file (in possession of author).

134. OSS Kunming, "Herbert Moy et al.," Jan. 12, 1945, p. 2, accessed Nov. 18, 2017, www.cia.gov/library/readingroom/docs/DOC_0000112812.pdf.

135. "Japanese Total Espionage in Manchuria, China, and the Netherlands East Indies," Apr. 5, 1942, p. 46, decimal file 894.20200, Records of the Department of State Relating to the Internal Affairs of Japan, 1940–1944, Archives Unbound (accessed June 25, 2013); Foreign Broadcast Intelligence Service, "Special Report #90: Radio Tokyo Commentators and Features," Aug. 16, 1943, p. 9, file "100155291 sec 5, 3 of 3," box 74, classification 100, RG 65, NARA-CP.

136. Japanese Embassy Intelligence Bureau, *Kokumin seifu kaku kikan shokushō hyō* [National government organization chart] (Nanjing: Intelligence Bureau, 1942); Burke, *China and Japan at War*, 286; *Wang wei "guo min zhengfu gongbao"* [Puppet Wang's "government gazette"], vol. 10 (Nanjing: Jiangsu guji chubanshe, 1991), 70.

137. Brook, *Collaboration*, 11–12.

138. Bernard Wasserstein, in *Secret War in Shanghai: An Untold Story of Espionage, Intrigue, and Treason in World War II* (New York: Houghton Mifflin, 1999), 186–93, discusses Kentwell's motives in detail, albeit with a few factual inaccuracies.

139. Madeline Y. Hsu, *Dreaming of Gold, Dreaming of Home: Transnationalism and Migration between the United States and South China, 1882–1943* (Stanford: Stanford University Press, 2000), 179.

140. Dai-ming Lee letter, c. 1942, p. 1, file 122, carton 13, Records of the Chinese World, Asian American Studies Library, University of California, Berkeley, CA; Sonia Tomara, "Famine Strikes in Kwangtung, Land Desolate," *New York Herald-Tribune*, July 20, 1943, 8.

141. Hsu, *Dreaming of Gold, Dreaming of Home*, 180; Jun-ke Choy, "Confidential Memorandum on the Macao Situation," July 17, 1943, p. 2, file "Caizengji zhi wutiecheng han," series ID *Tezhong dang'an*, file ID 1.26, Kuomintang Party Archives, Research Center for Digital Humanities, National Taiwan University, Taipei, Taiwan; Joel Mokyr and Cormac Ó Gráda, "Famine Disease and Famine Mortality: Lessons from the Irish Experience, 1845–50," in *Famine Demography: Perspectives from the Past and Present*, ed. Tim Dyson and Cormac Ó Gráda (New York: Oxford University Press, 2002), 31; Chinn, "Affidavit," 1.

142. Hsu, *Dreaming of Gold, Dreaming of Home*, 179–80; Lai-Chow Lau, "Affidavit by Native American to Explain Protracted Foreign Residence," Aug. 6, 1946, p. 1, Canton vol. 698; Chin Hing Shang, "Affidavit by Native American to Explain Protracted Foreign Residence," June 7, 1946, p. 1, Canton vol. 697.

143. See, for example, June Ting Yee, landing card, June 20, 1938, p. 1, June Ting Yee file (7030/5952), NARA-SEA; San Francisco District Director to Seattle Officer in Charge, Jan. 11, 1940, p. 1, Helen King Ying Yee file (7030/8271); Katie Yee, "Application for Registration," July 8, 1946, pp. 1–3, Canton vol. 700; Woo Kay Keong, "Affidavit by Native American to Explain Protracted Foreign Residence," Apr. 19, 1946, p. 1, Canton vol. 700.

144. Yee Wing, "Affidavit by Native American to Explain Protracted Foreign Residence," Apr. 12, 1946, p. 1, Canton vol. 700.

145. See, for example, Yee Chew-Man, "Application for Registration," July 25, 1946, p. 1, Canton vol. 700; Cheong Ching Ping, "Affidavit to Be Executed by a Person Born in the United States (of Alien Parents) Who Is Applying for the First Time for a Passport or Registration," Aug. 5, 1946, p. 1, Canton vol. 697.

146. Lee Yow-Lim, "Application for Registration," Sept. 11, 1946, p. 1, Canton vol. 698.

147. Hin Wong, "Reconstruction of West China Speeded Up by War," *CWR*, Jan. 22, 1938, 209.

148. *SCMP*, "Well-Known Chinese Journalist Mr. Hin Wong," Feb. 16, 1939, 11; *FRUS, 1943: China*, 301.

149. Graham Peck, *Two Kinds of Time* (Seattle: University of Washington Press, 2008), 237; Mitter, *Forgotten Ally*, 270–77.

150. Joe Tuey Soo-mon, "Affidavit by Native American to Explain Protracted Foreign Residence," Feb. 23, 1946, p. 1, Canton vol. 699; Ko-wong Hung, information blank, May 29, 1947, p. 4, file 3253, box 182, record group 11, United Board.

151. *Lingnan*, "Fundamental Problem," XI, no. 1 (Spring 1944): 4, file 3296, box 185, United Board; Mitter, *Forgotten Ally*, 274; Jung How-Jew, "Affidavit by Native American to Explain Protracted Foreign Residence," July 3, 1946, p. 1, Canton vol. 698; Woo Tuey-Far, "Affidavit by Native American to Explain Protracted Foreign Residence," Aug. 22, 1945, p. 1, Canton vol. 700; Peck, *Two Kinds of Time*, 554.

152. Soong, *Chinese American Refugee*, 62.

153. Ettie Chin letter, July 30, 1938, p. 3, accessed Aug. 28, 2017, divinity-adhoc.library.yale.edu/ChinaCollegesProject/Smith/bios/EC_3.html.

154. New York Guomindang Federation, "Gao zhu baxi gongshi xiongchongzhi nizhi wuneng qingxing" [Report on the situation of the incompetent and neglectful minister to Brazil, Samuel S. Young], pp. 1–2, file "Tezhong dang'an 5/23.32," Kuomintang Archives, Research Center for Digital Humanities. I have found no mention of Young's removal in the Foreign Ministry's papers; this seems to have been an entirely party-driven removal. *SCMP*, "Brazil and China," Aug. 23, 1941, 10, reported that Young would be serving within the Foreign Ministry in Chongqing; *DGB* (Hong Kong), "Xingzhengyuan jue zhaokai" [Executive Yuan decides to convene], Feb. 6, 1941, 3, describes his recall as a removal. By 1942 Young's name ceases to appear in Foreign Ministry records, suggesting that the latter report was correct.

155. *DGB* (Guilin), "Ju ban tanwu" [Arrests and dealing with corruption], Feb. 12, 1942, 4; *DGB*, "*Huaqiao kenqu*" [Overseas Chinese reclamation area], Sept. 1, 1938, p 5; *DGB* (Hong Kong), "Meiguangpei zuori dalian" [Mei Kuang-bi encoffined yesterday], May 22, 1940, 6.

156. Paddy Gully, *Shiguang feishi: zhongguo kongjun xianqu linfuyuan zhuan* [Time flies: The biography of Chinese aviation pioneer Art Lym], translated by Zhang Chaoxia (Guangzhou: Huacheng Publishing, 2013), 235–39. The regime did exploit Lym's popularity among overseas Chinese by sending him on a fundraising tour around the world in 1938, a few months after he helped shepherd the regime's aircraft repair facilities to Yunnan. After that, the government seemed to have little desire to use Lym's technical knowledge, so he remained in Hong Kong.

157. Seetoo interview, 13–16.

158. Soong, *Chinese American Refugee*, 82–84; Jan, *Unbound Spirit*, 209.

159. Choy, *My China Years*, 223–26.

160. Jan, *Unbound Spirit*, 171, 182; Soong, *Chinese American Refugee*, 90.

161. See, for example, F. B. Driscoll and Jacob Milwit to Ernest Moy, Apr. 17, 1944, pp. 1–2; Ernest Moy to Lewis P. Jordan, Apr. 29, 1944, p. 1; and Jordan to Moy, Apr. 17, 1944, p. 1, all in file "201—WASC Correspondence 1943-1945," container 14, RG 493, NARA-CP.

162. *Palo Alto Weekly*, "Richard Ming-tong Young," Nov. 6, 2009, accessed Sept. 22, 2017, www.paloaltoonline.com/print/story/2009/11/06/deaths; Barbara W. Tuchman, *Stilwell and the American Experience in China, 1911–1945* (New York: Macmillan, 1971), 883; Soong, *Chinese American Refugee*, 76.

163. Seetoo interview, 17–19; Emily Lee testimony, Aug. 5, 1927, p. 2, Emily Ying Wee Lee file (68/34), NARA-NY; *New York Herald Tribune*, "Chinese Waac Had to Increase Weight to Enlist," Sept. 19, 1942, 9; Emily Lee Shek, "Petition for Citizenship," Mar. 12, 1935, p. 1, New York Naturalization Records, Roll 942, petition 244165, New York, Naturalization Records, 1882–1944, online database (Provo: Ancestry.com Operations, Inc., 2012); Elizabeth P. McIntosh, *Sisterhood of Spies: The Women of the OSS* (Annapolis: Naval Institute Press, 1998), 231.

164. K. Scott Wong, *Americans First: Chinese Americans and the Second World War* (Philadelphia: Temple University Press, 2005), 162–92.

165. Jan, *Unbound Spirit*, 176–77; Soong, *Chinese American Refugee*, 90–91; Stephen C. Brown to Addison E. Southard, Aug. 17, 1940, p. 1, box 74, General Records of the Hong Kong Consulate; *Los Angeles Times*, "U.S.-Born Chinese Engineer Predicts Doom of Japanese," June 27, 1943, 5; Brown, "George Taikin Owyang," 1; Choy, *My China Years*, 227.

166. John W. Dower, *War without Mercy: Race and Power in the Pacific War* (New York: Pantheon, 1996), 164–70.

167. Wong, *Americans First*, 193–209; Charlotte Brooks, *Alien Neighbors, Foreign Friends: Asian Americans, Housing, and the Transformation of Urban California* (Chicago: University of Chicago Press, 2009), 144–58; Brooks, *Between Mao and McCarthy*, 69–74.

CONCLUSION

1. Eileen P. Scully, *Bargaining with the State from Afar: American Citizenship in Treaty Port China, 1844–1942* (New York: Columbia University Press, 2001), 194; Marie-Claire Bergère, "The Purge in Shanghai, 1945–46: The Sarly Affair and the End of the French Concession," in *Wartime Shanghai*, ed. Wen-hsin Yeh (New York: Routledge, 1998), 159. Vichy France ceded the French Concession to the Wang Jingwei regime in 1943 as well.

2. Felicia Yap, "Prisoners of War and Civilian Internees of the Japanese in British Asia: The Similarities and Contrasts of Experience," *Journal of Contemporary History* 47, no. 2 (2012): 328; Michael J. Green, *By More than Providence: Grand Strategy and*

American Power in the Asia Pacific Since 1783 (New York: Columbia University Press, 2017), 252–53; Aiyaz Husain, *Mapping the End of Empire* (Cambridge: Harvard University Press, 2014), 144–60; Wang Gungwu, "South China Perspectives on Overseas Chinese," *Australian Journal of Chinese Affairs* 13 (1985): 75–77.

3. Mae M. Ngai, *Impossible Subjects: Illegal Aliens and the Making of Modern America* (Princeton: Princeton University Press, 2004), 206–24; Charlotte Brooks, "The Chinese Third Force in the United States: Political Alternatives in Cold War Chinese America," *Journal of American Ethnic History* 34, no. 1 (2015): 68–73.

4. Peter J. Spiro, *At Home in Two Countries: The Past and Future of Dual Citizenship* (New York: New York University Press, 2016), 19–20.

5. Green, *By More than Providence*, 123–30, 151–56.

EPILOGUE

1. Jun-ke Choy, *My China Years: Practical Politics in China after the 1911 Revolution* (San Francisco: East/West Publishing, 1974), 198–99, 224–25, 227, 238.

2. *SCMP*, untitled, Sept. 7, 1946, 8. About two hundred applications for repatriation are included in Canton consulate vols. 697–700 and 740, RG 84, NARA-CP. A number of others who left were derivative citizens.

3. L. LaMarche, "American Evacuation," Oct. 2, 1945, p. 1, file "Clearance certificate, Lunghwa Camp, Oct. 1945," container 44, RG 493, NARA-CP; *Washington Post*, "John Y. Woo, Retired Physician," Jan. 28, 1976, B4; *Americans and American Firms in China: Directory* (Shanghai: Shanghai Evening Post and Mercury, 1946), 96, 122, 128; *SB*, "Benshi jianxun" [This city's news briefs], Oct. 22, 1947, 4; "Request for Report of Loyalty," Nov. 4, 1948, p. 1, Samuel Orne Moy FBI file (in possession of author); Flora Belle Jan, *Unbound Spirit: Letters of Flora Belle Jan*, ed. Fleur Yano and Saralyn Daly (Bloomington: University of Illinois Press, 2006), 224; Andrew Fong Zane, "Application for 'Certificate of Citizenship—Hawaiian Islands,'" Dec. 14, 1948, p. 2, Andrew Fong Zane file (1302/10981), NARA-SB.

4. Elizabeth P. McIntosh, *Sisterhood of Spies: The Women of the OSS* (Annapolis: Naval Institute Press, 1998), 231.

5. *SCMP*, "S'hai Lawyer Passes Away in America," Feb. 28, 1953, 10.

6. *SCMP*, "Death in U.S. of Mr. Frank Lee," Feb. 24, 1956, 7; *CWR*, "Chinese Abroad," March 1, 1947, 7.

7. K. Scott Wong, *Americans First: Chinese Americans and the Second World War* (Philadelphia: Temple University Press, 2005), 45–64; Shana Bernstein, *Bridges of Reform: Interracial Civil Rights Activism in Twentieth-Century Los Angeles* (New York: Oxford University Press, 2011), 72–99; Mary Dudziak, *Cold War Civil Rights: Race and the Image of American Democracy* (Princeton: Princeton University Press, 2000), 7–10; Ronald Takaki, *Double Victory: A Multicultural History of America in World War Two* (New York: Back Bay Books, 2000), 22–53; John Dower, *War without Mercy: Race and Power in the Pacific War* (New York: Pantheon, 1987), 164–71.

8. Elizabeth R. Escobedo, *From Coveralls to Zoot Suits: The Lives of Mexican American Women on the World War II Home Front* (Chapel Hill: University of North Carolina Press, 2013), 130–31; Michael B. Katz, Mark J. Stern, and Jamie J. Fader, "The New African American Inequality," *Journal of American History* 92, no. 1 (2005): 87–88; Madeline Y. Hsu, *The Good Immigrants: How the Yellow Peril Became the Model Minority* (Princeton: Princeton University Press, 2015), 200–3.

9. Francis B. Woo, *Highlights of Activities and Events of Former Hawaii Students at St. John's University, Shanghai, China* (Honolulu: Hawaii Chinese History Center, 1981), 19–23.

10. Directory of teachers, *Dance Observer* 13 (June 1946): 14; University of Washington Alumni Association, *Three Quarters of a Century at Washington* (Seattle: University of Washington Alumni Association, 1941), 336; Thomas Kirk Cureton, *Masters Theses in Health, Physical Education, and Recreation* (Washington, DC: American Association for Health, Physical Education, and Recreation, 1952), 148.

11. Woo, *Highlights of Activities and Events of Former Hawaii Students at St. John's University, Shanghai, China*, 16, 23.

12. H. K. Wong, "The Chinatownian Roams Around," *Chinese Digest* 3, no. 12 (Dec. 1937): 32; *New York Times*, "Buying Office Adds Stores," July 12, 1950, 38.

13. *The Michigan Alumnus* (Ann Arbor), "1944," Apr. 26, 1947, 348; Tin Chong Goo, "Application for Admission to Practice before the Board of Immigration Appeals and Immigration and Naturalization Service," Sept. 9, 1948, p. 1, Tin Chong Goo file (4500/650), NARA-SB.

14. William Yukon Chang, resume, c. 1963, p. 1, William Yukon Chang collection.

15. *Washington Post*, "Dr. Stephen Hu Dies, Noted Scientist," Sept. 1, 1977, C8.

16. Blossom Y. Tyau, "Sau Ung Loo Chan," in *Called from Within: Early Women Lawyers of Hawai'i*, ed. Mari J. Masuda (Honolulu: University of Hawaii Press, 1992), 178–89.

17. *Polk's Silver Spring, Bethesda, Chevy Chase, Kensington, Takoma Park and Wheaton City Directory, 1958* (Richmond, VA: R. L. Polk and Co., 1958), 156.

18. Robert D. Yee, email to the author, Dec. 12, 2017.

19. *New York Herald Tribune*, "Regal Lily Din, 5, Voted New Queen of Chinatown," June 17, 1956, 29; *Commercial Leader* (Lyndhurst, NJ), "Notice," May 17, 1973, 4.

20. *West Coast Sailors* (San Francisco), "In Memoriam," LXXX, no. 1 (Jan. 20, 2017): 6; Sacramento Directory Co., *Sacramento Suburban Directory, 1963* (Monterey Park, CA: Sacramento Directory Company, 1963), 773; Charles Hong Wong, landing card, Dec. 4, 1939, p. 1, Charles Hong Wong file (7030/10043), NARA-SEA; *Polk's Butte City Directory, 1945* (Salt Lake City: R. L. Polk and Co., 1945), 315; *Polk's Laramie City Directory, 1955* (Kansas City, MO: R. L. Polk and Co., 1955), 215.

21. *Malaya Tribune*, "Wan Wan San Revue Co," Oct. 21, 1939, 6; *Singapore Straits Times*, "Raffles Hotel" ad, May 14, 1949, 8; *Singapore Free Press*, "Capital Restaurant" ad, Jan. 25, 1952, 7; Edward and Nancy Wong family history site, accessed May 23, 2016, imedwong.yolasite.com/grandparents.php.

22. *San Francisco Chronicle*, "Lucille D. (Lim Poy) Chan," June 19, 2005, accessed Oct. 21, 2017, www.legacy.com/obituaries/sfgate/obituary.aspx?n=lucille-d-chan-lim-poy&pid=14276919.

23. John Jung, *Chopsticks in the Land of Cotton: Lives of Mississippi Delta Chinese Grocers* (Yin and Yang Press, 2011), 75–76.

24. Omar Wing, "Application for Registration," Apr. 17, 1946, pp. 1–4, and James Wing, "Application for Registration," Feb. 25, 1946, pp. 1–4, in Canton consulate vol. 699, RG 84, NARA-CP; *Washington Post*, "James Wing," Apr. 21, 2016, accessed Oct. 21, 2017, www.legacy.com/obituaries/washingtonpost/obituary.aspx?pid=179841005; Omar Wing faculty profile, accessed Oct. 21, 2017, www.ee.columbia.edu/omar-wing. Both brothers also taught at the Chinese University of Hong Kong, where James was briefly a Fulbright lecturer and Omar, after his retirement from Columbia, became the founding dean of the CUHK Faculty of Engineering.

25. *My Columbia Basin*, "WWII Soldier Gets Medals 70 Years Later," July 5, 2016, accessed Oct. 21, 2017, www.mycolumbiabasin.com/2016/07/05/ww-ii-soldier-gets-medals-70-years-later; Oregon Chinese Consolidated Benevolent Association, "Kelly Wong Scholarship," accessed Oct. 21, 2017, www.oregonccba.org/scholarships.

26. "Herbert K. Luke," in Honolulu, Hawaii, National Memorial Cemetery of the Pacific (Punchbowl), 1941–2011, online database (Provo: Ancestry.com Operations, Inc., 2011); University of Michigan, *Michiganensian 1955* (Ann Arbor: University of Michigan, 1955), 420.

27. Elsie Chin Yuen Seetoo, interview by Herman J. Trojanowski, Sept. 9, 2005, pp. 23–26, Women Veterans Historical Project, University of North Carolina, Greensboro, accessed Aug. 27, 2018, libcdm1.uncg.edu/cdm/singleitem/collection/WVHP/id/10300/rec/1.

28. Wong, *Americans First*, 55–56.

29. Robert S. Stevens, "Report of the Death of an American Citizen," Apr. 11, 1960, Reports of Deaths of American Citizens Abroad, 1835–1974, online database (Provo: Ancestry.com Operations, Inc., 2010).

30. Choy, *My China Years*, 149, 152–63, 248–49; Charlotte Brooks, "The Chinese Third Force in the United States," *Journal of American Ethnic History* 34, no. 1 (Fall 2014): 57–59; Charlotte Brooks, *Between Mao and McCarthy: Chinese American Politics in the Cold War Years* (Chicago: University of Chicago Press, 2015), 151–52, 191.

31. *Newsday* (Long Island), "Poy Lee 68, Architect In New York and China," Mar. 27, 1968, 64; *Chinese-American Times* (New York), "Architect P. G. Lee Bridged Two Cultures," May/June 1968, 1–3; Poy Gum Lee, "Questionnaire for Architects' Roster and/or Register of Architects Eligible for Federal Public Works," Oct. 24, 1946, pp. 1–4, Poy Gum Lee papers, collection of Kerri Culhane.

32. "George Kin Leung" in U.S., World War II Army Enlistment Records, 1938–1946, online database (Provo: Ancestry.com Operations, Inc., 2005); *Second Round Table Conference on Chinese-American Cultural Relations* (College Park: University of Maryland, 1956), 25; *Historical Register of Yale University, 1937–1951* (New Haven: Yale University, 1952), 209; *New York Times*, "At a Christmas Party in Chinatown," Dec.

21, 1951, 20; *New York Herald Tribune*, "Going on in New York," Oct. 4, 1951, 28; *New York Herald Tribune*, "Lonely Aged of Chinatown Hold Songfest," Oct. 24, 1951, 25.

33. Commissioner of Immigration and Naturalization, Honolulu, "Transmission of Records of Exclusion Proceedings," Jan. 19, 1949, p. 1, John Y. Woo file (1302/11266), NARA-SB.

34. Kenneth Young to Josiah McCracken, Nov. 4, 1953, p. 1, file 126, box 5, Josiah Calvin McCracken Papers, Yale Divinity School.

35. C. M., "Sportman's Sudden Death," *SCMP*, July 20, 1972, 14.

36. *DGB* (Hong Kong), "He tan jintian zai ping juxing" [Peace talks held today in Beijing], Apr. 1, 1949, 1.

37. *The Ring-tum Phi* (Washington and Lee University), "W&L Alumni Now Refugees, Need Assistance," Mar. 1, 1953, 2; *SCMP*, "Coming and Going," Apr. 22, 1950, 3. As the assistant manager of the Hong Kong Central Air Transport Corporation office, Louie also played a bit part in the "Two Airlines Incident" of 1949.

38. *SCMP*, "Deaths," Mar. 5, 1959, 10; *SCMP*, "Deaths," Dec. 4, 1966, 6.

39. *Wah Kiu Yat Po* (Hong Kong), "Daxia daxue xiaoyouhui ren lishizhang" [Daxia University alumni association appoints board chair], July 7, 1962, 14.

40. *Central Daily News* (Taipei), "Yao guanshun jiang jun: bingshi nanyang" [General George Y. S. Bow: dies of illness in Southeast Asia], Oct. 25, 1951, 1.

41. *New York Times*, "Lucy Pang Yao Seng Chang," Sept. 23, 1969, 47; *New York Times*, "Gladys Hardy Brazil," Oct. 19, 2014, 26.

42. I. F. Wixon to District Director, Ellis Island, Feb. 10, 1938, p. 1, Samuel S. Young file (61/526), NARA-NY; Woo Sing Lim, "Xianggang huaren mingren shilue" [Biographies of notable Hong Kong Chinese] (Hong Kong: n.p., 1937), 35–37; *SCMP*, "Sudden Death of Dr. Samuel S. Young," Jan. 9, 1958, 8.

43. Paddy Gully, *Shiguang feishi: zhongguo kongjun xianqu linfuyuan zhuan* [Time flies: The biography of Chinese aviation pioneer Art Lym], trans. Zhang Chaoxia (Guangzhou: Huacheng Publishing, 2013), 245–47; Lois J. Roork to Republic of China Ministry of Foreign Affairs, Jan.12, 1953, p. 1, file "120.2 Taipei Administration, 1953," Records of the Office of Chinese Affairs, 1945–1955 (Archives Unbound database).

44. Jan, *Unbound Spirit*, 225, 235, 244, 247.

45. In Young, testimony, Jan. 21, 1947, pp. 1–4, in In Young file (1300-47188), NARA-SB.

46. "Louie Posang," in California, Death Index, 1940–1997, online database (Provo: Ancestry.com Operations Inc, 2000).

47. Irma Tam Soong, *Chinese American Refugee: A World War II Memoir* (Honolulu: Hawaii Chinese History Center, 1984), 100–2.

48. Kim Liao, "Welcome to Girl Meets Formosa!," accessed Nov. 22, 2017, girlmeetsformosa.com; Kim Liao, conversation with the author, June 15, 2018.

49. Jack Theodore Young, *Yinshuisiyuan* [Never forget where you came from] (Taipei: Central Daily News, 1989), 259; *Philadelphia Enquirer*, "Deaths Elsewhere," June 5, 1977, 84.

50. Hsu, *The Good Immigrants*, 138–40.

51. "Herbert Moy, Active Collaborator," Nov. 3, 1944, p. 1, document 112811, CIA FOIA Collection, accessed Aug. 14, 2015, www.foia.cia.gov/sites/default/files/document_conversions/89801/DOC_0000112811.pdf.

52. "Information Concerning the Death of Herbert Moy," Nov. 3, 1945, pp. 1–3, WN24213, box 22, RG 226 (Office of Strategic Services), NARA-CP. Herbert Moy's mistress, who had also been the mistress of a Japanese officer earlier in the war, provided much of this information to investigators. They mistakenly recorded her name as "Marquita Kwong." She was, in fact, Marquita Kwan (aka Marquita Scott and Maraquita Kwan), a white British woman whose first husband was Hong Kong architect Kwan Wing Hong. Gordon Fortin, "Shanghai General Report No. 1," Oct. 12, 1945, p. 4, BFO 371/46246.

53. *Baltimore Sun*, "Yanks Hailed in Shanghai," Aug. 30, 1945, 3.

54. Harrison M. Holland and Anne B. Wheeler, "Ernest K. Moy," May 24, 1951, p. 1, file "450.2 Security Problems Involving Chinese, 1951," Records of the Office of Chinese Affairs; SAC Chicago to J. Edgar Hoover, Dec. 13, 1950, p. 1, Samuel Orne Moy FBI file (in possession of the author); *Zhongyang Ribao* (Taipei), "Qiaoling mei qiju zisha" [Overseas leader Ernest Moy commits suicide], Feb. 2, 1958, 3.

55. Edward Scheidt to J. Edgar Hoover, Dec. 29, 1950, p. 1; Richard W. Dow, "Samuel Orne Moy," Jan. 5, 1951, pp. 1–6; and Chief, Investigations Division to J. Edgar Hoover, Apr. 13, 1955, p. 1, all in Orne Moy FBI File.

56. Paxton to Drumright, "Additional Details in Regard to Imprisonment of Mr. Henry K. Chan in China," June 17, 1946, pp. 1–2, "War Crimes and Criminals" file, Records of the Office of Chinese Affairs.

57. *DGB* (Shanghai), "Shen ni siliang" [Traitor William Z. L. Sung], Apr. 11, 1947, 2.

58. Zheng Jiemin, report, June 17, 1946, pp. 1–3, file 002-080200-00307-001, Jiang zhongzheng zongtong wenwu, AH; Leonard Kiang, "Synopsis and Epilogue," in *Such a Life: Autobiography of Kiang Kang-hu*, Kiang Kang-hu, 137–39, 1948, Rare and Special Collections, University of California, Berkeley, East Asian Library, Berkeley, CA.

59. *SCMP*, "In Memoriam," Mar. 17, 1947, 6.

60. *DGB* (Shanghai), "Gan deyun zuo ji shenjie" [Kentwell investigation completed yesterday], July 18, 1946, 5; *DGB* (Shanghai), "Dierpi nichan" [The property of the second batch of traitors], Sept. 5, 1947, 4.

61. Hu Tu Tan to editor, *CWR*, Nov. 29, 1947, 396.

62. *Hong Kong Dollar Directory 1954* (Hong Kong: Hong Kong Dollar Directory Company, 1954), 1212; *Wah Kiu Yat Po*, "Zhangzhou wuyi xianghui tan chenzitang fu mei" [Zhangzhou Five Counties Association sees Russell Chen off to America], Oct. 22, 1962, 9; *SCMP*, "Chang-Chen Wedding," Apr. 4, 1961, 8;

63. *SCMP*, "People," Feb. 28, 1982, 11.

BIBLIOGRAPHY

Abend, Hallett. *My Life in China, 1926–1941*. New York: Harcourt, Brace and Company, 1943.

Academia Historica. *Zhonghuaminguo shishi jiyao, chugao, minguo ernian qi zhi shieryue fen* [Summary of historical events of the Republic of China, first draft, July–December 1913]. Taipei: Academia Historica, 1981.

———. *Zhonghuaminguo shishi jiyao, chugao, minguo liunian* [Summary of historical events of the Republic of China, first draft, 1917]. Taipei: Academia Historica, 1976.

Alba, Richard, and Nancy Foner. *Strangers No More: Immigration and the Challenges of Integration in North America and Western Europe*. Princeton: Princeton University Press, 2015.

All China Returned Overseas Chinese Federation. *Guiqiao qiaojuan guiguo huaqiao xuesheng xianjin shiji huibian* [A compilation of the meritorious deeds of the returned overseas Chinese, overseas dependents, and overseas Chinese students]. Beijing: All China Returned Overseas Chinese Federation, 1959.

Allerfeldt, Kristofer. "'And We Got Here First': Albert Johnson, National Origins and Self-Interest in the Immigration Debate of the 1920s." *Journal of Contemporary History* 45, no. 1 (2010): 7–26.

Altman, Albert A., and Harold Z. Schiffrin. "Sun Yat-sen and the Japanese, 1914–1916," *Modern Asian Studies* 6, no. 4 (1972): 385–400.

American Architects Directory, First Edition. New York City: R. R. Bowker LLC, 1956.

American Journal of International Law. "An Act in Reference to the Expatriation of Citizens and Their Protection Abroad." I, no. 2 (1907): 238–58.

———. "Dual Citizenship." 9, no. 4 (1915): 942–48.

American University Club of China. *American University Men in China*. Shanghai: Commercial Press, 1936.

Americans and American Firms in China: Directory. Shanghai: Shanghai Evening Post and Mercury, 1946.

Ancestry.com. California, Death Index, 1940–1997. Online database. Provo: Ancestry.com Operations Inc, 2000.

———. Consular Registration Applications, 1916–1925. Online database. Provo: Ancestry.com Operations, Inc., 2012.

———. Consular Reports of Births, 1910–1949. Online database. Provo, Utah: Ancestry.com Operations, Inc., 2010.

———. Honolulu, Hawaii, National Memorial Cemetery of the Pacific (Punchbowl), 1941–2011. Online database. Provo, Utah: Ancestry.com Operations, Inc., 2011.

———. List or Manifest of Alien Passengers for the United State. Online database. Provo: Ancestry.com Operations, Inc., 2008.

———. New York Naturalization Records, 1882–1944. Online database. Provo: Ancestry.com Operations, Inc., 2012.

———. 1940 United States Federal Census. Online database. Provo: Ancestry.com Operations, Inc., 2012.

———. Reports of Deaths of American Citizens Abroad, 1835–1974. Online database. Provo: Ancestry.com Operations, Inc., 2010.

———. U.S. Passport Applications, 1795–1925. Online database. Provo: Ancestry.com Operations, Inc., 2007.

———. U.S. Veterans' Gravesites. Online database. Provo: Ancestry.com Operations, Inc., 2006.

———. U.S., World War I Draft Registration Cards, 1917–1918. Online database. Provo: Ancestry.com Operations Inc, 2005.

———. U.S., World War II Army Enlistment Records, 1938–1946. Online database. Provo: Ancestry.com Operations, Inc., 2005.

———. Washington, Passenger and Crew Lists, 1882–1965. Online database. Provo, Utah: Ancestry.com Operations, Inc., 2006.

Archives Unbound. Policing the Shanghai International Settlement collection, Shanghai Municipal Police Files, 1894–1945. Online database. Farmington Hills, MI: Cengage/Gale Group, 2010.

———. Records of the U.S. Department of State, Office of Chinese Affairs, 1945–1955. Online database. Farmington Hills, MI: Cengage/Gale Group, 2010.

———. Records of the U.S. Department of State Relating to the Internal Affairs of Japan, 1940–1944. Online database. Farmington Hills, MI: Cengage/Gale Group, 2010.

Arnold, Julean. *Commercial Handbook of China, Vol. I.* Washington, DC: USGPO, 1919.

Austin, Denise. *"Kingdom-Minded" People: Christian Identity and the Contributions of Chinese Business Christians.* Leiden: Brill, 2011.

Azuma, Eiichiro. *Between Two Empires: Race, History, and Transnationalism in Japanese America.* New York: Oxford University Press, 2005.

Bailey, Beth L., and David Farber. *The First Strange Place: Race and Sex in World War II Hawaii.* Baltimore: Johns Hopkins Press, 1994.

Balderrama, Francisco E., and Raymond Rodriguez. *Decade of Betrayal: Mexican Repatriation in the 1930s.* Albuquerque: University of New Mexico Press, 2006.

Baldoz, Rick. *The Third Asiatic Invasion: Empire and Migration in Filipino America, 1898–1946*. New York: New York University Press, 2011.

Barrett, David P. "Introduction: Occupied China and the Limits of Accommodation." In *Chinese Collaboration with Japan, 1932–1945: The Limits of Accommodation*, edited by David P. Barrett and Larry N. Shyu, 1–17. Stanford: Stanford University Press, 2001.

Barrow, Ian J. "India for the Working Classes: The Maps of the Society for the Diffusion of Useful Knowledge." *Modern Asian Studies* 38, no. 3 (2004): 677–702.

Benedict, Carol. *Golden-Silk Smoke: A History of Tobacco in China, 1550–2010*. Berkeley: University of California Press, 2011.

Bergère, Marie-Claire. *The Golden Age of the Chinese Bourgeoisie, 1911–1937*. Translated by Janet Lloyd. Cambridge: Cambridge University Press, 1989.

———. "The Purge in Shanghai, 1945–46: The Sarly Affair and the End of the French Concession." In *Wartime Shanghai*, edited by Wen-hsin Yeh, 157–78. New York: Routledge, 1998.

———. *Sun Yat-sen*. Translated by Janet Lloyd. Stanford: Stanford University Press, 1998.

Bernstein, Shana B. *Bridges of Reform: Interracial Civil Rights Activism in Twentieth-Century Los Angeles*. New York: Oxford University Press, 2011.

Bickers, Robert. *Empire Made Me: An Englishman Adrift in Shanghai*. New York: Columbia University Press, 2003.

———. "Settlers and Diplomats: The End of British Hegemony in the International Settlement, 1937–1945." In *In the Shadow of the Rising Sun: Shanghai under Japanese Occupation*, edited by Christian Henriot and Wen-hsin Yeh, 229–56. New York: Cambridge University Press, 2004.

Bieler, Stacy. *"Patriots" or "Traitors"? A History of American-Educated Chinese Students*. Armonk: M. E. Sharpe, 2004.

Bouston, Leah Platt. *Competition in the Promised Land: Black Migrants in Northern Cities and Labor Markets*. Princeton: Princeton University Press, 2017.

Boyle, John Hunter. *China and Japan at War, 1937–1945: The Politics of Collaboration*. Stanford: Stanford University Press, 1972.

Brandimarte, Cynthia A. "Japanese Novelty Stores." *Winterthur Portfolio* 26, no.1 (1991): 1–25.

Bredbenner, Candice Lewis. *A Nationality of Her Own: Women, Marriage, and the Law of Citizenship*. Berkeley: University of California Press, 1998.

Bremmer, G. Alex. "Nation and Empire in the Government Architecture of Mid-Victorian London: The Foreign and India Office Reconsidered." *The Historical Journal* 48, no. 3 (2005): 703–42.

British Foreign Office. Foreign Office Files for China. Online database. Marlborough: Adam Matthew Digital, 2013.

Brook, Timothy. *Collaboration: Japanese Agents and Local Elites in Wartime China*. Cambridge: Harvard University Press, 2005.

Brooks, Charlotte. *Alien Neighbors, Foreign Friends: Asian Americans, Housing, and the Transformation of Urban California*. Chicago: University of Chicago Press, 2009.

———. *Between Mao and McCarthy: Chinese American Politics in the Cold War Years.* Chicago: University of Chicago Press, 2015.

———. "The Chinese Third Force in the United States." *Journal of American Ethnic History* 34, no. 1 (2014): 53–85.

Buckley, Kerry W. "A President for the 'Great Silent Majority': Bruce Barton's Construction of Calvin Coolidge." *New England Quarterly* 76, no. 4 (2003): 593–626.

Business Directory of Hong Kong, Canton, and Macao, 1938. Hong Kong: Far Eastern Corporation, 1938.

Campbell, James T. *Middle Passages: African American Journeys to Africa, 1787–2005.* New York: Penguin, 2007.

Canton Christian College. *Canton Christian College, 1919–1924: Report of the President.* New York: Trustees of Canton Christian College, 1924.

———. *Catalogue of the College of Arts and Sciences, 1921–1922.* Guangzhou: Canton Christian College, 1921.

———. *Catalogue of the College of Arts and Sciences, 1917–1918.* Guangzhou: Canton Christian College, 1917.

Carroll, John M. *Edge of Empires: Chinese Elites and British Colonials in Hong Kong.* Cambridge: Harvard University Press, 2005.

Chan Sui-jeung. *East River Column: Hong Kong Guerrillas in the Second World War and After.* Hong Kong: Hong Kong University Press, 2009.

Chan, Sucheng. "The Exclusion of Chinese Women, 1870–1943." *Chinese America: History and Perspectives* 8 (1994): 75–125.

Chang, Michael G. "The Good, the Bad, and the Beautiful: Movie Actresses and Public Discourse in Shanghai, 1920s–1930s." In *Cinema and Urban Culture in Shanghai, 1922–1943,* edited by Yingjin Zhang. Stanford: Stanford University Press, 1999.

Chang, William Yukon. William Yukon Chang collection, in possession of Dallas Chang.

Chau, K. L. "Present Weaknesses Found in the Life of the Returned Students." In *A Report of the Proceedings of the First North China Returned Student Conference Held at Peking,* 4–6. Beijing: Peking Leader Press, 1918.

Chen Anren. *Lingnan daxue nianjian* [An almanac of Canton Christian College]. Guangzhou: Canton Christian College, 1925.

Chen Cungong. "Zhongguo hangkong de faren: min qian liunian zhi minguo shiqinian" [The origins of Chinese aviation: From 1905 to 1928]. *Bulletin of the Institute of Modern History, Academia Sinica* 7 (1978): 371–420.

Chen Duxiu. "Xinwenhuayundong shi shenme?" [What is the New Culture Movement?]. *New Youth* 7, no. 5 (1920): 175–80.

Chen Fulin. *Liao Zhongkai Nianpu* [Chronicle of Liao Zhongkai]. Changsha: Hunan Publishing House, 1991.

Chen Min. *Minguo huaqiao mingren zhuanlüe* [Biography of prominent overseas Chinese of the republican era]. Beijing: China Overseas Chinese Publishing Company, 1991.

Ch'en, Jerome. "Defining Chinese Warlords and Their Factions." *Bulletin of the School of Oriental and African Studies* 31, no. 3 (1968): 563–600.

———. *Yuan Shih-k'ai*. 2nd ed. Stanford: Stanford University Press, 1972.

Chen, Jian. *Mao's China and the Cold War*. Chapel Hill: University of North Carolina Press, 2001.

Chen, Yong. *Chinese San Francisco, 1850–1943: A Trans-Pacific Community*. Stanford: Stanford University Press, 2000.

Chen, Zhongping. *Modern China's Network Revolution: Chambers of Commerce and Sociopolitical Change in the Early Twentieth Century*. Stanford: Stanford University Press, 2011.

Cheng, Chi-Pao, and W. T. Tao. "China's New System of Schools." *The Annals of the American Academy of Political and Social Science* 122 (1925): 100–10.

Cheng, W. K. "Enlightenment and Unity: Language Reformism in Late Qing China." *Modern Asian Studies* 35, no. 2 (2001): 469–93.

Chinese Overseas Collection. University Library, Chinese University of Hong Kong, Hong Kong SAR.

Chinese Students' Alliance. *Meizhou Liuxue Baogao* [Report of the American Returned Students]. California: Chinese Students Alliance, 1905.

Chinese Students' Alliance of Hawaii. *First Annual Journal of the Chinese Students' Alliance of Hawaii*. Honolulu: Chinese Students Alliance, 1909.

Chinese Students' Monthly (New York). 1908–1921.

Chinese World. Records of the *Chinese World*. Asian American Studies Library, University of California, Berkeley, CA.

Chinn, Thomas. "A Historian's Reflections on Chinese-American Life in San Francisco, 1919–1991." Interview by Ruth Teiser, 1990–1991. Regional Oral History Office, University of California, Berkeley. http://content.cdlib.org/view?docId=hb5779n97v&brand=calisphere.

Chow, Tse-Tung, *The May Fourth Movement: Intellectual Revolution in Modern China*. Cambridge: Harvard University Press, 1960.

Choy, Jun-ke. *My China Years: Practical Politics in China after the 1911 Revolution*. San Francisco: East/West Publishing, 1974.

Chun, Gloria Heyung. *Of Orphans and Warriors: Inventing Chinese American Culture and Identity*. New Brunswick: Rutgers University Press, 1999.

Clifford, Nicholas. "A Revolution Is Not a Tea Party: The 'Shanghai Mind(s)' Reconsidered." *Pacific Historical Review* 59, no. 4 (1990): 501–26.

Clymer, Kenton. *A Delicate Relationship: The United States and Burma/Myanmar since 1945*. Ithaca: Cornell University Press, 2015.

Coble, Parks M. *Chinese Capitalists in Japan's New Order: The Occupied Lower Yangzi, 1937–1945*. Berkeley: University of California Press, 2003.

———. "Debating War in China: The Decision to Go to War, July–August 1937" In *Debating War in Chinese History*, edited by Peter Lorge, 237–56. Leiden: Brill, 2013.

———. *The Shanghai Capitalists and the Nationalist Government, 1927–1937*. Cambridge: Council on East Asian Studies, Harvard University, 1980.

Cochran, Sherman. *Big Business in China: Sino-Foreign Rivalry in the Cigarette Industry, 1890–1930*. Cambridge, Harvard University Press, 1980.

Cohen, Lizabeth. *A Consumers' Republic: The Politics of Mass Consumption in Postwar America*. New York: Vintage Books, 2003.

———. *Making a New Deal: Industrial Workers in Chicago, 1919–1939*. New York: Cambridge University Press, 1990.

Cohen, Paul. *History in Three Keys: The Boxers in Event, Experience, and Myth*. New York: Columbia University Press, 1997.

Cohen, Warren I. *America's Response to China: A History of Sino-American Relations*. 4th ed. New York: Columbia University Press, 1990.

Colley, Linda. *Britons: Forging the Nation, 1707–1837*. New Haven: Yale University Press, 1992.

Cong, Xiaoping. *Teachers' Schools and the Making of the Modern Nation-State, 1897–1937*. Vancouver: University of British Columbia Press, 2007.

Corbett, Charles Hodge. *Lingnan University: A Short History Based Primarily on the Records of the University's American Trustees*. New York: Trustees of Lingnan University, 1963.

Cornell University. *Cornell Alumni Directory*. Ithaca: Cornell University, 1922.

Cureton, Thomas Kirk. *Masters Theses in Health, Physical Education, and Recreation*. Washington, DC: American Association for Health, Physical Education, and Recreation, 1952.

Dan, Shao. "Chinese by Definition: Nationality Law, Jus Sanguinis, and State Succession, 1909–1980." *Twentieth Century China* 35, no. 1 (2009): 4–28.

Darwin, John. "Orphans of Empire." In *Settlers and Expatriates: Britons over the Seas*, edited by Robert Bickers. New York: Oxford University Press, 2010.

Davidann, Jon Thares. "'Colossal Illusions': U.S.-Japanese Relations in the Institute of Pacific Relations, 1919–1938." *Journal of World History* 12, no. 1 (2001): 155–82.

Daxueyuan Gongbao [University Gazette] (Nanjing). 1928.

de Bary, Wm. Theodore, Wing-tsit Chan, and Chester Tan. *Sources of Chinese Tradition, Vol II*. New York: Columbia University Press, 1960.

DePastino, Todd. *Citizen Hobo: How a Century of Homelessness Shaped America*. Chicago: University of Chicago Press, 2014.

Diamond, Norma. "Women under Kuomintang Rule: Variations on the Feminine Mystique." *Modern China* 1, no. 1 (1975): 3–45.

Dikotter, Frank. *The Discourse of Race in Modern China*. Stanford: Stanford University Press, 1992.

Dillon, Nara, and Jean C. Oi. "Middlemen, Social Networks, and State-Building in Republican Shanghai." In *At the Crossroads of Empires: Middlemen, Social Networks, and State-Building in Republican Shanghai*, edited by Nara Dillon and Jean C. Oi, 3–21. Stanford: Stanford University Press, 2007.

Directory & Chronicle for China, Japan, Corea, Indo-China, Straits Settlements, Malay States, Siam, Netherlands, India, Borneo, the Philippines, &c. Hong Kong: Hong Kong Daily Press, 1914.

Directory and Chronicle for China, Japan, Corea, Indo-China, Straits Settlements, Malay States, Siam, Netherlands, Indies, Borneo, the Philippines, and etc. Hong Kong: Hong Kong Daily Press, 1905.

Dirlik, Arif. *The Origins of Chinese Communism*. New York: Oxford University Press, 1989.

Dong, Stella. *Shanghai: The Rise and Fall of a Decadent City*. New York: Perennial, 2001.

Dower, John W. *War without Mercy: Race and Power in the Pacific War*. New York: Pantheon, 1996.

Dryburgh, Marjorie. "Regional Office and the National Interest: Song Zheyuan in North China, 1933–1937." In *Chinese Collaboration with Japan, 1932–1945*, edited by David P. Barrett and Larry N. Shyu, 38–55. Stanford: Stanford University Press, 2001.

Duara, Prasenjit. *Culture, Power, and the State: Rural North China, 1900–1942*. Stanford: Stanford University Press, 1988.

———. "Nationalists among Transnationals: Overseas Chinese and the Idea of China, 1900–1911." In *Ungrounded Empires: The Cultural Politics of Modern Chinese Transnationalism*, edited by Aihwa Ong and Donald M. Nonini, 49–60. New York: Routledge, 1996.

———. *Rescuing History from the Nation: Questioning Narratives of Modern China*. Chicago: University of Chicago Press, 1995.

———. "Transnationalism and the Predicament of Sovereignty in China." *American Historical Review* 104, no. 4 (October 1997): 1030–51.

Dudziak, Mary. *Cold War Civil Rights: Race and the Image of American Democracy*. Princeton: Princeton University Press, 2000.

Eastman, Lloyd E. *The Abortive Revolution: China Under Nationalist Rule, 1927–1937*. Cambridge: Harvard University Press, 1975.

———. "Fascism in Kuomintang China: The Blue Shirts." *China Quarterly* 49 (1972): 1–31.

———. *Seeds of Destruction: Nationalist China in War and Revolution, 1937–1949*. Stanford: Stanford University Press, 1984.

Educational Directory and Yearbook of China, 1917. Shanghai: Educational Directory of China Publishing, 1917.

Edwards, Louise. "Policing the Modern Woman in Republican China." *Modern China* 26, no. 2 (2000): 115–47.

Elman, Benjamin A. "Naval Warfare and the Refraction of China's Self-Strengthening Reforms into Scientific and Technological Failure, 1865–1895." *Modern Asian Studies* 38, no. 2 (2004): 283–326.

English, Jim. "Empire Day in Britain, 1904–1958." *The Historical Journal* 49, no. 1 (2006): 247–76.

Escobedo, Elizabeth R. *From Coveralls to Zoot Suits: The Lives of Mexican American Women on the World War II Home Front*. Chapel Hill: University of North Carolina Press, 2013.

Esherick, Joseph. *The Origins of the Boxer Uprising*. Berkeley: University of California Press, 1988.

Feng, Liping. "Democracy and Elitism: The May Fourth Ideal of Literature." *Modern China* 92, no. 2 (1996): 170–96.

Feuerwerker, Albert. "China's Nineteenth Century Industrialization: The Case of the Hanyehping Coal and Iron Company Limited." In *The Economic Development of China and Japan*, edited by C. D. Cowan, 79–110. New York: Routledge, 1964.

Fitzgerald, John. *Awakening China: Politics, Culture, and Class in the Nationalist Revolution*. Stanford: Stanford University Press, 1996.

———. "Increased Disunity: The Politics and Finance of Guangdong Separatism, 1926–1936." *Modern Asian Studies* 24, no. 4 (Oct. 1990): 745–75.

———. "The Misconceived Revolution: State and Society in China's Nationalist Revolution, 1923–26." *Journal of Asian Studies* 49, no. 2 (1990): 323–43.

Fleegler, Robert L. *Ellis Island Nation: Immigration Policy and American Identity in the Twentieth Century*. Philadelphia: University of Pennsylvania Press, 2013.

Foner, Nancy. *From Ellis Island to JFK: New York's Two Great Waves of Immigration*. New Haven: Yale University Press, 2002.

Fox, Josephine. "Common Sense in Shanghai: The Shanghai General Chamber of Commerce and Political Legitimacy in Republican China." *History Journal Workshop* 50 (2000): 22–44.

Freyeisen, Astrid. *Shanghai und die Politik des Dritten Reiches* [Shanghai and the politics of the Third Reich]. Würzburg: Königshausen und Neumann, 2000.

Fu, Poshek. *Passivity, Resistance, and Collaboration: Intellectual Choices in Occupied Shanghai, 1937–1945*. Stanford: Stanford University Press, 1993.

———. "Projecting Ambivalence: Chinese Cinema in Semi-Occupied Shanghai, 1937–41." In *Wartime Shanghai*, edited by Wen-hsin Yeh, 86–110. New York: Routledge, 1998.

Gabaccia, Donna R. "Is Everywhere Nowhere? Nomads, Nations, and the Immigrant Paradigm of United States History." *Journal of American History* 86, no. 3 (1999): 1115–34.

Gerstle, Gary. *American Crucible: Race and Nation in the Twentieth Century*. Princeton: Princeton University Press, 2001.

Gilmartin, Christine K. *Engendering the Chinese Revolution: Radical Women, Communist Politics, and Mass Movements in the 1920s*. Berkeley: University of California Press, 1995.

Glazer, Penina Migdal, and Miriam Slater. *Unequal Colleagues: The Entrance of Women into the Professions, 1890–1940*. New Brunswick: Rutgers University Press, 1987.

Gong Bohong, ed. *Guangfu huaqiao huaren shi* [History of overseas Chinese from Guangdong]. Guangzhou: Guangdong Higher Education Publishing, 2003.

Gongshang Banyuekan [Industry Bimonthly] (Nanjing). 1929.

Goodman, Bryna. *Native Place, City, and Nation: Regional Networks and Identities in Shanghai, 1853–1937*. Berkeley: University of California Press, 1995.

Green, Michael J. *By More than Providence: Grand Strategy and American Power in the Asia Pacific Since 1783*. New York: Columbia University Press, 2017.

Gregory, James N. *The Southern Diaspora: How the Great Migrations of Black and White Southerners Transformed America*. Chapel Hill: University of North Carolina Press, 2005.

Grieder, Jerome B. *Hu Shih and the Chinese Renaissance: Liberalism in the Chinese Revolution, 1917–1937*. Cambridge: Harvard University Press, 1970.

Guangdong Provincial Archives. *Huaqiao yu qiaowu shiliao xuanbian (guangdong)* [Selected historical materials on overseas Chinese and overseas Chinese matters (Guangdong)], vol. 1. Guangzhou: Guangdong People's Publishing House, 1991.

Guglielmo, Thomas A. *White on Arrival: Italians, Race, Color, and Power in Chicago, 1890–1945*. New York: Oxford University Press, 2003.

Gully, Paddy. *Shiguang feishi: zhongguo kongjun xianqu linfuyuan zhuan* [Time flies: The biography of Chinese aviation pioneer Art Lym]. Translated by Zhang Chaoxia. Guangzhou: Huacheng Publishing, 2013.

Guoli Daxue Lianhehui Yuekan [National University Federation Monthly] (Shanghai). 1928.

Guominzhengfu [National Government] records. Institute of Modern History, Academia Historica, Taipei, Taiwan.

Hackworth, Green Haywood. *Digest of International Law, Vol. III, Chapters IX–XI*. Washington, DC: USGPO, 1942.

Haiwai Yuekan [Overseas Monthly] (Nanjing). 1933.

Hao, Yen-p'ing."A 'New Class' in China's Treaty Ports: The Rise of the Comprador-Merchants." *Business History Review*, 44, no. 4 (1970): 446–59.

Harvard University. *Quadrennial Catalogue of the Officers and Graduates, 1636–1920*. Cambridge: Harvard University, 1920.

Hauser, Ernest O. "Chinaman's Chance." *Saturday Evening Post*, Dec. 7, 1940, 14–87.

Hawaiian Department and Territory of Hawaii. *Digest of Information*. Honolulu: US Army, 1930.

He Guohua. *Minguo Shiqi de Jiaoyu* [Education in the republican period]. Chaoguan, Guangdong: Guangdong People's Publishing House, 1996.

Henriot, Christian. *Shanghai, 1927–1937: Municipal Power, Locality, and Modernization*. Translated by Noel Castelino. Berkeley: University of California Press, 1993.

Herzog, Ben. *Revoking Citizenship: Expatriation in America from the Colonial Era to the War on Terror*. New York: New York University Press, 2015.

Higham, John. *Strangers in the Land: Patterns of American Nativism, 1860–1925*. New York: Atheneum, 1963.

Hill, Michael Gibbs. "Between English and Guoyu: 'The English Student, English Weekly,' and the Commercial Press's Correspondence Schools." *Modern Chinese Literature and Culture* 23, no. 2 (2011): 100–45.

Hinckley, F. E. "Extraterritoriality in China." *Annals of the American Academy of Political and Social Science* 39 (1912): 97–108.

Hong Kong Census Office. *Report on the Census of the Colony for 1911*. Hong Kong: Hong Kong Legislative Council, 1911.

Hong Kong Census Office. *Report on the Census of the Colony for 1921*. Hong Kong: Hong Kong Legislative Council, 1921.

Hong Kong Census Office. *Report on the Census of the Colony for 1931*. Hong Kong: Hong Kong Legislative Council, 1931.

Hong Kong Collection. Special Collections, Hung On-To Memorial Library, University of Hong Kong, Hong Kong SAR.

Hong Kong Dollar Directory 1930. Hong Kong: Local Printing Press, Ltd., 1930.

Hong Kong Dollar Directory 1940. Hong Kong: Hong Kong Dollar Directory Company, 1940.

Hong Kong Dollar Directory 1954. Hong Kong: Hong Kong Dollar Directory Company, 1954.

Hong Kong Government Gazette. 1936.

Hong Kong Legislative Council. *Hansard/Votes and Proceedings, 1911*. Hong Kong: Hong Kong Legislative Council, 1911.

Hong Kong Legislative Council. *Sessional Papers*. 1924, 1928.

Hong Kong Young Men's Christian Association. *Qingnianhui shiye gai yao* [An outline of the purpose of the YMCA]. Hong Kong: YMCA, 1918.

Hongkong & Canton Business Guide, 1934 Issue. Hong Kong: The Publicity and Information Bureau, 1934.

Honig, Emily. *Sisters and Strangers: Women in the Shanghai Cotton Mills, 1919–1949*. Stanford: Stanford University Press, 1992.

Hsu, Madeline Y. *Dreaming of Gold, Dreaming of Home: Transnationalism and Migration between the United States and South China, 1882–1943*. Stanford: Stanford University Press, 2000.

———. *The Good Immigrants: How the Yellow Peril Became the Model Minority*. Princeton: Princeton University Press, 2015.

———. "Trading with Gold Mountain: *Jinshanzhuang* and Networks of Kinship and Native Place." In *Chinese American Transnationalism: The Flow of People, Resources, and Ideas between China and America during the Exclusion Era*, edited by Sucheng Chan, 22–33. Philadelphia: Temple University Press, 2006.

Hu Xiansu. "Shuo xinri jiaoyu zhi weiji" [Speaking of the crisis in education today]. *The Critical Review* 4 (Apr. 1922): 471–80.

Huang Jingchu. *Huaqiao mingren gushi lu* [Record of the stories of famous overseas Chinese]. Shanghai: Commercial Press, 1940.

Huang Meizhen and Yang Hanqing. "Nationalist China's Negotiating Position during the Stalemate." Translated by David P. Barrett. In *Chinese Collaboration with Japan, 1932–1945: The Limits of Accommodation*, edited by David P. Barrett and Larry N. Shyu, 56–76. Stanford: Stanford University Press, 2001.

Huaqiao Banyuekan [Overseas Chinese Semi-monthly] (Nanjing). 1933.

Huaqiao Yuekan [Overseas Chinese Monthly] (Nanjing). 1932–1936.

Huie Kin. *Reminiscences*. Peiping: San Yu Press, 1932.

Hunt, Michael H. "Americans in the China Market: Economic Opportunities and Economic Nationalism, 1890s–1931." *Business History Review* 51, no. 3 (1977): 277–307.

Husain, Aiyaz. *Mapping the End of Empire*. Cambridge: Harvard University Press, 2014.

Industrial and Commercial Directory of Shanghai. Shanghai: General Chamber of Commerce, 1927.

Israel, John. "The Beida-Tsinghua Connection: Yenching in the World of Beijing's Elite Universities." *Journal of American-East Asian Relations* 14 (2007): 61–77.

Jan, Flora Belle. *Unbound Spirit: Letters of Flora Belle Jan*, edited by Fleur Yano and Saralyn Daly. Bloomington: University of Illinois Press, 2009.

Japanese Embassy Intelligence Bureau. *Kokumin seifu kaku kikan shokushō hyō* [National government organization chart]. Nanjing: Intelligence Bureau, 1942.

Jiang Zhongzheng Zongtong Wenwu [President Chiang Kai-shek cultural relics]. Institute of Modern History, Academia Historica, Taipei, Taiwan.

Jiaoyu Zazhi [Education Magazine] (Shanghai). 1922–1927.

Johnson, Kay Ann. *Women, the Family, and Peasant Revolution in China*. Chicago: University of Chicago Press, 1983.

Johnston, Reginald F. *Twilight in the Forbidden City*. London: Victor Gollancz Ltd., 1934.

Jung, John. *Chopsticks in the Land of Cotton: Lives of Mississippi Delta Chinese Grocers*. Yin and Yang Press, 2011.

Katz, Michael B., Mark J. Stern, and Jamie J. Fader, "The New African American Inequality." *Journal of American History* 92, no. 1 (2005): 75–108.

Kelley, Rev. D. O. *History of the Diocese of California, from 1849 to 1914*. San Francisco: Bureau of Information and Supply, 1915.

Kiang Kang-hu. *Such a Life: Autobiography of Kiang Kang-hu*. Rare and Special Collections, East Asian Library, University of California, Berkeley, 1948.

Klapper, Melissa R. *Small Strangers: The Experiences of Immigrant Children in America, 1880–1925*. New York: Ivan Dee, 2007.

Krysko, Michael A. *American Radio in China: International Encounters with Technology and Communications, 1919–41*. New York: Palgrave Macmillan, 2011.

Kuhn, Philip A. *Chinese among Others: Emigration in Modern Times*. New York: Rowman and Littlefield, 2009.

Kuo, Ping-wen. *The Chinese System of Public Education*. New York: Columbia University Teachers College, 1915.

Kuo, Ya-pei. "'The Emperor and the People in One Body': The Worship of Confucius and Ritual Planning in the Xinzheng Reforms, 1902–1911." *Modern China* 35, no. 2 (2009): 123–54.

Kuomintang Party Archives. Research Center for Digital Humanities, National Taiwan University, Taipei, Taiwan.

Kwan, Stanley S. K., and Nicole Kwan. *The Dragon and the Crown: Hong Kong Memoirs*. Hong Kong: Hong Kong University Press, 2008.

Lai, Him Mark. *Chinese American Transnational Politics*, edited by Madeline Y. Hsu. Urbana: University of Illinois Press, 2010.

———. "Retention of the Chinese Heritage: Chinese Schools in America before World War II." *Chinese America: History and Perspectives* 14 (2000): 10–31.

Lamberton, Mary. *St. John's University Shanghai, 1879–1951*. New York: United Board for Christian Colleges in China, 1955.

Lamson, Herbert Day. "The American Community in Shanghai." PhD diss., Harvard University, 1935.

Lary, Diana. *Region and Nation: The Kwangsi Clique in Chinese Politics, 1925–1937*. New York: Cambridge University Press, 1974.

Lautz, Terrill V. "The SVM and Transformation of the Protestant Mission to China." In *China's Christian Colleges: Cross-Cultural Connections, 1900–1950*, edited by Daniel H. Bays and Ellen Widmer, 3–22. Stanford: Stanford University Press, 2009.

Lee, Edward Bing-Shuey. *Modern Canton*. Shanghai: The Mercury Press, 1936.

Lee, Erika, and Judy Yung. *Angel Island: Immigrant Gateway to America*. New York: Oxford University Press, 2010.

Lee, Erika. *At America's Gates: Chinese Immigration during the Exclusion Era, 1882–1943*. Chapel Hill: University of North Carolina Press, 2003.

Lee, Leo Ou-fan. *Shanghai Modern: The Flowering of a New Urban Culture in China, 1930–1945*. Cambridge: Harvard University Press, 1999.

Lee, Mary Bo-tze. "Problems of the Segregated School for Asiatics in San Francisco." Master's thesis, University of California, Berkeley, 1921.

Lee, Poy Gum. Poy Gum Lee papers, collection of Kerri Culhane.

Lee, Seung-Joon. *Gourmets in the Land of Famine: The Culture and Politics of Rice in Modern Canton*. Stanford: Stanford University Press, 2011.

Lee, Shelley. *A New History of Asian America*. New York: Routledge, 2013.

Lee, William Yinson. *World Chinese Biographies*. Shanghai: Globe Publishing Company, 1944.

Lemann, Nicholas. *The Promised Land: The Great Black Migration and How It Changed America*. New York: Vintage, 1992.

Lester Institute of Medical Research. *Annual Report, 1934*. Shanghai: Lester Institute, 1934.

Lew Williams, Beth. *The Chinese Must Go: Violence, Exclusion, and the Making of the Alien in America*. Cambridge: Harvard University Press, 2018.

Lin, Alfred H. Y. "Building and Funding a Warlord Regime: The Experience of Chen Jitang in Guangdong, 1929–1936." *Modern China*, 28, no. 2 (2002): 177–212.

Lin, Man-Houng. "Overseas Chinese Merchants and Multiple Nationality: A Means for Reducing Commercial Risk (1895–1935)." *Modern Asian Studies* 35, no. 4 (2001): 985–1009.

Linebarger, Paul M. W. Paul M. W. Linebarger papers. Hoover Institution, Stanford, CA.

Lingnaam Magazine (Guangzhou). 1919.

Lingnan University. *Bulletin No. 38: Catalogue of College of Arts and Sciences and Lingnan Agricultural College*. Guangzhou: Knipp Memorial Press, 1926.

Liu Boji. *Meiguo huaqiao shi, xubian* [History of the American Overseas Chinese, sequel]. Taipei: Li Ming Cultural Enterprises, Ltd., 1981.

Liu Shimu and Xu Zhigui, editors. *Huaqiao Gaiguan* [General survey of the overseas Chinese]. Shanghai: Chunghwa Book Co., 1935.

Liu, Haiming. *The Transnational History of a Chinese Family: Immigrant Letters, Family Business, and Reverse Migration*. New Brunswick: Rutgers University Press, 2005.

Liu, Yuzun, Dehua Zheng, and Larry Lam, editors. *Hu Jingnan Wenji* [The collected works of Gilbert Woo]. Hong Kong: Xiangjiang Publishing Company, 1991.

Loy-Wilson, Sophie. *Australians in Shanghai: Race, Rights and Nation in Treaty Port China*. New York: Routledge, 2017.

Lu, Hanchao. *Beyond the Neon Lights: Everyday Shanghai in the Early Twentieth Century*. Berkeley: University of California Press, 1999.

Lucken, Michael. *The Japanese and the War: Expectation, Perception, and the Shaping of Memory*. New York: Columbia University Press, 2013.

Lui, Mary. *The Chinatown Trunk Mystery: Murder, Miscegenation, and Other Dangerous Encounters in Turn-of-the-Century New York City*. Princeton: Princeton University Press, 2007.

Lum, Yansheng Ma, and Raymond Mun Kong Lum. *Sun Yat-sen in Hawaii: Activities and Supporters*. Honolulu: University of Hawaii Press, 1999.

Lutz, Jessie G. "Chinese Nationalism and the Anti-Christian Campaigns of the 1920s." *Modern Asian Studies* 10, no. 3 (1976): 395–416.

Ma, Debin. "Economic Growth in the Lower Yangzi Region of China in 1911–1937: A Quantitative and Historical Analysis." *Journal of Economic History* 68, no. 2 (2008): 355–92.

Ma, L. Eve Armentrout. *Revolutionaries, Monarchists, and Chinatowns*. Honolulu: University of Hawaii Press, 1990.

MacKinnon, Stephen R. *Wuhan 1938: War, Refugees, and the Making of Modern China*. Berkeley: University of California Press, 2008.

MacMurray, John V. A. "Opening Remarks." *Proceedings of the American Society of International Law at Its Annual Meeting*, Apr. 1932, 37–45.

Mar, Lisa Rose. *Brokering Belonging: Chinese Canada's Exclusion Era, 1885–1945*. New York: Oxford University Press, 2010.

May, Elaine Tyler. *Homeward Bound: American Families in the Cold War Era*. New York: Basic Books, 1988.

McCord, Edward A. "Burn, Kill, Rape, and Rob: Military Atrocities, Warlordism, and Anti-Warlordism in Republican China." In *Scars of War: The Impact of Warfare on Modern China*, edited by Diana Lary and Stephen McKinnon, 3–47. Vancouver: University of British Columbia Press, 2001.

———. *The Power of the Gun: The Emergence of Modern Chinese Warlordism*. Berkeley: University of California Press, 1993.

McCracken, Josiah. Josiah Calvin McCracken Papers. Yale Divinity School Library, Special Collections, New Haven, CT.

McIntosh, Elizabeth P. *Sisterhood of Spies: The Women of the OSS*. Annapolis: Naval Institute Press, 1998.

McKeown, Adam. *Chinese Migrant Networks and Cultural Change*. Chicago: University of Chicago Press, 2001.

———. "Conceptualizing Chinese Diasporas, 1842–1949." *Journal of Asian Studies* 58, no. 2 (1999): 306–37.

———. "Transnational Chinese Families and Chinese Exclusion, 1875–1943." *Journal of American Ethnic History* 18, no. 2 (1999): 73–110.

Mei, Hua Chuan. "Guomin duiyu sifa zhi guannian" [The people's concept of the court]. Translated by Cai Liucheng. *Faxue Jikan* (Shanghai) 1, no. 1 (1922): 25–30.

———. "Some Pressing Problems in China." *American Bar Association Journal* 7, no. 4 (1921): 179–82.

Minyi [Public Opinion] (Guangzhou). 1913.

Mitter, Rana. *Forgotten Ally: China's World War II, 1937–1949*. New York: Mariner Books, 2014.

———. *Modern China: A Very Short Introduction*. New York: Oxford University Press, 2008.

Mokyr, Joel, and Cormac Ó Gráda. "Famine Disease and Famine Mortality: Lessons from the Irish Experience, 1845–50," In *Famine Demography: Perspectives from the Past and Present*, edited by Tim Dyson and Cormac Ó Gráda, 19–43. New York: Oxford University Press, 2002.

Moltmann, Günter. "American-German Return Migration in the Nineteenth and Early Twentieth Centuries." *Central European History* 13, no. 4 (1980): 378–92.

Monroe, Paul. *A Report on Education in China (for American Educational Authorities)*. New York: Institute of International Education, 1922.

Morgan, William Michael. *Pacific Gibraltar: U.S.-Japanese Rivalry over the Annexation of Hawai'i, 1885–1898*. Annapolis: Naval Institute Press, 2011.

Murdock, Michael G. "Exploiting Anti-Imperialism: Popular Forces and Nation-State-Building during China's Northern Expedition, 1926–1927." *Modern China* 35, no. 1 (2009): 65–95.

Musgrove, Charles D. *China's Contested Capital: Architecture, Ritual, and Response in Nanjing*. Honolulu: University of Hawaii Press, 2013.

National Archives and Records Administration. Regional office, Boston, MA.

National Archives and Records Administration. Regional office, New York, NY.

National Archives and Records Administration. Regional office, San Bruno, CA.

National Archives and Records Administration. Regional office, Seattle, WA.

National Dr. Sun Yat-sen Memorial Hall. Collected Works of Sun Yat-sen Online Full Text Retrieval System database. http://sunology.culture.tw/cgi-bin/gs32/s1gsweb.cgi/ccd=8Aeomi/webmge?db=corpus&.

Ngai, Mae M. "The Architecture of Race in American Immigration Law: A Reexamination of the Immigration Act of 1924." *Journal of American History* 86, no. 1 (1999): 67–92.

———. *Impossible Subjects: Illegal Aliens and the Making of Modern America*. Princeton: Princeton University Press, 2004.

Office of the Law Revision Counsel. "An Act in Reference to the Expatriation of Citizens and Their Protection Abroad." March 1907. http://uscode.house.gov/statviewer.htm?volume=34&page=1228#.

Office of Strategic Services. Records, RG 226. National Archives and Records Administration, College Park, MD.

Okihiro, Gary Y. *Cane Fires: The Anti-Japanese Movement in Hawaii, 1865–1945*. Philadelphia: Temple University Press, 1992.

Ong, Soon Keong. "Chinese but Not Quite: Huaqiao and the Marginalization of the Overseas Chinese." *Journal of Chinese Overseas* 9 (2013): 1–32.

Pacy, James. "British Views of American Diplomats in China," *Asian Affairs* 8, no. 4 (1981): 251–61.

Pan Yihong. "Feminism and Nationalism in China's War of Resistance against Japan." *International History Review* 19, no. 1 (1997): 115–30.

Peck. Graham, *Two Kinds of Time*. Seattle: University of Washington Press, 2008.

Phelan, James D. "Why the Chinese Should Be Excluded." *North American Review* 173, no. 540 (1901): 663–76.

Phillips, Sarah T. *This Land, This Nation: Conservation, Rural America, and the New Deal*. New York: Cambridge University Press, 2007.

Polk's Butte City Directory, 1945. Salt Lake City: R. L. Polk and Co., 1945.

Polk's Laramie City Directory, 1955. Kansas City, MO: R. L. Polk and Co., 1955.

Polk's Silver Spring, Bethesda, Chevy Chase, Kensington, Takoma Park and Wheaton City Directory, 1958. Richmond, VA: R. L. Polk and Co., 1958.

Portes, Alejandro, and Ruben G. Rumbaut. *Immigrant America: A Portrait*. Berkeley: University of California Press, 2014.

Pott, F. L. Hawkes. *St. John's University, 1879–1929*. Shanghai: Kelly and Walsh, 1929.

Powell, John B. *My Twenty-Five Years in China*. New York: Macmillan, 1945.

Presbyterian Church in the USA. *85th Annual Report of the Board of Foreign Missions of the Presbyterian Church in the U.S.A.* New York: Presbyterian Church in the USA, 1922.

Pye, Lucian W. "How China's Nationalism Was Shanghaied." *Australian Journal of Chinese Affairs* 29 (1993): 107–33.

Qin, Yucheng. *The Diplomacy of Nationalism: The Six Companies and China's Policy Toward Exclusion*. Honolulu: University of Hawaii Press, 2009.

Qishier lieshi zhong de huaqiao [The seventy-two overseas Chinese martyrs]. Hong Kong: Haichao Publishing, c. 1950s.

Radtke, Kurt Werner. *China's Relations with Japan, 1945–83: The Rise of Liao Chengzhi*. Manchester: Manchester University Press, 1990.

Radziłowski, John. "Born a Gypsy: Secondary Migration and Spatial Change in Two Polish Immigrant Communities, 1880–1925." *Polish American Studies* 66, no. 2 (2009): 73–85.

Rankin, Mary Backus. "Nationalistic Contestation and Mobilization Politics: Practice and Rhetoric of Railway Rights Recovery at the End of the Qing." *Modern China* 28, no. 3 (2002): 315–61.

Regional Oral History Office. Bancroft Library, University of California, Berkeley, CA.

Remnick, Elizabeth J. *Regulating Prostitution in China: Gender and Local Statebuilding, 1900–1937*. Stanford: Stanford University Press, 2014.

Report of the Commission Appointed by His Excellency the Governor of Hong Kong to Enquire into the Causes and Effects of the Present Trade Depression in Hong Kong. Hong Kong: Noronha & Co. Government Printers, 1935.

Report of the Proceedings of the First North China Returned Student Conference Held at Peking. Beijing: Peking Leader Press, 1918.

Rhoads, Edward J. M. *China's Republican Revolution: The Case of Kwangtung, 1895–1913.* Cambridge: Harvard University Press, 1975.

Robertson, Craig. *The Passport in America: The History of a Document.* New York: Oxford University Press, 2010.

Rogaski, Ruth. *Hygienic Modernity: Meanings of Health and Disease in Treaty-Port China.* Berkeley: University of California Press, 2004.

Rolle, Andrew. "The Immigrant Experience: Reflections of a Lifetime." *Italian Americana* 19, no. 1 (2001): 36–41.

Romero, Roberto Chao. *The Chinese in Mexico, 1882–1940.* Tucson: University of Arizona Press, 2010.

Roy, Denny. *Taiwan: A Political History.* Ithaca: Cornell University Press, 2003.

Sacramento Directory Co. *Sacramento Suburban Directory, 1963.* Monterey Park, CA: Sacramento Directory Company, 1963.

Salyer, Lucy. *Laws Harsh as Tigers: Chinese Immigrants and the Shaping of Modern Immigration Law.* Chapel Hill: University of North Carolina Press, 1995.

Schoppa, R. Keith. *In a Sea of Bitterness: Refugees during the Sino-Japanese War.* Cambridge: Harvard University Press, 2011.

Schwarcz, Vera. *The Chinese Enlightenment: Intellectuals and the Legacy of the May Fourth Movement of 1919.* Berkeley: University of California Press, 1986.

Scully, Eileen P. *Bargaining with the State from Afar: American Citizenship in Treaty Port China, 1844–1942.* New York: Columbia University Press, 2001.

Second Round Table Conference on Chinese-American Cultural Relations. College Park: University of Maryland, 1956.

See, Lung-Kee. "To Be or Not to Be 'Eaten': Lu Xun's Dilemma of Political Engagement." *Modern China* 12, no. 4 (1986): 459–85.

Seligman, Scott D. *Tong Wars: The Untold Story of Vice, Money, and Murder in New York's Chinatown.* New York: Viking, 2016.

Shanghai Municipal Archives. *Jindai zhongguo baihuoye xianqu—shanghai sida gongsi dang'an huibian* [Modern China's department store pioneers—an archival compilation on Shanghai's big four companies]. Shanghai: Shanghai Municipal Archives, 2010.

Shao Yong. *Jindai huidang yu minjian xinyang yanjiu* [Research on modern anti-Qing societies and folklore]. Taipei: Xiuwei Science and Technology Ltd., 2011.

Shishi Yuebao [Current Affairs Monthly] (Nanjing). 1930–1931.

Shumsky, Neil Larry. "'Let No Man Stop to Plunder!' American Hostility to Return Migration, 1890–1924." *Journal of American Ethnic History* 11, no. 2 (1992): 56–75.

Simons, Sarah E. "Social Assimilation. V." *American Journal of Sociology* 7, no. 4 (1902): 539–56.

Sincere Co., Ltd., Twenty-fifth Anniversary, 1900–1924. Shanghai: The Sincere Co., 1924.

Sinn, Elizabeth. *Pacific Crossing: California Gold, Chinese Migration, and the Making of Hong Kong.* Hong Kong: University of Hong Kong Press, 2013.

Sklaroff, Lauren Rebecca. *Black Culture and the New Deal: The Quest for Civil Rights in the Roosevelt Era.* Chapel Hill: University of North Carolina Press, 2014.

Smith, Carl. Carl Smith collection. Hong Kong Public Records Office, Hong Kong SAR.

Soong, Irma Tam. *Chinese American Refugee: A World War II Memoir.* Honolulu: Hawaii Chinese History Center, 1984.

Soong, T. V., Papers. Hoover Institution, Stanford, CA.

Spalding, William F. *Eastern Exchange, Currency and Finance.* London: Pitman, 1918.

Spence, Jonathan D. *The Gate of Heavenly Peace: The Chinese and Their Revolution, 1895–1980.* New York: Penguin, 1981.

Spiro, Peter J. *At Home in Two Countries: The Past and Future of Dual Citizenship.* New York: New York University Press, 2016.

St. John's University Shanghai. *Catalogue, 1919/1920.* Shanghai: St. John's University, 1919.

———. *Catalogue of the Officers and Students of St. John's University, September 1921–June 1922.* Shanghai: Presbyterian Mission Press, 1921.

———. *The Johannean 1935.* Shanghai: The Johannean Board, 1935.

———. *The Johannean 1939.* Shanghai: China Press, 1939.

State of Illinois. *State of Illinois Official Register of Legally Qualified Other Practitioners.* Springfield: Illinois State Board of Health, 1917.

Strauss, Julia C. "Creating 'Virtuous and Talented' Officials for the Twentieth Century: Discourse and Practice in Xinzheng China." *Modern Asian Studies*, 37, no. 4 (2003): 831–50.

———. "The Evolution of Republican Government." *China Quarterly* 150 (1997): 29–351.

Subcommittee to Investigate the Administration of the Internal Security Act and Other Internal Security Laws of the Committee on the Judiciary. *Morgenthau Diary (China), Vol. 1.* Washington, DC: USGPO, 1965.

Survey of Race Relations on the Pacific Coast. Hoover Institution, Stanford, CA.

Takaki, Ronald. *Double Victory: A Multicultural History of America in World War Two.* New York: Back Bay Books, 2000.

Taylor, Jay. *The Generalissimo: Chiang Kai-shek and the Struggle for Modern China.* Cambridge: Belknap Press, 2011.

Thomson, John A. *A Sense of Power: The Roots of America's World Role.* Ithaca: Cornell University Press, 2015.

Todd, O. J. "The Yellow River Reharnessed." *Geographical Review* 39, no. 1 (1949): 38–56.

Trustees of Canton Christian College. *Lingnan: Our Alma Mater.* New York: Lingnan University Board of Trustees, 1927.

———. *Canton Christian College, 1919–1924: Report of the President.* New York: Trustees of Canton Christian College, 1924.

Trustees of Lingnan University. Archives of the Trustees of Lingnan University. Yale Divinity School Library Special Collections.

Tsai Chutung. "The Chinese Nationality Law, 1909." *American Journal of International Law* 4, no. 2 (1910): 405–11.

Tsai, Jung-Fang. *Hong Kong in Chinese History: Community and Social Unrest in the British Colony, 1842–1913*. New York: Columbia University Press, 1993.

Tsin, Michael. *Nation, Governance, and Modernity in China: Canton, 1900–1927*. Stanford: Stanford University Press, 1999.

Tsou Mingteh. "Christian Missionary as Confucian Intellectual: Gilbert Reid (1857–1927) and the Reform Movement in the Late Qing." In *Christianity in China: From the Eighteenth Century to the Present*, edited by Daniel Bays, 73–90. Stanford: Stanford University Press, 1996.

Tuchman, Barbara W. *Stilwell and the American Experience in China, 1911–1945*. New York: Macmillan, 1971.

Tyau, Blossom Y. "Sau Ung Loo Chan." In *Called from Within: Early Women Lawyers of Hawai'i*, edited by Mari J. Masuda, 172–90. Honolulu: University of Hawaii Press, 1992.

United Board for Christian Higher Education in Asia. Archives of the United Board for Christian Higher Education in Asia. Yale Divinity School Library Special Collections.

US Bureau of the Census. *Census Bulletin 127: Chinese and Japanese in the United States*. Washington, DC: USGPO, 1914.

———. *Census of Manufacturers: 1905—Earnings of Wage-Earners*. Washington, DC: USGPO, 1908.

———. *Census Reports, Vol. I, Twelfth Census of the United States, Taken in the Year 1900*. Washington, DC: USGPO, 1901.

———. *Compendium of the Tenth Census, Part I*. Washington, DC: USGPO, 1885.

———. *Fifteenth Census of the United States, 1930: Population Number and Distribution of Inhabitants*. Washington, DC: USGPO, 1931.

———. *Fifteenth Census of the United States: 1930. Population, Vol. II: General Report, Statistics by Subject*. Washington, DC: USGPO, 1933.

———. *Fourteenth Census of the United States, 1920: Population, Vol. IV: Occupations*. Washington, DC: USGPO, 1923.

———. *Twelfth Census of the United States—1900, Volume I: Population Part I*. Washington, DC: USGPO, 1901.

US Central Intelligence Agency, Office of Strategic Services Collection. https://www.cia.gov/library/readingroom/search/site/?f%5B0%5D=im_field_collection%3A1834887

US Commissioner-General of Immigration. *Annual Report of the Commissioner-General of Immigration to the Secretary of Commerce and Labor for the Fiscal Year Ended June 30, 1902*. Washington, DC: USGPO, 1903.

———. *Annual Report of the Commissioner-General of Immigration to the Secretary of Commerce and Labor for the Fiscal Year Ended June 30, 1904*. Washington, DC: USGPO, 1904.

———. *Annual Report of the Commissioner-General of Immigration to the Secretary of Commerce and Labor for the Fiscal Year Ended June 30, 1905*. Washington, DC: USGPO, 1905.

———. *Annual Report of the Commissioner-General of Immigration to the Secretary of Commerce and Labor for the Fiscal Year Ended June 30, 1906*. Washington, DC: USGPO, 1906.

———. *Annual Report of the Commissioner-General of Immigration to the Secretary of Commerce and Labor for the Fiscal Year Ended June 30, 1907*. Washington, DC: USGPO, 1907.

———. *Annual Report of the Commissioner-General of Immigration to the Secretary of Commerce and Labor for the Fiscal Year Ended June 30, 1908*. Washington, DC: USGPO, 1908.

———. *Annual Report of the Commissioner-General of Immigration to the Secretary of Commerce and Labor for the Fiscal Year Ended June 30, 1909*. Washington, DC: USGPO, 1909.

———. *Annual Report of the Commissioner-General of Immigration to the Secretary of Commerce and Labor for the Fiscal Year Ended June 30, 1910*. Washington, DC: USGPO, 1910.

———. *Annual Report of the Commissioner-General of Immigration to the Secretary of Commerce and Labor for the Fiscal Year Ended June 30, 1911*. Washington, DC: USGPO, 1911.

———. *Annual Report of the Commissioner-General of Immigration to the Secretary of Commerce and Labor for the Fiscal Year Ended June 30, 1912*. Washington, DC: USGPO, 1912.

———. *Annual Report of the Commissioner-General of Immigration to the Secretary of Commerce and Labor for the Fiscal Year Ended June 30, 1913*. Washington, DC: USGPO, 1913.

———. *Annual Report of the Commissioner-General of Immigration to the Secretary of Commerce and Labor for the Fiscal Year Ended June 30, 1914*. Washington, DC: USGPO, 1914.

———. *Annual Report of the Commissioner-General of Immigration to the Secretary of Labor for the Fiscal Year Ended June 30, 1915*, Washington, DC: USGPO, 1915.

———. *Annual Report of the Commissioner-General of Immigration to the Secretary of Labor for the Fiscal Year Ended June 30, 1916*. Washington, DC: USGPO, 1916.

———. *Annual Report of the Commissioner-General of Immigration to the Secretary of Labor for the Fiscal Year Ended June 30, 1917*. Washington, DC: USGPO, 1917.

———. *Annual Report of the Commissioner-General of Immigration to the Secretary of Labor for the Fiscal Year Ended June 30, 1918*. Washington, DC: USGPO, 1918.

———. *Annual Report of the Commissioner-General of Immigration to the Secretary of Labor for the Fiscal Year Ended June 30, 1919*. Washington, DC: USGPO, 1919.

———. *Annual Report of the Commissioner-General of Immigration to the Secretary of Labor for the Fiscal Year Ended June 30, 1920*. Washington, DC: USGPO, 1920.

———. *Annual Report of the Commissioner-General of Immigration to the Secretary of Labor for the Fiscal Year Ended June 30, 1921*. Washington, DC: USGPO, 1921.

———. *Annual Report of the Commissioner-General of Immigration to the Secretary of Labor for the Fiscal Year Ended June 30, 1922*. Washington, DC: USGPO, 1922.

———. *Annual Report of the Commissioner-General of Immigration to the Secretary of Labor for the Fiscal Year Ended June 30, 1923*. Washington, DC: USGPO, 1923.

———. *Annual Report of the Commissioner-General of Immigration to the Secretary of Labor for the Fiscal Year Ended June 30, 1924*. Washington, DC: USGPO, 1924.

———. *Annual Report of the Commissioner-General of Immigration to the Secretary of Labor for the Fiscal Year Ended June 30, 1925*. Washington, DC: USGPO, 1925.

———. *Annual Report of the Commissioner-General of Immigration to the Secretary of Labor for the Fiscal Year Ended June 30, 1926*. Washington, DC: USGPO, 1926.

———. *Annual Report of the Commissioner-General of Immigration to the Secretary of Labor for the Fiscal Year Ended June 30, 1927*. Washington, DC: USGPO, 1927.

———. *Annual Report of the Commissioner-General of Immigration to the Secretary of Labor for the Fiscal Year Ended June 30, 1928*. Washington, DC: USGPO, 1928.

———. *Annual Report of the Commissioner-General of Immigration to the Secretary of Labor for the Fiscal Year Ended June 30, 1929*. Washington, DC: USGPO, 1929.

———. *Annual Report of the Commissioner-General of Immigration to the Secretary of Labor for the Fiscal Year Ended June 30, 1930*. Washington, DC: USGPO, 1930.

———. *Annual Report of the Commissioner-General of Immigration to the Secretary of Labor for the Fiscal Year Ended June 30, 1931*. Washington, DC: USGPO, 1931.

———. *Annual Report of the Commissioner-General of Immigration to the Secretary of Labor for the Fiscal Year Ended June 30, 1932*. Washington, DC: USGPO, 1932.

US Department of Justice, Federal Bureau of Investigation, RG 65. National Archives and Records Administration, College Park, MD.

US Department of State. *Papers Relating to the Foreign Relations of the United States, with the Annual Message of the President Transmitted to Congress. December 2, 1902*. Washington, DC: USGPO, 1903.

———. *Papers Relating to the Foreign Relations of the United States with the Annual Message of the President Transmitted to Congress. December 6, 1910*. Washington, DC: USGPO, 1915.

———. *Papers Relating to the Foreign Relations of the United States, 1925, Vol. I*. Washington, DC: USGPO, 1940.

———. *Papers Relating to the Foreign Relations of the United States, 1926, Vol. 1*. Washington, DC: USGPO, 1941.

———. *Papers Relating to the Foreign Relations of the United States, 1927, Vol. II*. Washington, DC: USGPO, 1942.

———. *Papers Relating to the Foreign Relations of the United States, 1929, Vol. II*. Washington, DC: USGPO, 1943.

———. *Papers Relating to the Foreign Relations of the United States, 1930, Vol. II*. Washington, DC: USGPO, 1945.

———. *Papers Relating to the Foreign Relations of the United States, 1937, Vol. III.* Washington, DC: USGPO, 1954.

———. *Papers Relating to the Foreign Relations of the United States, 1937, Vol. IV.* Washington, DC: USGPO, 1954.

———. *Papers Relating to the Foreign Relations of the United States, 1938, Vol. III.* Washington, DC: USGPO, 1954.

———. *Papers Relating to the Foreign Relations of the United States, 1938, Vol. IV.* Washington, DC: USGPO, 1955.

———. *Papers Relating to the Foreign Relations of the United States, 1940, Vol. IV.* Washington, DC: USGPO, 1955.

———. *Papers Relating to the Foreign Relations of the United States, 1941, Vol. IV.* Washington, DC: USGPO, 1956.

———. *Papers Relating to the Foreign Relations of the United States, 1941, Vol. V.* Washington, DC: USGPO, 1956.

———. *Papers Relating to the Foreign Relations of the United States, 1943, China.* Washington, DC: USGPO, 1956.

———. Records of Foreign Service Posts of the Department of State, RG 84. National Archives and Records Administration, College Park, MD.

US Forces in the China-Burma-India Theater of Operations. CBI Records, RG 493. National Archives and Records Administration, College Park, MD.

US Office of Education. *1909 Bulletin, No. 2.* Washington, DC: USGPO, 1909.

University of Illinois. *University of Illinois Directory for 1929.* Urbana-Champaign: University of Illinois, 1929.

University of Michigan. *Michiganensian 1955.* Ann Arbor: University of Michigan, 1955.

University of North Carolina, Greensboro. Women Veterans Historical Project. http://libcdm1.uncg.edu/cdm/landingpage/collection/WVHP

University of Washington Alumni Association. *Three Quarters of a Century at Washington.* Seattle: University of Washington Alumni Association, 1941.

Van Norden, Warner M. *Who's Who of the Chinese in New York.* New York: Warner Van Norden, 1918.

Waijiao Pinglun [Foreign Affairs Review] (Nanjing). 1930.

Wakeman, Frederic Jr. *The Fall of Imperial China.* New York: The Free Press, 1975.

———. *Policing Shanghai, 1927–1937.* Berkeley: University of California Press, 1995.

———. *The Shanghai Badlands: Wartime Terrorism and Urban Crime, 1937–1941.* New York: Cambridge University Press, 1996.

———. *Spymaster: Dai Li and the Chinese Secret Service.* Berkeley: University of California Press, 2003.

Wang Gungwu. "South China Perspectives on Overseas Chinese." *Australian Journal of Chinese Affairs* 13 (1985): 69–84.

Wang wei "guo min zhengfu gongbao" [Puppet Wang's "government gazette"]. Vol. 10. Nanjing: Jiangsu guji chubanshe, 1991.

Wang Yixin. *Women huijia: Xin zhongguo chuqi huaqiao guiguo ji* [We returned home: Overseas Chinese memories of returning to the nation in the early years of New China]. Jinan: Shandong People's Publishing House, 2013.

Wang, Dong. *Managing God's Higher Learning: U.S.-China Cultural Encounter and Canton Christian College (Lingnan University), 1888–1952*. Lanham, MD: Lexington Books, 2007.

Washington and Lee College. *The Callyx XXXII*. Lexington, VA: Students of Washington and Lee, 1926.

Wasserstein, Bernard. *Secret War in Shanghai: An Untold Story of Espionage, Intrigue, and Treason in World War II*. New York: Houghton Mifflin, 1999.

Wasserstrom, Jeffrey. "Cosmopolitan Connections and Transnational Networks." In *At the Crossroads of Empire: Middlemen, Social Networks, and State-Building in Republican Shanghai*, edited by Nara Dillon and Jean C. Oi, 206–23. Stanford: Stanford University Press, 2007.

———. *Student Protests in Twentieth-Century China: The View from Shanghai*. Stanford: Stanford University Press, 1991.

Who's Who in China. 4th ed. Shanghai: China Weekly Review, 1931.

Who's Who of American Returned Students. Beijing: Tsing Hua College, 1917.

Wilbur, C. Martin. *The Nationalist Revolution in China, 1923–1928*. New York: Cambridge University Press, 1983.

Wilkerson, Isabel. *The Warmth of Other Suns: The Epic Story of America's Great Migration*. New York: Vintage, 2011.

Wilson, David A. "Principles and Profits: Standard Oil Responds to Chinese Nationalism, 1925–1927." *Pacific Historical Review* 46, no. 4 (1977): 625–47.

Wong, Edith, Eileen French, and Rose Estep Fosha. "Deadwood's Pioneer Merchant: Wong Fee Lee and His Wing Tsue Bazaar." *South Dakota History* 39, no. 4 (2009): 283–300.

Wong, Edward, and Nancy Wong. Family history website. http://imedwong.yolasite.com/grandparents.php.

Wong, K. Scott. *Americans First: Chinese Americans and the Second World War*. Philadelphia: Temple University Press, 2005.

Woo Sing Lim. *Xianggang huaren mingren shilue* [Biographies of notable Hong Kong Chinese]. Hong Kong: n.p., 1937.

Woo, Francis B. *Johanneans in Hawaii: Highlights of Activities and Events of Former Hawaii Students at St. John's University, Shanghai, China*. Honolulu: Hawaii Chinese History Center, 1981.

Wood, Frances. *No Dogs and Not Many Chinese: Treaty Port Life in China, 1843–1943*. London: John Murray, 1998.

Wray, William D. "Japan's Big-Three Service Enterprises in China, 1896–1936." In *The Japanese Informal Empire in China, 1895–1937*, edited by Peter Duus, Ramon H. Myers, and Mark R. Peattie, 31–64. Princeton: Princeton University Press, 1989.

Wu Lien-teh. *Plague Fighter: The Autobiography of a Modern Chinese Physician*. Cambridge: W. Heffer and Sons Ltd., 1959.

Wu, Ellen D. *The Color of Success: Asian Americans and the Origins of the Model Minority*. Princeton: Princeton University Press, 2014.

Wu, Shellen. *Empires of Coal: Fueling China's Entry into the Modern World Order, 1860–1920*. Stanford: Stanford University Press, 2015.

Wyman, Mark. *Round-Trip to America: The Immigrants Return to Europe, 1880–1930*. Ithaca: Cornell University Press, 1993.

Xing, Jun. "The American Social Gospel and the Chinese YMCA." *Journal of American-East Asian Relations* 5, no. 3/4 (1996): 277–304.

Xingzhengyuan Gongbao [Executive Yuan Gazette] (Nanjing). 1929.

Xinwen Zhoubao [News Weekly] (Shanghai). 1931.

Xu Guoqi. *Chinese and Americans: A Shared History*. Cambridge: Harvard University Press, 2014.

Xu, Xiaoqun. *Chinese Professionals and the Republican State: The Rise of Professional Associations in Shanghai*. New York: Cambridge University Press, 2001.

Yale University. *Achievements of the Class of 1902, Yale College*. New Haven: Yale University Press, 1908.

———. *Alumni Directory of Yale University Living Graduates and Non-Graduates*. New Haven: Yale University, 1926.

———. *Historical Register of Yale University, 1937–1951*. New Haven: Yale University, 1952.

Yang Xiangyi and Gladys Yang, trans. *Lu Xun: Selected Works, Vol. II*. Beijing: Foreign Languages Press, 1985.

Yap, Felicia. "Prisoners of War and Civilian Internees of the Japanese in British Asia: The Similarities and Contrasts of Experience." *Journal of Contemporary History* 47, no. 2 (2012): 317–46.

Ye, Weili. *Seeking Modernity in China's Name: Chinese Students in the United States, 1900–1927*. Stanford: Stanford University Press, 2001.

Yeh, Wen-Hsin. *The Alienated Academy: Culture and Politics in Republican China, 1919–1937*. Cambridge: Council on East Asian Studies, 1990.

———. "Introduction: The Struggle to Survive." In *Wartime Shanghai*, edited by Wen-hsin Yeh, 1–17. New York: Routledge, 1998.

———. *Shanghai Splendor: Economic Sentiments and the Making of Modern China, 1843–1949*. Berkeley: University of California Press, 2007.

Yellin, Eric. *Racism in the Nation's Service: Government Workers and the Color Line in Woodrow Wilson's America*. Chapel Hill: University of North Carolina Press, 2013.

Young, Elliott. *Alien Nation: Chinese Migration in the Americas from the Coolie Era through World War II*. Chapel Hill: University of North Carolina Press, 2014.

Young, Jack Theodore. *Yinshuisiyuan* [Never forget where you came from]. Taipei: Central Daily News, 1989.

Yu, Alice Fong. Papers of Alice Fong Yu. Stanford University Library Special Collections, Stanford, CA.

Yu, Henry. "The Intermittent Rhythms of the Cantonese Pacific." In *Connecting Seas and Connected Ocean Rims: Indian, Atlantic, and Pacific Oceans and China Seas*

Migrations from the 1830s to the 1930s, edited by Donna R. Gabaccia, 393–414. Leiden: Brill, 2011.

Yu, Renqiu. *To Save China, to Save Ourselves: The Chinese Hand Laundry Alliance of New York*. Philadelphia: Temple University Press, 1992.

Yung Wing. *My Life in China and America*. New York: Henry Holt and Co., 1909.

Yung, Judy. *Unbound Feet: A Social History of Chinese Women in San Francisco*. Berkeley: University of California Press, 1995.

Zanasi, Margherita. *Saving the Nation: Economic Modernity in Republican China*. Chicago: University of Chicago Press, 2006.

Zarrow, Peter. *After Empire: The Conceptual Transformation of the Chinese State, 1885–1924*. Stanford: Stanford University Press, 2012.

———. "Historical Trauma: Anti-Manchuism and Memories of Atrocity in Late Qing China." *History and Memory* 16, no. 2 (2004): 67–107.

Zhao, Suisheng. *Power by Design: Constitution-Making in Nationalist China*. Honolulu: University of Hawaii Press, 1996.

Zheng Zican, *Xianggang shangyeren minglu* [Hong Kong business directory]. Hong Kong: Zheng Zican, 1910.

———. *Xianggang shangyeren minglu*, v. 1 [Hong Kong business directory, v. 1]. Hong Kong: Zheng Zican, 1915.

Zhiyuanlu. "Qingli dang'anchu" [Organization archiving]. Beijing: Printing Bureau, 1920.

Zhonghua minguo weixinzhengfu gai shi [Record and history of the Reformed Government of the Republic of China]. Nanjing: Executive Yuan Propaganda Department, 1940.

Zhongguo Guomindang Records. Hoover Institution, Stanford, CA.

Zhongyang Dangwu Yuekan [Central Party Affairs Monthly] (Nanjing). 1930–1931.

Zhu, Liping. "Ethnic Oasis: Chinese Immigrants in the Frontier Black Hills." In *Ethnic Oasis: The Chinese in the Black Hills*, edited by Liping Zhu and Rose Estep Fosha, 3–43. Pierre, SD: South Dakota State Historical Society Press, 2004.

INDEX

Abend, Hallett, 99
African Americans, 8, 9, 133
Ahana, Edna, 133
Ahlo, Anthony Leefong: and Chen Jitang regime, 126, 150; death, 203; diplomatic career, 106, 217n82; early life, 44–45, 222n15; friendship with L.K. Kentwell, 101–102, 241n134; and New Policies, 47, 53; wartime collaboration, 171–172
Aid Refugee Chinese Intellectuals (ARCI), 202
alumni clubs, 59, 63, 64, 146
American Association of University Women, 59, 146
American Beauty Shop, 133, 144
American-Born Chinese Band, 100
American Emergency Committee, Shanghai, 159–160, 173
American President Lines, 173–174, 177–178. *See also* Dollar Steamship Company
American University Men's Club, 59, 103, 145
Anfu clique, 168–169
Asiatic Phosphate Corporation, 171
Au, Aida, 200
Au, David W.K., 35, 72, 108
Au, Duncan, 200
Au, Frances Yuk Yung Lui, 35, 73, 108, 176, 200
Au, Lincoln, 108, 200
Au Ben (Andrew Au Ben), 35

Balderrama, Francisco E., 149
Bank of Canton, 19, 86, 127, 178, 249n55
banking, 19–21, 71, 101, 185, 249n55
Beijing: as "Beiyang" government seat, 25, 57; capture by Yan Xishan, 106; Chinese Americans in, 158; Nanjing Decade and, 141; 1900 foreign occupation, 17, 46; returned students' conference, 58; during Second Sino-Japanese War, 152, 155, 157, 180
Beiping. *See* Beijing
Beiyang government: Chinese Americans in, 56–57, 100, 104–105; Chinese Maritime Customs Service and, 79–80; dual citizenship negotiations, 98; former officials, 168; international recognition, 25, 28, 93; Jinan University and, 121
Bergère, Marie-Claire, 71
Bieler, Stacey, 58
Bow, George Y.S., 77, 107, 200, 217n82, 243n164
Boxer Indemnity, 31
Boxer Protocol, 46, 218n96
Boxer Uprising, 17, 45
boycotts: of Japanese goods, 37, 39, 135; New Life Movement and, 143; 1905 boycott of US products, 47; 1924 boycott of British and US products, 80
British American Tobacco, 3, 70, 100
Brook, Timothy, 183
Bucknell, Howard Jr., 97

Cai Tingkai, 135

Canton Christian College: donors, 34, 38; feeder and branch schools, 23, 88; kidnappings at, 83; name change, 138; overseas Chinese students, 31–34, 36, 37–39, 72; target of anti-imperialists, 87–89; University Medical Center, 49. *See also* Lingnan University
Canton Daily Sun, 126
Canton Hospital, 87, 175–176
Cantonese Baptist Church of Shanghai, 100
Carroll, John, 16, 85
Central News Agency, 130, 177
Chan, Henry K., 181, 202
Chan, Hin Cheung, 128
Chan, Lem Fong, 198
Chan, Sau Ung Loo, 128, 196
Chan Shun, 91
Chang, Anna, 134
Chang, Eleanor I., 144
Chang, Hsin-hai, 142
Chang, Loy: escape from Hong Kong, 178; in Guomindang government, 105, 130, 150, 188; return to United States, 200; support for tariff autonomy, 101
Chang, William Yukon, 145, 166–167, 179–180, 196, 251n76
Char, Nicholas Wai Yuen, 61, 100, 109–113, 196, 217n80
Chen Duxiu, 69
Chen, Eugene, 142
Chen, Gladys, 203
Chen Jiongming, 25–26, 57, 76, 78–79, 82
Chen Jitang, 106, 121–124, 125–127, 150, 169, 188
Chen Kwong Department Store, 80
Chen Lianbo, 82
Chen, Russell Bates Shue (Chen Zitang): background and marriage, 61, 66–67; and Cantonese Residents Association, 64; changing politics of, 101–103; collaboration with Japanese, 168–172, 182–183; postwar life and death, 203
Cheng, Dorothy Fischer, 159
Cheshire, F.D., 28
Chew Wu, Gertrude, 63
Chiang Kai-shek (Jiang Jieshi): and Chen Jitang regime, 127, 142; Chinese American citizen views of, 200; Chinese Communist Party and, 138, 155; collaborators and, 168–169; Frank Lee and, 106; Li Jishen arrest, 107, 122; money-raising strategies, 107–109; New Life Movement, 117, 143; Nick Char case, 112; Nineteenth Route Army and, 136; Northern Expedition, 99, 118; Second Sino-Japanese War, 153–156, 161, 182, 187; Sun Yat-sen and, 77; Republic of China on Taiwan, 199; view of Japanese threat, 119; Wang Jingwei and, 104
Chin, Clara Bong, 177
Chin, Ettie Toy-Len, 185–186
Chin Din, Stanley, 196
China: aviation in, 50–51, 55–56, 126–127; chambers of commerce in, 47; civil war, 191, 200–201; debates over culture and identity in, 59–60, 67–71; diplomatic corps, 44, 98, 106; economic growth, 60, 71; embargo on weapons sales to, 55; emigration from, 4, 15, 38; examination system, 16, 17, 31, 47, 52; famine relief in, 63; governments and overseas Chinese, 71, 128; Great Depression, 116, 123–124, 132; inflation, 187; infrastructure and resource development, 51–53, 73; Japanese encroachment in, 118–119; Japanese-occupied areas of, 153, 162–166, 175–184; Ministry of Finance, 53, 54, 105, 111, 130; Ministry of Justice, 131; Ministry of Transportation, 142; new professional organizations, 64, 101; Railroad Ministry, 105, 131; relationship with United States, 76, 156; Second Sino-Japanese War, 154–189; standard of living, 134, 147, 151, 187; tariff autonomy, 101; unequal treaties, 60–61, 76, 101; unoccupied "Free," 153, 178, 179, 184–189, 194; Western and Japanese imperialism in, 17, 37, 60–61, 71, 192. *See also* Beiyang government; Chinese; Guomindang; People's Republic of China; Qing dynasty; Republic of China on Taiwan
China Agency and Trading Company, 34, 219n114
China Courier, 103
China Critic, 112
China Press, 110, 132, 145; Chinese American employees of, 64, 132, 144, 161, 167, 196, 251n76
China Weekly Review, 102, 108
Chinese: coastal and treaty port class, 32–36, 38–40, 59–61, 63–68, 70–74, 76, 79–80, 87–89, 91, 101, 108–109; 112, 115–116, 130, 175, 191; intellectuals, 35, 42–43, 60, 70, 119, 142; merchants, 14, 16–18, 21, 27,

31–40, 47, 59, 61, 75–76, 78–82, 85–89, 108, 116, 124, 154; merchants in the US, 1, 2, 7, 19, 22, 30, 43, 44, 62, 89–91, 100, 174; reformers, 3, 45, 50, 51–52; revolutionaries, 3, 51–52; US residents, 6–7, 21, 83, 115–116, 210n24

Chinese American citizens: anti-Japanese sentiments of, 124, 127, 136–138; as bridge between Chinese and foreigners, 63–64, 101–102, 147; Chen Jitang regime and, 121–127; Christians, 11, 48–49, 62, 64, 125; citizenship status of, 2, 74, 75, 78; college-educated, 43–44, 47, 72–74, 133; cultural orientation of, 134–135, 145, 149, 158, 252n92; doctors, 64, 70, 132, 136; downward mobility in the United States, 44; dual citizenship of, 10, 27–30, 38, 190–192; elite of, 1, 43; employees of foreign companies and agencies in China, 35, 38–39, 68–70, 76, 109, 113, 132–135, 151, 193, 245n6; engineers, 48, 69, 105; entertainers, 133–134, 145; exclusion from US protection in China, 93–99; feelings about America, 15, 149, 189; Great Depression and, 115–116, 121–124, 127–129, 133–134; hybrid identities of, 3–5, 8, 15, 39–40, 67–68, 76, 165, 193; idealization of China, 69, 147–148, 189, 190–191; imperialism and, 70–71, 74, 85–86; Japanese harassment of, 175–176; lawyers, 61, 70; loyalties, 153–154, 157, 168, 172, 180–183, 188–189; merchant emigrants, 9, 13–40, 51, 52, 71, 72–74, 83–84, 114, 124, 190, 198; "modernizers," 9, 15, 41–74, 105–107, 109, 117–118, 125, 130, 132, 149, 153, 188, 190, 195, 196; New Life Movement and, 143–145, 149; 1932 Shanghai incident, 135–136, 257n27; non-citizen spouses of, 263n112; in occupied China, 179–184; People's Republic of China and, 191–192; pilots, 50, 127, 136–138; politics and nationalism of, 100–103, 182, 217n82; population of, 2–3, 207n3; postwar lives, 194–203; refugees, 159–161, 178–179, 182, 184–188; relationship with Guomindang, 78–79, 83–84, 87–89, 104–107, 109–114, 116–117, 124, 139, 147, 158–159, 186, 249n55; resistance to Japanese occupation, 181; response to First United Front, 75, 78; return to United States, 11, 84, 88, 152–154, 158–159, 164–165, 176–177, 188–189, 193, 194–195; Second Sino-Japanese War and, 142–153, 156–158; Shanghai community, 61–71, 100–103, 129–136; in Shanghai *gudao*, 166–168; size of emigration to China, 3, 38–39, 122, 129, 259n66; social life and aspirations, 13, 21, 58–59, 64–67, 70–72, 76, 101, 129–130, 139, 145–146, 151, 210n24; stranded in wartime China, 177–178, 180, 183–184; student activism and, 37–38, 139; student emigrants, 9, 13–40, 51, 52, 71, 72–74, 83–84, 114, 124, 178, 188–189, 190, 194–195, 196–198; translators, 105; US immigration policy and evacuation, 174–175; US servicemen and women, 187–189, 198–199; views of strong state, 72–73, 83, 124, 148; wartime collaboration with Japan, 154, 168–172, 181–183, 202–203

Chinese American citizen women: athletes, 131; education, 22, 35–36; emigration statistics, 254n132; employment in China, 62–63, 70, 144; employment in Hong Kong, 128; employment in the United States, 44, 198; Great Depression emigration patterns, 115–116, 133; marriage, 63, 66–67; New Life Movement and, 143–146; 1932 Shanghai Incident and, 136; in Shanghai, 62–63, 129; in south China, 35–36; US immigration policy and, 4, 67, 174–175, 231n137; US servicewomen, 187–189, 198; wartime collaboration and, 171, 202–203

Chinese Christians, 17, 32, 46, 62, 64, 133, 237n66

Chinese Communist Party: Chen Duxiu and, 69; Chiang Kai-shek and, 99, 119, 155; Chinese American hostility towards, 7, 199; First United Front, 75, 77, 91, 99; founding of, 61; and Guomindang purge, 104, 107, 108; in Shanghai, 84–86; victory in civil war, 195, 202–203

Chinese communities outside China: in Boston, 67; fear of disorder in China, 26, 84; in Honolulu, 45; in New York, 21, 45, 196; in the Philippines, 20; response to Merchant Corps Incident, 81–82; in San Francisco, 46, 196; Second Sino-Japanese War and, 157; in Southeast Asia, 197; in United States, 22, 134–135, 147–148; views on gender, 22, 35–36, 62, 67, 133, 144

Chinese Constitutionalist Party, 79, 183, 199

Chinese Democratic Constitutionalist Party. *See* Chinese Constitutionalist Party

Chinese Exclusion Act of 1882, 1–2, 6, 43, 45, 154, 207n3
Chinese Exclusion Repeal Act, 11, 154, 189
Chinese Maritime Customs Service, 79–80, 144
Chinese Nationalist Party. *See* Guomindang
Chinese Outlook. See *Voice of New China*
Chinese Red Cross, 136, 186, 187
Chinese Students' Alliance, 47, 52, 58, 68
Chinese Women's Club, 146, 168
Chinese World, 50, 199
Ching, Michael Foon, 188, 196
Ching, Yue (Ching, Wah Yue), 53, 64
Chinn, Carolyn, 126
Chinn, Thomas, 132
Chiu James, Margaret, 62
Chong, Lois Loi-tsin, 156, 175
Chongqing, 129, 153, 155–156, 178, 185–188
Choy, Jun-ke: banker, 20; Cantonese Residents' Association and, 64; children, 176; Columbia University years, 48–49; marriage, 66; postwar life, 199; return to United States, 188, 194; Sun Fo and, 105; view of Guomindang, 27, 104, 187; work for Chinese governments, 83, 150, 217n82; during World War II, 178, 184, 187
Chu, Laurand, 91, 96, 238n74
Chu, Ow Wing, 91, 96, 238n74
Chu Shea Wai: arrest, 75; family, 89–92, 238n74; postwar life, 200; in Shanghai, 130, 143; US State Department and, 92–97, 99, 111, 192; work for Guomindang government, 178, 188, 192
Chu Su Gunn, 89, 91–92, 238n74, 238n79
Chuck, Sarah, 83, 186
Chui Cheong Loong Company (Tsue Chong Wing Company), 18
Chun, Young Chan, 48, 105, 136
Chung, Mon Yin, 83, 105, 166, 217n82
Chung, W.K. (Wing Kwong), 138
citizenship: Chinese governments' views of, 4, 10, 26–30, 54, 74, 78, 82, 109, 111–112, 117, 124, 141, 191; formal US versus racialized, 3–5, 11, 77, 89–97, 113, 176, 180, 192; overseas Chinese and, 38, 73, 97–99, 212n7; transmission of US to spouses and children, 38–39, 66, 174–175; transnationalism and, 15, 42–43, 67–68, 88–89, 191. *See also* dual citizenship; *jus sanguinis*; *jus soli*
Cixi (empress dowager), 17–18, 46–47
Cold War, 8, 191–192; 195
collaboration. *See* Chinese American citizens: wartime collaborators; Japan: collaborationist regimes in China; Reformed Government of the Republic of China; Reorganized Government of the Republic of China
colonies: and British identity, 97–98; Dutch East Indies, 119; European in Asia: 29, 78, 89, 120, 154, 191–192; French Indochina, 171–172; Philippines, 20, 41, 97, 133, 178. *See also* Hong Kong
compradors, 1, 19, 39, 82, 87, 100
Confucianism, 17, 42, 60, 143
Constitutional Protection Movement, 57
Coolidge, Calvin, 92, 93
Critical Review, 69
Cunningham, Edwin, 109, 111–112
Curtiss School of Aviation, 50, 57

Daxia University, 130, 200
denaturalization (denationalization), 98–99
Dillon, Nara, 147
discrimination: in education, 6–7; in employment, 44, 61, 116, 133, 148–149, 153, 176, 182–183, 187, 189, 195; racial, 2–3, 5–6, 10, 47, 61, 134, 154, 187, 189, 190, 193; social, 7, 35
Dollar Steamship Line, 158, 159, 160. *See also* American President Lines
Dong Toy, 19, 20–21
Dong Wing, 19, 20–21
Dongshan. *See* Tungshan
Du Yuesheng, 107–108
dual citizenship: Chinese governments and, 8, 10, 74, 78, 112–113, 191, 242n145; exploitation of, 28–29; international law and, 27–28; US government and, 8, 29–30, 93–99, 190–191, 192, 263n108
Duara, Prasenjit, 72–73
Dunn, Robert, 109, 147–148

education: of Chinese American children on the Chinese mainland, 10, 21–24, 30–34, 72, 115–117, 122–124, 184, 194–195, 218n92; of Chinese American children in Hong Kong, 7, 13–14, 21; of Chinese American children in United States, 7, 72, 134–135; college majors, 47–48; English-language in China, 23–24, 31–34, 39, 132; Guomindang government and, 23, 119–121; in Hong Kong, 16–17; postwar impact, 196–198; Qing initiatives, 47; reform of, 60; westernized, 16–17, 129–130

Emergency Quota Act of 1921, 76, 94
Expatriation Act of 1907, 4, 29–30, 92, 94–95, 192
extraterritoriality (extrality): Chinese Americans and, 27–29, 78, 89–90, 92, 96–97, 109–113, 191; exploitation of, 212n7; Guomindang opposition to, 76; international negotiations and, 97–99; US Court for China and, 70, 101

Filipino Americans, 133
First United Front, 77–84
Fish, Hamilton, 95
Fong, Eloise, 23, 164
Fong F. Sec, 32
foreign concessions: Chinese Americans and, 150–151, 191; Northern Expedition and, 76, 103–104; in Shanghai, 104, 135, 141, 143, 146–147, 165, 179–180, 193; Second Sino-Japanese War and, 153; symbolism of, 60–61, 117, 191. *See also* French Concession; International Settlement; Jiaozhou concession; Jiujiang concession; Shameen concession; Shanghai: foreign concessions
Form 430, 15, 26, 90, 212n4, 217n87
France: education of Chinese in, 132; ethnic Chinese colonial subjects, 192, 267n1; Vichy regime, 171–172, 179, 267n1. *See also* French Concession
French Concession: Chinese Americans in, 59, 95, 166; description, 61; Japanese control, 179; Pioneer Field, 109; refugees, 158; reversion to Chinese control, 267n1

Gauss, Clarence, 158, 160, 178
Gee, Dorothy, 69
Gee Chuck (Gee Ah Bow), 34
Germany, 36–37, 55, 192. *See also* Nazi Party
Ging Hawk Club of New York, xi, 147–148
Ginling College, 130, 185
Goo, Edna, 133, 144, 145, 146, 176–177
Goo, Evelyn, 133, 144, 145
Goo, Ting Cho, 144
Goo, Ting Chong, 166, 196
Goodman, Bryna, 64
Great Britain: Anthony Leefong Ahlo and, 44–45, 171; China and, 16, 60, 129, 191; fall of Hong Kong and, 178–179; Hong Kong Chinese elite and, 85; investment in China, 229n104; L.K. Kentwell and, 102–103, 169, 183; Northern Expedition and, 103–104; Shameen racial restrictions, 163, 228n92; Shanghai, 61; treatment of ethnic Chinese subjects, 97–99, 141, 192; United States policy in China and, 93. *See also* Hong Kong
Great Depression: in China, 124, 132; Chinese Americans and, 10, 115–117, 121–123, 129, 133–134, 194; in Hong Kong, 127–128; in the United States, 114; women and, 144–145
Great Migration, 9, 211n37
Greater East Asia Co-Prosperity Sphere, 180
Green Gang, 107–108
Guangdong: central government control of, 141; Chen Jitang regime, 106, 121–124, 125–127; Chinese American ancestral province, 64–65; Chinese Americans in, 9–11, 38–40, 75, 123–124, 153, 194–195, 218n92; early republican government of, 54; education, 22; emigrants from, 16; refugees from, 160; Second Sino-Japanese War in, 153, 162–165, 175–178, 183–184, 188–189, 259n66; unions of peasants and laborers in, 86, 99; US citizens in, 159, 162–163; warlord era in, 25–34, 72–73, 89
Guangxi, 25–26, 41, 55–56, 77, 79
Guangxu emperor, 17, 46
Guangzhou: aviation in, 41, 57, 83, 162; Chen Jitang era in, 122; Chinese Americans in, 9–11, 23, 34–40, 82–83, 194–195; elite of, 31–35; First United Front era, 75, 77–92; foreign concession, 61; foreign-registered companies, 80; Japanese occupation of, 155, 171; New Life Movement, 144; 1925–1926 strike and boycott, 76, 86–89; 1927 Commune, 114; Northern Expedition, 99, 124; Second Sino-Japanese War, 162–165, 184; Sun Yat-sen Memorial Hall, 130; US citizen population, 159, 163
Guangzhou Merchant Volunteer Corps, 81
Guangzhou Student Union, 37–38
gudao. *See* Shanghai: gudao period
Guomindang: accommodation of Japanese encroachment, 135, 138; air corps, 57; anti-communism, 104, 107–108, 119, 121, 136, 138–139, 148, 155; assassination of wartime collaborators, 168–169; Chinese Americans and, 10–11, 75, 78, 87–88, 97, 104–107, 127–128, 130–132, 134–135, 150–151, 153–154, 156–157, 168, 180, 185–189, 190; civil war and, 191, 200, 202–203; connections and patronage in, 106–107, 109, 126, 132, 148,

Guomindang *(continued)*
150, 186; corruption in, 141–142, 149, 154, 157, 184–187, 189, 257n27; death of Sun Yat-sen and, 84; economic policies, 107, 150–151; education policies, 138; exclusive citizenship views, 77, 98–99, 111, 141, 191, 193; factionalism, 99, 107, 191; and fascism, 117, 118, 142–143; First National Party Congress, 81, 82; flag, 50; international recognition of, 106; leftists, 75, 104, 122; New York City branch, 186; 1920s resurgence, 73–74, 85; 1927 purge, 104, 108, 130; Northern Expedition, 99–100, 103–104; overseas Chinese and, 1–2, 75, 112–114, 116–117, 119–121, 142, 147–148, 191, 247n21; relationship with Guangzhou business class, 25–27, 73, 79–83; repression of dissent, 138–141, 147; rightists, 100, 101, 104; Second Sino-Japanese War, 153–154, 184–186, 188–189; Standard Oil Co. and, 96; state-building, 118; Sun-Joffe agreement, 77–78; urges relocation to "Free China," 166, 168; US citizen members, 21, 54–55, 106–107, 200; views of state power, 73; views of Western cultural and political values, 118, 142–143, 148, 172; views of women, 143–146; Yuan Shikai's suppression of, 24.
See also Republic of China on Taiwan

Hankou, 61, 104, 159, 162
Hawaii: attorneys, 196; Chinese Americans in, 24, 44, 100, 123, 129–130, 131; economy, 116, 128, 129, 177; US annexation of, 45
Hay, John, 76, 95
Henriot, Christian, 108
Henry Lester Institute, 132, 196
Heungshan Benevolent Hospital, 125, 176, 198
Ho, Philip Lin, 66
Hoh, Mary Akwai, 156
Hong, Kaye, 147–148, 158
Hong Kong: centrality to "overseas Chinese world," 7, 16–17, 18–21, 127, 165, 200; Chinese Americans in, 9, 18–21, 51, 84, 117, 127–129, 148, 177, 193, 194; Chinese elite of, 7, 16–17, 85–86; economy, 127; government, 55, 101; history of, 16; 1925–1926 strike and boycott, 76, 84–86; political unrest in China and, 54–55; postwar, 192, 200–203; refugees, 160–161, 163–164, 177; and Second Sino-Japanese War, 152, 176–178, 195; wages in, 213n22; World War II, 178–179, 188
Hong Kong-Guangzhou boycott and strike, 76, 84–89, 96, 99, 101, 114
Hong Sling, 7, 21, 72
Hong Sling, Francis Yee, 176
Hong Sling, Harry, 7, 21, 72, 176, 200
Hong Sling, Jennie, 7, 21
Hong Sling, William: career, 127; education 7, 21, 72; Hong Kong strike and boycott, 85; marriage, 176; postwar life, 200; wartime imprisonment, 179
House, Herbert E., 32–33
Hsu, Madeline Y., 183
Hu Hanmin, 25, 84, 91, 92, 118, 238n79
Hu, Stephen M.K., 132, 196
Hu Xiansu, 69
huaqiao. *See* overseas Chinese
Huie, Alice, 62
Huie, Caroline, 62, 231n137
Huie Kin, 62
Huie, Louise Van Arnam, 62
Hull, Cordell, 163, 174–175
Hundred Days' Reforms, 17

Ilimokilani Club of St. John's University, Shanghai, 139, 140, 145
immigration: hostile views of, 15, 38, 76; push and pull factors, 154; race and, 92–93; from the United States, 5–6, 8–9, 211n34; to the United States, 5–6, 92–93
Immigration Act of 1917, 8, 94
Immigration Act of 1924, 66, 76, 92–94, 174
Immigration and Naturalization Act of 1965, 11
International Settlement: Chinese Americans in, 59, 95, 133, 145; government of, 61, 102–103; Japanese occupation of, 179–180; labor unrest in, 84–85; 1932 Shanghai Incident and, 135–136; refugees in, 158; Second Sino-Japanese War, 152, 166
Israel, John, 32

Jan, Flora Belle: citizenship, 263n108; clothing, 144; in Kaifeng, 134; marriage, 67; return to United States, 201; in wartime Chongqing, 186–187, 188; in wartime Beijing 175, 181; work, 145
Jang, Monroe, 196
Japan: anti-colonialism and, 191; attack on Pearl Harbor, 153, 154, 155, 178, 183, 194–195; Chinese Americans and, 176–184; collaborationist regimes in

China, 154, 156, 168–172, 181–183, 184–185; encroachment in North China, 118–119, 124; imperialism of, 17, 37, 60–61, 71, 192; internment of enemy aliens, 180; investment in China, 229n104; Japanese Americans and, 150; 1931 invasion of Manchuria, 119, 138; 1932 Shanghai Incident, 135–136; 1937 invasion and occupation of China, 11, 103, 118, 151, 152–153; 1945 surrender, 202; occupation of Guangdong, 30, 127, 175–178, 183–184, 189, 218n92, 259n66; occupation of Indochina, 171–172, 203; propaganda, 189; relationship with United States, 152–153, 156, 161, 173, 175–176; 21 Demands, 227n80; war crimes, 155, 179. *See also* Second Sino-Japanese War
Japanese Americans, 150
Jee, Henshaw, 83
Jee, S. Pond M., 53, 54
Jee, Shien-Yien Luther M., 53, 54, 83, 143, 195
Jenkins, Douglas S., 86, 93–97, 111
Jian Jinglun, 82
Jiang Kang-hu, 100, 171, 202–203
Jiaozhou concession, 37
Jimmy's Kitchen, 167
Jin Gun Oy, 115
Jinan Academy, 31
Jinan University, 120–121
jinshanzhuang, 18, 34, 39, 213n19, 219n114
Jiujiang concession, 104
Jo Nom Wing, 89, 91, 92, 238n74
Joffe, Adolph, 61, 77
Johnson, Nelson, 163
jus sanguinus citizenship, 27, 141, 191
jus soli citizenship, 27

Kang Youwei, 17–18, 45
Kau, Edward En-Young, 64, 83
Kentwell, Lawrence Klindt, 101–103, 169, 171, 183, 203, 241n134, 265n138
Kiang, Lillian Ying Loo, 100, 171, 202–203
Kiang Kang-hu. *See* Jiang Kang-hu
Kim, Peter, 201
King, Albert, 22
Kong Tet-en, 24
Kung, H.H., 105, 130
Kwok, T.W., 103
Kwok Min, 27

Lam, Richard, 125
Lau Waan-wai, 105, 131, 132, 166, 195
Law, Martha F., 144
Lee, Alfred Sy-hang, 143, 166, 181
Lee, Alice Moy, 136, 166, 168, 172, 181, 231n137
Lee, Dai-ming, 183, 199, 217n82
Lee, Doris Shoong, 139
Lee, Elsie, 100
Lee Fong. *See* Ahlo, Anthony Leefong
Lee, Frank William Chinglun: anti-communism, 100; death, 195; diplomatic career, 106, 132, 138; early life, 45; education, 224n39; politics, 217n82; rejection of dual citizenship, 78, 82, 216n74; Second Revolution, 54; Shanghai College, 83, 91
Lee, George, 134
Lee, Hazel Ying, 136–138, 198
Lee, Ida, 64
Lee, Jane Kwong, 148
Lee, Leo Ou-fan, 60
Lee, Minnie, 45
Lee, Pansy Choye, 100
Lee, Poy Gum: career, 64–65, 130–131, 251n71; marriage, 100, 175; return to United States, 199; during World War II, 181
Lee, Sarah Elaine, 125
Lee, Tom, 45
Lee Toma, Ethel, 62
Lee, William K., 134
Lee Yow-Lim, 184
Lee Yuk Sue, 7
Lem, George, 84
Lend-Lease program, 156, 173, 177
Leong, Ellen, 132
Leong, Ruby, 132
Leung, Edward Fook, 34, 83
Leung, George Kin, 83, 199
Lew, Don Geate, 152, 166, 174
Lew, Foot Jung, 34
Lew Kay, Marjorie, 152, 156, 166, 195
Li, T.M. (Tsing-meu), 24, 49, 57, 131, 146
Li Jishen, 107, 122
Li Zongren, 124, 243n164
Liang Hongzhi, 168–169
Liang Qichao, 17–18, 45
Liao, Anna Faith Lee, 160, 201
Liao, Thomas Wen-I, 160, 201
Liao Zhongkai: assassination, 75, 89–94, 238n79; citizenship, 233n1; education, 21; and Merchant Corps Incident, 81; and Second Revolution, 54–55; and Sun Yat-sen, 84
Liao Zhubao, 21

Linebarger, Paul, 105
Lingnan University: Chinese Americans students, 115, 123; Chinese American teachers, 125; Guomindang education policies and, 138; overseas Chinese students, 139; Second Sino-Japanese War, 162, 163. *See also* Canton Christian College
Linnell, Irving, 162–163
Liu, Flora Seu Tai, 130, 195–196
Long Jiguang, 25, 55
Loo, Henry Kong, 49, 156
Loo, Nancy Ngan Sin, 128–129, 188
Look King, 127
Look Poong Shan, 19–20, 86, 127, 178
Look Tin Eli, 19
Louey Shuck (Louey Po Sang): death, 201; early life, 1–2; family, 1–2, 31, 127, 200; in Guangzhou, 25, 31; in Hong Kong, 18–20; 1925–1926 Hong Kong-Guangzhou boycott and strike, 87; social status, 35, 72; target of Guomindang, 97, 108
Louie Hong How (Edward H.T. Louie), 31, 72, 127, 176
Louie Jung Yan (James J.Y. Louie), 31, 35, 72, 200, 271n37
Lowe, Bessie Ahtye, 48–49
Lowe, Chee S., 48–49, 54
Lu, Hanchao, 71
Lu Rongting, 25, 55
Lu Xun (Zhou Shuren), 42, 83
Lugouqiao incident. *See* Marco Polo Bridge Incident
Luke, Herbert K., 198
Luke, Samuel B., 128
Lum, Tsai Yan, 86, 132
Lym, Arthur Fook Yin: aerial bombing, 57; in Chen Jitang's aviation corps, 126–127, 150; early life, 50–51; Euro-American Returned Students' Association, 58; expatriation, 217n82; postwar life and death, 200–201; Second Sino-Japanese War, 186, 266n156; in Shanghai, 83; Tom Gunn and, 55

Ma Ying Piu, 38
Macao, 163, 177, 184, 187, 194
MacMurray, John V.A., 93–97, 111
Mao Dun, 60
Marco Polo Bridge Incident, 152–153, 155, 157, 161, 166
Mark, Stephen Gum, 125
marriage: Chinese American women and, 36, 63; into Chinese coastal and treaty port classes, 40, 145–146; companionate and monogamous, 43; into new elite, 109; US citizenship and, 66–67, 174; war and, 201
May Fourth Movement, 10, 36, 37–38, 60–61, 69–70, 142
May Thirtieth Incident, 76, 85, 100, 101–103
Mei, H.C. (Hua Chuan), 64, 68, 100, 132, 136, 195
Merchant Corps Incident, 81–83
Mexican Americans, 133, 149
Midnight (novel), 60
missionaries: as American emigrants, 8; Boxer Uprising and, 46; Chinese American, 48–49, 133; hospitals and institutions of, 64, 70, 124–125, 136, 146, 149; Northern Expedition and, 87–88, 103–104; residence rights in China, 29; schools, 17, 23–24, 31–34, 37–38, 59, 80, 129–131, 138, 144; and Second Sino-Japanese War, 159, 162, 173–174, 175–176, 183–184, 187
Mixed Court. *See* Shanghai Provisional Court
modernity and modernization: Chinese and Chinese American views of, 10, 42–43, 49–53, 57–58, 60–61, 68–71, 148, 190; education for, 47–48, 223n31; fascism and, 143
Moon, Kam Yee, 100
Moon, Nina, 100
Moy, Ernest Kee: death, 202; education, 49, 66, 224n43; employment in China, 105, 107, 132; and 1932 Shanghai Incident, 136; return to United States, 195, 201–202; Second Sino-Japanese War, 181, 187, 188; siblings, 172
Moy, Herbert Erasmus: death, 202; education, 66; mistress, 272n52; print journalism, 132; and radio station XGRS, 182; and radio station XMHC, 133, 172
Moy, Kenneth, 136, 159–160
Moy, Loring, 136, 159–160, 166, 181
Moy Quong-poy: arrest and trial, 75, 99; death, 186; expatriation, 92; in Guomindang, 217n82, 238n79; journalist, 49; Li Jishen and, 107; Second Revolution and, 54
Moy, Ruth Koesun (Ruth K. Kim): assists OSS, 181–182; in Chinese Women's Club, 146; and Medal of Freedom, 201; during

1932 Shanghai incident, 136; 1937 evacuation, 159–160; return to Shanghai, 166; return to United States, 195
Moy, Samuel Orne, 181, 202
Moy, William Taft, 132, 172

N.A. Tye and Brothers, 13, 19, 86, 127
Nanjing: as national capital, 104, 118; 1927 incident, 104, 242n145; Second Sino-Japanese War, 155, 161; Sun Yat-sen Mausoleum, 64–65, 130, 250n70
Nanjing Road, 60, 157
Nanyang Brothers Tobacco Company, 82
national goods movement, 61
National Revolutionary Army (NRA), 103–104
nationalism: anti-foreign, 63, 70–71; anti-imperialist, 38–39, 43, 101–103; economic, 47, 48, 61, 70–71, 227n80; Guomindang and, 75–76, 78–89, 96, 111–113, 191; racial, 3–5, 11–12, 28, 76–77, 92–96, 111–113, 149–150, 190–191, 193, 211n36; returned students and, 67–68
Nationality Act of 1940, 263n108
Naturalization Act of 1906, 4
Nazi Party, 143, 172, 181, 182
New Culture Movement, 10, 36, 60, 69–70
New Life Movement, 117, 142–147, 149, 150, 189
New Policies (xinzheng), 10, 46–47, 71–72
Ng Ah Tye, 13–14, 86, 127, 211n1
Ng Lee Ting Tye, 13–14, 211n1
Ngai, Mae, 92–93
1911 Revolution. *See* Xinhai Revolution
Nineteenth Route Army, 135–136
Northern Expedition, 76, 99–100, 103–104, 107, 124–125, 139
Noyes Memorial Academy. *See* Pui Ying School

Oi, Jean C., 147
On Leong Tong, 45
Ong, Soon Keong, 5, 35
"Open Door" policy, 76, 192
opium, 16, 45, 78, 79, 100, 178
Oriental Public School, 6–7, 46, 209n22
Overseas Chinese: attitude toward First United Front, 75, 78; Australian, 18, 35, 36, 72, 86, 144, 146; in British colonies, 97–99; Canadian, 16, 36, 72, 144, 146; in Chen Jitang era, 124; Chinese governments' views and policies, 4–5, 32, 112; department stores, 34–38; donations to Chinese governments and institutions, 125, 136, 157, 257n27; exploitation of dual citizenship status, 29, 111–112; and Guomindang government corruption, 141–142; Guomindang government policy and treatment of, 117, 119–121, 126, 141–142, 191; Guomindang views of, 81–82, 91, 108–109, 116–117, 135; imperialism and, 37–38, 70–83, 86–89, 113–114; investment in China, 17–18, 21, 34, 60, 84; marriages, 36, 40, 146, 175; merchants, 14, 16–17, 18, 21, 33–34, 36, 37–39, 73, 76, 78–79, 82, 88, 89; networks, 7, 9, 13–14, 16, 18, 21, 35–36, 39–40, 52, 73, 75, 80, 113, 127, 154, 165; northern elite views of, 35; political activities, 3, 18, 45, 51–52, 79, 199; political connections, 104; Qing dynasty and, 17, 212n17; remittances to China, 183–184; returnees, 247n21; social lives, 145–146, 151; in Southeast Asia, 72, 78, 197; students, 31–34, 37–38, 139, 162; targets of criminals and officials, 26, 30, 78, 83, 89, 185; terminology, xvi; views of citizenship, 89
"overseas Chinese world": central institutions of, 124–125; description, 73, 165; Guangzhou and, 34–36, 91; Hong Kong and, 16–17, 200; World War II and, 154, 191
Owyang, George, 132, 179, 188
Owyang, Maye Tom, 179, 188

Pacific War. *See* World War II
Panay incident, 161
paper sons, xvii, 38–39
patriotism: anti-Japanese, 136–138; Chinese American modernizers', 51–53, 56, 147–148; Chinese Students' Alliance and, 58; complexity of Chinese American, 77, 128–129; provincial loyalties and, 124; Second Sino-Japanese War and, 157, 166, 168, 169, 172; westernized lifestyles and, 68, 142
Pearl River Delta: banditry and piracy in, 82; Chinese Americans in, 9–11, 122–124, 148, 159, 193, 194–195, 218n92; during early republic, 25–26; education in, 23, 71; Second Sino-Japanese War and, 162–165, 175–179, 183–184, 195; warlord era, 29–34
Peking Chronicle (*Peiping Chronicle*), 166, 181

Peking Union Medical College (PUMC), 57, 146, 165, 180
People's Republic of China, 5, 7–8, 191–192, 199, 200
Phelan, James, 3
Pontius, Albert W., 28
Pooi To Academy, 32, 34, 59, 87, 178
Powell, John B., 102
Poy, Alfred, 177
Poy, Charles, 177
Poy, Lucille, 198
Pui Ching Baptist Academy: feeder school for Canton Christian College, 34; founding, 237n66; overseas Chinese students at, 37, 59, 83, 87, 123, 185; teachers at, 32, 125, 185
Pui Ying Middle School, 32, 34, 37, 87
Puyi (Aisin Gioro Puyi), 119
Pye, Lucien, 70

Qing dynasty: education initiatives, 22; end of, 1, 24, 53, 89; nationality law of 1909, 4; New Policies, 10, 46–47, 51–53; reform efforts, 17–18, 42, 108, 12; rights recovery campaign, 48; sale of titles, 212n17; Taiping Rebellion, 79
Queen's College, 21, 72, 85
Quong Lun Company, 19

railroads: Beijing-Zhangjiakou, 54; Canton-Hankow, 159, 160; Japanese bombing of lines, 163; Shanghai-Nanjing, 105; Sunning, 79; Yichang construction, 56
Reformed Government of the Republic of China, 168–172, 183
refugees, 135, 158, 159–164, 177, 185–187
Reorganized Government of the Republic of China, 168, 170, 183
Republic of China on Taiwan, 5, 7–8, 199, 200, 202–203
Returned Chinese Women's Club, 58
"returned students": Chinese Americans and, 57–59, 63, 64–72, 76, 104; in Great Depression, 132;
Rodríguez, Raymond, 149
Roosevelt, Franklin D., 156, 164

Salt Administration, 54, 107
San Francisco, California: 6–7, 35, 46, 213n19
schools: attendance rates, 43; Chinese language in United States, 22, 134–135; on Chinese mainland, 17, 21–24, 52; in Guangzhou, 31–39, 49; in Hong Kong, 16–17, 21, 123; missionary, 17, 21, 31–33, 37–38, 62, 70, 123, 124–125, 129, 138, 159; Qing-founded, 47; in Shanghai, 132; in Southeast Asia, 120; special overseas Chinese, 23, 31; village, 22–23, 30, 71, 122–123, 184
Second Revolution, 25, 41, 54–55
Second Sino-Japanese War: in central China, 161–162; and Chinese Americans, 10–11; Chinese casualties, 155–156; economic impact, 154; famine during, 183–184, 185; Guomindang retreat, 155–156, 186; Japanese treatment of civilians, 165, 166, 175–176, 179–180; at Nanjing, 161; outbreak, 152–153, 155; in Shanghai, 155–161, 165–168, 178–180; in south China, 162–165, 178–179, 183–184, 189
Second United Front, 155
See, Lung-kee, 69
Seetoo, Elsie Chin Yuen, 172, 186, 187, 198
Seid, Annie, 198
Seid, Lily, 198
Shameen concession, 59, 61, 80, 88, 162–163, 228n92
Shanghai: business classes of, 107–109, 115, 138; Cantonese compradors, 64–65; Chinese Americans in, 9–11, 61–71, 83, 100–103, 117, 129–136, 156, 179–180; evacuation of US citizens from, 158–161, 173–175; foreign concessions, 60–61, 95, 109–111, 193; Great Depression in, 129; *gudao* period, 165–168; modernity, 43, 60; movie industry, 63, 143; New Culture Movement and, 70–71; new elite, 65–67, 109, 132, 175; New Life Movement, 143–147; 1932 incident, 135–136, 155; racial discrimination, 102–103; radio industry, 133; refugees, 158; returned students' conference, 58; Second Sino-Japanese War, 153, 155, 156–161, 179–180; social life, 61, 63–64, 72; standard of living, 134; traditional networks, 64; US citizen population, 156, 159, 262n99
Shanghai College, 83, 91, 106
Shanghai Incident of 1932, 119, 135–136, 155, 157, 257n17
Shanghai Municipal Council (SMC), 61, 102–103
Shanghai Municipal Police, 76, 84–85, 103
Shanghai Provisional Court, 101, 103, 109, 111–112, 169

Shek, Emily Ying Wee Lee, 187–188, 195
Shew, Lynne Lee, 36, 125, 176, 198–199, 262n107
Shih Shih Hsin Pao, 68
Shim, Edward, 126, 248n4
Shue, Charles K., 66–67, 231n132
Sid Bock Yin, 34
Simons, Sarah E., 3
Sincere Department Stores: Guangzhou, 34, 35, 36, 37–38, 80; Hong Kong, 35, 86; owners, 35, 72; Shanghai, 34, 35, 70, 157, 175
Sinn, Elizabeth, 16
Song Meiling (Madame Chiang Kai-shek), 143
Song Qingling (Madame Sun Yat-sen), 77
Soo-hoo, Lily, 67, 171, 202
Soong, Irma Tam, 161, 177, 178, 185, 187, 188, 200
Soong, Norman, 132, 161, 177, 178, 188, 200
Soong, T.V., 104, 105, 130, 166, 249n55
South China Morning Post, 160, 203
Southard, Addison, 177
Southern Hospital, 57
sports, 59, 64, 100, 109–110, 131
SS *President Hoover*, 159
St. John's University, Shanghai: Chinese American students at, 72, 115, 130, 136, 139, 167, 195–196; Chinese Hawaiian students, 24, 129–130, 195, 199; Guomindang and, 138–139; medical school, 130; New Life Movement and, 145; 1911 revolution, 25; Second Sino-Japanese War, 166, 171, 181; teachers, 32; tuition, 250n65
Standard Oil Co., 35, 70, 96–97
Stillwell, Joseph, 187
Stimson, Henry, 112
student activism: at Jinan University, 120–121; in May Fourth era, 37–38; May Thirtieth Incident and, 84–85; in Nanjing Decade, 118–119, 135, 138–139
Student Volunteer Movement, 32
Sun Department Stores, 37–38, 80, 134
Sun Fo, 105, 142
Sun Yat-sen: anti-imperialism, 78, 122; anti-Qing activities, 18, 24, 52; attitude toward state power, 42, 73; Chen Jiongming and, 77; Chinese Americans and, 200; death, 84; early Guangzhou governments of, 10, 25–27; First United Front era government, 78–82; ideals of, 108; Joffe agreement, 61, 75; Mausoleum, 64; and New Culture Movement, 60; Second Revolution, 41, 54–55; Three People's Principles of, 120; Tom Gunn and, 50
Sung, Lily Soo-hoo, 67, 171, 202
Sung, William Z.L., 67, 171, 202
Sze, Alfred Sao-ke, 58

Taishan. *See* Toisan
Taiwan (Republic of China). *See* Republic of China on Taiwan
Tak Sang Hung, 34
Tak Shin Hung, 34
Toisan (Taishan): boycott movement, 37; Chinese Americans in, 9–11; economy, 123–124; Second Sino-Japanese War, 162, 164–165, 176, 177–179, 183–184, 198
Tom, Dora Kam, 62–63
Tom Gunn (Tom Duck Gunn), 41–42, 50–51, 55–56, 57, 100, 217n82
Tom Gunn, Lily, 55
Tong, Ah Huna, 144, 145
Tong, Julia Sih, 67, 103, 169
Tong Kai-cho, 169
Tong Shao-yi, 169, 183
Tongmenghui, 24, 50, 54
transnationalism, 15, 64, 89, 147
Treaty of Versailles, 37, 39
True Light Middle School, 31, 32, 34, 37, 87, 125
True Story of Ah Q, 83
Tsao, Y.S., 68
Tseu, Joseph Yuk Woon, 125–126, 127
Tsin, Michael, 81
Tsing Hua College, 31, 32, 68, 218n96
Tung Wah Hospital, 35
Tungshan (Dongshan), 59, 91, 162
Tyau, Philip Ahung, 24
Tye, Herbert Spencer, 13–14, 211n1
Tye, Leland Stanford, 13–14, 127, 211n1
Tye, Van Gesner, 13–14, 211n1

Union Middle School, 34, 83, 162
Union of Soviet Socialist Republics (USSR): advisors from, 77, 83, 91, 99; agreement to support Guomindang, 61; World War II, 156, 257n17
United States: anti-Chinese movement in, 1–2, 13; anti-Japanese movement in, 13; businesses and institutions in China, 61, 76, 87–88, 96–97, 159, 162–163, 165–166, 193; civil rights movement, 154, 189;

United States *(continued)*
commercial treaty with China, 106; decline of racial discrimination in, 195; economy, 61, 114, 115–116, 121–122, 128–129; gender discrimination, 198; immigration and national identity, 5–8; immigration and naturalization policy, 2–4, 15, 66–67, 92–93, 153, 174, 189; investment in China, 229n104; legal system, 11; military, 187–188, 198–199; People's Republic of China and, 191–192; racism and segregation, 97–98, 180, 187, 189, 190; relationship with China, 76, 112, 141, 156, 187, 191–192; relationship with Japan, 152–153, 156, 161, 173, 175–176; Second Sino-Japanese War and, 152–153; World War II and, 154, 178, 183, 187–189, 195, 198
University of Hawaii, 129, 250n65
University of Hong Kong, 72, 85
University of Nanking, 32, 130, 161
University of Shanghai, 130
US Army Fourteenth Air Service Group, 188
US Consulate, Guangzhou: and Chinese American protection issues, 26, 27–30, 78, 99, 141; Chu Shea Wai case, 89–97, 111; Merchant Corps Incident, 82; 1925–1926 Hong Kong-Guangzhou boycott and strike, 86–87; postwar, 194–195; Second Sino-Japanese War, 162–165, 177
US Consulate, Hong Kong, 18, 92, 160, 177–178
US Consulate, Shanghai, 109–112, 129, 159–160, 162, 173–175
US Court for China, 70, 100, 101–103, 262n103
US Legation, Beijing, 92, 158, 174
US Office of Strategic Services (OSS), 181, 187–188, 195
US State Department: Chinese American citizenship and, 11, 27–30, 75–76, 97–99, 139, 141, 193, 201, 242n145; Chu Shea Wai case, 89–97; cultural and racial criteria for protection, 94–95, 111, 192; and evacuation of US citizens from China, 158–161, 162–164, 173–175, 177; Guomindang regime and, 111–112; naturalization in China, 262n102; passports for Chinese Americans, 212n4, , 217n87; Standard Oil Co. and, 96–97
US Women Airforce Service Pilots (WASP), 198
US Women's Army Corps (WAC), 188, 195
US v. Wong Kim Ark, 2
USS *Augusta*, 157–158

Voice of New China, 169

Wa Kiu (Overseas Chinese) School of Canton Christian College, 31–33
Wai Wah Hospital and Medical College, 57
"Wan Wan San." *See* Wong, Tong Quong
Wang, C.T., 105
Wang Jingwei: collaborationist regime, 156, 168, 171, 182–183; rivalry with Chiang Kai-shek, 104, 118; Sun Yat-sen and, 84
Wang, Louis, 123
Wang, William, 123
War Area Service Corps, 187
War of Resistance Against Japan. *See* Second Sino-Japanese War; World War II
warlords: Chinese American employees, 42, 56–57; cliques, 56, 168–169; in Guangdong, 25–31, 73, 89; in central China, 56–57; in north China, 25, 85, 99
Wasserstrom, Jeffrey, 63–64, 147
Western Returned Students Association (Guangzhou), 58
Whampoa Academy, 75, 99
whiteness, 211n37
Wilson, Huntington, 95, 97
Wing, George D., 100
Wing, James, 198, 270n24
Wing, Omar, 198, 270n24
Wing On Department Stores, 34, 70, 103, 157
Women: education of Chinese and Chinese American, 16–17, 22, 31, 62; feminism in China, 144; film actors in China, 63; New Life Movement and, 143–145; "new women" in China, 36; organizations of in China, 63, 64, 143, 146; US immigration policy and, 4. *See also* Chinese American women
Women's New Life Movement Promotion Association, 143
Wong, Chan K., 88, 89
Wong, Charles Ahfook, 52, 217n82
Wong, Charles Hong, 164, 196
Wong, Edward, 23
Wong, George K.T., 166
Wong, Hin (Huang Hsien-chao), 27, 57, 58, 79–81, 130, 185, 235n24
Wong, Jay Lai, 144
Wong, Kelley Hong, 164, 198

Wong Pui, 179
Wong, Selma James, 143
Wong, Tong Quong, 196–198
Wong, Virginia, 136–138
Wong, Warren Achuck, 105
Wong, William A., 48
Wong Bok-yue, 141
Wong Fee Lee, 6–7, 21, 23, 197
Wong Yee-bong, 178
Woo, Gilbert, 11–12
Woo, John, 131, 132, 195, 199
Woo, Kay Keong, 196
Woo Ah Tin, 46
Woon, Sue, 197–198
World War I, 26, 36–37, 60
World War II, 154, 178, 183, 187–189, 191, 198. *See also* Second Sino-Japanese War
Wu, Andrew Gayson, 57, 64
Wu, Pei-tsung, 178, 187, 194
Wu, Pond Shuck, 48, 56–57
Wu Tiecheng, 135, 143
Wuhan, 56, 155, 162

XGRS, 172, 182
Xi'an Incident, 155
Xiguan (Sai Kwan), Guangzhou, 81–82
Xinhai Revolution, 24, 42, 53–54
XMHC, 133, 172
Xu Mo, 109–111
Xu Shichang, 169

Yam, Yau Sing, 123
Yan Xishan, 106, 124
Yarnell, Harry, 158
Ye, Weili, 52
Yee, Coon Ai, 48
Yee, Francis, 132
Yee, Herbert, 121–122, 123
Yee, James, 146, 180, 196–197
Yee, James Marion, 197
Yee, Marian Li, 146, 180, 196–197
Yee, Robert D., 180, 197
Yee Ting, 115
Yeh, Wen-hsin, 64, 139
Yen, Theodora Chu Li, 35
Yen, W.W., 35, 200
Yenching University: Chinese American students at, 72, 115, 130–131, 161, 166, 196; Second Sino-Japanese War and, 152, 165
Young, Ching Leong, 136, 195
Young, Clarence Wun, 133, 144
Young, Henry Joe, 91, 92, 238n74
Young, In: auto dealer, 133; engineering work, 48, 56, 227n80; in "Free China," 179, 188; relocation to Shanghai, 83; return to United States, 201
Young, Jack T., 181, 187
Young, Kenneth, 199
Young, Olive, 63, 100
Young, Paul Ball, 24, 195
Young, Richard Ming-Tong, 187
Young, Samuel Sung: in Beiyang government, 54, 57; death, 200; diplomatic career, 106–107, 132, 266n154; early life, 46; and New Policies, 53; Second Sino-Japanese War, 186
Young, Walter Ching, 46
Young Men's Christian Association (YMCA): in China, 70, 130, 142; in Guangzhou, 36, 48–49, 59; in Hong Kong, 35; in Shanghai, 59, 62, 64, 65, 103
Young Women's Christian Association (YWCA), 59, 62
Yuan Shikai, 24–25, 41, 53–55
Yung, Bartlett Golden, 48
Yung, Morrison Brown, 48
Yung Wing, 48

Zane, Andrew F., 24, 136, 179–180, 195
Zane, John, 64
Zhabei, Shanghai, 108, 135
Zhang Xueliang, 155
Zhao Hongdi, 56
Zia, Francis, 103

Founded in 1893,
UNIVERSITY OF CALIFORNIA PRESS
publishes bold, progressive books and journals on topics in the arts, humanities, social sciences, and natural sciences—with a focus on social justice issues—that inspire thought and action among readers worldwide.

The UC PRESS FOUNDATION
raises funds to uphold the press's vital role as an independent, nonprofit publisher, and receives philanthropic support from a wide range of individuals and institutions—and from committed readers like you. To learn more, visit ucpress.edu/supportus.